DATE DUE

NO 25 '98			
DE 6 '98			
DE 1 8 '99			
AP 24 '00			
DE 20 '00			
AP 23 '01			
MY 14 '01			
RENEW			
JE 07 '01			
OC 17 '01			
NO 07 '01			
DE 06 '01			
FE 7 '02			
JE 4 '03			
FE 12 '04			

DEMCO 38-296

LATIN JAZZ

The First of the Fusions, 1880s to Today

John Storm Roberts

Schirmer Books
An imprint of Macmillan Library Reference USA
NEW YORK

Schirmer Books
An imprint of Macmillan Library Reference USA
1633 Broadway
New York, NY 10019

Library of Congress Catalog Card Number: 98-42730

Printed in the United States of America

Printing number
1   2   3   4   5   6   7   8   9   10

Library of Congress Cataloging-in-Publication Data

Roberts, John Storm.
    Latin jazz : the first of the fusions, 1880s to today / John Storm Roberts
        p.   cm.
    Includes bibliographical references, discography, and index.
    ISBN 0-02-864681-9 (alk. paper)
    1. Jazz—Latin American influences.   I. Title
    ML3506.R63 1999
    781.65'16268—dc21   98-42730
                                                                CIP
                                                                MN

This paper meets the requirements of ANSI/NISO Z39.48—1992 (Permanence of Paper).

Contents

Introduction

Back in 1979, I wrote in the introduction to my book, *The Latin Tinge,* that Latin-American music was the most important outside influence on U.S. popular music of the last 100 years. The notion did not, to put it mildly, sweep the land from sea to shining sea, though on the whole it was received politely. I'm happy to say that over the past 20 years enough work has been done by a large number of musicologists to establish that, at the very least, I had a point. Certainly I've heard nothing to make me change my mind, and a good deal to cause me to believe that I may even have understated things.

If Latin music, and specifically, Brazilian, Cuban, Argentinian, and Mexican music, have been enormously influential in the U.S. in general—even setting up outposts in the shape of Cuban-derived salsa and Tex-Mex music—they have been particularly significant in jazz. Indeed, at the end of the 1970s it seemed that Latin-derived rhythmic processes, pure or Americanized, were about to take over jazz altogether, ousting the old four-to-the-bar shuffle beat—but it didn't happen.

On one level it's embarrassing to tackle a subject like this, because there is a small posse of people out there who know much more about even the most obscure aspects of it than I do, both on the practical and theoretical levels. If I'm not embarrassed, it's because I have met nobody who knows as much as I do about all the aspects involved. The issue, in other words, is breadth rather than depth. Besides, even if you added everything that all the experts know about almost anything, it's a drop in the bucket. Isaac Newton once said something to the effect that knowledge is like an enormous ocean, and all he ever did was poke around on the shore and pick up the occasional brightly colored shell. This book is the sum of the shells I've found on this particular beach.

I should make clear right away that this is not an ethnomusicological work, for one simple reason: I'm not an ethnomusicologist. I usually describe myself as a music journalist, because all my work (my two previous books aside) has been done for magazine, newspapers, radio, or (very rarely) television. Secretly, I'd like to think I can aspire to the title of music historian on my best days.

In any event, this book is music history and not ethnomusicology, and it is written for the famous "general reader," who couldn't read musical examples or decipher ethnomusicological lingo if I were to use them. But beyond that, I don't think this subject *could* be tackled ethnomusicologically. Any science (and ethnomusicology is half science and half metaphysics) needs to be able to test propositions. Much of what I believe to be significant is, at the moment, highly speculative. Some of it may be unprovable one way or the other, either at the level of analysis or at the level of historical documentation. The rest of it involves the kind of labor that any one person could only undertake in a minute area of my subject. Even to support the *likelihood* of a serious habanera/danza influence on ragtime and other pre-jazz, for example, one would have to ferret through thousands of pieces of sheet music from the 1870s through the 1890s. Only thus could one establish how much the danza was, so to speak, in the air in the United States of the late nineteenth century. That kind of undertaking takes serious time, and therefore serious money, neither of which I personally have to spare for it.

Both my previous books were based on premises that were widely regarded as out in left field when they were first published. So does this one: the idea that Latin music may have been much more influential in the earliest days of both jazz and ragtime than has yet been realized, and therefore shown. But unless somebody suggests there may be something to show for a particular line of research, the work won't get done. Looking back, the major merit of my *Black Music of Two Worlds* and *The Latin Tinge* was that they stimulated research that wouldn't otherwise have gotten done, some of which suggested I was wrong in places, but more of which suggested I was at least on the right path. Of course, academic careers have been ruined by being right about something that sounded off the wall, even if at least preliminary evidence was there. One of the merits of non-academic types like Paul Oliver, Ernest Bornemann, and myself is that we don't have to worry about tenure. It took 20 years for a grudging admission that Bornemann was right about the hidden Maghrebi factor in West African and Iberian links in Latin American music, and another ten for the notion to become commonplace. Imagine if he'd been going for a professorship with that round his neck! All this is another reason why I am a good person to write this book. I can follow my ears and my intuitions as much as I like without running up against a threat to my career from unacademic standards. I can take risks. I can postulate and speculate and suggest avenues for exploration.

That's more important than it may seem at first blush. Over the years I have read general-reader articles on many discoveries, historical, archeological, and anthropological. Added together, they make depressingly clear that all of us, "experts" included, are irredeemably addicted to assuming that people in the past (in our own as well as other cultures) were less sophisticated than they eventually prove to have been. Horses were ridden thousands of years earlier than was thought. The Neanderthals had some kind of music and therefore probably some kind of speech. Australian Aborigines seem to have run a substantial stone-axe manufactory, perhaps for export to Polynesia, a thousand years ago. The Tudors had certain navigational aids a century before they were thought to have been invented. We do it *all* the time—confuse "not established" with "wrong"—even if prior assumptions have meant nobody has risked derision by even testing whatever the concept may be.

Above all, this is a survey of a musical movement in the U.S. that has the odd property of being one of the most important, and at the same time the most neglected and even despised, of the twentieth century. Even though Jelly Roll Morton stated the obvious so long ago, the crucial relationship between jazz and Latin music of various kinds remains essentially unexplored, except by a handful of eccentrics writing for the most part in magazines with tiny circulations. Indeed, it's not long since it was worse than unexplored. With a very few honorable exceptions, an older generation of jazz critics who wouldn't know guaguancó from guacamole preceded the word "Latin" with the word "commercial" as infallibly as Homer preceded the word "sea" with "wine-dark." Nor is this kind of obtuseness confined to critics, those much maligned outcasts. An equal proportion of jazz fans, and a smaller but significant number of jazz musicians, have been just as happy to pigeonhole a rich and complex idiom without letting it clutter up the purity of their prejudices with inconvenient facts.

The fact is that knowing all about jazz or all about Latin music doesn't necessarily cut the mustard. Talking about Third Stream in his *West Coast Jazz,* Ted Gioia sums the issue up better than I could: "Like all hybrid musics—fusion, bossa nova, Afro-Cuban, even jazz itself—Third Stream is both more and less than its constituent parts and must be so treated. . . . An African griot and a nineteenth-century classical composer might have been equally unimpressed with the music of King Oliver or Jelly Roll Morton . . . any critical assessment of these works must approach them gingerly, careful not to apply blindly the various jazz pieties that have little bearing on such compositions."

Jazz at its best, of course, has never consisted of one style, or one generation. Having labored for years in the vineyard myself as both writer and editor, I have had experience of one of the most common distorting factors in jazz journalism. With the exception of a few writers important enough to be left alone, a music journalist has to sell an idea to an editor whose basic question will be, not just "why run this?" but "why run it now?" It is very tough to persuade an editor that "Group Playing For the Past Five Years Makes Terrific Recording Very Like the Last Six" will be a strong addition to the jazz press.

Nor is that editor merely being crass. Except for insightful people like you and me, magazine readers want to know what's happening, not what's existing. The news value of a story may be slight, but it has to be there. That works well enough for some levels of rock and pop. But jazz has always been a music in which several generations of musicians and music coexisted, each as lively in its own way as the next one. And one of the most admirable aspects of most Latin music is that the most avant-garde musicians, and even the music critics, have often been passionate in praise of older styles. So it's important to remember that while the Young Turks were taking the campuses by storm, a previous generation of Latin-jazz musicians continued to play older idioms as freshly as ever. As Ingrid Monson put it in her recent book *Saying Something,* "The jazz experience has always been more varied and cosmopolitan than any of the narratives that have been written about it."

Among the many problems of dealing with jazz, particularly in reference to Latin music, is that nobody can agree about what it is, because the word came out of nowhere and was used loosely until the first academic got to work on it. That means that perennial arguments—like whether jazz came from New Orleans and spread or popped up in various places—are literally meaningless, since both sides define "jazz" to suit their positions. If you define "jazz" as the mix of elements found in New Orleans, then jazz was a New Orleans creation. If you allow a simpler blues/ragtime/brass band mix into the canon, Hello Kansas City! It is important to remember that the first certain reference to jazz pops up in 1915. It wasn't until World War I Chicago, in other words, that anybody knew they were playing jazz, as opposed to ragtime, at all. Moreover, the distinction between "jazz" and "popular" music was a much later critical construct: the first jazz musicians played the hits. Early trumpeter Bunk Johnson shocked the earnest researchers who had found him working in a Louisiana rice paddy in 1939 by wanting to play "The Yellow Rose of Texas"!

Similarly, if ragtime is confined to the piano music we classy folk find approvable, then it's a very limited form. If we use the loose definition accepted by the people who originally listened to the stuff, it's a very different story. Luckily, the notion that we can't discuss anything without defining it to a fare-the-well is only marginally true. The music that causes most of the arguments is only perhaps five percent of the material we agree about. Music styles are like geography. If you could travel from France to Germany without seeing any frontier signs, you might get a little confused in Alsace, but nine-tenths of the time you'd know extremely well which country you were in.

Musical quality and personal taste are a different matter. As those who know me are aware, I have strong views on practically everything, many of them backed up by a good deal of solid evidence. But at the simplest level, I try never to forget that my disliking something doesn't mean it is bad (like all of us, I have a soft spot for some pretty dodgy stuff). When I was writing reviews, I stated my opinions freely, because doing so is a big part of the job description. But this book isn't about quality, or whether one person's borrowing was a rip-off and somebody else's was genius building on the trivial. Though I express my enthusiasms from time to time, and though I sure wouldn't be writing this if I weren't in love with the music, this is about mutual jazz/Latin influence, not about whether or when it's a good or a bad thing.

A friendly critic commented about *The Latin Tinge* that he wished it had been more interview-based. A fair comment, except that it was. It simply wasn't very direct-quote-heavy. This book is also based on hundreds of conversations and interviews, formal and otherwise, conducted over a quarter of a century by myself and by several people who have generously shared what they have learned—as well as on the recordings and live performances I've heard. I don't very often quote directly, first because direct quotes aren't necessarily relevant to a book of this scale, and second because an effective quote is a form of sound-bite, and relatively few interviews produce sound-bites.

As to the actual music, to a very large extent this book is based on recordings. I know very well that this provides its own kind of distortion, because live performances tend to be very different from recorded ones (although I recall an exception or two). But as this book covers roughly 110 years and hundreds of artists, there is really no way of giving adequate emphasis to club and concert gigs. Even if I was there, you weren't, and in almost all cases the performances either went unreviewed or were reviewed in terms that frankly don't help much at this date. At least you can listen to the recorded history, however lopsided it may be (just how lopsided, my first three chapters will make clear).

I recognize that this book may seem slightly monomaniacal at times, solemnly pursuing the Brazilianisms of a rhythm section and ignoring some blow-your-socks-off sax solo. But then, the book isn't about great solos, and it *is* about Brazilianisms. The fact that I stress a particular part of a performance doesn't mean I am oblivious to the other aspects involved. You will also certainly find some of your favorite recordings or artists undervalued, omitted, or treated in ways of which you disapprove. That may be because my judgment differs from yours, or because I can't listen to everything, or because I goofed. It happens. No book ever written has been without serious errors and omissions—certainly no book in such an undocumented area as this is. Somewhere somebody may get carried away and call this a definitive study. Not so: it's an initial exploration, and like all such it is tentative and probably takes more than a few turns that will eventually prove to be wrong. I hope readers will do what I try to do when not in a grouchy mood, which is to take from this book what seems sound and leave the rest behind in charity.

There are, of course, areas that I have necessarily omitted. The most important is the possible Latin influence brought in by the English-speaking Panamanians who are sprinkled through the history of jazz: a major example from the 1920s and 1930s was Luis Russell, who was born in Panama City and began his musical life there. The Anglophone Panamanians present a complex musical problem. Like the Anglophones of Costa Rica, they preserved British West Indian music as well as presumably absorbing the music of Panama (which is closely related to Colombian music). This means that a third strain enters into any possible jazz/Latin interaction in their work. If anybody has done any research on this particular issue I have not come across it, and I chose to set it aside in the body of this book. But it should be remembered as another possible subplot in this tangled tale.

On the subject of monomania, it is important to bear in mind that I am not arguing that Latin music's influence in jazz was necessarily huge, though I believe it to have been present at all times in the history of jazz, and it is perfectly clear to me that it has been far greater than jazz writers have allowed (which wouldn't be hard). Nor is this a zero-sum game. I am not arguing, for example, that the Latin elements I detect in ragtime displace the African-derived aspects of the music, or for that matter its important European elements (although some of those African and European elements may have reached jazz in part *through* Latin music). I am arguing that jazz has always been in some measure an Afro-Euro-Latino-American music.

Nor does it matter "how much" of any of these elements is present in jazz. As I've said before, it's impossible to say what is the "central" element of curried goat, the goat or the curry. Nor, therefore, is it relevant that there's a pound of goat to a gram of sauce. There's not much yeast in a loaf of bread either—just the crucial amount. Nor—in an ideal world it shouldn't need saying—does the fact that Latinos and European-Americans have played important creative roles in jazz detract from the centrality of African-Americans and African-American culture to the whole subject. It's hardly a derogation of the chefs to suggest that the dish called jazz is even richer and more varied than we knew.

I do believe that the Latin tinge was one of the crucial elements in the universality of jazz. The African elements in Latin music and the African elements in U.S. African-American music have supported and enriched each other in jazz. And so, too, the southern European elements in Spanish and Portuguese music (and of course their Middle Eastern tinge) have enriched the northern European—mostly British—elements. How exactly the Latin element related to the others is a subject for further arguing and research. The earliest Latin tinge was clearly a lot greater than has been recognized, and (as indeed Jelly Roll Morton remarked) it was also, from the beginning, a catalyst. Aside from enriching New Orleans and Mississippi delta ragtime, the earliest Latin tinge provided a bridge-head, so to speak, for the Latin influences that were to come in once jazz was starting to become part of the mainstream—and thus for the further fusions that were Afro-Cuban and Brazilian jazz.

In discussing relationships that haven't been considered much, occasionally I've had to adapt or invent a word or phrase to cover a concept that isn't discussed often. "Straight 4/4" and "straight 2/4" are examples, used to distinguish a rhythmic pulse in which the bass plays pretty much even beats, syncopated or not, as opposed to Latin montunos or funk-jazz grooves, which are based on a mix of longer and shorter pulses. I can't call this simply 4/4 or 2/4, because Cuban and Brazilian music commonly have a 2/4 pulse, or 4/4 when played in the U.S.

Another sort of definition presents other problems. Jazz has existed for maybe a century, depending on what you mean by jazz. The various Latin forms that fed and feed into it cover a slightly longer period and a much wider stylistic territory. Some readers know all the terminology and historical background; many do not. But the same problem arises in writing about "straight" jazz, in an era when many quite serious fans don't know who King Oliver is, let alone Freddie Keppard.

A glossary at the back of this book gives brief definitions of some of the most important concepts mentioned here. Most of them are Latin, because Latin-music fans tend to know more about jazz than the reverse. But I can't do an entry for everything, let alone everybody, because a penny-pinching publisher told me I have to stick to one volume. There are also a bibliography and a discography. As for anything that may be missing, there are a lot of jazz reference books out there, though still too few Latin ones. Use them well! Above all, listen to the music; otherwise this is all (you should pardon the word) academic. My not-very-well-hidden agenda isn't to educate you, anyway. It's to lure you into discovering a body of music as splendid as it is undervalued.

Acknowledgments

Any halfway honest author of a book covering the kind of ground this one does knows that all the acknowledgments due would take up a whole separate volume. Without the musicians mentioned in the text, the book wouldn't exist. Nor would it exist without the books, articles, and recordings I have cited, and the help of various people other than musicians and academics who are involved with the music professionally or personally (or both). All of them I also thank. Too many scholars and buffs have thrown in their two cents' worth over the Internet for me to list. You know who you are; importantly so do I, and I'm grateful.

I owe the following special thanks for forms of help that might not be obvious from reading the book.

Pianist George Winston for the loan of out-of-print Bola Sete albums.

Susan Stinson of the Belfer Archive, Syracuse University.

Anne Needham, my wife, best friend, and most tolerant critic, for a lot of editing and for putting up with my usual miscellaneous ranting as work proceeded.

Writer Ellen Collison for various forms of recondite information and contacts.

David Rumpler for sundry information on Brazilian music.

Phil Hoffman for putting me on to Jack Walrath.

Matthew Barton for dubbings and information connected with the Library of Congress Jelly Roll Morton interviews.

Tony Cox, BBC African Service, retired, and Kenton student, very much not retired.

David Carp, who knows more than anybody I have ever met about the details of New York Latin music and musicians, and whose generosity with precious information humbles me.

Joe Blum, writer, teacher, and former pianist, for insights on the complex relationships between jazz and Latin music.

Ed Lis for sharing his master's thesis on Brazilian jazz.

Terri Hinte of Fantasy Records for help of all sorts beyond the call of duty.

Mike Kieffer, collector and friend, for supplying copies of a large percentage of the early recordings I've cited as well as for unfailing patience with my habit of firing off discographical questions of all kinds by E-mail.

Dick Spottswood for his crucial discographical work in general, but also for supplying me with a dubbing of a rare Zutty Singleton recording discussed in the 1930s chapter.

Richard Zimmerman for information on ragtime tangos.

Dan Levinson for a rare Red Nicholls dubbing.

Professor Juan Flores for sharing his research and contacts.

◇ 1 ◇

Much More than Morton

The First Latin Tinge

The degree to which Latin musical styles affected ragtime, pre-jazz, and very early jazz will always be unclear because the historical record is scattered, confused, or most often of all, nonexistent. Journalists of the time (including African-American journalists) focused on "respectable" middle-class and mainstream music, pausing only to tut-tut occasionally about the vulgarisms of the masses who were busy creating one of the twentieth century's most vital musical styles.

Still, it seems plain that nineteenth-century New Orleans—and therefore early New Orleans jazz—was in more of a position to be influenced by Latin music than anywhere else in the U.S. As Alan Lomax put it in his biography of Jelly Roll Morton, *Mr Jelly Roll*, "French opera and popular song and Neapolitan music, African drumming . . . Haitian rhythm and Cuban melody . . . native creole satiric ditties, American spirituals and blues, the ragtime and the popular music of the day—all these sounded side by side in the streets of New Orleans. . . ." And Morton himself told Lomax: "New Orleans was the stomping ground for all the greatest pianists in the country. We had Spanish [read: "Latin"], we had colored, we had white, we had Frenchmen [mostly refugees from Haiti in fact], we had Americans, we had them from all parts of the world. . . ."

In a musical culture this complex, it is tough to disentangle the Latin influences from European-Spanish on the one hand and non-Latin Caribbean elements on the other—tough, and at times self-defeating, because all the various Caribbean idioms (including in all probability New Orleans idioms) had already been influencing each other for a century or more. It is also likely that many strains in the earliest jazz came from local musicians' combining disparate but

1

similar inflections, rhythms, or snatches of melody—using a memory of a Cuban pattern to juice a "native" New Orleans creole rhythm that might itself be a legacy of the Haitian refugees who were an important part of the nineteenth-century population, or throwing a phrase from a specific Mexican melody into a ragtime piece.

Even the dance forms popular in the 1880s and onward were more ambiguous than is often realized. In the 1890s, proto-jazzman Buddy Bolden played quadrilles (hotted up, according to pianist Armand Hug), mazurkas, and schottisches, as well as "slow-drags," which seem to have been a form of instrumental proto-blues. Slow drag aside, all this sounds very Euro-American. But the mazurka had already been creolized in both the Latin and French Caribbean; the quadrille was a mainstay of Jamaican country music; the polka and the waltz were the basic rhythms of northern Mexican music; and the Mexicans were also just as fond of the schottische (sometimes Hispanicized as "chotis") as were American ballroom dancers. In fact, several schottisches from a specifically Mexican source were issued by a New Orleans sheet music house in the mid-1880s. Given the proven popularity of Mexican music in New Orleans while Bolden was growing up, there's at least a strong possibility that some of the mazurkas and schottisches he played were Mexican compositions.

Confusing though all this is, the weight of evidence supports Jelly Roll Morton's famous dictum that if it doesn't have a "Spanish [i.e., Latin] tinge," it isn't jazz (my gloss, but his assessment). This is not empty theorizing. Even aside from any (I suspect small) influence that might have remained from the days when New Orleans was a Spanish domain, a major Latin—mostly Mexican—connection straddled the musical life of pre-jazz New Orleans. This connection was quite complex and developed over time, but one event was crucial. In 1884–85, New Orleans hosted the World's Industrial and Cotton Centennial Exposition. Of the various foreign exhibitors, none was more enthusiastic than Mexico, whose exhibit rivaled the U.S.'s itself. As part of its effort, the Mexican government sent over the band of the Eighth Regiment of Mexican Cavalry, a unit variously estimated between 60 and 80 musicians strong. This was the musical hit of the show, playing at the opening and at pretty much every major function. According to contemporary newspaper reports, its repertoire included Mexican waltzes and schottisches (some of which were published in New Orleans). But most importantly it included a number of danzas—a term that in Mexico covered pretty much anything with the bass known in Cuba as the danza habanera and in the U.S. as the habanera.

The "Mexican Band" hit New Orleans well before the birth of jazz. In 1884, Buddy Bolden (who is often described as the first jazz trumpeter) was seven

This Mexican octet entertained passengers on a Mississippi sternwheeler throughout the late 1880s. Documentation is still extremely sparse, but every fragment that emerges suggests more strongly that the number of Latin groups playing in the U.S. during the nineteenth century—and their influence on Anglo popular music—was considerable. *Author's collection*

years old and the first rag was more than a decade from publication. But, the band's musical impact continued after it went home. First, it set a particularly high standard of technical musicianship for local bands. Second, sheet music of pieces it had played at local concerts began appearing in 1885. Advertisements for the publishing house of Junius Hart alone show 35 Latin numbers, all Mexican, and many advertised specifically "as played by the Mexican Band." They included seven identified danzas, four schottisches, ten mazurkas, one danzón ("Ausencia")—also called a danza elsewhere—seven waltzes, two polkas, and various pieces not identified by rhythm. Several other numbers from the band's repertoire were published by Louis Grunewald in a collection with a cover offering "Souvenirs of the famous band of the Eighth Mexican Cavalry as played at the World's Exposition at New Orleans." Among them are at least two danzas and a mazurka.

Even if the band of the 8th Mexican Cavalry had been the only one to play Latin music in the New Orleans of the 1880s, that would be enough to support Jelly Roll Morton's assertion of a "Spanish" tinge in jazz. But there were in fact others, as New Orleans researcher Jack Stewart has documented in a couple of articles in *The Jazz Archivist*. How many, is not certain. As Stewart shows, press reports and other evidence of the time were vague enough that references to "the Mexican Band" and an Orquesta Típica Mexicana may have been to more than one group. Stewart argues that "one can safely conclude that Mexican music had a fairly large presence in New Orleans during an especially fertile period in the city's musical history," and even that the general region could have provided a larger market for Mexican music than Mexico itself. To that, I would only add that some of what the Mexican groups played was almost certainly of Cuban origin (as was the danza rhythm), and that there is enough circumstantial evidence to suggest that a Cuban presence in late nineteenth-century New Orleans is far more likely than its absence.

When the Mexican Band (or bands) went home, several of its musicians stayed in the New Orleans music scene. One was Florenzo Ramos, a sax player born in Mexico around 1865, who was one of the founders of the New Orleans musicians' union. According to writer Al Rose (*A New Orleans Jazz Family Album*), Ramos Senior "played with everybody" from the French Opera House to Stalebread Lacoume, leader of a street "spasm" band on the lines of the later jug and washboard groups. Another musician said to have arrived in New Orleans with the Mexican Band, Joe Viscara or Viscaya, later played with Jack "Papa" Laine's group, the leading white jazz band of the time. Viscara was a sax player of whom Laine said, "He could hardly speak American, but that son of a bitch could handle a horn!" Yet another member of Laine's band was an uncle of Alcide "Yellow" Nunez, the clarinetist with the white Original Dixieland Jazz Band, the first jazz group to record, in 1917 (though he had quit the ODJB by then). Nunez was apparently also part-Cuban, as he was related to Laine's wife, herself Cuban.

But the New Orleans/Latin connection in the pre-jazz days went well beyond the Mexican Band, or the other Mexican groups of whose presence in New Orleans there are hints. Of the musicians mentioned by early jazz interviewees, around ten percent had Spanish names. Of these, some were definitely Spanish-from-Spain; others had been in New Orleans or at least the U.S. for at least a couple of generations. But even some of these had links or experiences that could have exposed them to Latin influences. Perhaps the most important example was the Tio family, an impressive clan of reed players, one of whose members— Lorenzo, Jr.—at some time or other taught several of the leading black clarinetists of early jazz, including Sydney Bechet, Johnny Dodds, and "Big Eye" Louis Nelson. According to Professor Lawrence Gushee, the Tios had lived in Louisiana for generations, but had come to New Orleans in 1877 from Tampico, a seaport on the Caribbean coast of Mexico that borders the province of Vera

Cruz, where they had lived for around 15 years. The first language of clarinetist Lorenzo Tio, Sr., who was active musically in the New Orleans of the 1880s, was Spanish, and he and other family members are said to have studied at the Mexico Conservatory. According to Donald Marquis's *In Search of Buddy Bolden*, Lorenzo, Sr. and his brother Louis played with the Excelsior Brass Band.[1]

At one time or another Papa Laine hired other musicians with Latin connections. One of them, an important witness to the Latin element in New Orleans, was "Chink" Martin, a string-player whose parents (according to Martin himself) were Mexican and Spanish. A lengthy interview with Martin includes a host of passing references to a Latin music scene of some significance in the city around the turn of the century. Martin said that Royal Street between Dumaine and Esplanade was inhabited mostly by Mexicans and Spaniards as were several other blocks, and that Latin music was common in the Vieux Carré. He told of singing street serenades with Mexican and Spanish musicians (the songs he recalled singing were "La Paloma," "La Golondrina," and one from Puerto Rico called "Cuba"). He also remembered playing with a Mexican group in seamen's bars on Decatur Street around 1913 and working as a violinist with a Puerto Rican guitarist and a bassist of unstated origin with a Spanish name.

Compared with the Mexicans, relatively few individual New Orleans musicians are mentioned as having Cuban links, but even aside from the possibility that the word "Spanish" may have hidden some Cubans—which isn't certain, because immigration from Andalucia to the New World was at a peak in the last couple of decades of the century—various witnesses mentioned phenomena that sound intriguingly familiar. Guitarist Danny Barker describes times when ". . . the rhythm . . . would play that mixture of African and Spanish syncopation—with a beat—and with just the rhythm going." That sounds awfully like the Cuban street rumba. However, what does it mean? Did these groups perform a percussion jam in the middle of an instrumental piece? Or one of those Latin-shaded percussion-only segments that are heard in some of the later street brass band recordings? How much Cuban/New Orleans contact was there at street and popular level, anyway? Havana and New Orleans were on the same classical and theatrical tour circuits, and both cities were major Caribbean ports. The evidence is incomplete, but evocative.

All the Latin musicians I've mentioned played with white or creole bands (when segregation became more vicious with the 1894 tightening of the Black

---

[1] There is, of course, no telling how much Mexican music was absorbed by the pre-jazz generation of Tios, nor what that music was like in the nineteenth century. But recorded examples of the traditional harp and fiddle-led string band music of the Vera Cruz area are notably "hot," to use a handy though undeservedly unfashionable word, to describe their complex and markedly swinging rhythms.

Codes, most Latin musicians seem to have gone wherever they were accepted). I've come across no mention of identifiable nineteenth-century Afro-Cuban musicians in New Orleans. But there's a Louis Rodriguez, who seems clearly Afro-Latin, in an early photo of Jimmy Paolo's band. Another highly suggestive clue lies in the name of Perlops López, said to have run one of the city's first black bands in the 1880s. He exists as one passing mention turned up by Donald Marquis: nothing else remains. But I wonder: An African-American musician might be called López, of course . . . but Perlops? Classical names—even obscure ones—are popular among Latin Americans. If López was Afro-Latino, of course, he could have come from Puerto Rico, or even Colombia. But Cuba—as a port, a country already musically significant, and one that had strong general, political, and emotional links with New Orleans—seems to me the most likely bet.

It is also likely that some New Orleans musicians heard Cuban or Mexican music in their places of origin. The older Tios, of course, would have heard the music of Vera Cruz as children. And Manuel Mello, who played with one of Jack Laine's orchestras, is said to have worked for a while in a sugar house in Oriente Province—a particularly rich musical area and home of the Afro-Cuban *son* style which, under the name of rumba, was to sweep the U.S. and the world in the 1930s. Other direct connections were vaguer: Willie Cornish, Buddy Bolden's trombonist, served in the Spanish-American War, although for how long and in what conditions we do not know.

The early Latin influences in New Orleans (and elsewhere) seem to have been varied, but they have often been disguised by a number of factors. One is the way in which jazz history until recently has been written. An exclusive focus on jazz itself has left us with an overly narrow view of groups that usually played a range of dance music, of which jazz was only part. Moreover, much early jazz research was influenced by various political, ethnic, and romanticizing agendas that have disguised the complexity of the story. Mostly these have led them to overplay the working-class, black, and folk-oriented aspects of the music. Early jazz researchers to the contrary, neither ragtime nor jazz was some "pure" music set in sharp distinction to a "trivial" pop culture; they were part of that pop culture. Pianist Tony Jackson's composition "Pretty Baby" was not just a jazz classic but a New Orleans pop song.

A tendency toward loose terminology, though it can sometimes be helpful, can also be misleading. In an excellent article on the Creole origins of jazz, for example, Thomas Fiehrer often talks of Creoles from other parts of the Caribbean basin. But, while French and Spanish creole music had a good deal in common, there were equally important differences, and Fiehrer does not distinguish between the two. He does, however, point up a large number of telling factors, including the presence of many multiracial families headed by Cubans (as well as other Creoles) in the 1880 census. He also discusses the Saint-Domingue (Haitian) influence in nineteenth-century New Orleans, which seems to have been large. To what extent were the Haitian refugee musicians who reached New Orleans via Cuba influenced by Cuban music? Who knows? But they were trained players who spread a level of musical education in nineteenth-century New Orleans that has always been ignored.

They were not alone. Even in Puerto Rico, something of a backwater in colonial days compared with Cuba, bandleaders in the late nineteenth and early twentieth centuries were remarkable for both versatility and activity. Manuel Tizol (one of the Tizol dynasty that provided Duke Ellington with his famous valve-trombonist and composer of "Caravan") conducted open-air concerts and parades, organized chamber groups and cultural societies for the San Juan elite, and ran a dance orchestra. Bandleaders in provincial cities were at least as versatile. And If this was true of Puerto Rico and the Dominican Republic, how much truer of Cuba and Mexico! The rigid but very thorough solfeggio system that annoyed jazz pianist Ferdinand "Jelly Roll" Morton must have been widely taught in New Orleans, as it was—and to some extent still is—in the Latin Caribbean.

The issue of Latin influence in pre-jazz New Orleans is made far more complicated by the existence of local creole songs with clear links to the French-speaking Caribbean (a handful of these, notably "Eh Là Bas," ended up as minor jazz standards). Moreover, those French-Caribbean islands themselves, particularly Haiti, contributed greatly to the New Orleans mix. More than 10,000 Haitian refugees reached New Orleans in around 1810 after spending ten years in Cuba. They certainly introduced the Haitian version of the calenda, a dance found all over the Caribbean (and in Cajun Louisiana). And they and their immediate descendants, having helped in the Caribbeanization of Franco-New Orleans music, certainly would have found the early danzas less strange than Anglos.[2] Later recordings of New Orleans creole numbers such as "Eh Là Bas" by Kid Ory and the like, in fact, had rhythms very close to the *son*/rumba—though perhaps suspiciously so, given that they were mostly recorded after a decade of U.S. rumba mania.

If the degree of possible Latin influence in nineteenth-century New Orleans music has been less underrated than ignored, the same is true many times over

---

[2] Morton was of Haitian descent on both sides, according to Fiehrer.

for the U.S. as a whole. The New Orleans fixation of many jazz researchers led to a lot of interviewing, however narrow or unfocused some of it may have been. For the rest of the country, we have nothing but hints. About the only nineteenth-century black musician credited with a definite Latin tinge—in a passing reminiscence by Eubie Blake—was pianist Jess Pickett, who played in "The Jungle" near Hell's Kitchen on New York's West Side, as well as in Philadelphia. Pickett's most famous number (though some say it was composed by an even more shadowy figure, Jack the Bear) was variously called "The Dream," "Ladies' Dream," "Bowdiger's Dream," and "Digah's Dream," and Pickett himself had once called it the "Bull-Dyke's Dream," because, he claimed, it was popular with Lesbian prostitutes in the bordellos. The year of its composition isn't clear, but if Pickett played it at the World's Columbian Exposition in Chicago in 1893, as Rudi Blesh claimed, it would qualify as one of the earliest rags or proto-rags.

According to Eubie Blake, Pickett performed "The Dream" with a Latin-based first part and a section played (as far as we can tell the sense of the phrase "slow drag") at least moderately bluesy, which Pickett used to teach Blake to play ragtime! The version on Blake's 1969 Columbia recording, which he claimed was exactly as Pickett taught it to him, is a mix of Latin, ragtime, and bluesy elements: ragtime intro and breaks, a strongly ragtime right hand over a very marked habanera rhythm (so well integrated as to make it clear how admirably the rhythms meshed), phrases or short passages bluesy enough that I recognize some of them from later barrelhouse recordings (notably some fast triplet ripples used by Cow Cow Davenport in his "Cow Cow Blues"), and moody bass clusters.

Blake, incidentally, mentioned another piece of Latin influence on African-American music in a conversation with Rudi Blesh cited in his *Combo U.S.A.* Talking about how he learned to play ragtime on a parlor reed organ, he described losing his first girlfriend to a musician called Edward Dowell, who "played a doubled bass, da-da, da-da (two notes for each one I, or anyone else, played) and put it into a tricky Brazilian maxixe rhythm with wide jumps." What Blake called a maxixe many years later was probably a fast habanera (the maxixe, which was itself influenced by the habanera, was not yet in existence). But, alas, like virtually every jazz writer faced with a reference to a Latin tinge, Blesh failed to follow up this extraordinary description of an apparent boogie-woogie-cum-Latin bass in 1895!

Nineteenth-century proto-piano-blues is so undocumented that Pickett's habanera bass could have been common or a fluke. Either way, it was a genuine habanera bass in strong contrast to the universally steady one-two-three-four of ragtime basses. But I seriously doubt that he was the only proto-ragtime pianist who played with a Latin twist. "The Dream" may have been unique in its habanera bass, but it could equally well have been a typical slow-drag. After all, the phrase itself fits a slow tango type held-note rhythm as well as, if not better than, slow common time.

It is also possible that early ragtime itself, including both cakewalks arranged for piano and "classic ragtime," had a greater Latin element than has been recognized. The problem is that any links there may be are unprovable, because the only cakewalks we know are written compositions in the ragtime tradition, and because the danza habanera rhythm and its variants are similar to rhythmic patterns common in a very wide range of New World music. One of them, which any American would regard as quintessential ragtime, was in fact pretty much identical to the nineteenth-century Brazilian lundú rhythm. Because written cakewalks have the steady left-hand part of ragtime piano scores, any Latin elements are audible only in the right-hand patterns. "Smoky Mokes" (published in 1899) is a pretty obvious example of a Cuban influence in the right-hand rhythms, and the same Havanese ghost seems to hover over the 1897 "Mississippi Rag," which is both a cakewalk and the first published piece with the word "rag" in the title. One aspect of ragtime that has never been raised as far as I know is the possibility that the almost universal steady left hand of written ragtime was a publishing convention and that improvised ragtime may have been more varied. According to Rudi Blesh, Sam Patterson always played Scott Joplin and Louis Chauvin's "Heliotrope Bouquet" as a tango (read "habanera"). Because Patterson was a personal friend of Joplin, it's at least possible that this was the way its composers played it when they weren't producing a score to please a music publisher. And if so, why not others?

Just as the Mexican Band provided a smoking gun for early Latin influence on New Orleans, so another, smaller group provides a similar link for a Latin-ragtime connection. One of the most important crucibles of classic ragtime was the St. Louis area, where Scott Joplin, Louis Chauvin, and many others played. St. Louis, of course, is on the Mississippi. And a Mexican octet led by a Professor T. F. Gloria played for several years on one of the more luxurious Mississippi River steamers, the *Stella Wilds*, starting with her maiden voyage in 1886. A photo included by Joan and Thomas Gandy in their book *The Mississippi Steamboat*, shows the group to have consisted of a cornet, flute, valve trombone, two alto or tenor horns, violin, guitar, and double bass (bowed, in the photo). Gloria composed a "Stella Wilds Mazurka" to celebrate the band's booking, but I have no doubt at all that they also played the popular danzas. The *Stella Wilds* and any other steamers with Mexican groups aboard were travelling into the upriver ragtime heartland of the St. Louis/Sedalia area (which already had special cultural links with New Orleans, being part of French province of Upper Louisiana Purchase) and on up to Vicksburg, Memphis, and beyond, some of them traveling as far as Cincinnati. Given that the bands on the steamers frequently gave shipboard concerts for the locals where they docked (a source cited by Jack Stewart talked of hearing a Latin shipboard group playing at Natchez), it's quite likely that Professor Gloria's group reinforced the effect of any habanera sheet music that might have found its way to St. Louis.

At least one written claim of a Latin tinge in ragtime goes back to its very early days. An African-American composer, Benjamin R. Harney, published a *Ragtime Instructor* in the 1890s whose introduction states specifically that "Rag time (or Negro Dance Time) originally takes its initiative steps from Spanish music, or rather from Mexico, where it is known under the head and names of Habanara, Danza, Seguidilla, etc." Though he wrote at least one classic song, "You've Been a Good Old Wagon But You Done Broke Down," Harney is *persona non grata* with ragtime scholars for his self-billing as "inventor of ragtime," the fact that the arrangements in his *Instructor* were by somebody else, and his looseness in defining ragtime. But the mere fact that in the dawn of ragtime somebody—whether Harney or his ghostwriter—saw a Latin connection with any African-American music back when ragtime was in its formative stage, is critical. At the very least, he was there when it was happening.

More recently, the notion of any such link has, typically enough, come in for a less-than-benign neglect. In fact, Samuel Charters and Leonard Kunstadt make it an indictment in their 1966 book, *Jazz: A History of the New York Scene*, summing up the supposed "commercialism" of the remarkably talented crop of young, black pre-World War I New York composers with: "When tangos were popular they wrote tangos, when blues were popular they wrote blues" (surprise!). In reality, a habanera/tango tinge was part of the black popular and theater music that fed into ragtime from the start. William Tyers's "La Trocha" (see below) was an early example.

The examples of rags with habanera or, later, tango influences (stylistically there's very little difference, if any) are legion—not just in pop-ragtime and ragtime songs, but in so-called classic rags as well. One, cited by William J. Shafer and Johannes Riedel in their *The Art of Ragtime*, was Henry Lodge's "Temptation Rag," whose popularity they specifically attribute to a "persistent habanera-like rhythmic pattern developed through distinctive themes." Another

Ben Harney, composer and ragtime pianist, was one of the first to state in print that ragtime had a strong Latin element. He did so as far back as 1898! *Frank Driggs Collection*

musician Shafer and Riedel mention as having a Latin tinge is Artie Matthews, who "explored the uses of Latin rhythms and blues-derived bass lines in his series of 'Pastime Rags,' going well beyond anything in Joplin, Scott or Lamb."

"Heliotrope Bouquet" aside, Scott Joplin also showed signs of Latin influence. At least once it was conscious. His 1909 "Solace—A Mexican Serenade" opens with an habanera bass with a slow rag above it. Blesh and Janis see it as "a most unusual tango for the period: it avoids the minor mode, and its melodies are rather anticipatory of those of the Brazilian maxixe, which was to be introduced a few years later." In reality it has nothing to do with the tango—or the Brazilian maxixe, or in any precise sense the Mexican *serenada*. It's a pleasant mood piece with a mostly habanera bass, whose links with Mexican music are more a question of feeling than imitation or recreation. It was, in fact, a real and far-from-unusual example of a Latin tinge in an African-American piece of the era.

In addition to this overt reference to Latin rhythms, passages in several Joplin rags, including the famous "The Entertainer," may be habanera-inspired. In places there's a habanera pattern to the right hand itself; in others the right hand is so phrased that it seems to cry out for an habanera rhythm rather than the steady oom-pah written. But on the whole it is the slower or more reflective pieces that sound the most likely candidates for habanera influence. Some pieces fool the listener. The first strain of Joplin's "The Cascades" is without anything one might claim as an habanera influence, but the second strain sounds almost as though a memory of the rhythm had been built into it for contrast. Joplin's "Weeping Willow," "Eugenia," and "Reflection Rag" present a different version of the same notion. Much of the right-hand phrasing in both "Reflection Rag" and "The Easy Winners" is straight habanera, and in fact the melody line in one of the later sections of "Reflection Rag" sounds extraordinarily old-Cuban.

Over time, the relationship between ragtime and Cuban music was mutual. But it can't be argued that the first influence was from the U.S. south to Cuba, for the simple reason that the habanera reached the U.S. 20 years before the first rag was published, and New Orleans at least was awash with habanera-derived Mexican danzas in sheet music form in the decade leading up to ragtime's efflorescence. Absent analysis of sheet music published elsewhere, particularly in St. Louis—the first ragtime center and a major music-publishing center besides—we can only speculate on the degree of influence the habanera *might* have had. I believe there is at least preliminary reason to assume it was major.

Part of the problem with this whole subject is that the distinctions that are useful if kept fluid have come to be set in stone. As Jess Pickett shows, ragtime, blues, and whatever else went into the hopper were being mixed from the start. Jelly Roll Morton is a key figure in understanding the process, both because he is exceptionally well-documented and because he was born in New Orleans but travelled widely, and decades later talked intelligently into a recording machine about what he heard.

Pretty much the only universally quoted evidence for a Latin element in early jazz was Jelly Roll Morton's comment (made in the late 1930s, when such a notion was not fashionable) that a "Spanish tinge" was what distinguished jazz from ragtime: "if you can't manage to put tinges of Spanish in your tunes, you will never be able to get the right seasoning, I call it, for jazz." In his famous Library of Congress interviews with Alan Lomax, Morton uses "La Paloma"— already a standard when he was a young man—to illustrate the process. His commentary further confirms that there was plenty of Latin music to be heard in the New Orleans of the period.

Morton commented: "I heard *a lot of Spanish tunes* [my emphasis], and I tried to play them in correct tempo, but I personally didn't believe they were really perfected in the tempos. Now take 'La Paloma,' which I transformed in New Orleans style. You leave the left hand just the same. The difference comes in the right hand—in the syncopation, which gives it an entirely different color that really changes the color from red to blue."

Morton might have said the syncopated right hand turned the piece red, white, and blue. As he plays, the piece's Latin-ness disappears and something emerges that would be heard time and again from ragtime into jazz-funk: American-Latin. What makes Morton's demonstration particularly interesting is the (distractingly loud) straight-4/4 foot-tapping, which shows eloquently how easily the danza patterns could be blended with ragtime's steady 4/4 bass.

"La Paloma" was far from being the whole story. Morton wrote and recorded several numbers with a habanera bass over the years, and in fact it was while talking to Lomax about the first of these that the "Spanish tinge" came up. The problem with discussing Morton's own "Spanish tinge" is that his earliest solo piano recording dates from 1923, by which time an awful lot of water had flowed under everybody's musical bridge. However, the fact that there's a good deal of underlying consistency in his solo recordings between the early 1920s and the more extended versions he recorded for Alan Lomax and the Library of Congress in 1938 make them at least partially reliable as evidence.

His first recording, suitably enough, was "New Orleans Blues" in a fairly fast version lightly disguised as "New Orleans Joys." This shows a complex interlinking of Latin, ragtime/stride, and blues elements. It opens with a bright tango rhythm in the left hand under a right hand with ragtime rhythms but adds bluesy intonations, and at one point a wonderful treble equivalent of a barrelhouse walking bass, before moving into a straight-stride style towards the end, including an Earl-Hines-like "trumpet style" right hand.

The longer and somewhat slower Library of Congress version allows for more variation but the elements are similar. Again a loose ragtime opening gives way to a habanera bass set against bluesy stride right-hand patterns, but the habanera is contrasted a couple of times with a descending semi-walking four-to-the-bar bass pattern usually associated with deep barrelhouse playing. Again, there is a right-hand "walking treble" passage, and again the piece in general gets more bluesy as it goes on. Morton begins tapping a straight 4/4 beat contrasting with the habanera left hand, and finally abandons the habanera bass for barrelhouse-like patterns.

At least judging by 1920s recordings, the Spanish tinge was milder in Morton's next relevant composition, the 1905 "Jelly Roll Blues." Neither in his 1924 piano solo nor the 1926 version by the Red Hot Peppers (this time called

"Original Jelly Roll Blues"), is there much that is Latin about the opening strains: a ghostly memory in rhythms with touches of the Black Bottom, some overtones in the stop-time passages, a passing hint of a tango bass in a bridge. Here, unlike the more complex approach of "New Orleans Blues," Morton uses a device similar to W.C. Handy's "Memphis Blues," by setting a section with a habanera bass—accented in the band version by the out-of-place castanets so beloved of 1920s groups playing anything Latin—as a contrast to kicking stride passages.

The possible influence of Latin music is relatively easy to track in piano ragtime because it was written down, and in Jelly Roll Morton because he was so self-aware and consistent over time. The issue becomes a lot tougher in the case of bands playing early or pre-jazz, because their music has not survived either as scores or recordings. But there are hints. As I have already mentioned, bands led by Buddy Bolden played different material depending on circumstances, including waltzes, mazurkas, and polkas, all of which existed in New Orleans in Mexican forms, as well as rags and what sound from contemporary descriptions like early blues. There is, of course, no way of knowing what the Latin music "in the air" did for the embryonic styles of jazz. Not only are there no recordings and no transcriptions, but influence—even profound influence—is often unrecognized by the people undergoing or witnessing it. Moreover, some of the basic rhythmic phrasings of ragtime and early jazz—notably the cakewalk's ta-tum-ta-ta-tum—crop up frequently in earlier U.S. styles; and lastly, influences have a tendency to be mutual and set up a complex of cross-currents that would drown the hardiest researcher.

By the turn of the century, New Orleans was getting its habanera influence from the New York theatre as well as the ships from Havana. From the 1890s to 1915, New York saw an extraordinary upsurge of black musical theater. The shows that came out of this flowering were written by a dozen or more once-famous black composers. Many of them contained at least one habanera or habanera-influenced piece, and they all took these songs across country on more or less extended tours. One example of a song with an habanera-style bass was "Under the Bamboo Tree," written for *Sally In Our Alley*, and included also in the 1903 *Nancy Brown*. By July 1903, according to Schafer, William J. Braun's Naval Brigade Band was playing it at Audubon Park. Thereafter the jazz bands picked it up, and it was still sufficiently remembered for Kid Ory to record it in 1945.

And that was just one example with a particularly clear jazz link. The 1906 show *The Shoo-Fly Regiment* by James Reese Europe and Bob Cole included a "filipino" number, "On the Gay Luneta," with a habanera bass. The 1908 *The Red Moon* included "On the Road to Monterey," another habanera-influenced piece.

The group run by the semi-legendary New Orleans trumpeter Buddy Bolden is sometimes called the first jazz band. But in common with many others it also played whatever dance rhythms its patrons wanted. Trombonist Willie Cornish spent several months with a military band in Cuba after the Spanish-American War. *Frank Driggs Collection*

Bob Cole and James Weldon Johnson's 1904 "Mexico," with an intermittent but dominant habanera ostinato bass, was the hit song of *Humpty Dumpty*, which played to white audiences on Broadway. And in 1911, James Tim Brymn's "Porto Rico," from the show *His Honor the Barber* (which toured the Midwest before opening in New York City, and later went to San Francisco) used a rhythm which though not a habanera, has a very similar pulse.

The theatrical connection is important here. As Riis remarks in *Just Before Jazz*, "No style or genre in popular music could be isolated from all others, and the amount of borrowing and imitation was considerable." Riis was talking of black theater musicals, but the same was equally true of ragtime and jazz, both of which were merely a part—even if the most creative part—of a much wider popular music scene. Musical shows went on tour. Many musicians known to us as jazzmen not only heard them but adopted some of them, and even played in their pit orchestras. And whether played throughout the country in the black (and probably also in white) musicals, or in New Orleans in the formative years of

The Reliance Brass Band in 1910. Cornet player Manuel Mello heard proto-rumbas when he spent some years in Cuba. Tuba player Chink Martin, by his own account, played with Latin groups and musicians in new Orleans. Moreover, there's some evidence Cuban danzas were a permanent part of the repertoire of bands like this. Certainly they played danza-inspired U.S. show tunes like "Under the Bamboo Tree." *Frank Driggs Collection*

jazz and band ragtime, or travelling up-river on the sternwheelers, the habanera was a minor but a permanent part of African-American popular music for all of the 35 years during which ragtime and proto-jazz were forming and developing.

The stage shows were not the only New York influence on early jazz, nor the only one with a Latin tinge. William Tyers, who wrote dance tunes as well as musical comedy pieces, composed "Panama" (1911), which had a habanera-like bass in its original scoring. It became one of the most enduring of early jazz classics and brassband pieces, and though it soon lost its habanera rhythm, it was played in its original form in the orchestral arrangement of the New Orleans society ragtime orchestra run by Armand J. Piron. And even where the original habanera bass was long gone, its effect sometimes lingers. You can still hear it in a recording of the Olympia Brass Band of New Orleans. A fairly straight common-time holds sway for a while. Then the marching drums break into a long passage remarkably like common conga-drum patterns, and the final choruses fuse habanera and march-band rhythms in a fascinating hybrid. "Panama" became so well-known among New Orleans bands that William J. Schafer, in his *Brass Bands and New Orleans Jazz*, calls it a "grand old New Orleans march," which indeed it had become. Nevertheless, its origin was the early days of U.S.-Latin music.

Tyers was working with the habanera long before "Panama," and it seems likely that some of his work influenced early ragtime composers. In 1896 he wrote a piece called "La Trocha," described on the score as a "Cuban Dance," that appears to have been widely played. In 1908, he wrote another Latin-influenced work with legs, "Maori—A Samoan Dance" (yes, that's right!). This had a particularly interesting rhythm, not strictly a habanera but reminiscent of what Americans were to call the rumba. "Maori" is thoroughly forgotten now, but it was around long enough that Duke Ellington recorded three versions in 1930.

By happenstance, "Maori" also influenced another key black composer. W.C. Handy had already encountered Cuban music by 1900, when his band played some gigs on the island. He included an arrangement of the Cuban national album, "El Himno de Bayames," in his repertoire, and he also was struck by a much more rootsy Cuban idiom played by small groups in the back streets. Many years later, Handy wrote, "These fascinated me because they were playing a strange native air, new and interesting to me. More than thirty years later I heard that rhythm again. By then it had gained respectability in New York and had acquire a name—the rumba."

That might, of course, have been that. But in 1906 or thereabouts, he had an experience that struck him forcibly and with permanent results on jazz. As he tells it in his autobiography, he was playing at a black carnival site called Dixie Park in Memphis (a town without any overt Caribbean links, be it noted, but one at which the *Stella Winds* and Professor Gloria probably docked). Among the numbers the band played was Tyers's "Maori," and it triggered something in black dancers that Handy found remarkable. He noted, "When we . . . came to the habanera rhythm, containing the beat of the tango, I observed that there was a sudden, proud and graceful reaction . . . White dancers, as I had observed them, took the number in stride . . ."

Suspecting some kind of unexpected ethnic response, Handy had the band play "La Paloma" as a reality check, and got exactly the same response from black dancers. It was this experience, according to Handy himself, that led him to introduce the rhythm (which he called a "tangana") into the instrumental piano version of "Memphis Blues," the chorus of "Beale Street Blues," and most famously the opening of "St. Louis Blues" (though this was published in 1916, at the height of the tango craze—so perhaps there were other reasons for Handy jumping on the Latin bandwagon!).

Yet another African-American style with at least occasional habanera influences was New York stride piano, a flamboyant amplification of jazz and ragtime which may have been influenced by composers like Tyers or by earlier players like Pickett, Dowell, and their long-forgotten peers, or (my guess) both. One surviving example is the 1910 "Spanish Venus," by the great ragtime/stride pianist Luckey Roberts (a version of which was recorded by Eubie Blake in 1969). In 1939, Roberts—born Charles Luckeyth Roberts in 1893, so that he was 20 when the tango craze hit—turned this into an unpublished *Spanish Suite* for piano and orchestra along with two other movements, "Spanish Fandango" (which he later recorded for the Good Time Jazz label) and "Porto Rico Maid." It seems to me fairly obvious that these both stemmed from the same period as "Spanish Venus." The titles alone are something of a giveaway, and the copyright notice in the Goodtime Jazz recording gives "Spanish Fandango" as "Public Domain." As Roberts played it on the album, "Spanish Fandango" is highly ornate in the fashion of the stride style, with florid right-hand runs and a definite tango feel, though the rhythm is broken up. It was a show piece, not one for dancers.

Morton may have been a special case, "Panama" may have been another, Jess Pickett another, Handy's experience a fourth, and on and on. But there comes a point at which skepticism becomes a state of denial. Evidence is scattered, in large measure because until recently interviewers have consistently failed to follow up passing references to habanera and maxixe influences made by early jazz musicians, and it is hard to disentangle Latin influences from somewhat similar African-American rhythmic patterns—not to mention later players' habit of ironing out Latin elements originally present in some compositions. But I believe it to be highly likely that both rhythms were a persistent—even if minor—element at the heart of ragtime's (and therefore early jazz's) development, as well as showing up as a strain in mainstream popular music.

As far as that mainstream was concerned, in fact, this strain was soon to become anything but minor. Thanks to the fact that an American touring company had left an Anglo-American dance team stranded in Paris in 1912, the first (or was it second?) Latin Revolution was about to break out.

2

Tango Land

The 1910s–1920s

The popularity of the habanera's one-measure clave pattern was given an enormous boost on February 3, 1913, when a musical comedy called *The Sunshine Girl* opened at the Knickerbocker Theatre on Broadway with a new singing star, Julia Sanderson, and a young husband-and-wife dancing team, Vernon and Irene Castle, in the cast.

Within months, the tango (whose rhythm was basically a faster habanera) was a national mania. The Castles were pulling down a thousand pre-World-War I dollars for single appearances and running a dance school whose orchestra was (very remarkably for the time) conducted by two of New York's most famous African-American composers, W. H. Tyers and James Reese Europe, who was also the Castles' musical director. For a while, the Castles also featured the Brazilian maxixe (which was similar enough to the tango that it was sometimes called a "tango brésilien" on sheet music). The maxixe had nothing like the phenomenal lifespan of the tango, which (its current revival aside) was still going fairly strong in the early 1950s, but it did surface occasionally as the first U.S. Brazilian tinge in jazz.

The degree of the tango's influence on jazz depends to a large extent on whether you consider ragtime as a tributary of jazz or a separate stream. Ragtime and ragtime songs were at their popular peak at the time the tango hit, and a number of "ragtime tangos" soon joined the earlier habanera-based rags in the repertoire, among them the archetypally named "Tango Rag" by Abe Olman; "Everybody Tango" by a white pianist from Indianapolis called Paul Pratt; and a "Chicken Tango," published by the dean of ragtime publishing, John Stark, who despite his rather austere approach to ragtime—he issued only "classic" piano

James Reese Europe's Clef Club Band was essentially the group with which he backed the Castles. The banjos grouped at front were part of a deliberately Afro-American sound and considerably influenced American versions of the tango. *Frank Driggs Collection*

rags—also published an Ed Hallaway piece called "Tango Tea." Ragtime com-posers, in fact, now used tango elements in their work, just as they had earlier used the virtually identical habanera. More than one "classic" ragtime composer also composed tangos. Henry C. Lodge wrote a forgotten piece called "Tango Land" full of rather adventurous progressions, which was popular enough at the time to appear on an Edison cylinder recording, and Cincinnati ragtime pianist Joe Jordan composed another called simply "The Tango." Thomas Turpin, anoth-er "classic" composer, wrote a "Pan-Am Rag" in 1914 that Dave Jasen and Trebor J. Tichenor describe as having an implied tango rhythm and feeling—not surprisingly in this case, as it was written for the Pan-American Exposition. And Artie Mathews, whom Jelly Roll Morton considered one of the best black pianists in St. Louis, wrote a five-part series called "Pastimes." Only the first of these is much played by ragtime revivalists, but two of the other parts were strongly tango influenced: "Number Three," whose A section has what Jasen and Tichnor call a "beautiful, reflective tango"; and "Number 5," which in places uses "dotted" or held rhythms alternating with straight 4/4. This technique, which Jasen and Tichnor describe as typical of late ragtime, was still being used by bass players in proto-Latin-jazz numbers throughout the 1920s and into the 1930s.

It is easy to laugh at the tangos the Edison company was recording by 1913, using a small brass band to slightly odd effect. But they provided a valuable early example of the way in which America's Latin tinge was processed. The 1913 recording of "La Bella Argentina," for example, was already a hybrid, with a tango rhythm, but melody lines, and particularly bridges, that would fit straight into a ragtime pianist's right-hand patterns. And more generally, the Edison cylinders show that rags works and tangos were seen as two sides of one coin. Several recordings back a tango with a rag (or one-step, which is a rag in false whiskers): "Muy Lindo Tango," the most Argentinian of the early Edison tangos, was paired with Henry Lodge's "Pastimes Rag."[1]

Oddly perhaps, very few piano tangos were recorded in the early days, though so many were published. One that did appear was Paul Riess's 1914 "Hacienda." Riess maintained a typically crisp, strutting (and far from inauthentic) tango rhythm in his left hand. His right-hand part was a lot more complex; many of its melodic patterns were pure tango, but much of the phrasing was essentially rag-time, while other phrases would fit into any rag even though they retained the tango's held notes. The harmony was another matter. "Hacienda"'s chord changes

---

[1] Not to be confused with the Mathews set.

were simpler than the multi-strain structure of classic ragtime, merely modulating into a second section in a different key, a common tango technique.

The tango rage was by no means a specifically white phenomenon. From 1913 on, Harlem's *New York Age* was full of advertisements and news items that make the tango's popularity in Harlem plain. The Astoria Cafe offered tango teas that included dancing lessons, and the Palace Casino and Manhattan Casino organized tango picnics, contests, and balls. Reports from the time suggest that the tango generated a number of songs mentioned as sung specifically at tango teas, including "I'm Crazy About My Tango Man," "That's Why I'm Loving Someone Else Today," "Back to the Carolina I Love," and "Every Girl is My Girl." Other reports mention a piece called the "Carolina Maxixe" and a "Darky Tango" described as a "new concept." These songs all suggest an instant African-American/Latin fusion of some sort. They may not have been jazz, but they were just the sort of black popular music on which jazz drew. And like their earlier relatives, they were part of an extremely active music scene, along with ragtime, black vaudeville, and early jazz. Most importantly for jazz, Harlem was the cradle of the virtuosic stride piano of musicians like James P. Johnson, Willie "the Lion" Smith, and Lucky Roberts (who was at the Astoria Cafe shortly before the tango teas were introduced there).

Recordings of the African-American take on the tango at this time are rare, but some do exist (along with a maxixe), featuring the band with which James Reese Europe backed the Castles. They are crisp and buoyant, but above all they reflect the specifically "African-American" sound that Europe targeted in all his bands, notably by the use of several banjos, which gave the rhythm a very distinctive throb lacking in all the other U.S. tango recordings of the time.[2]

Europe's was not the only African-American band playing tangos for white dancers. *Modern Dance* magazine for March 1914 mentions editorially, "Van Houten's colored orchestra at the Sans-Souci, with instrumentation a little out of the ordinary for Tango and Turkey Trot Orchestras, has proven one of the best combinations for this kind of work." I think it is a reasonable bet that the "out of the ordinary" instrumentation included a banjo. The same issue carries

---

[2] Thanks to Europe's and the Castles' popularity, the use of banjos in tango orchestras seems to have caught on to become one of the earmarks of the tango's indigenization. *That Half Barbaric Twang* (a history of the banjo in America) shows that U.S. banjo makers began plugging a new instrument called the "tango banjo" (with four strings tuned in an open fifth like the banjolin but a fifth lower), and reproduces an advertisement for the banjo in *The Crescendo* claiming that tango bands using it were paid double and adding "for the teacher this Tango craze should prove a Bonanza if properly handled."

Composer/pianist Charles "Lucky" Roberts was a leading spirit in the New York stride piano style. He composed several stride pieces with tango basses. *Frank Driggs Collection*

an advertisement for Oliver White's Select Society Orchestra offering music for tango teas, which specifially mentioned, seemingly as an ethnic hint, "that indispensible quality in its playing called rhythm, swing etc."

As with the habanera, African-American stage shows also helped spread the tango. A 1913 revival of *My Friend from Kentucky* included a couple, and there was a "Tango One-Step" in the *Ziegfeld Follies of 1914* that seems to have involved black dancers and to have been borrowed from the Harlem show. The composers of the early Harlem Renaissance also continued to write Latin-influenced material, and, in 1914, the Castles—at the height of their fame—traveled uptown to support James Reese Europe and his National Negro Orchestra in a concert that included tango and maxixe demonstrations and compositions by W. H. Tyers, Ford Dabney, and others. A full one quarter of the pieces performed were tangos or otherwise Latin-inspired.

In fact, it is certain that the tango was as big a deal among blacks as among whites at a time when ragtime was still at its popular peak and shading into or blending with jazz. Importantly, middle- and upper-class African-Americans often danced it to ragtime accompaniment. And though the press lost interest, the tango continued to be popular among blacks as well as whites: popular enough that it surfaced as a joke in a 1917 recording by the vaudeville star Bert Williams, "You Can't Get . . . What?," which includes the couplet: "Even village preachers/have engaged their tango teachers." Williams's joke would not have been funny if the tango's popularity had waned.

The most famous of all the early jazz/tango mixes, of course, is W.C. Handy's "St. Louis Blues," published in 1916. The tango rhythm is upfront and center, not buried in a third strain like the habanera passage of his earlier "Memphis Blues"; this was the most obvious of all W.C. Handy's "Latin" sections. But it was not the only number played by the embryonic jazz bands of the mid-teens to use the same format. Another was the particularly attractive "Egyptian Fantasy," used by the Original Creole Band to introduce their vaudeville act with which it toured the U.S.

At this juncture, there is no telling whether "Egyptian Fantasy" came out of the tango fashion or was resurrected from the New Orleans habanera tradition. It seems only to have been recorded once, in 1941, by Sidney Bechet. In his version, it is a beguiling number with a low-register clarinet opening (apparently almost identical to one originally played by George Baquet in the teens), whose easy, opening rhythm sounds to me more like the slower habanera than the crisper tango rhythm. But Bechet's recording, after all, was made more than a quarter century later. As to the way it was originally played, there is no hint.

The Harlem stride pianists took to the tango early, adopting and adapting it as enthusiastically as a previous generation of pianists did the habanera, presumably because they played for dancing cabarets—and even perhaps for tango teas—and also because it served as a tool in the virtuosic cutting contests in which they established their pecking order. "Tango la Caprice," by Willie "The Lion" Smith, was just such a show piece that the stride master used to wipe out the opposition. It was not for ordinary dancers (at least as he played it on a much later recording), and was full of complex playing in both the left and right hands, but you can clearly hear the crossover between stride and tango patterns in the right hand. Stride pianist/composer James P. Johnson, who was just starting his professional career during the first tango boom (his first professional gig was in 1912, when he was 18 years old) also may have picked up the tango elements around this time that were to surface on his solo and band recordings from 1921 to 1956.

If the tango was so dominant in the 1910s, why did jazz musicians, other than pianists, ignore it? In all probability, they didn't: as with so many things, we simply lack information. But "Egyptian Fantasy" was the theme tune of an important early jazz band on a major vaudeville tour, and there is no reason to suppose it was unique. After all, the first jazz-band recording was not made until 1917—four years after the tango hit—and the first African-American bands recorded around 1921, almost a decade after its arrival. By the time African-American bands went into the studio, in other words, the tango was no longer particularly hip, even though it was still popular with dancers. Moreover, not only were the early jazz-band recordings closer to vaudeville than the dance hall—they tended to have a deliberately hokey tinge—but they may have been affected by record-executive pressure to be novel. Certainly working jazz groups were playing tangos on the dance floor. In a 1948 interview in *Jazz Journal*, in fact, trumpeter Mutt Carey specifically mentions them as part of the repertoire of the Kid Ory band in its early days.

Only Jelly Roll Morton, the original Mr. "Spanish Tinge" himself, recorded many habanera/tango-bass solo piano pieces during the early 1920s. These recordings remain as particularly subtle and effective examples of a jazz/Latin blending that by now was certainly not a Morton monopoly. We have already noted his "New Orleans Joys" recorded in 1923 as an example of a ragtime-tango-stride mix (see Chapter 1). In April (or possibly May) of 1924, Morton recorded "Mama Nita," a later composition than his other Latin-tinged pieces, inspired by a (presumably Latina) girlfriend named Anita whom he met when he was working in California. The first recording of this composition opened with a series of fast, rather flashy interlinked breaks, then kicked into a crisp

Jazz pianist Ferdinand "Jelly Roll" Morton claimed jazz was not jazz without a "Spanish tinge", and put the theory into practice with a number of danza-based compositions. Here he is with Anita Gonzales, the inspiration for one of them, "Mama Nita." *Frank Driggs Collection*

tango/habanera bass with Morton's signature delayed rhythms in the right hand. Again, as was the case in "New Orleans Joys," his left hand mixed Latin and African-American elements, contrasting a tango rhythm with a four-to-the-bar barrelhouse-like rising bass figure.

Morton went back into the studio on June 9, 1924 and recorded three more habanera/tango numbers. One was another version of "Mama Nita" marginally slower than the first version (though a bit faster than his 1938 Library of Congress performance). In both these versions, one strain of the melody sounds very Brazilian. In the second, equally interestingly, the rising four-to-the-bar bass passage has an almost clave-ish feel, laid over a two-measure one-two-three-four/one-two pattern.

Next came a solo version of his "Jelly Roll Blues," which (like Handy's "Memphis Blues") used a habanera/tango section as a second-strain contrast to an opening strain, with touches of the Black Bottom (which had been introduced the same year in the Harlem musical *Dinah;* see Chapter 1). The third Latin-

Kid Ory's Original Creole Jazz Band in San Francisco in 1922, two years before it became the first black jazz group to record. Trumpeter Mutt Carey has testified that the group regularly played tangos and other popular dance rhythms on demand. *Frank Driggs Collection*

influenced piece of the session was "Tia Juana," whose opening sounded more like a popular song of the period than either jazz or any sort of Latin music. A light tango rhythm in the opening bars gave way to stride bass and ragged right hand. The second strain had a fast, almost nervous left-hand part that by moments sounded more like a Cuban *son*/rumba than a tango. The third strain returned to a 4/4 rhythm and, after a quick tango contrast, the piece rode out in common time. The effect was almost as if Morton were letting the two rhythmic traditions duke it out (the tango won by a nose in a perfunctory coda).

If it was rare to find a jazz pianist recording so many overtly Latin-tinged pieces in so short a period during the 1920s, it was even rarer among bands, though Morton himself recorded a band version of one of the numbers, now called "Original Jelly Roll Blues" (see Chapter 1). Other than this, I have come across only one other overtly Latinate late-1920s jazz piece by any group in the standard jazz pantheon: "Rumba Negro (sic)—Stomp," recorded by Benny

Moten & His Kansas City Orchestra in 1929 and credited to Moten and Count Basie (who had just joined the band from the Blue Devils). "Rumba Negro" was a charmingly eccentric number in a marked 2/4 time with a delicious-verging-on-hilarious rhythmic overlay that hinged on the joint efforts of Latinish castanets and a mildly hyperactive tuba. The piece soon kicked into a stomp rhythm with a nice trumpet solo and fine guitar work, under which the tuba moved repeatedly between 2/4 and tango, like the early ragtime-tango basses. A snatch of piano in Basie's early, by later standards almost florid style, was set off by vaguely Latin instrumental riffs. The whole thing combined slightly perverse ingenuity with a certain silliness typical of Latin-influenced recordings at the time.

Overt Latin elements are one thing. But given the degree to which the habanera and tango had been part of the milieu in which jazz grew up, an equally important issue is the degree to which Latin elements infiltrated early "straight" jazz itself and the styles of its individual players. I have run across only one specific reference to this whole topic. In 1988, Don Cherry specifically linked the playing of trumpeter Jabbo Smith with Morton's famous "Spanish tinge" remark and added: "Jabbo, he always had that in his trumpet." But many 1920s jazz and blues recordings with no ostensible Latin links showed what sound like tango influences, including numbers by one of the most famous studio groups in early jazz, Louis Armstrong's Hot Five. The most obvious example is the rhythm that opened "Heebie Jeebies," a straight tango that intermittently resurfaced—straight or modified—later in the piece. The stop-time chorus under Johnny Dodds clarinet solo in Armstrong's "My Heart" implied a skeletal tango rhythm, and the patterns of piano solo and parts of the banjo-playing in "Gut Bucket Blues" sound tango-ish. An effect that recurred more than once was a stomp-rhythm alternating with a more tango-influenced passage for contrast. And in one of the most famous of all the Hot Five recordings, "Muskrat Ramble," the front line and the banjo developed a subtle tango feel, not in any one instrumental part but (in a technique reminiscent of West African group drumming) in the interplay between them.

Other musicians' recordings also showed this minor but recurring Latin strain. A couple of extremely obvious tango sections occurred in a 1925 recording of "Rampart Street Blues" by Lovie Austin and Her Blues Serenaders, with a lineup that includes the wonderful blues trumpeter Tommy Ladnier and Johnny Dodds, one of the greatest of all New Orleans jazz clarinetists.[3] In incorporating intermittent, specifically tango sections, the intention was the usual one: novelty and con-

---

[3] Its tango sections deviate slightly from the standard "St. Louis Blues" pattern by showing up in the middle and at the end of the number instead of the beginning and end.

trast. But the rhythm of the rest of the number is particularly intriguing. Austin often favored a quick upbeat after the main beats, rather like a proto-boogie, eight-to-the-bar figure. In many of her recordings this seemed to come casually from the intermittent up-beats that banjoists threw into their accompaniment. But in "Rampart Street Blues" the extra upbeat falls only after the first beat of the measure, as if it were a tango trying to get out.

"Rampart Street Blues" was not the only Lovie Austin recording to show tango influences. Nor was it a passing fancy. Her "Steppin' on the Blues", recorded a year earlier, made a similar use of contrasting tango sections and stop-time. Moreover, in a version of "Jackass Blues" she recorded a year later, her piano took on seemingly tango-influenced rhythms in places, and the tango rhythm patterns, even though Americanized, were even stronger in her "Frog Tongue Stomp." These tango references weren't confined to black bands. A composition by new Orleans trombonist Santo Pecora called "She's Cryin' For Me," which has an intrinsic tango section, was recorded by the finest white New Orleans jazz band of the period, the New Orleans Rhythm Kings (with which Pecora played).

Doubtless many more tinges of tango, and maybe danzón and other Cuban rhythms, lurk unrecognized in the enormous body of (mostly unavailable) record-ed jazz of the time. One final example of jazz-band Latin-moving-into-Black rhythms is a 1929 recording by the Spencer Williams Orchestra with King Oliver, "I'm Going To Take My Bimbo Back to the Bamboo Isle," whose intriguingly frenetic rhythm section hangs between Charleston and tango.

Morton aside, the jazz musician whose 1920s recordings showed most signs of tangification was James P. Johnson, who had started his career playing stride piano in New York when the Harlem tango was young. Throughout the 1920s, both as soloist and bandleader, Johnson used what appear to be tango touches—and sometimes more than touches—on a range of recordings for both solo piano and band. It might seem that the remains of ragtime phrasing (and ragtime's own habanera tinge) in stride piano would make subtle tango elements impossible to distinguish. But as with ragtime recordings, a mental "tango matrix" placed over certain pieces fits like a glove, whereas with many others it jars badly. Take "The Harlem Strut," which Johnson recorded in August 1921. There is no convincing way you can impose Latin phrasing on the playing here—until the coda, when suddenly a rhythmic pattern appears that is an only slightly modified tango.

There was a more obvious tango influence in Johnson's 1921 solo version of "Carolina Shout." After the clear tango echo in the intro, the body of the piece had little or no Latin influence at first. But as it progressed, Johnson moved between a bass that would fit a habanera rhythm nicely and one that cut right across it.[4] The influence was even more obvious in the band recording of the same piece made in the name of Jimmie Johnson's Jazz Boys the same year. The intro was again tango-inflected, and the first chorus or so moved back and forth between semi-tango and straight 2/4 beat (though the effect was not always obvious because elements of the tango rhythm were parceled out among different instruments).

The blend of jazz and Latin elements could be complex even at this early stage. The coda of the 1928 "Daylight Saving Blues," recorded with what was essentially a Duke Ellington small band minus Ellington, came over as a Charleston/black-bottom/tango blend. And another recording from the same period illustrated how the tango may have infiltrated jazz via the theater. "Dear Old Southland," a version of a Henry Creamer composition by James P. Johnson's Harmony Eight, used straight-tango sections as a contrasting feature. Besides a passage in the first chorus that sounds like an Americanization of some other Latin rhythm, the second theme was a straight U.S.-style tango, and choruses or half-choruses of tango and straight-rhythm alternated pretty much throughout. It is also interesting that the piece, which was by now a standard, did not have any overt "Latin-American" theme in its lyrics.

The issue of Latin influence in the blues has been even less researched than Latin influences in jazz, though a few blues scholars are beginning to be aware of its existence. Based on decades of listening, I'd have to say that early country guitar blues had little or no Latin influence, though I suspect that some of the 12-string-guitar playing of Huddie Ledbetter (Leadbelly), a Texan, may have had Tex-Mex and Mexican elements, including influences from the Mexican 12-string bajo sexto. I have heard some of his bass runs in early Tex-Mex playing (specifically in some of the recordings of singer/guitarist Lydia Mendoza), and it's even possible he took a fancy to the 12-string guitar itself from hearing Latino players: it's a very rare instrument among blues players.[5]

All of this raises the intriguing possibility that the same Mexican influences that went up the river to St. Louis and fed into ragtime could have surfaced at second hand in the rag-based blues of Memphis and elsewhere. After all, Memphis, like St. Louis, is on the Mississippi, and may have been exposed to those Mexican groups on the paddle-steamers. Certainly piano blues, or barrel-

---

[4] Once again the coda was also pure tango/habanera.

[5] Other than this, the only likely candidate is a melody called the "Spanish flang dang," popular with guitarists out of the Southeastern rag-blues tradition.

house, players drew from a wide range of sources including ragtime. Perhaps they would have absorbed some habanera influence in the right hand from that source, and also tango during its general popularity, as well as (depending on where they lived) from more general creole/Latin tinges. If, as seems likely, Jess Pickett's "The Dream" (see Chapter 1) was not unique, there may have been a direct link between early habanera-tinged slow-drag players and later piano blues. That would provide two or even three or more different conduits for a Latin influence to enter barrelhouse. In any event, the patterns in the left hands of a number of barrelhouse players seem to show vestigial or Americanized habanera or tango influences.[6]

One influential piano blues player, Jimmy Yancey, was exceptional in that his "habanera bass" has been acknowledged, if only vaguely, by pretty much every jazz writer who has studied him. Yancey's father was a professional guitarist, and his brother Alonzo a ragtime piano player. Yancey himself followed a different career. By the age of ten he was appearing on the Orpheum Vaudeville Circuit as an "eccentric dancer" and he toured Europe in his early teens. He left showbiz at the age of 16, and spent most of his adult working life as a groundsman at Chicago's Comiskey Park. Yancey apparently started to learn the piano only after he quit vaudeville, and never became a full-time professional, though he played occasional local club dates and was popular on the rent-party circuit. Nor did he record until he was "rediscovered" in the late 1930s.

Yancey's basses were all individual, and some of them were clearly tango-derived. Why, is not entirely clear, because Chicago piano as a whole doesn't show as much overt tango influence as the New York stride style or more southern blues piano. My own theory is that he may have picked the rhythm up as a dancer and translated it to the piano. If he was in Europe in 1912 or 1913, he was almost certainly exposed to the tango, which was a rage in France and England before it ever hit the U.S.

Yancey raises the question of a Latin influence on individual musicians, and the related effect on an individual jazzman of particular Latin musicians, rather than a Latin style as a whole. Many jazz musicians worked opposite tango bands, both in the U.S. and in Europe. Noble Sissle (with Sidney Bechet), Sam Wooding, and many other big bands preferred Europe to the U.S., because European audiences treated them like honored artists. And given that in Europe

---

[6] One is Montana Taylor, whose 1929 recording of "Indiana Avenue Stomp" (not his later recording of the same piece), is a case in point. Even more obscure examples include Charles Avery's "House Rent Scuffle" and a passage in Charlie Segar's "Boogie Woogie."

the so-called "jazz age" was more accurately a tango age, this meant many black American musicians worked in a Latin-soaked environment. In his autobiography *I Guess I'll Get the Papers And Go Home,* Doc Cheatham cites as a personal influence the important Argentinian tango artist Francisco Canaro, who was leading the great Canaro Brothers Tango Band in Biarritz opposite Sam Wooding's orchestra in 1929. "He showed me things I'd never heard of," Cheatham wrote. "His own playing was outta sight, and for some sets we would swap trumpet players, and he and I would alternate between the bands."

Because the tango never went out of style, while famous dances like the Charleston rose and fell as more or less short-lived novelties, a tantalizing question is the degree of Latin influence in African-American dance (and thus on jazz). The possibility of Latin origins or influence in several 1920s dance rhythms have struck more than one writer. In a discussion of W.C. Handy in his America's Music, Gilbert Chase says of the habanera/tango used by W.C. Handy, "a variant of this pattern . . . produces the rhythm of the once popular . . . Charleston." And it has also been suggested that the shimmy had part-Latin origins (indeed Cuban bandleader Don Azpiazu claimed it was essentially Cuban, for what that's worth). The problem with this theory is that it clashes with the evidence that the basic moves of Charleston and the black bottom existed, even if not under that name, in nineteenth-century African-American rural communities, where a habanera influence would have been unlikely. On the other hand, it is possible that the tango fused with earlier proto-Charleston moves to produce the 1920s version. Many of the urban African-American dances developed in competition. Several decades later, Maya Angelou described concocting a solo dance from "a little rhumba, tango, jitterbug, Susy-Q, trucking, snake hips, conga, charleston and cha-cha." That, it seems to me, sums up the indissoluble bond of Afro-U.S. and Afro-Latin music, as well as dance. True, Angelou was talking about a period later than the 1920s, but common sense suggests that when a particular Latin rhythm had been enormously popular for more than a decade it was more likely to rub off. (In fact the opposite notion, that African-American dancers and musicians lacked the creativity and open-mindedness to scoop up and turn to their own purposes anything going, verges on the insulting, as well as being obvious nonsense).

The one African-American dance of the 1920s that had a life rivaling the tango was the Lindy hop, which surfaced around 1927 at Harlem's Savoy Ballroom. To judge from old "how to" photos, the early Lindy borrowed at least some of its steps and breakaways from the maxixe and tango as danced in the U.S., and in the early 1930s the Lindy coexisted with the rumba at the Savoy.

Camped on the steps of the jazz pantheon was a vast rabble, the purveyors of pop jazz or dance music with jazz elements, some of whom from time to time have been granted at least postulant status in the jazz pantheon itself, depending on the personal taste of individual historians. These bands recorded tangos and tango-influenced numbers throughout the 1920s, presumably because their recordings were aimed at the roll-up-the-living-room-carpet dance public. In 1926, Doc Cook & His Dreamland Orchestra—a jazz-oriented danceband rather than a strictly jazz group, but one which included outstanding jazz musicians—recorded a piece called "Spanish Mamma" that was typical in both its high and its low spots. A brief tango opening and coda book-ended a hokey arrangement whose only interest is nifty clarinet work from the New Orleans creole master, Jimmy Noone, and a nice duo break for trumpet and clarinet in which Noone's partner was the great and sorely under-recorded New Orleans trumpeter Freddie Keppard (the supposed stylistic link between the legendary Buddy Bolden and Louis Armstrong's mentor King Oliver).[7]

Not all the dance pieces with both Latin and jazz elements were as simple as "Spanish Mamma." Under its "hey-hey" overlay, the 1927 version of "One Night in Havana" by Hoagy Carmichael and his Pals had some remarkable playing—mostly from Carmichael himself—including an interesting two-handed take on a tango/habanera rhythm and a really effective version of the common jazz-Latin rhythm section alternating measures of 4/4 and tango rhythm.

Another recording with more than a touch of originality and a definite jazz connection was the 1928 "Lady of Havana" by an obscure group run by bassist Thelma Terry, known as her Playboys, among whose members was a future swing superstar, drummer Gene Krupa. Terry's group was typical of a whole class of groups that tend to be classified as dance bands, but which also had jazz connections. Chicago-style tenor player Bud Freeman, for example, played with Terry, and the solo trumpet on "Lady of Havana" was probably played by Johnny Mendel, who was to play with Charlie Barnet in the late 1930s. So "Lady of Havana" may have been typical of the way working jazz-oriented groups tackled Latin material in the 1920s. The first section contained a piece of rhythmic byplay between trumpet and the bass-player (Terry herself) that managed to be both humorous and complex. The second section went into a tight tango, cas-tanets and all. In the third section, Terry gave a sophisticated display of mixed-

---

[7] Cooks's "So This is Venice," also with Keppard, is another piece with stop-time choruses that sound tango-derived.

Chicagoan bassist/bandleader Thelma Terry. In 1928 she recorded a couple of the few examples of jazz-Latin crossover from the period to make it onto wax, with a band that included tenor saxist Bud Freeman and other notables of the white Chicago jazz scene. *Frank Driggs Collection*

rhythm bass playing behind a banjo passage, and there was also a fluid trumpet solo over the castanets. This was not, in other words, simply an off-the-shelf chart played on sufferance.

Just as the tango played in the U.S. was thoroughly Americanized, so were performances of the many Cuban, Mexican, and Brazilian songs published in the U.S. during the 1920s. Most of these songs were in a generalized Latin vein (Mexican composers in particular turned these out with workmanlike regularity), and most of them were picked up by dance rather than jazz groups. Still, some were to have considerable jazz legs. One—published in 1924—was Joseph M. LaCalle's "Amapola" ("Little Poppy"), which was to be a big-band hit for all sorts of people in the 1940s. Another was "Siboney," by one of Cuba's most famous composers, Ernesto Lecuona. This began life as a danzón, sidled onto the U.S. stage in two bet-hedging forms—it was published both as a "tango foxtrot" and a "danzón cubano"—had at least a minor Tin Pan Alley success in various recorded versions, and, much later, sprang back to life in a wonderful 1950s recording by Dizzy Gillespie and Stan Getz. Moreover, a marvelous 1950s recording by the trumpeter Kid Thomas gives an idea of how the New Orleans bands may have played the Latin pieces in their repertoire.

A significant factor in the relationship between jazz and Latin music in the teens and 20s was the fact that musicians from Puerto Rico and Cuba were arriving in the U.S. in ever greater numbers.[8] The best-known to most jazz buffs is San-Juan-born valve-trombonist Juan Tizol, who arrived around 1920 with an orchestra that played the black TOBA circuit and settled in Washington. But Tizol was neither the only, nor the first, Puerto Rican to be involved with black U.S. bands. As Ruth Glasser documents at length in her book *My Music Is My Flag*, Puerto Rican musicians were crucial to James Reese Europe's 369th Infantry "Hellfighters" Band, back in 1917. Faced with the need for sight-reading musicians who could play military-band instruments, Europe went straight to Puerto Rico, where every provincial city had a brass band, most of which contained musicians who could both sight-read and play several instruments. Europe's military orchestra, in fact, contained no less than 18 Puerto Rican musicians, including trombonist Rafael Hernández, who was to become a major composer, and clarinetist Rafael Duschesne, who played with several early African-American swing bands. It is only when you see the list of musicians in this band

---

[8] Because of the complications involved in identifying them, I am not even attempting to discuss the issue of Panamanians in jazz. Band leader Luis Russell was only one of a number of Panamanians, many of them with English names because they came from the Anglophone Panamanian community descended from Jamaicans and others working on the Panama Canal.

Benny Peyton was one of several African-American band leaders who worked consistently in Europe during the 1920s and 1930s. In 1928 his septet included two Europe-based Latino saxists as well as clarinet/alto player Horace Eubanks (next to drum kit). Eubanks later recorded a couple of tracks with the Sid Catlett band (check) that blended the rumba and biguines he had heard in Paris and Nice. *Frank Driggs Collection*

that you can grasp how important the Puerto Rican or at least Latino input was: among others, the entire seven-man clarinet section, most of the mid-range and bass brass players, a bassoon player, and two mellophone players. Glasser also believes that Hernández and the rest were "almost certainly" involved in Reese's 1919 recordings. And if Europe had to recruit Puerto Ricans for the Hellfighters, how about Brymn's 350th Infantry band or the 807th Pioneer Infantry Band led by another well-known African-American composer (and arranger for Ziegfeld), Will Vodery?

At least some of the Puerto Rican musicians in the black military orchestras stayed on in the States, to be joined by an increasing flow of new arrivals. According to Ruth Glasser, Rafael Hernández went to Cuba when Europe's band broke up, then returned to New York City in 1925 to form an ensemble of Puerto Rican musicians, besides touring with stride pianist Lucky Roberts. Other Puerto Rican musicians, Glasser has established, worked with Fletcher Henderson and Don Redman, "careful orchestrators and arrangers who resented being categorized as 'hot' musicians. Their enthusiasm for Puerto Rican musicians probably represented their desire to combat prevalent stereotypes by producing an atmosphere where training often counted more than improvisational ability."

These men were what early New York Puerto Rican bandleader Ray Coen has called "music stand" musicians. Glasser quotes Coen as adding, "the black American orchestras were very good musicians, but they didn't have the training that the Puerto Rican musicians had . . . The African-American orchestras used Puerto Ricans a lot to read the parts of the Broadway shows." Among these musicians were Moncho Usera, who later ran an excellent mambo band, and bassist/tuba player Rafael Escudero (also known as Ralph Escudero). Escudero worked with Duke Ellington in 1922, when both of them were briefly in Wilbur Sweatman's band. He also played with Fletcher Henderson until 1924, as did trombonist Fernando Arbello.

Naturally enough, both Puerto Rican and Cuban musicians with reading skills were also in demand for the black musicals that were influenced by jazz. As early as 1922, Noble Sissle (who had been the lead singer with Europe's Hellfighters band) hired a number of Puerto Rican musicians, most of them probably alumni of the Europe band. The hugely popular Broadway show *Shuffle Along*, written by Sissle with pianist Eubie Blake, had a Francisco Tizol in its orchestra earning $70 a week (double what Josephine Baker, then a chorus girl, was making). Rafael Escudero played in the pit band of *Chocolate Dandies* of 1928, and Moncho Usera was in the Blackbirds orchestra about the same time—as was Cuban flutist Alberto Socarrás.[9]

The Puerto Ricans, of course, were American citizens, and could come to New York by right. The flow of Cubans was much smaller during the 1920s, but at least several were similarly involved in the late-1920s New York jazz scene. One of them was Alberto Socarrás. He arrived in New York in 1928, and within a few weeks had made a minor, though anonymous, mark on jazz by recording the first jazz flute solo, on a version of "Have You Ever Felt That Way" by Clarence Williams, on which he also played sax. (This solo, which had nothing Latin about it, was evidence that at least some of the Cubans coming to the States were perfectly at home in mainstream jazz.) Another Cuban who both played and recorded with Clarence Williams was a clarinetist named Carmelito Jejo, mentioned by trumpeter Rex Stewart in a 1960s *DownBeat* interview as playing at Small's Sugar Cane Club in Harlem around 1928. Others with a more fleeting impact on jazz were important musicians in their own right, including bandleader Nilo

---

[9] Some American bands that played regularly in Europe also from time to time hired Cubans there.

Even before the rumba craze hit, there was a Latin dance band playing at Harlem's Savoy Ballroom. Here are the seminal San Domingo Serenaders in one of their earliest avatars, photographed in 1929. Their lineup was about one-third African-American, and included at least two Cubans. *Frank Driggs Collection*

Melendez. While working as a staff musician for Columbia Records in the late 1920s, Melendez wrote a number called "Aquellos Ojos Verdes" that enjoyed some success at the time and—under the English title of "Green Eyes"—was to be a hit both in the early 1930s and (along with its contemporary, Joseph LaCalle's "Amapola") in the early 1940s.

These musicians might not have had any major long-term effect on jazz if they had been isolated individuals. But they were part of an increasing number of immigrants—mostly Cubans and Puerto Ricans—who established themselves as recognizable and growing colonies in various cities in the Eastern United States, above all in New York. Starting in the 1930s, these immigrants were to provide an infrastructure for U.S.-based Cuban and Puerto Rican music that proved enormously important. Thanks in part to their presence, what might otherwise merely have been another Latin ripple would become a riptide that eventually transformed jazz in ways that are still not fully recognized.

3

Rumbatism

The 1930s

On the afternoon of Saturday, April 26, 1930, the post-intermission curtain rose before a full house at New York's Palace Theater and the course of both Latin music and jazz in the United States was irrevocably changed. The opening number played by Don Azpiazú's Havana Casino Orchestra at that matinee, "Mama Inez," was to be a major U.S. hit with at least a few jazz versions (including one by Charlie Parker). And the third item on the menu would prove to be a catalyst of what eventually would be called Latin jazz: "El Manicero,"or "The Peanut Vendor."

I have written in the past that this was the first rumba band to play a midtown New York date. Technically I may have been wrong, though it was certainly the first to play a vaudeville gig. *La Prensa* preannounced the opening of a club called The Rumba on Broadway and 70th on April 5th, with a band called the Orquesta Royal Rumba de la Habana ("the first of this kind in New York") playing rumbas, danzónes, and tangos. Moreover, advertisements and articles in La Prensa show that the band the paper usually billed as Don Justo Azpiazú y Su Famosa Orquesta del Gran Casino Nacional also appeared in various theaters around town before hitting Broadway, along with a "Fantasia de policromatico esplendor Hispano-Cubano."[1] Still, Azpiazu's first Broadway appearance was significant less for what he played than for how he played it and to whom.

---

[1] The the various advertisements include a schedule change, but the band seems to have played the RKO Proctor Theater on 86th Street as well as houses in the Bronx and Queens before arriving at the Palace Theater.

The *norteamericano* public had long been familiar with one fairly straightforward Latin rhythm, played U.S.-style. Now, for the first time, it was hearing Latin music in a version whose African element made it far more complex than the elegant but straightforward tango rhythm. "Mama Inez" and "The Peanut Vendor" had been published in the U.S. in the late 1920s along with other new Cuban compositions. They had even gotten some play . . . but hardly authentic play! The original U.S. sheet music for "The Peanut Vendor" called it a "New Cuban Melody Made Famous By Major Bowes' Capital Theatre Radio Library. Yasha Bunchuk and His Band Will Serve It Piping Hot."

Don Azpiazú's band, by contrast, served its pieces with as much authenticity as zip and charm. In so doing it introduced the U.S. music world not only to a true Cuban dance sound, but to a rhythmic arsenal such as the States had never envisaged: the maracas, claves, bongos, and timbales of Cuban percussion.[2] The Havana Casino Orchestra was a class act; Azpiazú was known in Cuba for playing jazz, itself very upmarket in Latin America, although he had ruffled the waters in the posh Havana Casino by introducing what were regarded as lower-class Cuban pieces into his repertoire there. When he hit New York, he played the first true Afro-Cuban music—indeed, the first stylistically genuine Latin music—ever heard in mainstream U.S.A. Things would never be the same again.

Azpiazú's "Peanut Vendor" was a polished but authentically Cuban piece: a type of *son* called a *pregón*, derived from Havana street-vendors' cries. His recording of it, moreover, was a ground-breaker in more than just its success. Back then, when recording at least, Cuban bands normally simply repeated the sung melody in unison between verses. According to Azpiazú's son, Raul, one of the band's two trumpeters "was fooling around in the studio, playing variations. My father told him, 'Why don't you put that in the record?'" The results became a fundamental part of the tune, and a major contributor to its success.

That success didn't happen overnight. The band recorded "The Peanut Vendor" for RCA Victor in May 1930. Then, typically, the record executives got cold feet. The rhythms would be too strange for the great American public, and it would never sell. Couldn't Don Azpiazú record some jazz? No, Don Azpiazú couldn't: he played jazz in Havana, but for a foreigner to do so in its native land would be ridiculous. So it went, back and forth, until the recording was finally issued in September as part of a compromise: two Cuban pieces; two pieces with American singers. The general uproar that ensued has never been matched by any single title before or since.

---

[2] The conga drum that now symbolizes Afro-Cuban music to most people had not yet been brought into the dance bands.

The impact of Azpiazú's version of "The Peanut Vendor" was only part of the sudden-seeming Latinization of the early 1930s popular-music scene. But the huge national success of "The Peanut Vendor" and "Mama Inez" opened the floodgates. Azpiazú himself later commented that "within a week there existed a Havana Royal Orchestra, a Havana Novelty Orchestra, and a Havana God Knows-What." Many were ghost-bands created by a quick name change, sometimes for a single recording session. The Havana Novelty Orchestra, for example, was a confection of Nat Shilkret, a successful commercial dance band leader of the time.

In fact, the rush was on—and not for the rumba bands alone. The trickle of non-tango Latin sheet music released in the '20s became a flood. By September 1932, the noted music publisher E.B. Marks listed almost 600 Latin American songs in its catalog. Most—tangos aside—were Cuban or Mexican numbers, but they included a Venezuelan pasillo ("Anhelos"), as well as at least a couple of Brazilian numbers, a samba ("Batente"), and a choro ("Com que Roupa").

Many early recordings of "The Peanut Vendor" were strange at best. One Phil Fabello played a version that according to *Metronome* "used a symphonic arrangement retaining all the flavor of the original Cuban piece and yet dressing it up in the most modernistic jazz style." More typical was a recording made by Lou Gold & His Orchestra, lightly disguised as Don Carlos & His Rumba Band. This was a hack dance band doing its uncomprehending best, serving up a tame version of the world-famous opening riff, a soupy English vocal, an accordion left over from a tango session, irrelevant modulations, corny woodblocks, and a rhythm section that was to swing as anti-matter is to the ordinary stuff. But the recording did have its moments: until you've heard a tuba gallumphing all over a Cuban *son* rhythm, you haven't lived!

Like the tango, the rumba hit Harlem with quite as big a bang as white-oriented midtown. In late summer and early fall of 1930, two Cuban rumba groups played the Lafayette Theater, Harlem's main vaudeville house, alongside various black acts. In July 1931, Azpiazu lead vocalist Antonio Machin and his Royal Havana Troupe headlined in a Lafayette revue called "Rhumba-Land" that included vaudeville-blues singer Mamie Smith and jazz drummer Kaiser Marshall's Czars of Harlem. In September, a new edition of a show called *Rhapsody in Black*— which featured singers Ethel Waters, Adelaide Hall, Eddie Rector, and the dancing Berry Brothers—included a crossover-sounding number called "Harlem Rhumbola" by one Bessie Dudley.

The *Amsterdam News* also reported, in September 1931, on what sounds like the first piece of Cuban-derived Latin jazz created in the U.S. It was included in a show called *Fast and Furious* at Brandt's Theatre, Jackson Heights, with music by Broadway composers Mack Gordon and Harry Revel. The reviewer didn't think much of the show as a whole, but commented, "an outstanding song number is 'Rhumbatism,' a frenzied jazz affair with scraps from 'The Peanut Vendor' serving as an undercurrent. This is something new and worth more play . . . than it is given here."[3]

The rumba also penetrated very rapidly to that temple of 1930s black swing, the Savoy Ballroom. A passing comment by an *Amsterdam News* columnist makes it clear that by September 1931 the rumba was already a well-established staple at the Savoy: "Just a Glance Here and There" by Romeo L. Dougherty, has jocular and cryptic references to rumba, including a reference to an attack on "indecent dancing" by the Rev. Frazier Miller of St Augustine's Church, Brooklyn, and a comment about a "careful study" of rumba at the dance hall, all in a tone that takes everybody's awareness of the rumba's presence there for granted.[4]

One of the most fascinating and most totally forgotten of all episodes in the history of jazz/Latin relations is hinted at in the advertisements for dances at the Savoy Ballroom and other Harlem dance halls that appeared from around 1932 to 1934. These consistently listed a group variously referred to as the San Domingans, the San Dominicans, and the San Domingo Serenaders.[5] The San Domingans were not the only Latin group to play for dancing in early 1930s Harlem: an equally mysterious band called the Original Havana Orchestra alternated with Fess Finlay's dance band at the Renaissance Casino in March 1933. But the San Domingans consistently played on equal terms with some of the most important black swing bands of the early 1930s for black dancers. Not all

---

[3] One for trivia buffs: "Rhumbatism" was sung and danced by Jackie Mabley, who was to become famous as the comedian Moms Mabley.

[4] Intriguingly, the same column refers to a "marenga," which looks awfully like a misspelling of merengue, and it may very well have been just that.

[5] In January 1932, the San Domingans were playing at the Harlem Opera House. In May they were featured in a "Depression Dance." In December the San Dominican Band got top billing (not alphabetical) at Harlem Opera House, on a bill with blues singer Clara Smith among others. In October 1932 the Savoy Ballroom advertised Paul Tremain & His "Lonely Acres" Band, Chick Webb's Chicks, and the San Dominicans. The same month the San Domingans were part of a Savoy breakfast dance featuring Isham Jones, Luis Russell, and Chick Webb. In December they were part of an all-night benefit organized by the Rhythm Club at the Savoy along with Cab Calloway, Claude Hopkins, Don Redman, Luis Russell, the Blue Rhythm Boys, and Teddy Hill. In April 1933, as the San Domingo Serenaders, they were at the Lafayette Theater in a revue headlining singer Baby Cox and comedian Pigmeat Markham. And at an April 1934 benefit for the Needy Families' Emergency Fund emceed by the famous dancer Bojangles, the San Domingans was one of only two bands to play (unnamed "Prominent Stars" aside), the other being Teddy Hill's Serenaders (and it was the San Domingans who were listed first).

A deeply mysterious group, Napoleon's Alhambra Ramblers may have been the San Domingans under a temporary alias while playing the Alhambra Ballroom. What is certain is that it included both jazz-oriented Latinos (pianist Rod Rodriguez and trombonist Fernando Arbello) and at least one African-American with a swing resume, Ernest "Bass" Hill. *Frank Driggs Collection*

the Puerto Rican arrivals worked with African-American bands. Trumpeter Louis "King" García, who moved to the U.S. in the early 20s, played with the Original Dixieland Jazz Band for a while, and recorded with the Tommy Dorsey big band as well as a lot of dance orchestras. Here is evidence that important black swing players were, night after night, hearing rumbas, merengues, and other Latin rhythms at close quarters during the crucial years of the black swing golden age. It hardly seems too much of a stretch to suppose that some of what they heard may have rubbed off on their own playing![6]

Moreover, though jazz groups didn't record Latin music throughout most of the 1930s, they certainly played it, both for dancers and behind featured cabaret acts. One of the leading African-American dance duos during the 1930s and

---

[6] While the rumba and other new Latin dances were hot in black Harlem, the tango also lived on there. It was too familiar to get much press, but an October 1930 *Amsterdam News* photo of dancer Henry Weasels, stepson of the composer Henry S. Creamer, called him the "outstanding exponent of color of the Argentine tango" (which implies that there were others) and mentioned that he had been playing the Cotton Club steadily for five years. And three years later, a show at the Harlem Casino headlining classic blues singer Clara Smith also featured The Six Argentinos in a section called "A Night in Buenos Aires."

1940s, Harold Norton and Margo Webb, worked extensively with Earl Hines—who was at the top of the ladder about then—at Chicago's Grand Terrace. And even after the San Domingo Serenaders vanished from the Savoy Ballroom, older musicians like Panama Francis recalled playing rumbas for dancers during ordinary public sessions. White bands did the same, willingly or perforce. Woody Herman tells in his autobiography of a seven-month gig at the Roseland Ballroom in 1936: "The blues were the best thing we knew how to play, but we had to do a lot of fighting to play them. The management preferred that we play mostly dance music—fox trots, rumbas and waltzes—to satisfy the dancers."

It is of course possible that all these dance bands, black and white, simply played from stock arrangements, and some surely did. But the fragmentary evidence provided by the few relevant recordings that exist suggest that many bands did not find the demand for Latin material a chore, and that they met it with a certain amount of originality.

Along with the San Domingans, and the swing bands playing tangos and rumbas as part of a larger gig, there were African-American bands playing Latin music for black dancers. One Wilbert Griffith ran a black rumba/tango band during the 1930s, besides playing with a veteran Uptown Latino bandleader, José Budet (as Doc Cheatham was to do later). The various advertisements in the *Amsterdam Age* that mention Griffith's band do so without giving any further detail, so all we know is that it existed. Griffith's group was not the first African-American band to play Latin material regularly, nor would it be the last. But it does serve as further evidence that the African-American Latin scene was far more significant and complex than has been realized.

Dances were one thing, recording was another. There was no need for most jazz or swing bands to record the rumbas and tangos that dancers wanted, or even play them on the radio. This was the job of the dance bands and for specifically "Latin" groups like Xavier Cugat's Waldorf-Astoria Orchestra. But Latin-jazz recordings did appear from time to time. One early one was a version of the "Peanut Vendor" by Duke Ellington, no less. Recorded in January 1931, this was a remarkable exercise in sometimes subtle but real transformation. It opened with a measure or so of straight 4/4 under the opening theme, then kicked into a *son* rhythm with the bass actively participating in the classic "Peanut Vendor" groove. The "call" ("Mani!") was taken by Freddy Jenkins on trumpet with clarinet by Barney Bigard underneath. Harry Carney's splendid baritone sax solo was essentially a calypso melody. By the time Ellington came in with a short stride-piano romp, bassist Wellman Braud was mixing in 4/4 with the Cuban montuno pattern while drummer Sonny Greer kept the rumba rhythm going on traps. By the latter

Don Azpiazú's best-selling recording of "The Peanut Vendor" solidified the rumba in the U.S. and also introduced an authentic Cuban sound. It was from Azpiazú's band that Americans first met the panoply of percussion that surrounds him here. *Courtesy Raul Azpiazú*

part of the recording, Ellington totally abandoned Azpiazú's version in favor of a return to the calypso-like theme, though he did reprise the number's original montuno toward the very end.

Ellington's "Peanut Vendor" was striking for its straightforwardness—its lack of "Ellingtonisms"—compared with his handful of later Latin-inflected recordings. In this it contrasted strongly with a couple of numbers he had recorded the year before, both of them compositions by W.H. Tyers. One of these was a tango, "Admiration," which Tyers had written in 1915.[7] In many respects, Ellington's "Admiration" was like many other U.S. tango recordings, though (unsurprisingly) more interesting. Rhythmically, the second strain was more strongly tango in pulse than the first, and later on a fusion feel was set up by the familiar use of alternating tango and 2/4 rhythms, given an unusual tinge by the use of a tambourine, instead of the customary castanets, to mark the rhythm. Ellington himself contributed a nifty solo very much in the vein of tango (rather than ragtime) piano, and some of the ensemble sax writing sounded ten or 15 years ahead of its time.

The other Tyers's composition Ellington recorded was "Maori," the same piece that had woken W.C. Handy to an African-American affinity with the habanera a quarter-century earlier. The piece had remained popular among dance bands; the house band of the small Cameo label, in fact, had recorded it only a few years earlier, as had that paradigmatic crooner Rudy Vallee. Ellington made three takes of the number on two different dates. All three were broadly similar, but there were nevertheless some marked differences between the two sessions. The first version was recorded in February 1930, with solos from trumpeter Arthur Whetsol, trombonist Joe Nanton, and clarinetist Barney Bigard. The arrangement was quite Ellingtonian, and the solo work had some of the lushness and faux-exoticism of the 1937 "Caravan." Early in the recording, as in Ellington's "The Peanut Vendor," the rhythm section blended a straight jazz beat (4/4 this time, not 2/4) with the rhythm Tyers had originally used. This was a 3/8 pattern—very like the bass-lines the Central African rumba groups were to favor 30 years later—with an overall effect like a 4/4 loosened up by a Latin tinge (and a ghost of the common African mix of triple and duple rhythm). By around halfway through, the 4/4 rhythm was alternating fairly regularly with something nearer to a tight tango.

By March, when the two later takes of "Maori" were recorded, any Latin feel in the rhythm section (and most notably the double-bass line) had vanished.

---

[7] Ellington's "Jazz Convulsions" of 1930 also opened with a rather frenetic tango rhythm, but this was more of a garnish than an integral part of the piece.

Unlike the first version, the rhythm under Whetsol's early trumpet solo starts out as a basic 2/4 before turning to alternative measures of 2/4 and a somewhat amorphous, though attractive, skipping beat. Later on, the arrangement moves between sections with the skipping beat and choruses of straight 4/4. The rhythmic patterns are much the same in the second take, except that the 2/4 feeling in the bass surfaces more in the later stages of the number.

"Admiration," "Maori," and "The Peanut Vendor" were exceptions in the Ellington book and on 1930s jazz recordings in general. As had been true of the tango period, the rumba on disc mostly remained the perquisite of the dance bands, and all too many of the recordings they produced were novelty items at best. Mainstream jazz musicians did not record many rumbas: Cab Calloway's 1931 "Doin' the Rumba" (which was heard by a whole lot of people because it was the B-side to his huge hit, "Minnie the Moocher") had lyrics about the dance, but no musical hint of anything Latin.

However, there were exceptions to the general vapidity of 1930s Anglo-Latino recordings. Three days after Ellington recorded his "Peanut Vendor," white trumpeter Red Nicholls took his Five Pennies into the studio to make his own version. In the ebb and flow of jazz politics, Red Nicholls was once over, and is now under-rated. Nicholls' "Peanut Vendor," like Ellington's, was obviously modeled on Azpiazú. But if the usually unfaultable discographer Brian Rust is right, it included one major first: the presence of what Rust describes only as "three Cuban drummers" added to the traps playing of Gene Krupa. The reality, judging from the third-generation dubbing I've heard, is even more authentic: a percussion trio of claves, maracas, and bongó. But even without Cuban participants, which put Nicholls 15 years ahead of those more famous Afro-Cuban experimenters, Dizzy Gillespie and Stan Kenton, this would have been a remarkable recording. Unlike Ellington, Nicholls maintains the rumba rhythm throughout, pegged to a tumbao that is remarkably authentic for a jazz bassist in 1931, and short but punchy trumpet and bluesy clarinet solos from Charlie Teagarden and Benny Goodman respectively. The backing, "Sweet Rosita," has a more conventional dance band arrangement, but even here Jack Teagarden's trombone plays with the theme engagingly. Even more remarkable—indeed seemingly unique— was a 1934 guitar duet called "Danzón," by Carl Kress (a pioneer of chordal jazz guitar) and Dick McDonough. There was nothing too danzón-like about this, but it was a fine piece like some of the postwar Brazilian guitar playing, with plenty of often advanced-sounding chording set against picked runs, and an ostinato bass from the second guitar that was at times a little like an uptempo bossa nova with more edge.

In late January 1931, Red Nicholls and his band recorded a jazz version of "The Peanut Vendor" that anticipated Dizzy Gillespie and Stan Kenton by 15 years by including three Cuban percussionists in a jazz group, and was equally advanced in maintaining the rumba rhythm throughout. *Frank Driggs Collection*

In 1937, another guitar duo, John Cali and Tony Gottuso, recorded a couple of even more eclectic pieces. Their starting point seems to have been Italian, but they ranged a long way from home. "Violetta" opened with a "Malagueña"-type intro, moved into flamenco-inspired runs, and remained Spanish in tone for a while before shifting into a wonderful South American sounding melody on the bass strings and developing into a piece more reminiscent of some Spanish-inspired Mexican playing than of Spain itself. The reverse, "Carina," opened with a slightly tentative rumba rhythm and then switched into a more emphatically *son*/rumba pulse.

Though mainstream jazz musicians recorded very little that could be called Latin jazz in the 1930s, there was at least one magnificent exception, a 1935 recording by a band led by the outstanding African-American drummer Zutty Singleton. The A-side is a stunning number, built out of the Spanish chorus of Don Azpiazú's 1930 "Wanna Lot O' Love," called "Runenae Papa." It opens with solos by clarinetist Horace Eubanks that are almost identical to the clarinet work on 1930s Trinidadian calypso recordings (virtually all of which were made in

New York), along with flashes of a melody reminiscent of calypsonian Lord Beginner's song "Anacaona" (which itself seems to have been a truncated version of "Olvido," by the great Cuban composer/bandleader Miguel Matamoros). There is, however, nothing calypsonian about the lead vocal, which clearly is sung by a Cuban. Eubanks's magnificent clarinet work after the vocal blended calypso, Martiniquan biguine, echoes New Orleans creole jazz.

The B-side of this remarkable pairing is "Look Over Yonder," which may have come partly from a biguine, and according to discographer Richard Spottswood also has echoes of a Trinidad paseo recycled in a number of calypsos.[8] Certainly the instrumental parts sound almost pure calypso with some New Orleans phrasing, insofar as they are distinguishable: besides having common roots, 1930s biguine was influenced by both jazz and Cuban music. Certainly the rhythm is pure 1930s Trinidad calypso. The vocal is also exceptional: it opens in a gibberish that could be a phonetic attempt at a creole French lyric but is calypsonian in feel, switches into an African-American semi-chanted chorus with preaching overtones, then back into gibberish. After the vocal and a brief ensemble, Eubanks returns with a solo in which the jazz and calypso/biguine elements are astonishingly tightly intertwined.

The biguine element in this recording was presumably no fluke. When both the rumba and the biguine were hitting France in 1929, Eubanks was playing in both Paris and Nice in a septet run by Benny Peyton, who led bands in Europe throughout the 1920s and 1930s. Along with Eubanks, this group had two apparent Latinos, Fred Coxito and Alcide González. He was not alone. I've already mentioned Doc Cheatham's friendship with Francisco Canaro. But since tango and jazz were the two most popular styles in France, it wasn't unusual for a jazz group to share the bandstand with a tango orchestra. Wooding and Peyton aside, jazz violinist Eddie South did so for several months in more than one Parisian nightclub, as did the Noble Sissle orchestra at the Ambassadeurs in 1931.

Don Azpiazú himself was not merely the accidental vector for the U.S. rumba fever. According to his son, Raul, he had a vision of an intermarriage between Cuban music and jazz that prefigured the actual ceremony by a decade. He introduced a wide range of Cuban music to the U.S., including what must have been

---

[8] The Parisian connection is worth exploring. Eubanks was not the only jazz musician to be beguiled by Caribbean music in the early 1930s. According to his son, Fats Waller's favorite hangout on his 1931 Paris trip was a club called La Rumba. Waller's style was probably far too well established to be influenced by what he heard, but who would bet he didn't sit in with the resident Cuban band. The Trinidadian connection could have reached the Singleton band direct in the U.S., since most of 1930s calypso recording sessions were held in New York.

Boogie woogie pianist Jimmy Yancey was playing tango-inspired barrelhouse piano throughout the 1920s and 1930s. With classic simplicity, he wove a sound that clearly stemmed from two traditions but was also extraordinarily individual. *Frank Driggs Collection*

one of the earliest guajiras issued here. And he was a constant, though not wild-eyed, experimenter. He recorded purely Cuban numbers—not just "El Manisero," but the even better, though much more obscure, "El Panquelero." He recorded a somewhat schmaltzy but rhythmically tight "Green Eyes" with English-language vocalist Chick Bullock (forgotten now, Bullock was supposedly the most widely recorded singer of the 1930s). And he recorded at least one cut that was unique. His original version of "Wanna Lot O' Love" was entirely Cuban in style, both vocally and instrumentally, but the vocals were sung in English (the only example I've ever encountered of this particular version of crossover, and a fine recording instrumentally in the bargain).

Don Azpiazú's career in the U.S. was bracketed in ironies. Among the numbers he recorded in his first sessions was a version of "Mama Inez," which Cuban composer Eliseo Grenet has called "a symbol of our most noble and unquestionable past" and *Metronome* called "the most famous of all rumbas and the Cuban equivalent to a lowdown 'hot' number." Azpiazú's version was rejected, so that one of more-than-usual tackiness by Nat Shilkret's "Havana Novelty Orchestra" became the first issued recording of this classic though it was made almost six months later. Shilkret's "Mama Inez" was a grab bag of corn until the final chorus, which—despite a rhythm more like a vaudeville sand-dance than a rumba—was a nice pop-jazz ride-out with clarinet lead. (The U.S. public, which took the fine Azpiazú "Peanut Vendor" to its heart, also kept the awful Shilkret "Mama Inez" in print till 1938.) But then Don Azpiazu couldn't win. He never really benefited as much as he should from the rumba craze, he was forgotten later, and—in the biggest insult of all—just before Azpiazú's death, Cuban dictator Battista presented Xavier Cugat (!) with an award for services to Cuban music, while entirely ignoring the man who more than anybody launched Cuban music's international fame.[9]

With all that, Don Azpiazú operated musically in the cracks of the U.S. musical map. He was known in Cuba for playing jazz, but what Cubans of the time called "jazz," and what Azpiazú played (or at least recorded), was essentially dance music. And like so much Latin music before and since, his recordings often contained mixes of the sublime and the silly. It was typical that his Cuban singer was the outstanding Antonio Machin, but his English vocalists were the prolific but uninspired Chick Bullock and Bob Burke. Recording after recording burst with purely and often brilliantly Cuban inspiration—in the singing, in the trumpet playing, in the rhythm section, often in the guitar work—cheek-by-jowl

---

[9]Azpiazú's neglect was also probably due in part to the fact that he spent much of the '30s in Cuba, coming to the U.S. for occasional tours, while other bands stayed put and built a public.

with bland U.S. sweet dance-band ensemble writing and even (notably in the case of the gorgeous "Guajira," with its downhome guitar accompaniment and singing) rooster noises and other silliness. As so often, before and since, the two cultures' patterns of tradition, esthetics, and popularism were so out of sync that they sometimes seemed like a cat and a dog who, wanting to play together, are baffled by each other's body language.

"The Peanut Vendor" was one of those hits so great that they tend to be treated as fads or one-off items. But, in reality, the 1930s was a decade of solid and intensifying Latin presence in the U.S. Most of it was not obvious in jazz itself, but it was omnipresent in the larger musical scene of which jazz and swing were part. Not only did the rumba sweep the entire country, but the tango remained firmly entrenched on the nation's dance floors, and towards the end of the decade both the conga (the nearest thing to a short-lived fad that early U.S.-Latin dance produced) and the Brazilian samba arrived.

While the Anglo dancers—black and white—were discovering Latin music, the growing Latino population of New York was discovering swing. The New York Latin scene was symbolically launched in 1930, when a Puerto Rican civic association rented the Golden Casino on 110th Street and Fifth Avenue. By the early 1930s, an East Harlem dentist and musician called Julio Roque was presenting local artists on Radio WABC (at that time an independent station) playing Puerto Rican plenas, boleros, and some Mexican material. Most important of all in an area and an era when most people could not afford to attend nightclubs, the formerly Jewish theaters of East Harlem were turning Latin throughout the 1930s, providing steady work for musicians playing in many styles.

Many of the "uptown" bandleaders playing in the theaters were at least somewhat influenced by African-American music in general and jazz in particular. According to music historian Max Salazar, Alberto Socarrás—the same man responsible for the first jazz flute solo—organized a group in 1934 to play jazz at the Savoy Ballroom, the Cotton Club, Smalls Paradise, and Connie's Paradise in Harlem, while at the same time he was leading a Cuban group that played in East Harlem at the Campoamor Theatre and the Cubanacan and "midtown" at the Park Plaza. I was told by one veteran of East Harlem, "In one show I saw, Maestro Socarrás took an American tune—I believe it was 'I Can't Give You Anything But Love'—and transcribed it in a Latin way, though of course it had the jazz idiom to it."

The recordings by Socarrás's Cubanacan Orchestra show relatively little jazz influence—predictably, since they were presumably aimed at a "Latin" audience, whether Latino or not. But there are hints in his 1935 rumba "Masabi."

Alberto Socarrás was part of the first wave of Cuban musicians who reached New York in the 1920s. Throughout the 1930s Socarrás led both Latin and jazz-oriented groups (including a stint at the Cotton Club) besides working with several black swing bands. He was also in the pit orchestra for the famous Blackbirds revue on Broadway. *Courtesy Alberto Socarrás*

This opens with a calypso melody and includes some flutter-tongue and other jazz-sounding touches in Socarrás' flute playing, even though overall it is strongly Cuban. The drumming also sounds to me like crossover: there are no timbales, but a jaunty traps style that also cropped up in some of the "Latin" numbers by jazz groups of the period. And the B-side, "Africa," has a trombone solo which, while it essentially hews to the melody, sounds jazz-derived in its tone and inflections.

Socarrás operated in the jazz world and both branches of the New York Latin scene, uptown and midtown. In between running his own bands, he played with Benny Carter, Erskine Hawkins and Sam Wooding among others. But others more associated with uptown also had at least some jazz links. According to Max Salazar, the Cuban reedsman and violinist Alberto Iznaga played jazz jobs before settling into the East Harlem scene, where he became a major bandleader with a violin and sax frontline, playing danzónes. As a result of this interchange, some of the bands in El Barrio were training grounds for musicians who were to become important on the crossover scene. The most successful of all, a group run by Augusto Coen, provided early work for a young Puerto Rican pianist called Noro Morales, whose first gig in New York had been in the pit band of the Teatro Hispano on 116th and Fifth Avenue, and who was to become a major name of the 1940s.

The uptown Latin music scene was far from simple. After all, Latinos of a dozen nations lived there. There were, of course, conservative bands that played "pure" music from a dozen back-homes for nostalgic immigrants. But many of the bands in El Barrio were highly eclectic. Just like black Harlem dances, Puerto Rican dances featured a wide variety of music, Latin and Anglo. While Anglo rumba dancers wanted exoticism, which meant something at least vaguely authentic, younger *barrio* residents wanted something hip, which meant swing. And some *barrio* bands were more Americanized than some midtown groups. Ruth Glasser observes that Coen was among the first to use a modified big-band approach to Latin dance music. Around 1934 he formed a band of musicians with experience in the African-American groups, using two or more trumpets and saxes, and without Latin rhythm instruments. And in 1936 Augusto Coen's band-boy Federico Pagani, who was later to become an important promoter, launched another swing-oriented group, Los Happy Boys.

In fact, as Glasser remarks, Cugat and Azpiazú, playing midtown for Anglo dancers, used more Latin American instruments than uptowners Coen and Socarras, who "played Latin tunes with the sounds of a smooth, refined, highly arranged orchestra, which closely resembled the style of Duke Ellington or Cab Calloway." Coen's 1938 plena recording "El Ratón" uses panderetas but also full jazz orchestration, bluesy trumpet, and a singing style apparently modeled on Cab Calloway. And Glasser believes his 1938 "Ño Colá" was influenced by Ellington's "jungle jazz" sound. She sums up: "These musicians did not journey on a relentless path toward assimilation into a vaguely defined mainstream: they travelled 'backwards' to form Latin bands. They also traveled laterally, utilizing artistic elements from several subcultures within the United States. Rather than a simple, romanticized return to roots, their musical creations were actually new syntheses of jazz and Latino, mainly Cuban, music." East Harlem musicians, in fact, were developing the groundwork for the crossover that conventional wisdom credits as springing fully armed from the heads of Machito and his brother-in-law, Mario Bauzá, in the following decade.

Mario Bauzá, who arrived in the U.S. from Cuba in 1930, was to be one of the most important figures in the development of Cubop during the 1940s. He was a conservatory trained clarinetist and oboist. His first job was a recording for Antonio Machin's Cuarteto Machin for which he learned the trumpet (in two weeks he claimed), and he remained a trumpeter the rest of his life. Bauzá was an Afro-Cuban who identified strongly with African-Americans and lived in a black area of Harlem. He spent the whole of the 1930s working in major swing bands. In 1930 he joined Noble Sissle's orchestra, which already contained the Puerto Ricans Moncho Usera and Rafael Duchesne, but for most of the decade he worked in the trumpet section of Chick Webb's famous band, which headlined for years at the Savoy Ballroom.

Bauzá may have been more deeply involved in the swing scene than most, but he was by no means alone. Many of the old hands from the 1920s black big bands (and even the Hellfighters) were still around, and more were arriving every

Cuban trumpeter Mario Bauzá (fourth from right) spent the 1930s playing the Savoy Ballroom with the Chick Webb band, and later wove what he had learned into the New York Latin sound of Machito. He wasn't the only Latino in the Chick Webb band. Puerto Rican trombonist Fernando Arbello is second from right. *Frank Driggs Collection*

day. Trombonist Fernando Arbello, who had been with Fletcher Henderson in the 1920s, joined Bauzá in working with Chick Webb in Harlem in 1937. Other musicians played midtown, including three members of the Radio City Music Hall pit band. Miguel Angel Duchesne spent some years as Paul Whiteman's "hot Spanish trumpet"; Louis "King" Garcia, who was white, performed with Benny Goodman and the Dorsey Brothers orchestra. Pianist Roger "Ram" Ramirez, who was born in Puerto Rico but raised in New York City, had a long career with jazz musicians, including Rex Stewart in 1933, Ella Fitzgerald, Sid Catlett and on and on (including, on organ, blues singer T-Bone Walker!). He was, moreover, the composer of "Lover Man," a minor bebop standard and classic Sara Vaughan vehicle, and "Mad About You." In Europe, Don Marino Barreto—Don Azpiazú's brother—played with Noble Sissle's orchestra. And a spell at Harlem's Audubon Ballroom had been the first U.S. job for Augusto Coen, who also (like many other Latinos) worked in the pit bands of various Broadway shows, including *Blackbirds* and *Rhapsody in Black*, and for bandleaders Ellington and Eubie Blake as well as Sissle and Henderson. By contrast, Machito, who arrived in New York in 1937, first found work with fairly orthodox Cuban groups. He came to the city to work with Las Estrellas Habaneras, a *septeto*-type group, and also recorded with the Cuarteto Marcano.

Not only were the uptown Latino dance bands vacuuming up new influences, but the popular dance idioms of Cuba, Puerto Rico, and the Dominican Republic that were taking root in East Harlem and would be the backbone of Latin jazz were themselves recent developments that changed rapidly all the time, both under the influence of local factors and by absorbing elements of other music that were compatible, interesting to the island musicians and audiences, or deemed hip. Ragtime, jazz, and the jazz-related pop and dance music of the 1920s and 1930s had heavily influenced Cuban music. Nor was Cuba, the largest and most cosmopolitan of the three main Latin-Caribbean nations, the only one to be influenced by jazz. In the Dominican Republic (where, as in Cuba, jazz was associated with the upper crust), the more upmarket ballrooms of the two main cities developed a jazz-tinged form of merengue that was, in the words of merengue scholar Paul Austerlitz, "characterized by a novel fusion of rustic and sophisticated stylistic elements." Jazz/Latin blending, in fact, was far from confined to the U.S. East Harlem simply provided a different sort of melting pot, where the same complex of factors and styles intertwined under the influence of musicians from New York, Cuba, or both.

By the end of the decade, jazz-Latin crossover was picking up steam. One of the bandleaders to sidle into the area was Cab Calloway, who was quite unintentionally to have an important effect on the Latin-jazz explosion of the 1940s. In 1938, Calloway recorded "The Congo-Conga," a nod to a new dance fad that was starting to make it into the mainstream. This was a lighthearted piece, and Calloway's vocal may sound dated, but it was also solid early Latin-jazz in an enduring format: a rumba rhythm section with claves prominent that really swung, under fine jazz solos and swing band section-work. In an equally historic moment, Dizzy Gillespie arranged a number for Calloway's band which contained the embryo of the famous "A Night in Tunisia" riff. This was "Pickin' the Cabbage," one of Gillespie's earliest recordings. Its bass opening really does sound like "Night in Tunisia," and as a bonus you can hear a couple of bop-like touches and a nice Gillespie solo.

Several white swing bands—mostly the young up-and-comers—were also starting to record occasional Latin-inspired numbers. Charlie Barnet recorded a "Cuban Boogie Woogie" in 1939. The same year, Artie Shaw dipped his toe in the water with some sides that were fairly important in the mass popularization of Latin music, even though other Anglo bands had usually recorded the titles before him. "El Rancho Grande," under its correct title of "Alla en el Rancho Grande," had been a big regional success for Texas-Swing star Milton Brown in 1935, before Shaw made a hit of it. Another Artie Shaw recording, the 1938 "Jungle Drums," was based on Ernesto Lecuona's "Karabali." Finally, a third number that was to be a huge hit for Shaw in 1940, "Frenesi," was recorded in 1939 by three Latin groups, including a version by the Sexteto Victoria with pianist Noro Morales that was released on the general Columbia pop list.

Despite the fact that Shaw was not an innovator (in this area at least), these revivals were significant, reflecting a growing interest in Latin music in mainstream U.S. pop. One was particularly so, if only symbolically. This was his version of the Brazilian-derived "Carioca"[10] a revival of a hit song from the 1933 movie *Flying Down to Rio* (the film that made stars of Ginger Rogers and Fred Astaire). This too had been recorded by various Anglo dance groups and U.S.-based Latino artists in the early and mid-'30s, but Shaw's version greatly increased its popularity. And it was a very early example of the Brazilian/jazz fusion that was to become such a major part of jazz a few decades later.

Up to this point, the samba had not made any mark in the U.S., though at least a handful had been published in the U.S. But in 1938, things began to change. First, the samba was extensively played in the Brazilian pavilion at the 1939 New York World's Fair. As a result, a handful of U.S. bandleaders as well as Shaw

---

[10] Incidentally one of the last maxixes to reach U.S. dance floors.

made Brazilian-inspired recordings. By late in the year there was enough of a bandwagon that the U.S. sheet music to a piece called "Brazilian Night" described it as a U.S. version of "the New Brazilian Samba Craze." Then, in fall of 1939, Carmen Miranda bowled audiences over with her "South American Way" (performed, with true showbiz logic, in an Abbott and Costello vehicle called *The Streets of Paris*), setting the stage for the first major Brazilian rage in U.S. musical history.

◇ 4 ◇

Swing Shift

The 1940s

Two separate but interrelated processes made the 1940s the crucial decade for Latin music in the U.S. The first was the development, from mostly Cuban sources, of a distinctively U.S. Latin dance idiom. The second was the first consistent, conscious blending of Latin and jazz elements since Jelly Roll Morton's habanera-based compositions. Both of these processes were typical of the complex relationship between jazz (and jazz-related dance music) and Latin styles, in that they existed separately, with largely separate audiences, and yet intertwined, each feeding off and nourishing the other.

Historians (myself among them) have sometimes written as though Latin-jazz emerged abruptly in the mid-1940s, with the Dizzy Gillespie/Chano Pozo collaboration and the interaction between Stan Kenton and Machito. In point of fact, a groundswell was building throughout the early 1940s.

As we've seen, black and white swing bands were adding Cuban and other Latin pieces to their repertoire steadily by the 1930s (though not at the rate of the "sweet" dance bands). And the process picked up in the early 1940s. Even "The Peanut Vendor" by no means vanished between Don Azpiazú's seminal version and the powerhouse Stan Kenton arrangement of the mid-1940s. Bassist John Kirby was best known for his backing of Maxine Sullivan in "Loch Lomond" and various other improbable hits. But at the beginning of the decade, Kirby's outstanding small combo—with Charlie Shavers on trumpet, Buster Bailey clarinet, and Russell Procope on alto sax—worked out a highly original version of "The Peanut Vendor," including one that bounced between echoes of Azpiazú and a slyly driving boogie woogie beat. The same group also came up with a mellow

Lindy Hoppers at the Savoy Ballroom some time in the '40s. Born with apparent Latin influences, the Lindy was to be a major element in the New York mambo from the mid-'40s on, just as the swing that propelled it was a major ingredient of the big-band mambo sound. *Frank Driggs Collection*

semi-New Orleans take on LaCalle's 1924 "Amapola" that was a lot more durable than the big-band, cheek-to-cheek treatment it usually received during its 1940s revival.

Few of the Latin-tinged compositions played by the swing and dance bands of the time were up to Kirby's standard, and many were in pretty much of a novelty vein. One of the biggest of these was "Rhumboogie," launched by the Will Bradley–Ray McKinley band in April at the Famous Door on 52nd St, with a vocal by McKinley ("It's Harlem's new sensation with the Cuban syncopation. It's a killer!") and fine piano by Freddy Slack. "Rhumboogie" was a big enough hit that an Los Angeles club was named after it, but both the original and Woody Herman's cover were a lot less Rhum than boogie, with no Cuban rhythm until a few bars at the ride-out.

Several other white swing bands featured similar mixes, often with mainstream pop vocals that undermined what little Latin flavorings they had. Glenn Miller had "The Rumba Jumps" with vocal by Tex Beneke and Marion Hutton (this came from a Broadway show, *Walk With Music*). Charlie Barnet's theme, "Redskin Rhumba," was also not particularly Latin except in name. There were also some oddities. In a Brazil-meets-boogie mix, Bob Crosby recorded an anachronistic-seeming "Boogie-Woogie Maxixe" for Decca. Much of this was hit-of-the-week stuff, with the usual knockoff element. The 1941 film *Six Lessons from Madame La Zonga*, with James "Ragtime Jimmy" Monaco and the Mexican star Lupe Velez, included a song called "Jitterhumba" that obviously owed its existence to the success of "Rhumboogie." But some of the big successes of the time were rather less fluffy, notably "Para Vigo Me Voy"—recorded under that name or its English version of "Say Si"—which was a piece by the leading Cuban composer, Ernesto Lecuona. Charlie Barnet scored a major hit with it in 1941, and so did several other groups around the same time—which indicates that it was a dancehall staple, not some piece of onetime exotica. Another staple of both swing and dance groups was Lecuona's "Lamento Africano" (also known as "African Lament").

Older songs were also resurrected and given similar treatments. I've mentioned "Amapola," which was a hit for Jimmy Dorsey with Helen O'Connell. So were "Maria Elena" and "Green Eyes," both treated as cheek-to-cheekers (with a jazz-ballad O'Connell vocal on the latter). Harry James reached back into the nineteenth century to cover "La Paloma." And (no doubt mindful of the Brazilian wave that was just starting to build with the first movie or so starring Carmen Miranda), Artie Shaw resurrected and recorded "Carioca" (see Chapter 3). Interestingly, once Shaw had moved it into the jazz canon, so to speak, both Coleman Hawkins and Buddy Rich's band made versions of it.

The swing bands' Latinization process was given a boost by the popularity of the conga. Cab Calloway's August 1940 recording, "Goin' Conga," a follow-up to his "The Congo-Conga" (see Chapter 3) and "Chili-Con-Conga," was better than either of its novelty-tinged predecessors: fast, brassy, with a lot of conga-drumming from the start. The lyrics were as lightweight as ever, but the percussion was excellent and Calloway's imitation vocal soneos near the end were engaging in their own right. This was among the hottest neo-Latin recordings by a non-Latin group of the time. It is surely no coincidence that it was recorded during the one year when Calloway's trumpet section included two musicians with a respect for Cuban music: Dizzy Gillespie and Mario Bauzá.

The conga also inspired Duke Ellington's first truly Cuban-flavored piece since his 1930 "Peanut Vendor." The 1940 "Conga Brava" is typical of Ellington's forays into the field in being a piece of highly effective mood-music. It opens with vaguely montuno-ish piano, and the 4/4 rhythm of the theme has at least a suggestion of the fourth-beat kick of the conga, but the band soon shifts into straight 4/4. There are fine solos—notably by Ben Webster—but such Latin elements as the piece contains are a garnish (there's a faint odor of "Caravan" about the solos by Juan Tizol, who was no improviser). In October, Ellington mined a rather similar vein with "The Flaming Sword." Professor Lawrence Gushee, in his notes for the Smithsonian release *Duke Ellington 1940*, suggests this was essentially a version of W.H. Tyers's "Panama" with a harmonic side-debt to "Tiger Rag"—hardly avant-garde sources. Throughout the Latin jazz era, in fact, Ellington continued to use Latin elements—often no more than Latin echoes—to create generalized and highly personalized mood music, in a tradition going right back to Tyers's 1908 "Maori."

Although Bauzá had by then moved on, Cab Calloway continued his light-Latin experimentation in 1941, branching out from the conga with "Rhapsody in Rhumba," and "Conchita," also a rumba. Both were in a vein fairly standard at the time: a fast rumba rhythm turning faintly calypso-like under ensemble brass and sax riffs, followed by a driving, swing 4/4 under a jazz vocal and mostly ensemble riffs.

The 1940s were also the first time that a substantial number of Latinos formed successful bands of their own to perform for Anglo audiences and became part of the midtown mainstream rather than an exotic fringe, spreading the novel notion that Latino bands were an excellent source of Latin music.[1] Flutist Alberto

---

[1] Both Cugat and Enric Madriguera, who preceded him in the Anglo market were Spaniards. Much of their success came from their being outside the tradition from which they were borrowing.

Socarrás' dance band played opposite Glenn Miller at the Glen Island Casino in New Rochelle, NY—a double first, in that Socarrás had worked on the black U.S. scene, and his band was (in the words of the time) "the first sepia orchestra of its history"—and also played the Tropicana in 1943 opposite the newly formed Ella Fitzgerald Orchestra.

Just as Azpiazú had done in the previous decade, these Latino bands were expanding mainstream awareness of something approaching real Latin music. And they were starting to be well-received by the more enlightened critics as well as by the public. A review in the *Boston Life* summed up the process pretty neatly: "If two weeks ago anyone had told us that Boston would go strongly for a flute player with rumba rhythms we might have been polite, but not impressed. Yet after one session at the Beachcomber with Socarrás and his magic flute, even our jaundiced expression changed to one resembling joy everlasting."

For the first three years of the decade, what Stan Kenton expert Tony Cox has defined sublimely as "commuters'-bounce rumba" still ruled the Anglo big-band world. But under the surface things were stirring. Three events were particularly important:

- One of the new crop of white would-be bandleaders formed a rehearsal band with a prophetic slant to his book.
- A singer/maraca-player three years from Havana opened at the Club Cuba with a band having a one-to-two trumpet, three-sax front line.
- A young African-American found himself sitting next to an older Cuban in Cab Calloway's trumpet section.

The white would-be bandleader was Stanley Newcomb Kenton, born in Wichita, Kansas, in 1911, whose family moved to California when he was a child. During the 1930s, he played mostly with local and/or short-lived groups. In 1940 he formed a rehearsal band with a book of 17 titles, three of which were Latin of a sort. (True, "La Cumparsita," "Lamento Gitano," and "Ay, Ay, Ay" were not "the real McCoy," but they still comprised almost 20 percent of this new band's book—an indication of sounds to come.)

The Cuban with the sax section was Francisco Grillo, Jr., a man known to the world as "Machito." His 1940 band has been described as run-of-the-mill (though the frontline suggests that it was at least run of a cutting-edge mill), but to judge by its first hit record, the 1940 "Sopa de Pichon," it was already a cooking band. And more important, it was the embryo of an ensemble that was to prove more central to the Latin-jazz revolution in the making than any other single group— even Dizzy Gillespie's mid-1940s big band.

The Machito bands of the 1940s were at the heart of both the developing New York Latin sound and Afro-Cuban jazz or Cubop. Orchestral director Mario Bauzá's swing-band experience was a crucial factor in Machito's development from Cuban conjunct to New York mambo big-band, but so was the jazz-influenced playing of pianist Joe Loco (left). *Courtesy Mario Bauzá*

The young African-American was Dizzy Gillespie, who was playing in Cab Calloway's 1940 trumpet section alongside Machito's brother-in-law, Mario Bauzá, whose decade of experience in swing bands was what turned Machito's sound into the enormous influence it was to become.

An important development that affected the entire U.S. music scene, and was the next big step in the general naturalization of Latin music in the U.S.—carrying it into areas relatively unaffected by the tango and rumba and indeed to every town big enough to support a cinema—was Hollywood's sudden interest in musicals with Latin or part-Latin themes. The major reason was the need to replace European markets lost to World War II with Latin American ones. But the fact that Hollywood was willing to risk producing so many Latin musicals also reflected an awareness that Latin (or at least Latinoid) music was saleable to a U.S. mass audience. It was this that made nationally familiar faces of such disparate artists as Carmen Miranda (a major Brazilian singer), Cuba's Miguelito Valdés, and Desi Arnaz (a man with impressively little knowledge of Cuban music but a lot of showbiz talent), let alone Xavier Cugat (who turned out to be an excellent character actor).

Hollywood, of course, needed music that would appeal to both U.S. audiences and Latin American markets that, language apart, were extremely different one from another. The solution was twofold: on the one hand, generic Latin balladry, and on the other—mostly in nightclub scenes—both rumbas and sambas that were at times reasonably authentic (though it tended to get swamped on movie sound tracks, Carmen Miranda's backup group, the Banda da Lua, played wonderful Rio street samba).

Hollywood also needed all this fast. The result was the revival of songs that either had been hits earlier or were generic enough to appeal to wide audiences. Given that songs taken up by Hollywood also provided hits for the dance bands of the era, this meant a flood of not particularly distinctive recordings that nevertheless continued the softening-up process toward Latin music in the mainstream U.S. musical landscape started by the tango and rumba fads.

Carmen Miranda's movie success gave the samba equal status with the tango and rumba, the first time Brazilian music impinged on the U.S. in any significant way. Hollywood also popularized a few songs that, however watered down or camped up, stemmed from deeper zones of Latin music, as well as outstanding musicians. A classic example was "Babalú"—named after a leading member of the Cuban Yoruba pantheon—first sung on film by Miguelito Valdés (a major star in Cuba before he came stateside) with Xavier Cugat. "Babalú" may seem hokey nowadays, but it was no Hollywood invention: Valdés's first recording of it was with the Orquesta Casino de la Playa, one of Cuba's finest groups.[2]

 Though they caused no stir at the time, three important events took place in 1942, although not all were recognized as monumental at the time:

- Dizzy Gillespie wrote "A Night in Tunisia" for the Earl Hines big band.
- Stan Kenton's new band issued its first four recordings, no less than three of which were Latin-oriented: "Taboo," "Adios," and "The Nango" (a corruption of "Nañigo," one of the many Afro-Cuban religious groups). And, although he didn't record it, Kenton's first book also included the classic tango, "El Choclo."[3]
- The most important band in the history of Latin-jazz, Machito's Afro-Cubans, made its debut.

[2]At one time Damaso Pérez Prado was its pianist.

[3]Though the tango was still danced, it was mostly ignored by the "progressive" swing bands, but not by the working dance bands. In fact a long-forgotten sweet orchestra, Ray Herbeck and His Modern Music with Romance (I kid you not) featured a "Tango Moderne" in its radio broadcasts that was clearly targeted to dancers.

The creation of the Afro-Cubans was no ad-hoc affair. Its roots went back to 1941, when Mario Bauzá joined Machito's conventional *conjunto* as musical director. Machito's own resume included small groups like the Cuarteto Caney and Cuarteto Marcano (with both of which he recorded), and polished dance bands like Alberto Iznaga's Orquesta Siboney. His experience was solidly Cuban-straight, both in Cuba and in New York, though he did record a handful of sides with Xavier Cugat. All in all he had qualifications for New York City Latin-band leadership—but not for the kind of thorough-going melding of Afro-Cuban and Afro-American styles that was to become his band's trademark. But Bauzá, besides being a much more complete musician, came out of a decade-long dual Cuban/jazz experience.

For many years, Bauzá's enormous contribution to Machito's band, and thus to Cuban-based Latin jazz as well as to the developing New York Latin sound, went grossly under-recognized, at least in the jazz world. More recently the pendulum has swung a bit far in the other direction. But by even the most conservative estimate, Bauzá's makeover of the original Machito band was epochal. First, he upgraded its formal music skills by firing the band members who couldn't read music. Second, he enlarged the group and fleshed out its sound. In an interview in the late 1970s, Bauzá told me: "Our idea was to bring Latin music up to the standard of the American orchestras. So I brought a couple of the guys that arranged for Calloway and Chick Webb to write for me. I wanted them to give me the sound—to orchestrate it."

The process began while he was still working for Cab Calloway. He and Calloway arranger John Bartee worked nights after gigs, writing for the proposed group, along with Edgar Sampson, who worked regularly for Chick Webb and was to play with many of the major New York Latin bands in the late 1940s and 1950s. The formula was simple but enormously powerful: to blend a Cuban repertoire and a Cuban rhythm section (with its crucial formal underpinning, the two-bar offbeat call-and-response rhythmic pattern called clave) and a trumpet and sax frontline with the power of the black swing bands.

The early Afro-Cubans drew their power much more from this balance of jazz and Cuban music than from the additional instruments: in fact, the band started out with much the same instrumentation as its predecessor, though with better players. One of Bauzá's innovations was to hire non-Latino horn players, because his jazz-inflected sound would come not just from jazz voicings in the arrangements but from the details of phrasing. Crucially, at a time when most big-band jazz built complexity on a very simple structure (basically chorus-bridge-chorus) and small swing groups simplified matters even further with head arrangements and solos, Bauzá preserved a multi-section structure of the kind that jazz had largely abandoned around the time of King Oliver's Creole Jazz Band. Cuban dance music had already developed a *son*-based, two-part structure with a "head" that presented the basic theme and a section in which the lead singer improvised over the unvarying response of the two-or-three-voice *coro*. Preserving that, along with the far more vocal-oriented thrust of Cuban music of all kinds, kept the Afro-Cubans close to their roots.

The result of this dual outreach/preservationist strategy was what Max Salazar describes perfectly as "the *típico* big-band jazz sound."[4] The Afro-Cubans' essence was not the instrumentation—José Curbelo, after some time spent with Cugat, played opposite the Afro-Cubans at La Conga in 1942 with a group whose instrumentation was identical—but the embryonic enriching of the black, and thus largely African-derived, elements of the highly complex Cuban tradition by the use of the *African*-American stream of swing at a time when other Latin bands were still drawing mostly from the whiter and more pop-oriented aspects of the jazz and dance scene.

The changes in the Afro-Cubans took place over several years. Stage two took place in 1943. Several factors came together that year, but perhaps the most important was the arrival in the band of pianist Joe Estevez, better known (in fact at one time extremely well known) as Joe Loco. Loco, a New Yorker of Puerto Rican descent, had worked not only as a pianist with Latin groups but as a dancer at the Apollo Theater, where he appeared with the Chick Webb Orchestra (a link, be it noted, with Bauzá). According to bongo player Jose Mangual his piano work gave the band a more jazz-oriented swing, noticeable enough that dancers began calling the group "the Latin Count Basie Orchestra."[5]

That same year, the number that Salazar considers the first Afro-Cuban jazz work was composed, "Tanga." It became the signature tune of the Afro-Cubans' WOR radio broadcasts from La Conga in fall 1943,[6] at a time when Bauzá was upping the degree of the jazz voicings in the ensemble writing—a move that, along with Loco's more jazz-oriented soloing, began to get the group occasional jazz-club gigs. But Bauzá always kept one foot firmly planted in the group's contemporary-*típico* home base. It was typical of the Afro-Cubans that during the year that the jazz elements in the band were strikingly enhanced, the Cubanism of its rhythm section was solidified by the hiring of conga-player

---

[4] From his notes to *The Original Mambo Kings* compilation

[5] Quoted by Salazar in notes to the Tumbao CD *Joe Loco.*

[6] "Tanga" later became part of a major Latin-jazz suite.

Carlos Vidal.[7] Innovative though it was, it is important to bear in mind that at this time the new sound of the Afro-Cubans was not seen as "Afro-Cuban jazz," Cubop, Latin-jazz, or any other jazz-related music. It was simply one hip New York Latin band among several.

The first half of the 1940s was a time of coalescence. On the jazz side, Dizzy Gillespie, who had already discussed with Bauzá the idea of combining jazz with Cuban rhythms while they worked together in the Calloway band (or so at least both Gillespie and Bauzá both claimed in later years), was engaged in a kind of public woodshedding, learning the ins and outs of playing over Cuban rhythms. In 1942 he sat in with the Afro-Cubans at the Park Plaza on and off (mostly in afternoon sessions, Bauzá told me—presumably because he worked his regular gig in the evenings). In 1943, according to Alberto Socarrás, he also played with Socarrás's band for a few weeks.

Throughout the jazz world, everybody was learning the ropes before setting out on a voyage that nobody would have predicted at the time. In January 1945, the Boyd Raeburn big band, including Shelly Manne on drums, made the first recording of "A Night in Tunisia." That August, Woody Herman recorded the most famous of his infrequent excursions into the Latin tinge, "Bijou" (subtitled "Rhumba à la Jazz"), by the important Ralph Burns. To my ears this was the first recording to combine embryonic bebop elements in the bass and guitar opening and in "progressive" sax work with a Latin rhythm more or less throughout.[8] In 1946, Harry James recorded a Juan Tizol composition called "Keb-Lah," essentially a "Caravan" clone notable for a fine trumpet solo by James. Charlie Barnet recorded another piece of exotica, "The New Redskin Rhumba." Pianist Mary Lou Williams was playing a piece called "Rebop Rhumba" about this time. And, Nat "King" Cole recorded an album called *Rhumba à la King* in Cuba with a group that (according to producer/Latin music scholar René Lopez) included the great *conjunto* trumpeter Armando "Chocolate" Armenteros, one of a generation of Cubans who were remaking the old *septeto* solo style with strong jazz elements.

In 1946, several events signaled the beginnings of a true Latin-jazz movement (the word Cubop hadn't been coined yet). In New York, that March, Charlie

---

[7] An example of how "authentic" does not necessarily mean "traditional." The great Cuban bandleader Arsenio Rodriguez had only recently brought the conga into his Havana-based conjunto from the voices-and-percussion street rumbas and religious drumming.

[8] The handling of the Latin rhythm was a little clumsy, but these were the early days. Herman himself made no exaggerated claims for "Bijou." In his autobiography, he explained that he gave it the subtitle because "I was trying to explain why we were abusing the Latin rhythm," and added engagingly if not accurately, "I guess you could call it 'a stone-age bossa nova.'"

From the jazz viewpoint, the seminal pairing of Cubop came in December 1947, when Mario Bauzá sent the newly arrived conga-player Chano Pozo to joint Dizzy Gillespie's bebop big band for a concert. The collaboration lasted less than a year before Pozo was murdered, but though undeveloped it was the first time a serious jazz form had blended with "deep" Afro-Cuban percussion. Here they are in full flight along with tenorist James Moody. *Frank Driggs Collection*

Parker recorded his first version of one of the classics of early Latin-tinged bop, Dizzy Gillespie's "A Night In Tunisia." In May, composer/dancer/conga player Luciano Pozo y González, aka Chano Pozo, was lured to New York by Mario Bauzá. His arrival was unnoticed by the bebop community, but not by the Latin musicians. He had been a big deal in Havana ever since he appeared in a show called *Congo Pantera* at the Sans Souci cabaret in 1940, and had already composed a series of numbers that brought him both money and fame, among them a hardy perennial, "Blen-Blen-Blen."

Things were also stirring on the West Coast. Veteran Cuban bandleader Rene Touzet hired the jazz drummer Jackie Mills, and Mills persuaded him to hire Art Pepper, Pete Candoli, and a couple of jazz players, then brought in Johnny Mandel to play bass trumpet and write arrangements.[9] Along with experiments with jazz arrangements of Latin numbers, Mandel produced a 12-bar blues with a mambo rhythm, "Barbados Blues," which was later recorded (as "Barbados") by Charlie Parker.

But the year's most major transformation came with the Stan Kenton Band's move from Latin-Lite material to something a lot more important, not just within the jazz-oriented world of Cubop, but in its effect on the new Latino dance music. The story of how Kenton got religion depends to some extent on who is telling it, but it happened over the course of 1946. Kenton himself told it this way: "As far as the Latin-American influence on me goes I must credit one guy only. I was with [Pete] Rugolo at the Embassy Club in New York, where Noro Morales and his band were playing, and I became so excited by the Afro-Cuban music that Noro was playing and I wanted to hear more."[10]

Rugolo, whose compositions and arrangements were a major influence on the Kenton sound, was an early example of a new type of (at that time mostly white) jazz musician, one who not only had conservatory training but drew overtly or indirectly from contemporary conservatory composers. Like several other West Coast musicians of the time, Rugolo had studied with Darius Milhaud at San Francisco State University. (Tony Cox considers that Rugolo's "Artistry in Bolero," which Kenton recorded in July of 1946, had more to do with Ravel than with Latin America.)

Cox also holds that Kenton was first "seriously connected with Latin music" in July, when he recorded "Ecuador" (a Gene Roland composition) for Capitol

---

[9] According to Marshall Stearns in *The Story of Jazz*, the first major jazz history to take note of the Latin influence on jazz bands.

[10] Quoted by Chris Pirie in his Kenton biography, *Artistry in Rhythm*.

Transcription Service, which produced 16-inch discs distributed to radio stations. "Ecuador" was not released commercially for a couple of years, during which reports surfaced in the U.S. musical press that Kenton was proposing a suite comprising musical portraits of Latin-American countries.

The impact of the New York Latin bands on Kenton was major and decisive. Besides providing him with a number of major hits, Latin music would remain a significant part of his campaign to become a leader of what he would later call progressive jazz. By January 1947, in fact, he had a clear view of what he thought was involved for both sides of the equation. "Rhythmically," he told *Metronome*, "the Cubans play the most exciting stuff. We won't copy them exactly but we will copy some of their devices and apply them to what we are trying to do. And while we keep moving toward the Cubans rhythmically, they're moving toward us melodically. We both have a lot to learn."

While the jazz world was developing Cubop, the Latin-band scene was also continuing to undergo a great deal of change. Most importantly for the long term, a new rhythm that was to revolutionize both the mainstream and Latino dance scene was surfacing in New York around 1946. The origins of the mambo are not altogether clear, but it was to become the New York Latin idiom par excellence. Though Machito rightly became known as one of the New York troika of "mambo kings," and his swing-inflected style was of the essence of the style, Machito's was not necessarily the band that first played New York-style protomambos. The first use of the word on a record by a New York-based band seems to have come on José Curbelo's recording "El Rey del Mambo." This was recorded at the end of November 1946 (two years before the first Perez Prado mambos were released in the U.S.!).

Curbelo's band was an extremely interesting example of the changes in Latin music that were feeding both into and off swing and other non-Latino dance music. Curbelo had arrived in the U.S. in 1939 and formed his group in 1941 after a stint with Cugat, working the midtown circuit using much the same mix of U.S. and Cuban elements as Machito's band. His band reached its peak in 1946, when he hired two young New York Latinos who were to become leaders of the New York mambo school—singer Tito Rodriguez and *timbalero*-vibist Tito Puente—along with a rhythm section that included Chino Pozo (not to be confused with Chano, the conga-player) on bongos and long-time Machito sideman Carlos Vidal on conga, both of whom were to record extensively with jazz musicians.

Curbelo's 1946–47 recordings clearly show the genesis of the New York mambo style in the mid-1940s. They included several rumbas as well as guarachas of the type whose third section was to become the basis of the instrumental mambo's building riff and counter-riff, and which in Curbelo's hands already prefigured the classic mambo's stabbing trumpets and rolling sax riffs. There were also two Brazilian-inspired cuts, "Ed Sullivan Samba" and the interesting fusion piece, "Boogie Woogie na Favela."

Another seminal band of the period was founded in 1945 by Cuban Marcelino Guerra, who had been brought to the U.S. as an arranger by Robbins Music. Some claim that Guerra's unit was better than the Machito group of the time. It was certainly similar, to judge from the few recordings that it made for the small Verne label, but it broke up in 1947 for obscure reasons. African-American trumpeter Doc Cheatham and some other members at the time say the band's musicians were too black for midtown bookings.

1947 brought an intensification of the mambo buildup. Most importantly, both Tito Puente and Tito Rodriguez left Curbelo's group and formed trumpet conjuntos and soon expanded them to big bands in order to satisfy Anglo dancers' expectations (in Puente's case, specifically, the expectations of the Catskill resort-hotel scene). Puente's group, the Piccadilly Boys, signed with Tico Records and had a hit with its second release, "Abaniquito," which included Mario Bauzá on trumpet as well as the singer Vicentico Valdez, a major name in Latin music who never really crossed over into the Anglo musical consciousness. Rodriguez's Mambo Devils, which also signed with Tico, soon grew into a big band, but even as a conjunto it reflected the embryonic mambo idiom in recordings like "Mambo Mona," whose ensemble trumpet work included occasional heavy Kenton-influenced shakes.

In February, Tito Rodriguez took this group into the studio to back Chano Pozo in his first New York recordings, "Rumba en Swing," "Porque Tu Sufres," and "Cometelo To'," on which Pozo sang as well as playing conga. Tito fronted quite a team, including Arsenio Rodriguez, Machito's great arranger/pianist René Hernández, Mario Bauzá among the trumpets, and African-American alto player Eugene Johnson, as well as Machito's rhythm section. A slightly different group recorded a follow-up a few days later, and later still Pozo went back into the studio for two sessions with his own *conjunto*. Pretty much all the cuts reflected the classic Cuban *conjunto*-based sound of the time. But along with heavy, street-style, Afro-Cuban Pozo vocals, "Todo el mundo lo sabe" included his conga on what must have been one of the earliest recorded percussion rumbones. Other numbers also included horns with obvious swing influence, and in one case a mix of mambo-style riffs and a swing-voiced reprise. "Paso a Tampa" had swing voicings particularly well integrated into the Cuban elements of the trumpets, and the trumpets in "Seven Seven," from a second session by the same group, were even more jazz-influenced in places.

One of the crucial factors in the growth of a true Latin-jazz style was the increasing degree to which Latino musicians were playing in Anglo bands, and vice versa. Though Latinos had been playing in African American bands since before the 1920s, they had almost always been there to play the charts as written, or to provide trimmings like a Cuban-style trumpet solo in a rumba. Now they were starting to be equal partners in a separate and self-subsisting hybrid—call it Latin-jazz, Cubop, or what you will—that coalesced so rapidly because of the crossover of musicians and not just stylistic elements. Put bluntly, without Mario Bauzá—just as much as without Kenton or Gillespie—Cubop would in all probability not have happened.

It was, in fact, very much a two-way street. By the end of 1947, both Dizzy Gillespie and Stan Kenton had moved from fringe involvement to a continued experimentalism. Both men brought members of Machito's rhythm section into the studio. Kenton did so for the first time on January 2, 1947, by including bongo player Jose Mangual Sr. and Pedro Allendo on maracas on the calypso, "His Feet's Too Big For de Bed" (the Latin bands were also playing calypso, which was having one of its many short stints in the pop sun).

The following month, Kenton returned to the studio for a more significant session. One of the cuts, "Down in Chihuaha" with Kenton's vocal group, the Pastels, is in the old Latin-trivial vein. But the other cut is the first version of an eponymous tribute to Machito. This has no Latino instrumentalists on it, a lack that is obvious: the crisp, fast montuno with which the piece opens is weighed down by not-too-adept drumming from Shelly Manne. Manne did better later on, but the whole thing is a little heavy—particularly considering the honoree—with extremely busy brass and a Kai Winding trombone solo leaning toward "Caravan"-style exoticism. Kenton soon re-recorded the piece, partly to get a more authentic rhythm section by adding Ivan Lopez on bongos and Eugenio Reyes on maracas, and partly because trombonist Bill Harris wanted to redo a trumpet-trombone duet near the end of the piece.

The week after this recording Kenton disbanded, to reform in September for a concerts-only tour opening at the Rendezvous Ballroom at Balboa Beach, California. Tony Cox dates Kenton's really serious push into Latin rhythms to this group: "Both Kenton and Rugolo were seriously committed to exploring the rhythmic elements of Latin/Afro-Cuban music and to discovering how these elements could be successfully blended with the sort of jazz composition with which they had been experimenting over the previous year or so. They were searching for, and in my view found, hybrid vigour." His new repertoire, as Cox writes, "contained quite a lot of Latin-styled Progressive jazz numbers and also made use of various Latin percussion instruments in some non-Latin pieces." Between September and December, when an American Federation of Musicians ban put the kibosh on studio work, the new Kenton orchestra recorded 26 numbers, including up-tempo Latin dance pieces ("The Peanut Vendor," "Cuban Carnival") and more ambitious works using Latin rhythms for effect ("Introduction to a Latin Rhythm," "Journey to Brazil," "Bongo Riff"). Kenton also included bongos in many of the avant-garde concert compositions that were to form a significant part of his repertoire until the orchestra disbanded at the end of 1948.

"The Peanut Vendor," recorded in early December, was an early Cubop classic. Arranged by Kenton, it included Carlos Vidal on conga, Machito playing maracas, and Jose Luis Mangual on bongos. It opened with a fine acoustic guitar version of the piece's by-now-classic montuno by Laurindo Almeida, newly arrived from Brazil, with Milt Bernhart's trombone taking the main melody over it. The early part of the recording presented a brisk version of the classic "Peanut Vendor," punctured by subversive trombone smears. But above all the whole recording cooked in a way that the earlier "Machito" barely achieved. Bassist Eddie Safranski's imaginative lines provided the percussionist with the underpinning for a fine choppy swing full of counter-rhythms, while Kenton's aggressive brass, including a hair-raising four-trumpet section, deconstructed the classic logic of the piece. The result was a blend of the charm of Azpiazú's original with ensemble writing that was both startling and exciting. What made it important historically is that—for the first time on a studio recording—it blended serious and experimental jazz writing with an authentic Latin rhythm section and a classic Latin composition.

Kenton's "Peanut Vendor" was a well-deserved hit. Three pieces recorded just before Christmas had less popular appeal, but provided contrasting examples both of Kenton's dedication to the genre and of the different ways in which it was already possible to approach it. "Interlude" was not ostensibly a Latin theme, but Kenton's opening piano work had a clear Latin feel, mostly from the left-hand patterns that he sets against a lush right hand; in later stages, Safranski intermittently threw in montuno-like phrases to offset and spark the basic 4/4. "Bongo Riff," as you would expect, featured percussion soloing, this time by Jack Costanzo without the support of Machito's men. The whole piece was in swing 4/4, at least after an opening with a slightly odd rhythmic pattern. Costanzo's bongos, though busy and effective, lacked a certain something you might call clave discipline. Nonetheless, a case could be made that this was just about the first straight-jazz piece on record to incorporate a Latin percussion instrument.

The main motivator of Kenton's move into both concert pieces and Latin-jazz was Pete Rugolo, the man who had taken him to hear the real thing the previous year. In the view of Ted Gioia, author of *West Coast Jazz*, "Rugolo's ventures into Latin music are perhaps the most striking of his works from this period . . . 'Cuban Carnival' and 'Introduction to a Latin Rhythm' have none of the rarefied flavor of the academy to hamper their exuberance. While not up to the caliber of the Kenton classic *Cuban Fire* release of some years later, these charts showed that progressive music could boast a heady rhythmic flair and an earthy flavor."

Given his partially conservatory/avant-garde background, Rugolo's role in moving Kenton toward a more ambitious vision (there were those, including Gerry Mulligan, who called it grandiose) was hardly surprising. The commitment to more serious Latin experiments was less predictable, and it would have been less successful if the new group had not also included a couple of permanent Latin-American musicians. One was Kenton's long-term bongo player, Jack Costanzo; the other, much more importantly for jazz/Latin fusions in general, was Brazilian guitarist Laurindo Almeida. Almeida became featured acoustic guitarist for Kenton through 1948, and, clearly, part of the inspiration for a continuing Brazilian tinge in Kenton's Latinisms. He was a particularly good fit with Kenton's new group: far from being a hardcore samba player, he had extensive classical training as well as popular music experience.

If Kenton was ahead by a nose in the Cubop stakes, it was a very slight lead. While Kenton was playing the first gigs with his new orchestra, Dizzy Gillespie—the man who was to be credited, for very good reasons, with founding the whole Cubop movement—presented the Latin-jazz "Afro-Cubano Drums Suite," at a Carnegie Hall concert on September 29, 1947. This was a really substantive first on a couple of grounds, including being the first time a multi-movement Latin suite had been played in public, thus launching a trend that (Duke Ellington excepted) largely lived and died with Cubop.

All in all, 1947 went out in a blaze of glory—and not just thanks to Gillespie and Kenton. In late October, Charlie Parker recorded "Bongo Bop" with Miles Davis, Duke Jordan, Tommy Potter, and Max Roach. This is a fairly straight bop piece, without the montuno opening of "Night In Tunisia," though in its place Roach imitates somewhat bongo-like patterns on traps. His playing in the intro is an early effort to incorporate Cuban rhythms into jazz drumming. There is no attempt at anything overtly Latin by anybody else, a pattern that was fairly standard in very early Cubop. A companion piece, "Bongo Beep," was recorded by a group adding trombonist J.J. Johnson in late December. Here Roach's drumming, though in a similar opening, flows more smoothly and colors the whole intro rather more emphatically. His drum solo in the body of the work has no overt Afro-Cuban influence, but the bongo-inspired patterns return for an outro the earlier recording had lacked. Again there is no attempt at anything overtly Latin by anybody else in the group.

Meanwhile, Dizzy Gillespie presented a big-band concert at New York's Town Hall theater featuring *conguero* Chano Pozo that turned out to be one of the seminal moments of Cubop. And on December 30, Gillespie cut the first recorded version of Chano Pozo's "Manteca," featuring its composer. The importance of this did not lie in a perfect fusion of the two idioms. In his admirable study of bebop, Thomas Owens comments that ". . . once the theme ends and the improvisations begin . . . Gillespie and the full band continue the bebop mood, using swing eighths in spite of Pozo's continuing even eighths, until the final *a* section of the theme returns. Complete assimilation of Afro-Cuban rhythms and improvisations on a harmonic ostinato was still a few years away for the beboppers in 1947."

The same could have been said of another Gillespie classic of the period, "Woody'n You." This moved between sections in which Pozo was virtually playing solo and passages with jazz rhythms in which he sounded out of his depth. But while Kenton, however boldly, was mixing two styles that already had been intermingling, however peripherally, for a couple of decades, Gillespie was working to blend avant-garde, big-band work with a form of Cuban music more rootsy, more African, and less assimilated: the Afro-Cuban percussion of the religious cults, treated with respect rather than as the floor-show exoticism of "Babalú" and its ilk. Nevertheless, inchoate and sometimes awkward though the musical results were during the short time in which Gillespie and Pozo worked together, they confirmed Gillespie in his Latin-jazz experimentalism, gave the whole Cubop hybrid a cachet, and helped dent Latin music's previous "fun-time" image. They also inspired other musicians to follow the same path—and not only in the U.S. It was hearing the Gillespie/Pozo recordings that induced Cuban composer/arranger Chico O'Farrill, who was to become one of the most talented arrangers in Latin jazz, to move to New York. How the collaboration would have grown as both men developed more understanding of each other's idiom is one of the great tragic questions of jazz, because the partnership was ended almost before it started when Pozo was shot dead on December 12th.

For Gillespie, his bandsmen, and his admirers, however, Chano Pozo was something more than a mere conga-player, and in jazz writing his name is still mentioned with awe. Marshall Stearns quotes Gillespie as calling him "the greatest drummer I ever heard"; Teddy Stewart, Gillespie's drummer, as saying that "Chano was way ahead of us all"; and bassist Al McKibbon as describing how "Pozo used to parcel out rhythms to us while we were on the road and, man, we knocked out some terrific combinations on the backs of the seats." Mario Bauzá, who goodness knows had enough credibility for ten, concurred. "Chano Pozo's one of the greatest things that ever happened in Cuba, all round," he once told me. "He created more hit songs than anybody else and he created more rhythms than any conga players. . . . You know what Dizzy said to me? 'I don't want to have no more conga players in my band, because I hear all these so-called great guys, and they ain't nowhere close to Chano Pozo.'"

Underneath this praise lay a certain ambivalence that goes to the heart of the weaknesses in the Gillespie/Pozo recordings. Gillespie was a leader in a revolutionary style whose innovations had a strong harmonic element; Pozo was a *típico* traditionalist. Writing of "Manteca" in his biography, Gillespie says, "Chano wasn't too hip about American music. If I'd let it go like he wanted it, it would've been strictly Afro-Cuban, all the way. There wouldn't have been a bridge. I wrote the bridge. I . . . thought I was writing an eight-bar bridge. But after eight bars I hadn't resolved back to B-flat, so I had to keep on going and ended up writing a sixteen-bar bridge." Fair enough, but if Pozo didn't understand bebop, Gillespie's knowledge of Cuban music, though greater than that of other jazzmen, wasn't at that point very deep, and neither had time to figure out quite how to bridge the gap.

While the jazz world was unanimous in its admiration of Pozo's drumming, some Latino musicians considered him more important as a composer than conga-player. Mongo Santamaria, himself no slouch as a conga player, once commented to me that "When I was playing in Cuba, Chano Pozo was dancing. Dancing and composing. He used to play but he really wasn't dedicated because he wasn't a good player." Other Latinos who heard him perform in person vary in their assessments. Older Cubans tend to describe him as a good player among many. Younger New Yorkers like Barretto regard him as an inspiration. He played single conga in the old one-drum style, and whatever his limitations, he was in at least in one sense a complete player. "Where most conga players are top-heavy or bottom-heavy," as Roger Dawson wrote, "Pozo could do both—providing rhythmic support or melodic improvisation."[11] Whatever his talents, Pozo's background in the Abakwá religious sect gave him the kind of knowledge

---

[11] From an appreciation in *Latin New York* magazine.

Gillespie was seeking. And if he had some problems fitting in with jazz rhythms, many jazz musicians in this period had just the same problem playing over clave.

A few non-Latino players were already working regularly with Latin groups. Aside from the hornmen associated with Machito, and for Billy Taylor—who had once found himself holding down the Machito piano chair for a week while the band waited for René Hernández to arrive from Cuba—Tony Scott was playing in the sax section of the Lecuona Cuban Boys by early 1948. But most jazzmen still had a lot of learning to do. Trumpeter Doc Cheatham was to appear regularly with both Machito and Marcelino Guerra. But he told me that the first time he joined the band, Machito fired him after two nights because he couldn't cope with clave.

Despite all that had come before, if any single year has a claim as the birth year of Cubop, it is 1948. And if there was a common thread, it was still Machito—and, more particularly, his éminence grise, Mario Bauzá. The year began with a bang when Machito and his Afro-Cubans played a Town Hall gig that Max Salazar has called the first Afro-Cuban jazz concert. "The first" is always a tricky concept, and the Gillespie/Pozo concert the previous year might seem to have a major claim to the title. But both on a casual and a deeper level, Salazar has a point. First, the Gillespie concert consisted largely of big-band bebop without Latin connections. And more fundamentally, the Gillespie/Pozo collaboration at the first two concerts was unlike any other—unlike even Gillespie's later Latin-jazz work. The mainstream of Cubop/Latin jazz (where it wasn't simply a hip, add-a-conga version of the old Latin tinge) was to follow the lines of Machito's early collaborations with jazz musicians: collaborations like the one in August, in which bop trumpeter Howard McGhee soloed with Machito at the Apollo Theater, providing ad libs to "Tanga." This August concert provided the basis for what is arguably the first true Latin-jazz recording, and remains one of the greatest, "Cubop City," recorded under the band name of "Howard McGhee and his Afro-Cuboppers." This was the whole nine yards, with inspired solos by McGhee and tenor player Brew Moore over an arrangement for the full Machito band that perfectly fulfilled Bauzá's vision of a true blend of Cuban and African-American music, all held together by the clave laid down by one of the finest Afro-Cuban rhythm sections ever.

1948 also saw another seminal bop/Latin collaboration, when Norman Granz took the Machito band into the studio with Charlie Parker and former Woody Herman tenorist Flip Phillips. This was not the first time Parker and Machito had played together: Granz had previously taken Parker to a rehearsal at the Palladium. But it was the first time the public was heard the results.

The 1948 Parker/Machito session produced four numbers, "Mango Mangüe" the amiable "Okidoke," and the two-part "No Noise" and "Tanga." "Mango Mangüe" opens with superb tight, cohesive reed-playing in the intro. In solo Parker is, as always, Parker. Where his style worked best, interestingly, is during a solo over the *coro* that is like an instrumental substitute for the *sonero*'s vocal improvisations—perhaps because the *coro* acts as a formal bridge between the rhythm and the alto.

The first part of "No Noise" is a vehicle for a long solo by Flip Phillips (who sat out "Mango Mangüe"), with rather banal brass punctuations. Part Two has Parker soloing in one of his serener moods, slightly more legato than usual. The basic rhythm is a mildly eccentric tata-poum tapa*ka* that dovetails very effectively with Parker's patterns.

Even at this juncture, not every Latin-jazz mix was a fruit of the avant-garde. The great boogie-woogie duo of Albert Ammons and Pete Johnson made a recording of the early '40s hit "Rhumboogie," which was an echo of frivolities past. Overall, though, the scene was deepening and widening. The committed aside, beboppers in particular were increasingly looking to spice up a gig or a recording date with some Latin percussion. Pozo himself, as vocalist and conga-player, recorded a version of his own "Tin Tin Deo" with a group that included trumpeters Dave Burns and Elmo Wright, saxists Ernie Henry, James Moody, and Cecil Paine, drummer Art Blakey, and other jazz musicians. Charlie Parker cut perhaps the archetypal version of "Night in Tunisia," using most of Gillespie's arrangement from a septet recording a month earlier, in which he played a four-bar solo break (Gillespie's original had been half the length) that Thomas Owens has described as "as stunning as any in recorded jazz." Like the Louis "Big Eye" Nelson "High Society" clarinet solo half a century earlier, this became a defining element of the defining characteristics of the piece.

Many fine Cubop recordings of this period are totally forgotten. In March 1949, bandleader Jerry Wald, who led a competent big band in the early and mid-1940s, recorded four Cubop sides, "Bah'n Du Dah," "Afrocubalibra," and "Rhumbolero, Parts I and II." "Bah'n Du Dah" is a 12-bar piece with a scat vocal and improvised bop solos over strong Cuban percussion. "Afrocubalibra" and the six-minute "Rhumbolero" were, despite their silly names, uncompromising, big-band Cubop. The ensemble (which may have been a pickup group) included two musicians who were to play a leading role in Latin-jazz until the present day: Al Porcino and Frank Socolow.

One of the best of the Cubop-tinge recordings—those in which an otherwise orthodox jazz group adds a single percussion instrument—was also one of the earliest: trumpeter Fats Navarro (who was, perhaps not incidentally, part-Cuban and grew up in Florida's Key West) joined tenorists Wardell Grey and Allen Eager, pianist Tad Dameron, drummer Kenny Clarke, and bongosero Chino Pozo. Despite a cavalier attitude to clave and the presence of only one percussionist, "Lady Bird," "Jahbero," and "Symphonette" were remarkably successful for their time.

While many of these recordings were enormously influential, Machito's club dates also became a significant part of the scene, particularly in their effect on fellow musicians. Playing opposite Machito at the Club Clique, later renamed Birdland, pianist George Shearing was so bowled over by the band that, as he told it later, he was "then and there" inspired to launch his Latin jazz career.

The Latin scene, meanwhile, was (Machito aside) as effervescent as the bop world. Cuban musicians, who had always been marginally influenced by jazz, were incorporating more jazz elements into theoretically *típico* performances. A beautiful example came in a recording by Arsenio Rodriguez's conjunto called "Tumba Palo Cucuye," in which trumpeter Chappotín fused septeto-derived Cuban elements with jazz in a style that was to revolutionize both Cuban music and New York salsa, while pianist "Lili" Martinez's brilliant accompaniment breathtakingly integrated jazz chords with typical Cuban *floreos*. In particular, a number of the young musicians beginning to form their own groups had a particularly strong liking for jazz—among them the fine pianist Charlie Palmieri, older brother of the better-known Eddie.

1949 brought an intensification of the already burgeoning Cubop scene and some significant activity on a wider front. Machito, apparently feeling ready to expand on the Cubop side of his activities, cut instrumental sides without guest soloists from the bop world, among them "U-Ba-Bla-Du," "Gone City," and "Tea for Two." These last two were the first Latin arrangements by Chico O'Farrill, who was to be associated with the multi-movement suites that formed a fairly substantial part of the Cubop scene for a while. Why O'Farrill was hired for this date, rather than one of Bauzá's old swing-band colleagues, is not clear. Though his first job in the U.S. was with Noro Morales, and despite the fact that he was Cuban-born and raised (though he attended a military academy in the U.S.), O'Farrill's first musical interest was jazz, both in Cuba and in the U.S. His first U.S. compositions were straight jazz charts, "Undercurrent Blues" and "Shish-mabop," commissioned by Benny Goodman, who was engaged in a flirtation with bebop at the time. And he knew very little about Cuban music; much later, he told Max Salazar that Machito and Bauzá gave him "most of my knowledge about Latin music"—including that crucial building block, the clave rhythm.

Machito's live performances in jazz clubs were at least as influential as his recordings. He was appearing steadily in the various jazz spots midtown, including the Clique and (sponsored by Symphony Sid Torin—the only deejay with a song named after him!), the Royal Roost and Bop City. A recent re-release on the Tumbao label of airshots from radio broadcasts gives a rich picture of his performances in these clubs. Perhaps the most extraordinary tracks came from a February 11 broadcast from the Royal Roost intended to promote a forthcoming Jazz at the Philharmonic (JATP) concert. The first, "Bucabu," featured Flip Phillips fronting the Machito rhythm section. This opens with a stunning vocalization of deep Afro-Cuban percussion by (presumably) Machito and members of the band, into which the drums enter with a virtually pure street rumba over which Phillips plays a sliding, winding, oblique solo that balances bop inflections with the kind of high-energy jamming for which JATP soloists were famous (or infamous).

This was followed by something equally, though differently, mind-boggling—a piece named (apparently on the spot) "One O'Clock Leap" that put Machito's men behind trombonist Will Bradley's band, with vocals by Ella Fitzgerald! This heavy jam—no bebop subtleties here—opens with a hell-for-leather raver in which Machito's men are momentarily inaudible, segues into a brief scat vocal with Afro-Cubans under, then continues riotously with solo after the-hell-with-refinement solo from musicians and Ella that graphically illustrate just what jazz lost when it went respectable. There is no conveying the quality of this visceral performance, a perfect example of what the recording studio never could catch.

The Royal Roost broadcasts featured various different jazzmen, and combined instrumental Latin-jazz and jazz-inflected Afro-Cuban vocals. A March 19 broadcast, shortly after Machito had appeared at the Apollo, included a version of Chano Pozo's "Blen, Blen, Blen," that mixed a classic Machito vocal with brass-heavy arrangements that are much more big-band-jazz oriented than Machito's more downhome offerings. A piece called "Vacilando," featuring tenorist Brew Moore, offered an even heavier big-band-bebop-cum-swing approach to the mambo. Moore aside, flashes of René Hernández's piano blend jazz and Cuban playing nicely. Moore (like pretty much all the jazzmen involved in the Cubop of the time) soloed in a booting style that wouldn't have varied at all over a straight jazz 4/4. (Incidentally, one difference in the ensemble writing for Machito's Latin jazz and more *típico* avatars is that the former involved more chordal modulation, presumably to give jazz soloists a familiar grounding.)

As well as Moore, broadcasts in late March and April featured bop trumpeter Howard McGhee. These recordings gave a clear picture of a much more varied

Latin-jazz hybrid than one gets from the relatively few studio recordings of Cubop, and one in which the Cuban elements were given full measure. "Howard's Blues" opens with a brisk percussion *rumbón* that made no concession whatsoever to the supposedly rhythm-challenged Anglo audience, and moves into a classic bop head arrangement and solos that blended bop fluency with a certain pre-bop warmth of tone and inflection. Moore was consistently fine in Cubop surroundings; McGhee played a purer bop that sparked against both Moore's mellowness and the surging drive of the Machito riffs, and when the two soloists began trading fours, heaven set in. The program's theme tune, "How High the Moon," was perhaps the most perfect balance of bop and Cubop, with a rhythm section subtler and more complex than the others (partly thanks to an overlay of traps) and an amazing display of the loose-tight ensemble work that is big-band at its best.

As striking as the club numbers involving the jazz soloists were a couple of pieces in which the Afro-Cubans sans jazzmen played vocal mambos. The horns in "El Rey del Mambo" showed a clear jazz influence, but one that—here and to an even greater extent in "Bop Champagne"—was absorbed into what was already unarguably a big-band mambo sound. This was Cuban music, New York version, which meant a music of surpassing richness in influences and roots, both Caribbean and North American, Afro and Euro, Anglo and Latino.

All this innovation made considerable waves in the Latin-dance scene. Musicians who had made their mark in the midtown rumba bands of the early 1940s, like Noro Morales, found themselves facing the challenge of major change, and met it as best they could. Morales himself was not a jazz-oriented player, nor was he particularly in tune with the new mambo sound. His forte was an older quintet style blending Cuban elements with American Tin Pan Alley material. But at times he rose effectively to the occasion. His 1949 big-band arrangement of "The Peanut Vendor" managed to be both busy and generic, as if he was trying too hard to be hep (though it had its moments—notably some bluesy voicings in the second part of the original theme, a fine vocal by Pellin Rodriguez, and Morales's own piano solo). Two originals he recorded at the same time worked much better: "110th St & 5th Avenue" (named for the site of the important Park Palace/Park Plaza dance hall) was a tight mambo with a fast, nervous beat, an arrangement piling up ensemble trumpets à la Pérez Prado, excellent piano, and a nice alto solo faintly reminiscent of the Ellington/Tizol standard "Caravan." Better yet was "Ponce," whose section writing was more original than most of Morales's work, contrasting fairly standard mambo sax riffs with less conventional brass passages.

Pupi Campo's band was one of the hottest big Latin groups of the late 1940s and early 1950s, with a sound influenced by Stan Kenton. With Campo here are singer Luis "Puntillita" Kant and bongo player Johnny "La Vaca" Rodriguez, Sr. *Photo by Popsie Randolph © 1989 Frank Driggs Collection*

Another old hand who met the future head-on was the excellent pianist
Anselmo Sacasas, who had come to the U.S. in 1940 with singer Miguelito
Valdez after a distinguished career in Cuba. His was a "midtown" group which
played La Conga, the Havana Madrid, and other *New Yorker*-certified nightspots.
An excellent compilation on the Tumbao label, *Sol Tropical*, shows the impact of
bebop-era, big-band swing in general and the Kenton sound in particular on
Sacasas. Tracks like the 1945 guajira "Sol Tropical" essentially expanded on the
slightly self-conscious "exotic" wing of Cuban conjunto sound with sweet dance-
band trumpets, and classic post-sexteto Cuban trumpet in the uptempo numbers.
But by 1949, Sacasas was recording such Kenton-influenced mambos as "Opus
13," which blended Rubén Gonzalez's classic Cuban vocal with very Kentonian
brass, and "B Flat Mambo" (along with "El Salon del Rey del Mambo," based on
the first suite of Grieg's "Peer Gynt Suite"!).

Vocalist Miguelito Valdéz, the original Mr. Babel, had managed to keep one
foot in the Latino and the other in the non-Latino camp throughout the 1940s. He
maintained this pattern in 1949, running yet another band that mixed some
Cubop in with its proto-mambo (Stan Getz played with him for a while that year,
honing his Latin-jazz chops). Another fine but almost totally forgotten band was
run by Pupi Campo. Campo maintained a Latino-about-town image, straw boater
and all. But his band, heavily influenced by Stan Kenton, was a match for much
better-known groups. Campo's bandsmen were a roster of both jazz-oriented
Latinos (including Tito Puente and two outstanding pianists, Joe Loco and Al
Escobar) and mambo-minded non-Latino sidemen—among them Frank Socolow,
whom Campo lured away from Artie Shaw, and Kenton arranger Johnny Mandel,
whose shadow over Latin jazz was a very long one. Campo, incidentally, had an
interesting twofold, take on the Kenton influence: directly, and via Pérez Prado.

All in all, 1949 was a gateway year for Latin jazz, and like most gateways it
sat squarely between very different landscapes: the rumba, still going strong both
uptown and midtown, and the mambo, which by 1949 had broken out of midtown
and been discovered by the young Jewish dancers of Brooklyn and the Bronx,
who were among Latin music's most important non-Latino fans. Meanwhile the
future arrived in "Spanish" Harlem when two of the most influential Cuban percussionists in U.S. musical history, Mongo Santamaria and Armando Peraza,
appeared together at the Teatro Hispano as the Black Cuban Diamonds. And
most important of all, though a long way from Broadway and pretty much unnoticed at the time, in March Victor recorded a batch of mambos in Cuba played by
a band with a new sound run by a fairly successful pianist and bandleader called
Damaso Pérez Prado.

❖ 5 ❖

Mambo Comes to Cubop City

The 1950s

In the early and mid-1950s, Latin New York was booming musically as never before. Charlie Palmieri once told me that at one point in the early 1950s a particular crossroads on 52nd Street had four clubs, one on each corner, each with a Latin-oriented group of one kind or another (one night, he claimed, he switched gigs with another pianist halfway through the evening, after a cigarette-break kvetching session under a lamppost).

The mambo would greatly boost the fortunes of Latin bands in general, who were already benefiting from Machito's success. By 1951, the mambo, which was infiltrating New York City and the hipper reaches of the upstate New York Catskill resort area by the late 1940s, was starting to go national. And despite the talent and success of the New York big three—Machito, Tito Puente, and Tito Rodriguez—the musician most responsible for the mambo's rise was without question Damaso Pérez Prado.

The story goes that bandleader Sonny Burke heard a Pérez Prado recording while on holiday in Mexico, and persuaded RCA Victor to release it for the mainstream U.S. market. Pérez Prado's first major impact on the U.S. came in 1950 with his "Mambo Jambo," whose original title was "Que Rico el Mambo." Then, in 1951, his band played a legendary gig in Los Angeles at which the dance floor was so crowded that nobody could move, let alone dance, and he was off and running.

Pérez Prado is irredeemably associated with two numbers, "Cherry Pink" and the instrumental version of "Patricia," both essentially novelty arrangements. But his early recordings were genuinely powerful mambos with a distinctive sound

In the 1950s, Tito Puente's band formed one point of the New York mambo triable. Puente himself is not only a fine timbales and vibraphone player (he seems to have introduced the vibes to mambo) but a talented arranger with a sound strongly influenced by swing. *Frank Driggs Collection*

achieved not only by his trademark grunt but by Kenton-influenced arrangements featuring screaming high-register trumpets against rolling bass trombones (Maynard Ferguson was Pérez Prado's high-note technician for some of his recordings). The features of Pérez Prado's band that most struck West Coast musicians were a bright octave sound, a simple but inventive use of the usual contrast between brass and reeds, and a rhythm section that provided kick without too much complexity. British critic Ernest Bornemann once wrote: "Damaso Pérez Prado is first and foremost a showman." That may have become so as time went on, but he was far too good at his best to be dismissed as the Xavier Cugat of the 1950s.

With the groundwork laid in New York during the late 1940s, Pérez Prado's national success, the extraordinary Big Apple troika of Machito, Tito Puente, and Tito Rodriguez, and a supporting cast of bands—some of which were pretty much the equal of their more famous counterparts—the mambo revived a big-band tradition that was suffering from changed economic realities. Its national peak came in 1954, when a show called "The Mambo-Rhumba Festival" with a cast that included the bands of Tito Puente, Pupi Campo, the Joe Loco Quintet, vocalist Miguelito Valdes, and the Phillips-Fort Dancers, played 56 cities across the U.S. A major booking agency, Mercury Artists, had a whole department launching mambo groups not just to the big cities but to towns like Vegas, Albuquerque, Chester, Penn., and Indiana Harbor, Ind. All six listings in the "Everybody Dance" section of a December 1954 *DownBeat*'s "best-recordings" list were mambos. And most extraordinary of all, Latin bands touring the hinterland were, for probably the first and last time, paid more than their Anglo counterparts. Equally remarkably, the mambo was not monopolizing the dance floors. According to a Nat Hentoff *DownBeat* piece on the mambo, the rumba was still holding its own and people were still learning the tango four decades after it first hit the U.S.[1]

Pérez Prado was not the only Latin musician to owe a stylistic debt to Kenton, though his was particularly obvious. Pupi Campo has been quoted as saying in 1950: "We all think he's the greatest: we're all trying to copy Kenton." And though that was an exaggeration, it was a significant one. However, the fusion of big-band jazz and Cuban music pioneered a decade earlier by Mario Bauzá was the essence of the mambo. All the mambo bands of the time drew from jazz, and

---

[1] The jazz world continued largely to ignore the tango, though Stan Kenton had recorded an interesting and unusual album, *Artistry in Tango*, in 1951. The piece's exaggerated tango rhythm came over as a slightly sinister parody; the album's dark, brooding chord changes and mega-brass passages seemed more appropriate to the mambo than the tango.

at times crossed over into Latin jazz territory, however marginally. And unlike the
rumba groups, all were big bands. By 1953, even the veteran Noro Morales was
running a band that included former Woody Herman trumpeter Bernie Glow and
even featured the great swing trumpeter Charlie Shavers on a couple of recordings.

But many older musicians like Morales were only tourists in Latin-jazz territory. The younger men—above all Machito, Tito Puente, and Tito Rodriguez—
made it their home turf with a steady flow of pieces that, while indisputably Latin
rather than Cubop, equally indisputably drew constantly and effectively from the
sister discipline.

Puente was particularly well-equipped to do so. As well as mean timbales, he
played fine vibraphone. In fact, it was Puente who first introduced vibes into the
Latin lexicon in the late 1940s, first for Anglo ballads and soon also for mambos.
And he was also a highly talented arranger, confident in both the Cuban- and
swing-oriented sides of his material. By 1951, Puente had expanded his conjunto

Throughout the 1950s, the Machito band continued to play jazz-
influenced big-band mambo, and many jazz musicians were charter
members of his and other mambo groups. Doc Cheatham, seen here
around 1956, was a featured soloist with Machito for several years.
Photo Phil Newsum

into a big band (by some accounts, for a gig at Grossingers' Catskill resort hotel), adding sax and trombone sections, as well as a torrid rhythm section including Puerto Rican timbales player Manny Oquendo, who was later to become a mainstay of the Cuban-roots movement in New York, and the under-recognized pianist Al Escobar.

Mambo riffs tended to be based on the clave-oriented montunos at the heart of Cuban *típico* dance music. Cuban music is both harmonically simpler and rhythmically more complex than jazz. New York mambo arrangers often used far more complex chordings than the Cuban *típico* groups, but they were still building complexity onto a harmonically simple structure. Puente consistently played both Latin versions of jazz material and swing-inflected mambos, and it's revealing to compare the two. When he tackled the Billy Strayhorn classic "Take the A Train," he gave the contrasting and counterbalancing brass and sax riffs common to swing and big-band mambo lusher voicings and greater harmonic complexity. His arrangement of "Swingin' the Mambo" was an excellent example of his take on the big-band mambo. A nice opening for claves, bass, and piano gave way to an exercise in mambo ensemble writing with the recurrent *cierres* (many of them here for piano and bass) that Puente used for both excitement and variation.

So far as Cubop was concerned, the 1950s arguably opened on January 9, when the Dizzy Gillespie big band recorded "Carambola" and three other cuts with tenorist John Coltrane, conga-player Carlos Duchesne, and Francisco "Chino" Pozo, who had appeared on Gillespie's first Cubop performances, on bongos. The following month, Stan Kenton took his new band into the studio before a national tour and recorded a number of Latin-jazz tracks, including "Mardi Gras" (subtitled "Playtime in Brazil"), which featured Laurindo Almeida. But the most important event of the Latin/New York/Cubop year took place on December 21, when producer Norman Granz recorded *Afro-Cuban Jazz Suite*, arranged by Chico O'Farrill (his biggest U.S. commission so far), and featuring the Machito band backing Flip Phillips, Harry Edison, Buddy Rich, and Machito pianist René Hernández.

Though this was not the first Afro-Cuban suite to be recorded, it set the tone for what was to become a feature of 1950s Cubop. Its first section, "Cancion," opens with a Kentonianly massive brass chord leading to a pretty solo trumpet theme from Edison, interspersed with more pile-driver chords over a lazy bolero-like rhythm. This segues into "Mambo," which in turn kicks into the classic interweaving riffs of grunting saxes and stabbing trumpets. Then Parker takes off, playing hard, fast, and lyrical, backed by smoking, hard-driving percussion. As always, he made no attempt to adapt his style to his surroundings, but he fit in fine because the entire Machito band provided his work with a solid clave frame.

Afro-Cuban Jazz Suite transformed O'Farrill from a comer to a major player in the field. Most immediately, it led to commissions from Kenton and Gillespie; O'Farrill's work for Kenton, "Cuban Episode," featuring Carlos Vidal on vocal and conga, was quickly recorded. Another commission for a Latin suite came from Granz, this one for O'Farrill's own band. This group was the result of O'Farrill's migration to Los Angeles, where he was playing for a while with a big band run by Tito Rivera—an experience O'Farrill, with his new knowledge of Cuban music, found frustrating because, he told Max Salazar, Rivera's men didn't understand clave.[2]

It also led to O'Farrill's getting a commission for another multi-section work with the confusingly similar name of *Afro-Cuban Suite*. It consisted of six movements that were also self-standing numbers: "JATAP Mambo," "Havana Special," "Cuban Blues," "Avocado," "Almendra," "Fiesta Time," and "Carioca." A fine mambo featuring vocalist Bobby Escoto, "Freezelandia," was recorded at the same session but doesn't seem to have been counted toward the suite. There's some dispute as to who was involved in the sessions, but in 1977 O'Farrill gave Max Salazar a list that included many Machito sidemen, Machito's rhythm section, and Jazz at the Philharmonic's Flip Phillips. The arrangements were fairly typical of the time, pitting brass against saxes with percussion breaks for contrast—the Latin-jazz end of the mambo, but lacking the variety of the vocal versions and the flair of fine jazz soloists, though "Havana Special" had a fine piano solo by René Hernández. But "Cuban Blues" was an attractive theme and arrangement, as is "Avocados," with its occasional echoes of Ellington ensemble techniques and its varying mini-movements. The other attractive number is Vincent Youmans' durable "Carioca," from the 1933 movie *Flying Down to Rio*.

Not all Cubop, even by major artists, worked. Norman Granz issued a depressing set, *Charlie Parker South of the Border*, whose titles included "My Little Suede Shoes," "Un Poquito de Tu Amor," and the Brazilian "Tico Tico" (original Brazilian title "Tico Tico No Fubá"). Despite the presence of percussionists José Mangual and Luis Miranda, the performances were lame at best, given the caliber of the musicians and in comparison with much of what else was going on at the time. Parker's solos showed all his usual "damn the torpedoes" flair and indifference to vagaries of rhythm section, but his statements of

---

[2] Rivera's group, which is remarkably obscure, did record one powerful piece, "Gin & Seven."

the theme often sounded embarrassed and the overall effect was mildly depressing.[3]

Such lapses notwithstanding, Cubop was mostly exciting, varied, and constantly changing. It even gained variety from the fact that, specifically Cubop-oriented groups aside, bebop musicians were beginning to include at least one Latinish number on gigs and albums. Even pianist Bud Powell, perhaps the least Cubop-minded of the seminal bebop musicians, composed a well-known Latin-inflected number, "Un Poco Loco," of which he recorded several takes in 1951, with Curly Russell on bass and Max Roach on drums.[4]

Nor, by now, was Cubop confined to New York. The West Coast had several things needed for a healthy Cubop scene of its own, including a flourishing and a large and growing Latino population that (though it had a lively Tex-Mex musical life of its own) was discovering the newer sounds from Cuba. It also had a mambo role model in Pérez Prado, whose main U.S. turf was California. While the big-band mambo style was inherently jazz-influenced, Pérez Prado's reciprocated admiration for Stan Kenton gave him a particular West Coast flavor.

Kenton was by no means the only game out West. Various of his sidemen had coalesced as Howard Rumsey's Lighthouse All-Stars, a loose conspiracy of performers recruited by former Kenton bassist Rumsey to play at a Los Angeles jazz joint called the Lighthouse. The All-Stars developed an individual stance toward Latin-jazz early on. Trumpeter Shorty Rogers's "Viva Zapata," a regular part of the band's repertoire, was twice recorded by various of the All-Stars' avatars. "Viva Zapata No.1," a studio recording, in some ways set the pattern for the Lighthouse All-Stars' take on Cubop: a fast percussion/drums passage led into a clave-pattern for the horns, and then into mambo riffs. Machito (and Kenton) veteran Carlos Vidal's conga played a prominent part in a rhythm section with a strong sense of clave. Over this Latin base, the various horn and piano solos (and to a large extent drummer Shelly Manne's tomtom-heavy solo also) were straight, hot jazz.

---

[3] A later Charlie-Parker-meets-the-profit-motive album, called *Fiesta*, was even worse. This far-from-festive offering is a mixed bag of old Latin favorites—many of them perfectly fine material in the right context—from the elderly classics "La Paloma" and "Estrellita" via "La Cucaracha" and the bolero-ish "Begin the Beguine," to the 1930s Cuban hit "Mama Inez." Once again a group of outstanding bop musicians produced an LP redolent mostly of intense lack of involvement.

[4] Thomas Owens remarks that his was "but one of many Latin-style pieces affording extended sections for improvisation on the Mixolydian or other scales." That is, Powell adopted the harmonic simplicity of Cuban music which so many jazz critics found wanting. McCoy Tyner and Miles Davis were to do the same thing later and gain avant-garde brownie points for their experiments, while the Cuban originals were being regarded as simplistic, primitive, or cute.

A club performance of the same piece, called simply "Viva Zapata" and recorded live at the Lighthouse sometime in 1953, stands as a symbol of how much juice is missing from studio recordings. The whole performance is powerful jazz underlain by grooves of clave pattern with all the drive of Afro-Cuban/salsa. The opening percussion passage is taken a little faster than the studio version and, urged on by the audience and an uncredited cowbell player, Vidal and Manne create a cross-cultural rumbón of enormous urgency. The horn solos, though broadly similar to the earlier recording, are a lot harder, and Rogers's solo in particular flies over a rhythm section that includes dominant claves. Most interesting of all is a piano solo by Frank Patchen that (unlike his work on the first version) interweaves jazz patterns and rhythms with constant references to Latin piano montunos.

A more fully Latin tack was taken by Hampton Hawes, who played with the group at the Lighthouse the same year. Hawes's comping in places was based on specifically Cuban montunos, while elsewhere he built on them by blocking jazz chords in clave rhythm. In the 1956 "Mambo Las Vegas," Sonny Clark also maintained a fast mambo *guajeo* under the ensemble and in solo moved progressively from bop runs over a very sparse left hand part into a montuno pattern. By contrast, several 1953 recordings featured Claude Williamson, who often alternated a very full piano style—almost like stride with bop overtones (!)—with bop single-note runs and constant but oblique references to Cuban keyboard.

The remarkable range of approaches to the piano in the Lighthouse All-Stars Latin-jazz numbers underline the fact that the piano tends to have a defining role in the ensemble. Pianists playing straight jazz tend to tilt the whole band in the direction of jazz-with-Latin-trimmings; clave-based pianists favor the Latin aspects; and pianists working with both traditions have developed a real hybrid and sometimes full fusions that are both rich and self-standing.

The lively West Coast Cubop scene largely obscured the first of two extraordinary recordings of what would become Latin-jazz's extremely important Brazilian wing. Originally released in 1953 as *The Laurindo Almeida Quartet*, but reissued as *Brazilliance*, this album featured a quartet of Almeida, reed player Bud Shank, bassist Harry Babasin, and drummer Roy Harte that grew from a 1952 duet (subsequently trio) gig at a Sunset Strip club involving Almeida and Babasin. Shank and Almeida were an odd pairing in that Almeida was at least as much a classical as a samba musician, and despite his stint with Stan Kenton was not particularly jazz-minded. Nor was Bud Shank's usual style, which author Ted Gioia has called hard-nosed, entirely suited either to Almeida or to Brazilian music as a whole.

Conventional wisdom has it that *Brazilliance* was based on the baiao, a regional Afro-Brazilian rhythm that had very recently been introduced to the

Brazilian pop scene. In reality, the album was quite rhythmically varied. The only overt baiao in fact was the final track, "Blue Baiao," a typical composition by the great popularizer of the style, accordionist/singer Luiz Gonzaga. This was the disc's finest hour. The first section, based on the baiao rhythm itself, suggests a magnificent jazz road not taken, and the entire cut was a highly distinctive blend of jazz, Brazilian idioms, and jazz-elegant playing—quite how distinctive it takes imagination to hear, after four decades of Brazilian/jazz interaction. Two cuts had a prophetic ring. "Atabaque" moved between a somewhat generic samba and jazz 4/4 under gentle sax/guitar work—an interesting prefiguring of jazz-bossa.[5] A version of "Stairway to the Stars" also featured the sort of rich guitar chording that was to be associated with the bossa nova. And so it went, with "Baa-Too-Kee" (a phoneticization of "Batuque"), which Almeida had originally written for Kenton, a preponderance of compositions by well-known Brazilian composers such as Ary Barroso, and a couple of lesser-known U.S. numbers, in all of which Almeida and Shank swung toe to toe.

In September 1952, Kenton recorded one of my favorite Cubop pieces, "23°N–82°W" (the map reference for Havana). This opens with fat, clave-based, bullfrog-bop trombone riffs reproducing a classic piano *guajeo* and then continues with rich trombone from Frank Rosolino and a soaring Lee Konitz solo.

One of the great moments of 1953 came when producer Norman Granz (who liked putting together unlikely seeming musical matches) paired Dizzy Gillespie with tenorist Stan Getz. This first session, in December, included two-part version of a Cuban classic, "Siboney" (as far as I know, the first time Getz had recorded anything even remotely Latin), over a familiar mix of montuno and straight 4/4 rhythms. During the first part, Ray Brown gives a lesson in adapting bass montunos to bop mood, and Gillespie's muted trumpet statement of the melody is a masterly fusion of Latin and bop phrasing. Part Two opens with Max Roach imitating a cencerro rhythm on cymbal before Brown again lays down a bass montuno. Getz solos with a warm delicacy that foreshadows his jazz-samba persona, and Gillespie shows a total absorption of Latin rhythmic procedures just five years after the inchoate experiments of his Chano Pozo era.

By now, all sorts of jazz musicians were trying at least one Cubop number when they went into the studio. Most simply added a conga-player, who too often ended up as a fifth wheel when deprived of the call-and-response logic of clave. Others were more ingenious. Two cuts of Sonny Stitt's 1952 album *Kaleidoscope* were jazz-mambos with a three-trumpet front line and a timbales player rather

---

[5] According to one theory, it was copies of this album that inspired early Brazilian bossa nova. Whether or not this is true, the West Coast sound played a role. João Gilberto once told me that the greatest influence on bossa nova was baritone saxist Gerry Mulligan.

than the usual congas or bongos, which gave an unusual crispness to the rhythm section and blended well with the drummer. Nor did it hurt that the lead trumpeter was Joe Newman, who already had recorded with Machito. Like Parker (from whose over-arching influence he was trying to break away at the time), Stitt himself made no attempt to Latinize his soloing.

The enormous popularity of Cubop even affected Duke Ellington, who usually operated in his own musical cosmos. A 1953 recording of "Caravan" and "Bakiff" with Charles Mingus on bass made use of more genuine Latin elements than the earlier version. Just before the reprise of the theme of "Caravan," Ellington himself plays an interesting blend of tango and montuno bass, while the rhythm takes on something of a jazz-habanera feel, abetted by inexpert claves. "Bakiff" also uses a tango/habanera rhythm with free-form claves and a passage of equally imprecise castanets. Mingus also got some more authentic Latin experience the same year when he played a Birdland gig with a group that included Charlie Parker and Candido Camero on "Moose the Mooche" and "Cheryl." In 1954 he took part in a session with a quartet run by an organist called Vin Strong, which recorded two sides for Savoy Records, "Swinging the Mambo" and the unreleased "New Orleans Mambo."

In 1954, Woody Herman was also moved by the prevailing mania to include several mambos in his book, among them a mambo version of his theme "Woodchopper's Ball" called "Woodchopper's Mambo" (of which *DownBeat* thought highly); "Mambo the Most," a basic fast mambo with an intriguing intro in which the bassist played an odd montuno-like pattern on a straight 4/4 rhythm, and an effective piano montuno from Nat Pierce; and "Mambo the (Ut)most," which was most notable for offbeat clarinet from Herman, which floats almost dreamily over the mambo riffing.

A feature of the early 1950s was the rise, on both sides of the jazz/Latin divide, of the Latin-jazz piano and piano-and-vibraphone quartet or quintet. It was a distinctive format, flexible, cheap to run, and therefore long-lived. New though it was, the Latin-jazz quintet had deep roots. Not only did piano-and-rhythm trios and quartets go back a long way in jazz and blues (as did their kissing cousins, the piano-and-rhythm-group with one wind instrument), but on the Latin side these groups dated from at least the mid-1930s, when (mostly New York-based) string *cuartetos* added to their hipness quotient by bringing in a piano.[6]

---

[6] Machito recorded some vocals with one of the best-known of the early New York-based piano groups, the Marcano Quartet, as a new arrival in the late 1930s.

The early Latin piano quintet had moved into the midtown New York rumba scene and made a star of Noro Morales. But Morales was not jazz-minded, though he could do a fair imitation. The most important individual musician in turning this Latin subset into a Latin-jazz idiom was Joe Loco, whom we have already met helping to propel Machito's band toward Cubop in the mid-1940s (see Chapter 4). By 1951, Loco was fronting a piano group far more jazz-oriented than its predecessors.

Loco's repertoire fell into two distinct categories: his own mambos; and Latinizations of various Anglo standards or semi-standards. Both types mixed jazz and Afro-Cuban elements liberally. In "Band Stand Mambo," for example, Loco constructed classic Cuban-cum-jazz chordings of considerable rhythmic complexity, set off by occasional single-note runs. He began "Colony Mambo" with largely jazz-based chordings, then worked in more and more Cuban patterns before cutting back to locked-hands jazz playing toward the end. And his "Monticello Mambo" was rich in restrained, strongly Cuban piano with a lot of subtlety and interesting chord progressions.

Some of Loco's versions of "American" material were little short of wonderful. His version of the 1930s Andrews Sisters hit, "Bei Mir Bist Du Schoen," with a fast, punchy piano exposition and a terrific Cubano-klezmer rhythmic approach, to me outdid Cal Tjader's later reworking of the piece. His take on "Why Don't You Do Right?," which had made the young Peggy Lee a star, opens with a montuno reminiscent of a Jimmy Yancey bass line. Then he begins breaking the melody up Cuban-style, using the same Yancey bass as a counterweight, in a display that moves progressively into Cuban mode while always coming back to the melody. Even his version of the well-worn "How High the Moon" is quite original, with its highly decorated melodic right hand and busy left, capped by complex chorded variations that are neither standard jazz piano nor really Cuban.

Various claims on who can take the title of the originator of the vibraphone in mambo and Latin jazz have been made. The man with the best claim appears to have been Tito Puente, who began using it for "American" ballads on Catskill gigs, perhaps as early as the very late 1940s, and not much later in Latin-jazz contexts. By the early 1950s he was recording numbers like "Autumn Leaves" and "Tea For Two" with a vibraphone quartet.

On the jazz side of the Latin-jazz equation, the nursery group was surely George Shearing's popular piano/vibraphone quintet. Shearing dated his interest in Latin mixes to a 1949 Club Clique date opposite Machito, but he did not form his first Latin-oriented group until 1953, when he enlisted the vibraphonist Cal

During the mid-50s mambo fever, Erroll Garner recorded an entire album devoted to an idiom he clearly didn't understand very well. As so often with talented musicians, the result was perhaps more interesting than something more "authentic." *Columbia Records*

Tjader and a percussion dream team of timbales player Willie Bobo, bongo player Armando Peraza, and congacero Mongo Santamaria. Even then he played only a minority of Latin-jazz numbers (his first all-Latin recording was in 1957, when most of his best-known sidemen were gone). Nevertheless, it was Shearing who first popularized the sound, even if he never exploited his own creation.

Shearing's group was not the only piano-led, Latin-jazz style group at the time. New York's Billy Taylor was recording Latin material by 1953. In May, Taylor recorded four numbers, "I Love to Mambo," "Candido Mambo," "Early Morning Mambo," and "Mambo Azul"—all of them his own compositions— that paired his then-trio with Machito's rhythm section (more or less: Taylor's regular drummer switched to congas). As usual in such circumstances, the percussionists provided enough Cuban bottom that there was at least an equal balance between jazz piano and Latin rhythm. When (as in "Candido Mambo") Taylor threw in momentary references to classic montunos in his left hand under a barrage of single-note runs, and when he moved from a contrapuntal section into straight *guajeos* followed by some Latin-type chording, a new form of fusion was coalescing.

The twin popularity of the mambo and the piano quintet tempted a number of pianists with fewer Latin chops than Taylor to take a shot at a mambo (or sub-mambo) repertoire. One of these was Erroll Garner. To judge from his 1954 album *Mambo meets Garner*, a quartet recording that included Candido Camero on congas, Garner did not know clave from kielbasa, and his seeming ill-ease with the rhythms produced some very clunky moments. Candido also had some problems with the clave-less setting. But when his rhythm part and Garner's left hand began a dialogue, as they did in "Old Black Magic," Garner's very inexperience with the genre produced some intriguing moments.

Garner never really moved close to Latin authenticity, but he was a lot more plausible by the mid-1950s, when he recorded "Mambo 207" on his 1956 trio recording, *The Most Happy Piano*, even without a conga player. "Mambo 207" was fairly generic, but it worked on its own level, with Garner in form and bass and drums providing a kind of Cubano-Brazilian background that pretended to nothing more than a different way to back a jazz performance.

The involvement of most 1950s jazz musicians—even Shearing—in Latin jazz was a small part of their total activity. In fact, one could argue that Shearing's greatest contribution to the music was hiring Tjader. When Tjader quit Shearing's group after only a year, he formed the first American group on the jazz side to play almost exclusively Latin jazz.[7] Why Tjader split from Shearing so quickly he never specified. But he told John Tynan in a 1957 interview in *DownBeat* that "one of the chief compensations of being with Shearing was that back East I got to hear a lot of Machito, Tito Puente and Noro Morales. Those bands had a tremendous effect on me. Immediately I wanted to reorganize a small combo along the same lines, only with more jazz feeling incorporated in the Latin format." It was a desire for which we can all be grateful.

Tjader's Modern Mambo Quintet, consisting of vibes, piano, bass, timbales doubling with bongos, and conga, went straight to a six-month stint at the Macumba Club. His first release, *Mambo With Tjader*, consisted almost entirely of Latinized American standards, of which the wittiest was a version of "Sonny Boy," a lugubrious ballad that bounces from a parodied sentimental vocal-and-vibes opening into a classic Spanish-language, charanga-style duet vocal—funny and effective. In general, Tjader's fluent vibraphone playing over a solid rhythm

---

[7] The first band to play almost exclusively Cubop was British. Tenor saxist Kenny Graham formed his Afro-Cubists (which also played African- and Jamaican-inspired music) in 1950.

section generates considerable drive, enhanced by touches like a brief bop-style vibes break answered by a typical percussion *cierre*. But the effective mix of Latin and jazz elements was not all that makes even this early Tjader album so effective. There is also musical imagination in the way the ballad "Tenderly" jumps into a fast mambo-type section, or the two-voice vocal arrangement, part charanga-style, part-close-harmony, in "Chloe." Interestingly, Carlos Duran's piano was mostly more jazz- than Latin-oriented, though he shows flashes of Cuban style behind Tjader in "I'll Remember April."

Tjader's second 1954 issue, *Tjader Plays Mambo*, includes some cuts with the trumpet section from Woody Herman's Third Herd, a kind of jazz-conjunto that works particularly well in "Mambo Macumba," a fast, timbales-driven number whose punchy ensemble trumpet work is clearly conjunto-derived. Equally effective is a "Fascinating Rhythm," in which—after a short percussion passage—the trumpets pile in two-against-two with different voicings from even the most jazz-influenced conjuntos of the time, though they picked up later with a much more mambo-ish sound.

Tjader, in fact, was never bound to the quintet lineup. Though it appeared in 1955, his *Los Ritmos Calientes* contained cuts recorded even before he had quit the Shearing group. These included flutist Jerome Richardson, a San Francisco musician with a resume that included stints with Lionel Hampton and Earl Hines as well as Charles Mingus and Oscar Peterson. Aside from the fact that it predicted the imminent flute boom in Latin jazz and *típico* music, the most striking thing about the whole LP was its freedom and flexibility. It took a more creative approach to the percussion, and the whole thing was looser, than either of the *Mambo* releases. One of the later sessions eventually included on *Los Ritmos Calientes* (recorded in November 1955) was particularly interesting. The pianist on this session was again Carlos Duran, along with McKibbon, Peraza, Tjader, and (on some cuts) flutist Richardson. Once more, the feeling was similar to the later '50s, flute-led recordings, notably some of Herbie Mann's earlier efforts, with percussion contrasting effectively with light and dancing flute.

While Tjader was establishing a conspicuously warm and mellow West Coast Latin-jazz style, the Lighthouse All Stars were still playing a hotter version. A concert at the Irvine Bowl in June 1955 gave a fine sense of the fire and looseness that Latin-jazz could develop free of recording-studio pressures.[8] "Mexican Passport" is a particularly imaginative piece, with a montuno opening that leads into a contrastingly pretty, slightly satiric-seeming passage in which Bud Shank

---

[8] The session was recorded, and has been reissued on the *Mexican Passport* CD.

on flute duets with Bob Cooper on oboe (!) while the piano provides what sounds almost like a parody of earlier rumba-is-fun idioms. The band then kicks into bop playing while Shank returns with pure jazz flute against Cooper's sometimes lyrical, sometimes sour oboe obbligato. At a Rosolino trombone break, Shank and Cooper switch to alto and tenor, the bass kicks into straight 4/4, and there is a general mood-swing.

On the East Coast, meanwhile, Gillespie returned to a large canvas in a major multi-movement Latin-jazz composition, *Manteca Suite*, with arrangements by Chico O'Farrill and a phenomenal band that included Quincy Jones and Ernie Royal in the trumpet section, trombonist J. J. Johnson, and tenorists Hank Mobley and Lucky Thompson on the jazz side, and a percussion section with both Candido Camero and Mongo Santamaria on congas. The suite opens with "Manteca Theme," a tight and fierily brass-laden piece in which Gillespie flies lyrically over the basic theme before handing over to Hank Mobley's booting tenor. The well-named "Contraste" has all the richness and delicacy of Gillespie's solo ballad style, along with creamy sax work that makes a rhapsodic theme out of the Manteca bridge. "Contraste" segues straight into the 6/8 "Jungla," which kicks the "Manteca" theme around in a marvellous shouting variant from Gillespie, waist-deep in *inspiraciones*, before a restrained yet passionate trumpet solo over first a percussion *rumbón* and then occasional supporting chords. A straight-4/4 "Rhumba Final" joyously tosses the theme back and forth like a basketball until heavy riffs sparked by drummer Buddy Rich suddenly lead to a fast *rumbón*. Finally, the frenetic brass typical of big-band Cubop brings Gillespie back in a lyrical mood over occasional stop-chords, in an ending that harks back to "Jungla."

Manteca Suite was a major work, but Gillespie's Latin jazz recordings also included many smaller-scale but equally effective works in a number of formats. Only a week after the recording of *Manteca Suite*, in fact, he took a very different combo into the studio and recorded several cuts for an album called *Afro*. This was small-group music and a rarity for Gillespie in that it involved him with an all-Latino band consisting of Gilberto Valdez on flute, Machito pianist and arranger René Hernández, and several musicians who had also played on *Manteca Suite*: bassist Roberto Rodriguez and percussionists Mangual, Candido, Ralf Miranda, and Ubaldo Nieto.

Afro, a collector's item these days, was superb throughout, but two particularly interesting tracks were the Latin-jazz standards "Caravan" and "A Night in Tunisia." The band takes "Caravan" unusually fast, with a heavy rhythmic treatment notable for deep conga playing from Candido, while Gillespie plays havoc with the famous theme in a muted and very fast workout that strips it of all its usual pseudo-exoticism. Hernández contributes a solo fine even by his standards, mixing old-Cuban and jazz chording, and the rhythm section does its bit to turn the piece into something truly Latin with a long and devastating percussion *rumbón* section.

"A Night in Tunisia" is almost equally iconoclastic. Flutist Valdez takes a very free approach to the opening montuno, and Gillespie sounds freer than on most of his interpretations of the piece, as if the presence of so many Latinos had given him license to cut loose. The underlying rhythm is also atypical of the piece. After the usual tango opening, bassist Rodriguez plays an interesting mix of montuno and straight 4/4, often using an on-beat three-note montuno overlaying the 4/4 pulse.

By the mid-1950s, the addition of a conga to groups otherwise playing straight jazz was becoming commonplace, at least on recordings. One of the finest of all such recordings was Kenny Dorham's *Afro-Cuban*, with trombonist J. J. Johnson, Hank Mobley, and Cecil Payne on saxes, Horace Silver playing piano, and Oscar Pettiford on bass, along with drummer Art Blakey and Carlos "Patato" Valdes on congas. A year earlier, J. J. Johnson had made a recording that included a Latinized version of "Old Devil Moon" among other mid-tempo ballads, backed by Wynton Kelly on piano, Kenny Clarke on drums, Charles Mingus on bass, and Sabu Martínez on congas.

Another of the best—though not best-known—bop trombonists was featured on *Benny Green Blows His Horn* along with Charlie Rouse (who later became more deeply involved with Brazilian music) on tenor sax, Cliff Smalls on piano, Paul Chambers (long associated with John Coltrane) on bass, and drummer Osie Johnson; four out of nine tracks featured Candido Camero on congas. Like Sabu, Valdes, and Barretto, Candido had by now a good instinct for avoiding the pitter-patter that the lack of clave imposes on lesser musicians. As was usually the case, it was the slower numbers that allowed the conga player elbow-room: the ballads "Laura" and "Body and Soul" gave him more scope, moving as they did between a conga-less standard ballad pace and uptempo conga-backed passages during which Smalls played a lilting montuno. But this recording's most interesting track was the almost prophetic "Say Jack." Basically a riffer with vaguely Louis Jordanish group vocals and jump-blues touches backed by Candido's conga, it foreshadowed the later three-way latin/jazz/R&B funk fusion in which Candido's fellow conga player Mongo Santamaria would be so influential.

The touch-of-percussion approach sat particularly well with piano ensembles like Red Garland's recording groups of the late 1950s. Garland's long experience with the beboppers and liking for good old-fashioned swing served him well in April 1958, when he made the LP *Manteca* with bassist Paul Chambers, drummer Arthur Taylor, and the young Ray Barretto (the conga-player's first recording according to Barretto himself). Though other conga-players had learned to work effectively in jazz, Barretto's musical background was uniquely suited to it. A New Yorker of Puerto Rican descent, he grew up, by his own account, listening to his mother's Machito recordings by day and jazz on the radio by night. His musical experience did not begin in the Latin community, but with African-American musicians he met while serving in the army. Once back in New York, he continued his contacts with the African-American jazz scene, jamming with the likes of Roy Haynes, Max Roach, Sonny Stitt, and Charlie Parker. At the same time he acquired Latin experience working for Jose Curbelo's big band, Tito Puente, and the vibraphonist Pete Terrace. Thus rather than being locked into the strong clave-based Cuban tradition, with rules, fixed rhythmic patterns, and weight of the past, he was free to adapt elements of Cuban-style conga to an experience that was at the time entirely jazz-based.

Manteca was a classic example of the use of a conga to enhance what was essentially straight jazz. Except in the opening choruses of the title track, neither Garland nor his regular rhythm section showed any disposition to Latin elements in his playing. Barretto mostly follows the group's lead, providing a low-key part that often closely resembled a line that a trap drummer might have played, with only the distinctive sound of skin-on-skin adding a Latin feel. The same was broadly true of two follow-up sessions, *Rediscovered Masters, Vol.1*, and *Rojo*. Along with Barretto's presence, *Rediscovered Masters* contains bows to Latinity in "Blues in Mambo" and the old standard "Estrellita," but "Blues in Mambo" hardly even pretended to have links with the real thing, and "Estrellita" is treated as a straight ballad. The mix is much the same as in *Manteca*: essentially mainstream jazz with an extra rhythmic tang provided by Barretto.

For the most part, *Rojo* followed the same pattern as the earlier recordings, but the title cut was a very different kettle of fish. The drummer here was Charlie Persip, and he opens with clave-influenced work into which Barretto could interweave far more effectively than on the earlier recordings. Bassist George Joyner, too, starts off with a clearly montuno-inspired pattern, and while both drummer and bassist move on to patterns that are much less Latin, they provide a mini-demonstration of new rhythm sections, breaking away from straight 4/4 approaches. "Rojo" is altogether a more original piece than what came before it, and its Latin elements—overt and transmuted—are a crucial part of that originality.

As was the case in previous decades meanwhile, the critic-certified jazz immortals were not always the ones contributing to jazz/Latin crossover. The 1960s and 1970s were to be the decades of Latin-jazz-funk, to which musicians like Mongo Santamaria, George Duke, Deodato, and Herbie Hancock were all in different ways to contribute mightily. But there were forerunners, almost totally ignored in print but significant in their day. Just as Willard Griffith had played tangos and rumbas for black dancers in 1930s Harlem, so as also a series of largely African-American bands in the 1950s played a mix of Latin, jazz, and black popular music for Harlem dancers. They were important musicians in their community, but their history and personal tastes also shed light on the tastes of a substantial public of African-American Latin-music fans.

The big mambo bands played the Apollo regularly. That helped create a market for Latin dance music in Harlem clubs like Small's Paradise and the Celebrity Club.[9] It was filled by a number of bands, but the three most imprtant were a 12-piece band run by Hugo Dickens; the Joe Panama Sextet;[10] and the group that Henry Lee "Pucho" Brown formed out of the Joe Panama Sextet's ashes in 1959, which was originally called Pucho and the Cha Cha Boys. The only one of these bands to record was Pucho's and that was in the 1960s. Dickens himself was an r&b-oriented tenor saxist. His first group, which played stock arrangements, was set on a Laitn course by an African-American timbales player, Peter Sims (known professionally as Pete La Roca), soon to be joined by bongo player Ernest Philip "Phil" Newsum. By the mid '50s, the Dickens band was a sextet playing more Latin-jazz material. It was also notable for the presence of trombonist Barry Rogers, who was later to be so influential on Eddie Palmieri's seminal band of the 1960s. At this point, according to Phil Newsum, the band was an improvising ensemble with a full Latin rhythm section but a liking for hard-bop à la Art Blakey. This would place the sound squarely between the hard-bop-plus-conga ensembles and the more integrated Latin-jazz sound of a Cal Tjader. In the social clubs of Harlem, numbers like Dickens' "Old Man River Mambo" and "Nica's Dream" were solid hits. The band was, incidentally, always multi-ethnic, with white players like Rogers and trumpeter Marty Sheller, and important jazz names like Ted Curson and Chick Corea as well as Latinos such as Willie Bobo and Patato Valdés.

Joe Panama was a pianist whose major inspiration was clearly Joe Loco. His groups differed from Dickens' not in the places they played but in that he had a

---

[9] Though according to Henry Lee "Pucho" Brown, patrons in these clubs danced anything the bands cared to play, giving the musicians rather more freedom than their white equivalents.

[10] Joe Panama, real name David Preudhomme, was indeed part-Panamanian.

The most thoroughly ignored of all Latin-jazz phenomena were the mostly African-American bands that played a mix of mambo, bebop, funk, and Latin jazz for black dancers. The dean of them all was Hugo Dickens, seen here in the mid-1950s. Among the musicians present at this dance was trombonist Barry Rogers, a rare WASP on the Latin scene and the later the chief architect of the Eddie Palmieri two-trombone sound. *Photo Phil Newsum*

fairly settled preference for the vibraphone/piano front lines that Cal Tjader was starting to popularize on the West Coast.

There was considerable crossover between these Harlem bands and various Latino groups. Joe Panama's first band became the nucleus of Joe Cuba's successful group, and several members of Mongo Santamaria's first Latin-soul-jazz outfit came from Pucho's band. But there were also some subtle differences between the Harlem and East Harlem scenes. One was the width of taste of African-American dancers. As Pucho put it, "You had to be able to play Latin and jazz and funk. And there weren't too many musicians who could do that."

Pucho himself was converted to mambo around 1950 when he attended a junior-high school with a large Latino as well as African-American student body. One day a couple of his classmates were singing a version of Damiron and Chapuseaux's "Anabacoa" and drumming on their desks. This was Pucho's epiphany. "Anabacoa" is a fine recording, but it was not one of the great mambo hits of the time. One of the factors that made for subtle differences in the Harlem and East Harlem scenes was the recordings that were popular among the respective audiences. According to David Carp, the numbers that recur constantly in the reminiscences of mambo-minded African-Americans are Tito Puente's "Mambo Birdland," Joe Loco's "Stomping at the Savoy," and an obscure recording called "Brooklyn Mambo" by one Elmo Garcia. This last seems to be one of those quirks of taste, because Latinos tended not to think highly of it. But the others suggest an important truth about the coalescing of future fusions: while the Cuboppers were mostly still adding Latin percussion trimmings to bebop, the dancers of Harlem wanted something with a more solid Latin jolt. The Latinos with jazz chops could provide it, and a generation of Anglo musicians, both black and white, was immersed in the real thing, clave and all.

On the Latin side of the highly permeable fence, meanwhile, the mambo had been joined by a new dance rage, the chachachá. Though its origins lay in the flute-and-fiddle charangas, in the U.S. the chachachá essentially provided the big bands with a rhythmic and stylistic contrast to the mambo. Meanwhile, Tito Puente, Tito Rodriguez, Machito, and Pérez Prado were all riding high. It was in the 1955/1956 cusp, in fact, that Puente recorded what Puente buffs generally consider one of his two finest albums *Cuban Carnival*.[11] Two cuts on *Cuban Carnival,* "Yambeque" and "Cuban Fantasy," moved beyond big-band rumba into Latin-jazz territory, with tenor solos by Marty Holmes and, in the case of "Cuban Fantasy," Puente on vibraphone rather than timbales. By now, jazz and mambo were clearly overlapping styles with a large common pool of ideas.

Yet despite the mambo's strong swing element, particularly in the brass and sax writing, the mambo kept its identity because it was still rooted in the whole Cuban musical language of melodies, phrasings, and rhythmic procedures. Above all, it remained based in clave and therefore beholden to an offbeat, two-measure pattern that lurked within every aspect of even the most swing-oriented arrangements. The ensemble writing, in fact, often consisted of basic guajeos gussied up with augmented chords. Compared with late swing and above all post-bop big-band arrangement, the basic mambo construction remained rhythmically based and harmonically spare. Puente and the various arrangers working for Rodriguez and Machito might amplify mambo with swing, but they did not dilute it. They even avoided bridges of the complex harmonic sort standard in jazz and Anglo popular song, getting a similar effect through complex ensemble *cierres*: two- or four-bar breaks that were more complex and more varied than their jazz equivalents. A real aficionado could often identify an arranger simply

---

[11] Incidentally, it included the first version of the "Pa' Los Rumberos" that was to help make a star of Carlos Santana.

by his style in *cierres*: few or many; subtle or blow-you-down; solo (very rare) or ensemble.

The ways in which the mambo arrangers used their twin tradition were almost endlessly inventive and varied. Puente's "Cuban Nightmare" of November 1955 opens with a brass intro that could have been played by pretty much any swing band, but once paired with the rolling mambo saxes the (still swing-related) trumpet riffs take on a different feel, and by the second chorus Puente is squarely in mambo-land, where he remains even behind the jazz sax solos. "Que Sera Mi China," another chachachá recorded at the same session, has a more Cuban sound, partly because the singing is in the classic charanga duet vein and the instrumental work is paced by a charanga-style flute (very Cuban despite being played by the non-Latino Jerry Sanfino). The section work provides a perfect framework, despite owing a great deal to swing and very little to charanga fiddle *guajeos*.

Despite the decline in the swing-based big bands, Stan Kenton now recorded one of the last major multi-section Latin jazz suites for 20 years. *Cuban Fire,* written by Johnny Richards, was a 26-plus-minute piece with six movements, each based on a different rhythm or style: "Fuego cubano," a bolero; "El Congo Valiente," an abierta out of the street rumba tradition; "Recuerdos," a guajira; "Quien Sabe?," a guaracha; "La Guera Baila," an afro; and "La Suerte de los Tontos," a ñañigo.

Richards had a slight background in the music from which he was drawing. As he told Bill Coss, "people like Willie Rodriguez [the percussionist] . . . and his friends took me to dances, weddings, festivals, and quite literally introduced me to every aspect of the Latin American musical life available in New York. I spent those several weeks not writing a note of music, just listening and asking questions." It worked. Despite some pompous moments, Richards's combination of standard big-band writing with techniques brought in from conservatory music has a cohesion and musical logic that holds together what might have been overly pretentious and artificial.

Cuban Fire was not quite the last of the 1950s latin-jazz suites. In June 1958, Shorty Rogers recorded a "Wayacananga Suite" with lead vocals by Modesto Duran, as part of an LP called *Afro-Cuban Influence.* "Wayacananga Suite" has fine percussion and authentic-sounding, roots Afro-Cuban singing, and an arrangement with interesting moments. But overall, four decades later it sounds more dated, and more Hollywood-oriented, than the more modest cuts on the same LP: a punchy "Manteca" with wonderfully fat trombones and an effective tomtom part played by Shelly Manne; a flute- and oboe-driven version of

Ellington's little known "Moon Over Cuba" (Bud Shank and Bob Cooper reprising the sound); an honorific "Viva Puente," rather oddly hung from a straight 4/4 beat but with splendid solos; and a slightly grandiose version of Bud Powell's "Un Poco Loco."

The current of both jazz and Latin music was flowing away from the Third Stream, with its large-scale and ambitious compositions, and moving toward the unpretentiously effective approach of the small combos. Yet even they were showing some signs of being locked into a format that success risked turning into a formula. In June 1956, Cal Tjader was reported to be reorganizing his mambo quintet into a jazz group. He certainly played straight jazz in club dates. But if he was worried about being boxed in by the success of his mambo quintet, he chose rather to amplify than to abandon it: there was evidence in 1955's *Tjader's Latin Kick* of a search for flexibility both in the sound (tenorist Brew Moore substitute for Tjader himself on some tracks) and in a willingness to move away from his basic mambo format.

Characteristically, Mingus's 1957[12] *Tijuana Moods* took an approach to the Latin-jazz style as highly personalized as Duke Ellington's, though Mingus's understanding of Latin rhythms was surely greater, given the Cubop dates he had played as sideman. Some passages in "Ysabel's Table Dance," according to Mingus, represented a stripper collecting cash from tables. But the whole piece had a more Spanish than Mexican undertone, with castanets and echoes of the bullring in Clarence Shaw's trumpet work. "Tijuana Gift Shop" opened with a kind of sub-montuno trumpet pattern and broken-up and busy post-bop drumming with no apparent clave influence, while Mingus himself soon moved into straight-4/4 bass. "Los Mariachis" opened with a free-rhythm trio for horns, and the bass line includes a groove over two measures, but not one with the call-and-response feel of clave. There was, moreover, more Caribbean influence here than Mexican, or Latin of any sort, though in later passages Mingus's bass-playing developed flashes of it.

1957 was quite a year on a number of levels. Tjader's attempts to broaden his sound got a big boost when he recruited pianist Vince Guaraldi, who, though not Latino, had a solid understanding of Cuban piano. And crucially, while Tjader's group was playing opposite Tito Puente at New York's Palladium, Willie Bobo mentioned that he and Mongo Santamaria were planning to leave Puente to go West. Tjader snapped them up, and in a double coup added the newly arrived Cuban tenor player Chombo Silva. The effect of this infusion of new blood was obvious in some of the pieces included on the LP *Mas Caliente*. These were

---

[12] Recorded in 1957, that is. It was not issued for a further five years.

From the early 1950s until his death in 1983, Cal Tjader led the small-combo Latin-jazz pack with a tight vibraphone based sound and a series of groups that at one time or another included most of the best musicians in the field, Latino and non-Latino. *Courtesy Fantasy Record Group*

obviously designed to showcase Tjader's James-Moodyish mellowness. Aside from his extensive soloing, Guaraldi was in particularly good Latin form, with solos full of stabbing chords and broken montunos. Bobo was loud and powerful in a New York-timbales vein, and Santamaria's work was complex and classic, driving it all. For a studio recording, the drive and looseness was amazing.

Meanwhile, the flute, which had been a relatively small part of the Latin-jazz scene throughout the 1950s, was becoming increasingly significant. In August 1957, Herbie Mann cut a couple of sides with a group that included guitarist Laurindo Almeida. Their version of the Ary Barroso tune "Baia" was agreeable,

During the 1960s, percussionists Mongo Santamaria and Willie Bobo essentially created the Latin-jazz-funk that was the basis of the 1970s disco sound. But if they did so successfully, it was because of their grounding in hard-core mambo. Here they both are before their days of fame, playing at the Palladium around 1957. *Photo Phil Newsum*

though with percussion rather too heavy for the genre. But their take on "The Peanut Vendor" was unusual and highly effective. The combination of flute and guitar restored the piece's original elegance in a new guise, after Kenton's and Morales's brass-heavy 1940s renderings. Almeida's guitar work is intriguing in detail, and most importantly the whole thing had a lot of life.

A theme that ran through the Latin-jazz of the 1950s was the increasingly central position of Afro-Cuban percussion and a growing emphasis on its most African elements. The key to this was the multiplying presence of conga-players who came out of either Cuba's Yoruba- or Congo-Angola-derived religions (like Francisco Aguabella) or the street rumba of the black *barrios*, like Armando Peraza and Mongo Santamaria. Gillespie's earlier involvement with Chano Pozo might seem the root cause, but the connection is probably not that direct given that Pozo was killed a decade before a serious outbreak of percussion-centered recordings started appearing.

Activist percussion was nothing new or daring; even Cugat's 1930s recordings were often heavy on the bongos. What was fresh was letting the percussion take center stage. It began, as far as Latin jazz was concerned, with conga-playing within the ensemble that was deeper and more African in flavor than earlier work. Next came increasingly extended percussion rumbones, and then recordings in which percussion was the main event. They mostly had one thing in common: the name Santamaria, Peraza, Candido, Sabu, or Patato on the credits.

An early and influential example was Tito Puente's *Top Percussion*, recorded in July 1957. This is essentially a 11-number percussion rumbón with bass, with an impressive set of percussionists representing both Cuban roots and New York Latino branches: Puente himself, Willie Bobo, Mongo Santamaria, Francisco Aguabella, Enrique Martí, and Julito Collazo. Three vocalists are on hand: Marcelino Guerra, a highly talented jack-of-all-styles; El Viejo Macucho, a traditional vocalist of an older generation; and Mercedita Valdes, a leading singer of Afro-religious material. About half the cuts come from the religious tradition, presented straight—no "Babalú" ersatz-exotica here. Then the secularists take over with a powerful timbales-oriented but heavily street-Afro cut, "Four by Two Pt. 1," and an even more rootsy "Conga Alegre." Only on the ninth cut is bass player Evaristo Baro let loose, and then he contrives to sound like the Afro-Cuban street marimbula, a bass instrument like an overgrown African finger piano. The final cut, "Hot Timbales," lets Puente and Bobo loose, but even then the underlying conga tumbao is about as African as Cuban secular music gets. At the time the whole phenomenal LP was a stunning exercise in authenticity, and it still stands as one of the great percussion workouts.

Perhaps the most remarkable recording of 1957 had, strictly, no Latin-jazz links. Indeed, that is what makes it remarkable, along with the fact that it was issued on the Blue Note label. The title was *Palo Congo,* the leader was Sabu Martinez, and the format was essentially vocal and percussion (though the great Arsenio Rodriguez played tres as well as conga). The cuts included a plena called "Choferito," a piece for tres called "Rhapsodia del Maravilloso" that borrowed liberally from "The Peanut Vendor," and a classic *son* "Tribilin Cantore," as well the well-known "El Cumbanchero" which featured some heavy Afro-Cuban religious percussion. That a jazz label should have put this out in the late 1950s suggests that it had a far higher opinion of the jazz audience's rhythmic sophistication than was generally acknowledged.

Sabu also was involved in a recording with Art Blakey and His Jazz Messengers on the Jubilee label. Like Barretto and all the other conga players who were successful in Latin jazz settings, he had a very clear idea of the differences between the two styles. "I often leave more spaces in jazz," he said, "And I put more pressure on two and four. Actually, I feel jazz in two while in Latin music I have to feel the beat on all four beats pretty evenly. Another thing I do in jazz conga is to stretch my notes. I can deepen and stretch the beat by placing my hand heavier on the skin."

In 1958, Santamaria was still with Cal Tjader, and his effect on the band's live playing can be heard on a September date recorded at the Blackhawk, in San Francisco, *Cal Tjader's Latin Concert.* It featured one of his finest basic bands: Tjader, Santamaria, Guaraldi, McKibbon, and Bobo. This was a group with more *típico* elements than earlier versions, and it performed more self-composed numbers (six out of eight-and-a-bit). Once more Guaraldi's piano was as much Latin as jazz, and his largely montuno-based approach, on equal terms with Tjader's jazz vibes, was in sharp contrast to the old jazz-frontline/Latin-rhythm formula. Santamaria's effect was obvious more or less throughout. The Tjader standard "Lucero" uses the same conga/bass opening as earlier versions, but Santamaria gave it more snap, and he plays a strong supporting role throughout without overshadowing the other musicians. In his "Tu Crees Que?" (a composition with a calypso edge, a recurring minor strain in U.S. rumba and mambo), as he did in "Mi Guaguancó," which opened with a mix of two tumbaos, one is classic and the other rises as a thematic melody. "A Young Love," by contrast, had a percussion pickup into double tempo while Tjader maintained the slower pace over Santamaria's tight congas. It's an example of Santamaria's talent for adapting his down-home style to non-Cuban material, matched by Bobo on timbales.

The swing big bands had been having an increasingly hard time throughout the 1950s, and the booming mambo orchestras provided semi-permanent refuge for many a competent section man and soloist. As a result, fusions between the two were more and more viable. One of the more intriguing recordings of 1958 was a get-together between Tito Puente and Woody Herman, *Puente's Beat/Herman's Heat*, with guitarist Charlie Byrd as "guest artist." The standout here was Byrd's extensive soloing: particularly in "Prelude Ala Cha Cha" and "Mambo Bambo," partly because acoustic guitar was so rare in this kind of ensemble, partly because Byrd was so talented, but also because some of Byrd's phrasing was already strongly Brazilian in feel.

Dizzy Gillespie, no surprise, continued to lead one of the more experimental of the remaining jazz big bands—though only for recording sessions. Despite having been one of its most important pioneers, Gillespie was not entirely wedded to an Afro-Cuban sound. In 1958, he recorded Johnny Richards's "Interlude in C" for Savoy with a group that included six violins, alto flute, flute, oboe, bassoon, the trumpet, French horn, two cellos, harp, bass, drums, and bongos. And one of the first Latin-jazz recordings of 1959 was his small-group recording, "Ungawa," with Les Spann on flute, Junior Mance on piano, Sam Jones on bass, Les Humphries on drums, and Patato Valdez on conga. This kicked off with a fairly standard piano montuno, but it soon developed a fast Brazilian samba feel that was, in retrospect, prophetic.

The 1950s ended in as much of a creative ferment as it had begun, and as always, the most obvious events were not always the most significant. Two developments in particular were to create a tipping of the balance in jazz/Latin relationships for the next several years. By 1959, the balance in Cuban-U.S. music was moving subtly away from fusion toward the *típico*, in one of those half-unconscious shifts that seem to take place when the outside influences that had been enriching a particular style appear to be swamping it. Probably not coincidentally, two of the developing trends in Latin jazz were also reflected in the hardcore Cuban-Latin world: the move toward the flute; and the ever-greater stress on percussion.

Mongo Santamaria was closely involved in this movement, on two fronts. On one hand, while still with Tjader, he made a pair of highly influential albums for Fantasy: *Yambu* (December 1958) and *Mongo* (May 1959). *Yambu* was somewhat reminiscent of Puente's drum-dominant *Top Percussion* from the year before and even involves several of the same percussionists, and uses a slightly similar mix of sacred and secular material.[13] But there was one significant difference: *Yambu* was released on a West Coast jazz label and therefore introduced the jazz audience to a new level of Afro-Cuban percussion.

---

[13] Though the CD reissue claims this was Santamaria's first session as leader, he had recorded two earlier percussion sessions, the first for the ultra-obscure SMC label, the second for Tico.

Mongo, which added Paul Horn on flute and Emil Richards on vibes and marimba, is more significant on a couple of levels. First, its opening track was "Afro Blue," which became a Latin jazz standard. Second, it signaled Santamaria's intensifying interest in combining jazz with deep Afro percussion. It was also a fine recording, not just for its flute jazz and its street percussion tracks, but for a very charming *típico* cut with tres, "Ayenye." And, far from insignificantly, its prominent flute sound accentuated what was already a growing phenomenon.

On the Latin side of the aisle, not just the flute but the entire charanga sound was starting a dominance that would last almost five years. Even the archetypal Latin-jazz Latino, Charlie Palmieri, formed a charanga: the Duboney, fronted by a young flutist of Dominican background who was to become one of the biggest names of 1960s and 1970s salsa, Johnny Pacheco.

Suddenly the flute and the charanga were almost everywhere. Ray Barretto's breakthrough to bandleaderhood came when Riverside Records approached him to record for the Anglo market. Herbie Mann used Latin-jazz flute as a vehicle for at least semi-stardom in a series of outstanding recordings, both Latin- and African-influenced. In 1958, Machito made a recording with Mann that was reissued as *Super Mann*, though it originally bore only Machito's name. This was a remarkably powerful big-band recording. Some of the cuts, like "Love Chant"—a piece of exoticism with 6/8 percussion and a fine, breathy flute solo—encouraged Mann's lusher side. But he rode high, sharp, and convincing over the ensemble in numbers like "Brazilian Soft Shoe" (!), "Ring a Levio," "Carabunta," and "African Flute," built on a version of the 6/8 rhythm that is one of the most common across Africa.

The following year Mann fronted a powerful small group including Shearing alumnus Johnny Rae on vibes and trombone, Nabil "Knobby" Totah (a Jordanian by birth), and three Latino percussionists: Santo Miranda on drums, José Mangual on bongos, and Patato Valdez on conga for a session at Basin Street East also issued on a Verve recording. Aside from indulging Mann's liking for exotica (particularly in the Ellington/Tizol vehicle "Caravan," to which it was entirely suited), this shows him as a powerful and individual soloist capable of swinging effectively off the outstanding rhythm section, whose extensive percussion-only rumbones on a couple of tracks may have owed more than a little to Santamaria.[14]

The charanga and the flute-led Afro-Cuban-jazz group were not the only flute-driven sounds around. Among the various undercurrents in the late 1950s

---

[14] These, incidentally, confirm that jazz-club audiences could by now relate to a complexity of percussion that would have been foreign to most jazz musicians, never mind the listening public, a few years earlier.

A veteran of soul-jazz and mambo-inflected piano trios, Red Garland hired conga-player Ray Barretto for Barretto's first Latin-jazz recording sessions. *Courtesy Galaxy Records*

was an increase in the Brazilian component of Latin jazz in general. In March 1958, Laurindo Almeida and Bud Shank went back into the studio to follow up their early-1950s collaboration, this time with Gary Peacock on bass and Chuck Flores (who had worked with Shank in the Herman band) on drums. Oddly, more cuts of this followup (including several Almeida compositions) used straight 4/4 rhythm than had the original recordings. But Almeida and Shank also mined the Brazilian vein again, including a choro as well as a *baiao*.

Nor was this nascent Brazilian tide simply a vehicle for flute solos. In December 1958, the great John Coltrane used a by-now quite well-known Ary Barroso composition as the title track of his album *Bahia*. Like Charlie Parker before him, Coltrane made no attempt to Latinize his own style (whose boisterousness is pretty much the opposite of the light and lifting sounds of most Brazilian music), playing over a rhythm section that moves between an insistent montuno-like pattern and straight 4/4. Red Garland's extensive soloing also shows no inclination to move away from his usual mellow bop style except in a reprise of the theme. But there it was, after years of pretty much solid Afro-Cubanism: an album by a rising jazz star not just using a Brazilian theme but slapping it on the front of the album for all to see. A foundation was being laid, five years in advance, for one of the most important developments of 1960s jazz.

The arrival of the charanga did not signal the death of the classic mambo-based big-band sound. Machito, Puente, and Rodriguez were to continue to pack 'em into the Palladium for a few more years. But even they were affected by fashion. One result of the charanga craze was an increased use of a flute in the big band sound, in recordings like Tito Puente's June 1959 "El Bajo," which featured flutist Johnny Pacheco. This was a remarkably effective recording, mixing the trumpet flares of the old swing-band sound with a Pacheco solo exploring the rhythmic possibilities of a single repeated note, a hauntingly repeated three-note phrase for the saxes, and a güiro pattern (highly unusual: the güiro, associated with very *típico* music, almost never surfaced in big-band mambo).

As is not always the case in the future-gazing business, the situation at the end of the 1950s could well have led anybody reasonably savvy to predict what the 1960s would bring: a return to Cuban roots, and an increased Brazilian influence. However, even the wisest seers would have been surprised to discover just how accurate such prophecy would be. The *típico* movement would eventually, for a while at least, appear to overwhelm Cubop and jazz-oriented mambo. And the Brazilian wave was to prove something of a tsunami.

◇ 6 ◇

Everything's Coming Up Bossa:

The 1960s, Part 1

There can be no disputing that it was the huge success of the jazz-bossa that made Brazil the leading Latin-jazz source of the 1960s, after so many decades on the periphery. It is ironic that one of the last mass-popular movements in jazz to date also should have been one of the very few 1960s phenomena whose roots in the 1950s were tenuous, and that it should at one and the same time have intrigued musicians by its rhythmic and harmonic subtlety, and the general public by its extreme accessibility. The huge success of the jazz-bossa tends to be treated as if it were some short-lived 1960s fad, like the Twist. Perhaps this is because few revolutionaries have ever had so much charm. But charm or no, the jazz-bossa began a process that has, over three decades, brought the Brazilian tinge in jazz from an intermittent fringe activity to a role as important as that of Cuban music, though in a rather different way.

Whether the kind of proto-jazz-samba that a number of groups were recording during the 1950s would have remained as an enduring jazz fringe without the bossa novas's popularity is anybody's guess, though it seems likely, because Brazilian musicians—and not just Almeida, who had been around since the late 1940s—were already getting gigs and even regular jobs with U.S. bands before the jazz-bossa hit. (Mongo Santamaria hired João Donato as pianist for the first version of his influential fusion band.)

But the bossa nova, which had brought a new melodic, harmonic, and rhythmic approach to Brazil itself, was far more attractive to the jazzmen of the day—especially those associated with the so-called West Coast cool school—than the rhythmically ebullient, but harmonically relatively simple samba. Arranger Gary

McFarland, who made one of the first U.S. jazz-bossa recordings, summed up a widespread attitude: "There seemed to be more underplay, more subtlety than in other Latin rhythms, but with just as much buzz or intensity. The songs had interesting chord progressions, and the melodic intervals were more modern than in traditional samba melodies."[1] Certainly, the reasons for the jazz-bossa's development, popularity, and endurance went deep. True, jazz being as novelty-prone as any popular music, and Cubop having been around for 15 years or so, a style with a new take on all the elements that made Afro-Cuban jazz so attractive in the first place, plus the chordal subtleties that were still popular with jazz musicians, was a natural. From the viewpoint of the audience, meanwhile, jazz-bossa was in part a rediscovery of mellowness, lightness, and a subtle but irresistible tunefulness in a jazz context that seemed to have been lost. It was, in fact, the last jazz-based idiom to find a place in the Top Ten. It should not need pointing out that this does not automatically make it a "fad" as (like the tango) it has at times been called. After all, if "fad" carries any meaning except a certain snobbish disapproval, it implies something shallow-based and short-lived. Jazz-bossa, which brought significant and apparently permanent changes to much of jazz, fails the fad test on both counts.

The jazz-bossa movement owed its existence at least partly to the U.S. State Department. Guitarist Charlie Byrd toured South America for the United States Information Service with Keter Betts and Buddy Deppenschmidt, in Spring 1961; they played with Brazilian musicians and brought back "scores" of recordings. By later the same year, Byrd was playing jazz samba at the Show Boat club in Washington and tried unsuccessfully to sell various record companies on the idea of a jazz-samba recording.

Byrd was only one of several musicians who toured Brazil that year. Among the most important were Dizzy Gillespie and Herbie Mann, who first toured Brazil in July 1961. Mann later commented on the impact the trip had on him in terms like McFarland's. "Up till that point my success had come from having an Afro-Cuban type jazz band with four percussionists," he said. "But Afro-Cuban music was so simplistic melody-wise that it really got boring. When I went to Brazil I saw that their music could be as rhythmically involved as other ethnic music, but with it they had these melodic masterpieces. So as a jazz person, it was the best of both worlds—to have great melodies to improvise with combined with these rhythms."

---

[1] When jazz musicians began to take note of the new idiom is not altogether clear. McFarland claimed in the notes to his August 1962 Big Band Bossa recording (from which this quote comes) that a friend had played him a bossa-nova recording in the spring of 1960. If so, it must have been an import. The first bossa nova LP released in the U.S. was *Brazil's Brilliant João Gilberto*, issued by Capitol in 1961.

The jazz-bossa period produced a wealth of different approaches spanning the bossa/jazz spectrum. Ella Fitzgerald recorded a collection of Antonio Jobim numbers that both preserved the Brazilian flavor and gave a swing oomph to a vocal style that sometimes went beyond ethereal to alienated-sounding. *Courtesy Pablo Records*

1962 was the year in which jazz-samba and jazz-bossa moved from infiltration to Blitzkrieg. The catalyst was the overwhelmingly famous Charlie Byrd/Stan Getz version of "Desafinado." As we've seen, Byrd had been aware of Brazilian music for years and, following his 1961 State Department Latin America tour, had been playing bossa nova in Washington. "Desafinado" originated as a cut on a session recorded on February 13th at All Souls Unitarian Church, Washington, D.C., with Getz on tenor, Byrd on guitar, Byrd's brother Gene on bass and guitar, Keter Betts on bass, and Buddy Deppenschmidt and Bill Reichenbach on drums. (Byrd explained his use of two drummers in the notes to the album: "This is what the Brazilians do. Both drummers play simple patterns, and together they swing.")

Even though he knew nothing of the bossa nova until Byrd introduced him to it, Getz was a masterly choice for Byrd's experiment. Getz had a relatively light, legato approach, a tone that could move instantly between biting and mellow, and on-and-off experience with Latin groups going back to the mid-1940s. The album *Jazz Samba* was released by Verve Records in April, and the single of "Desafinado" spent 10 weeks in the *Billboard* Top 40, reaching number 15 at one point, besides (somewhat ironically) winning Getz a Grammy for best solo performance of the year.

Critics and musicians have sometimes bickered about whether this was the first U.S. jazz-bossa album, or indeed a jazz-bossa album at all. Given the close relationship between samba and bossa nova, this seems to me a futile debate. Certainly the recording is called *Jazz Samba* and the rhythms are mostly less glancing than Gilberto's in particular. But "Desafinado" is the quintessential bossa-nova composition. Jazz-samba or jazz-bossa, Byrd's solos were extremely interesting, with their combination of rich bossa-nova chording and bluesy bent notes, especially in "O Pato," "Samba de Uma Nota Só" (which was to become a standard as "One Note Samba"), and (my own favorite) "Baia." And though it may stem from unfamiliarity, even the fact that Getz in solo sometimes sounded as if he was feeling his way oddly matches the just-wondering quality of João Gilberto's remarkably offhand vocal style.

Whether or not *Jazz Samba* was the "first" U.S. jazz-bossa recording, it's clear that the U.S. jazz world as a whole was discovering the idiom at about the same time. A month after the release of the Byrd/Getz version of "Desafinado," Dizzy Gillespie recorded another version in New York, though it appeared on an LP called *Dizzy on the French Riviera*.[2] The recording as a whole caught the mellow

---

[2] The actual recording information for this album is confused; the tracks and data given in Dizzy's autobiography do not correspond with the actual LP release.

quirkiness of bossa nova without merely imitating it: the boisterously uptempo "Pau de Arara," for instance, featured powerful cymbal work taking the place of the shaker patterns in Brazilian roots samba.

More significant, though, was another Brazilian number Gillespie recorded in May. For "Pergunte ao Joao," he added two Brazilian singer/percussionists, Jose de Paula and Carmen Costa (who may have been the first person to play a cabaça in New York since the days when the Banda Da Lua was backing Carmen Miranda). Unlike any previous U.S. jazz-samba or jazz-bossa recording, this included a very carioca vocal duet by de Paula and Costa, to which Gillespie played muted-trumpet responses *à la* classic blues. In addition, Gillespie effectively worked samba rhythms into his customary solo idiom.

By mid-1962, the rush was on: musicians were travelling south to check out the source, and record companies were cranking out jazz-bossa and/or jazz-samba recordings good, bad, and indifferent. Herbie Mann cut an album in Rio with trumpeter Kenny Dorham and a bunch of carioca heavies—Sergio Mendes's Sexteto Bossa Rio, Baden Powell, Jobim, Bebeto, Helcio Milito—that was released in October as *Do the Bossa Nova With Herbie Mann*. Paul Winter also heard the famous Gilberto LP and, inspired by it, recorded in Rio and New York an album, *Jazz Meets the Bossa Nova*, that was more deliberately "Brazilian" than the Getz/Byrd recording, using Brazilian percussionists. Winter essentially fell for the same qualities as Gary McFarland before him: "We were hearing a very gentle voice that had the kind of soul and harmonic beauty that we loved in jazz. But as opposed to the hard-driving bebop that we were playing then, it was astounding to find a very quiet, gentle music that had an equal amount of magic."

Much of *Jazz Meets the Bossa Nova* was cool jazz with a jazz-bossa underlay. But if Gerry Mulligan and the earlier cool jazz sound were roots of bossa nova as João Gilberto later claimed, the cool arrangements as well as the solo work were certainly in the spirit of the Brazilian original. And the cuts recorded in Rio were ahead of their time in their use of Brazilian percussion instruments (presumably played by Brazilians). "The Spell of the Samba/Samba da Minha Terra," "Foolish One/Insensatez," and "Little Boat/Barquinho" had at least as solid a small-percussion section as most Brazilian urban samba recordings, and a couple of short rhythm-section solos setting jazz traps against the Brazilian percussion were emblematic of rhythmic blends to come. Paul Winter's second recording made in Brazil was a collaboration with Carlos Lyra, though Lyra was in fact one of the most jazz-minded of the early bossa nova composers.[3] The *Sound of Ipanema* did

---

[3] Indeed he formed a school with Roberto Menescal with the stated purpose of experimenting with cool-jazz harmonies.

not ignore Lyra's jazz interests or his affinity with older U.S. songwriters, but the album leaned heavily on the Brazilian side of his work, particularly his vocals. The result was a Brazilian bossa nova recording with Americans aboard, though the instrumental sections bridged the rather complex gap between the two styles with considerable panache.

Mann was another of the jazz musicians to record with Brazilian artists early on. Mann's continued involvement with bossa nova is hardly surprising. Aside from the fact that it was a happening thing, it was superbly suited to the flute, whose history in Brazilian popular music goes back to the nineteenth century. Mann was extremely prolific in the early 1960s, and most of his recordings mixed Brazilian and Afro-Cuban jazz. Aside from the title cut, a Latinized Twist (!), 1962's *Right Now* was squarely in the jazz-bossa version of a Latin-jazz tradition going back a decade, with single-string solos by guitarist Billy Bean on "Desafinado" and "Barquinho" (wrongly spelt on the label), and Mann playing alto flute to give a remarkably warm sound to a classic piece of jazz-samba. But then the whole album was imaginative. The quirky, not to say witty, "Jumpin' With Symphony Sid" mixes an Afro-Cuban 6/8 with a subdued soul-jazz feeling, electric piano and all. A couple of tracks even have a Jewish component, including the largely Afro-Cuban jazz "Free For All."

Mann continued to explore both Brazilian and Cuban influences in his 1964 *Latin Fever*. This was split between Afro-Cuban jazz, performed mostly with a big band, and Brazilian numbers recorded in Rio with Brazilian musicians. It opened with a superb big-band version of the haunting "Harlem Nocturne," a melody made for Mann's alto flute; "Not Now—Later On" was early Latin-jazz-funk fusion, female chorus and all. But the crown jewel of the album was "The Golden Striker," a sensational remake of John Lewis's number as a kind of funk charanga piece, with Mann overdubbing a fine duet with himself. Most of the Brazilian cuts were recorded with the Sergio Mendes Sextet, which included the great jazz-choro alto player Paulo Moura in cool-jazz form and Dom Um Romao on drums. These cuts had the typical Mendes nose for a hook, upbeat jauntiness, touches of jazz voicings (notably in Moura's solo work and Mendes's own piano), and general air of being determined to appeal to the audience while having fun. With Mann's flute on top, the result verged on the irresistible.

Though Mann continued to work on and off with existing Brazilian groups, his own recordings were jazz-bossa or jazz-samba fusions.[4] And though they con-

---

[4] As were many Brazilian recordings, the main difference being that the Brazilians referred to the style as "samba jazz" rather than jazz-samba!

tinued to come in for a good deal of sneering from purists, the musicians who—
rather than treating the original Brazilian form with overmuch reverence—took
the bossa nova and ran with it in sometimes weird but often wonderful directions
had the right idea. What would be the point of U.S. wannabe bossa recreationists,
when the real thing played by its creators could easily be imported?[5] In fact, the
music's long-term influence was entirely due to the so-called "dilution"—really
absorption—process.

It would be hard to beat Stan Getz's second bossa nova outing, *Stan Getz Bossa
Nova Arranged and Conducted by Gary McFarland*, for originality—or eccentricity. McFarland was one of the West Coast's most promising arrangers in the 1960s
(he wrote for Gerry Mulligan, Johnny Hodges, and Anita O'Day, among others).
His work on this album was about as far from João Gilberto's casual, oblique, cool
music as one could imagine, though. His heavily composed big-band arrangements
were written for an ensemble group that included—besides Getz—several musicians with long experience of Latin music: trumpeters Doc Severinsen and Clark
Terry; guitarist Jim Hall; pianist Hank Jones; and valve trombonist Bob
Brookmeyer; as well as the percussionists Jose de Paula and Carmen Costa, who
had recorded with Gillespie in May. Oh yes, and a bass clarinet!

Whether you regard this recording as ridiculously inappropriate or interestingly experimental is really a matter of taste. Their version of "Manha de Carnaval"
was notable for fine acoustic guitar from Hall, and while the lushness of its
arrangement might seem like overkill, it was no more overblown than the work of
the Brazilian Claus Ogerman, with whom Antonio Carlos Jobim so often worked.
The fast "Balanço No Samba" moved from a percussion opening to an intriguing
half-jazz/half-Brazilian rhythm off which Getz grooved mightily. Overall,
McFarland's arrangements were grandiose but interesting, and nicely offset
Getz's high, sharp soloing. McFarland's version of the song that started it all,
"Chega de Saudade," was given a rather Kentonesque opening with dramatic
trumpet by Doc Severinsen before a gorgeous contrasting section for Getz and
rhythm, echoed and amplified later by contrapuntal interplay between Jones,
Getz, and Brookmeyer, and ensemble work reminiscent of the Miles Davis/Gerry
Mulligan nonet recordings.

Percussionists de Paula and Costa were providing a touch of authenticity to a
remarkable number of jazz-bossa recordings at this time. They also cropped up

---

[5] Some of the least "authentic" examples of Brazilian influence pointed the way very early to its
future role in jazz. Forgotten now, guitarist Grant Green's unpromisingly titled *The Latin Bit* is a case
in point: among several bossa-nova-influenced numbers there was a wonderful version of "Tico
Tico," taken slower than usual and gradually turned into a long, slow, soul-jazz stomper.

Stalwarts of early jazz-bossa: American saxist Stan Getz and Brazilian guitarist João Gilberto appeared regularly together during the height of the bossa fever. *Columbia Records/Frank Driggs Collection*

on Herbie Mann's Brazil Blues, which included Patato Valdez on conga and Willie Bobo on timbales. By now certain bossa nova compositions were already being established as instant standards, but Mann mixed these with less-familiar numbers, whether older or self-composed. Notable among the former was the opener, Ary Barroso's "Brazil," given an unusual stomping straight-4/4 treatment with fine bass-playing, quick-silver flute, and an excellent piano solo. "B.N.Blues" was based on a shuffle riff neither blues nor Brazilian, with bluesy guitar, flute, and vibes. But the most interesting cut of all was the last one, "Me Faz Recorar," which opened with prominent cabaça shaker, with tambourim and moody chorded guitar underneath. The front line solos were again basically jazz, but the piece was transformed by its underlying cabaça—heavy street-shuffle— especially when the bass lays down a straight 4/4 line as a link between the two percussion instruments.

It was not just the jazz world that was picking up on Brazilian music. On the whole, the hardcore Latin scene had other fish to fry. But Mongo Santamaria— who was already showing signs of the major role he would play in jazz/Latin fusions of all sorts—was quick to pick up on the popularity of Brazilian music.

On his *Go Mongo* album, he used José de Paula (here playing guitar as well as percussion) and Carmen Costa on "Tumba Le Le," a stunning street samba with a superb rootsy vocal, a frontline of one trumpet and two saxes doubling on flute, and Chick Corea in the piano chair.

By mid-1962, the notion that the samba and bossa-nova offered rhythms that could work effectively in a jazz setting, particularly under a ballad, was taking firm hold. In September and October, Charlie Byrd recorded *Bossa Nova Pelos Passaros*. Most of the cuts involved the basic trio of himself, Keter Betts on bass, and Bill Reichenbach on drums; some cuts added Earl Swope on trombone, Charlie Hampton on flute and alto sax, Gene Byrd on guitar, and percussionist Willie Rodriguez (and some suffered from a somewhat banal string section added at a later session). The trio featured Byrd's usual fairly intricate chording and often bluesy single-string runs. The band tracks "Voce e Eu," "Ho-Ba-La-La," and "O Passaro" used cool-jazz ensemble heads before moving into solos that, with the exceptions of Byrd's subtle blends, were also cool jazz colored.

The steady arrival of Brazilian musicians in the U.S. was important to the continued development of jazz-bossa. American adaptation of the habanera, the tango, and the Brazilian maxixe had gradually diluted the borrowed elements into a tinge almost unrecognizably pale. By contrast, the presence of a separate Caribbean-Latin public in the U.S. had given Cubop and its predecessors enduring local role models. In the case of the jazz-bossa, such a roots public didn't exist; but many of the Brazilian musicians who originated bossa nova—Sergio Mendes, João Gilberto, Luiz Bonfá, Jobim, Oscar Castro-Neves—were by now on hand in the U.S., and many more of every ilk were to come.

One of the first Brazilian musicians other than percussionists to play a major role in a jazz-bossa recording was—suitably enough—Laurindo Almeida, who had been partly responsible for the early 1950s jazz-baiao. In a sense, Almeida was hardly closer to the original bossa nova than Charlie Byrd: not only was he basically a classical guitarist, but he had been working in the U.S. during the style's entire formative period.

He was also no purist, as is made clear by his late 1962 recording under the name Laurindo Almeida and the Bossa Nova All Stars, *Viva Bossa Nova!* The album includes the by-now expected "Desafinado" and "One Note Samba," along with an odd mix of minor standards and cover-band bottom-feeders: "Naked River Theme"; "Lazy River"; "Rambling Rose"; "Maria"; "Petite Fleur"; "Teach Me Tonight"; "Lollipops & Roses," "Moon River," "Mr. Lucky"; and "Theme from *Route 66*." But the results were far from uninteresting or unoriginal. On "Petite

Fleur," Almeida soloed on the small Brazilian cavaquinho guitar (plucked single-string rather than strummed in the usual way). The group also included Jimmy Rowles playing electric organ—almost certainly a jazz-bossa first!

The first major Brazilian guitarist with serious bossa-nova chops to move onto the U.S. jazz-bossa scene was Djalma de Andrade, known professionally as Bola Sete. He shared classical training with Almeida (as with most bossa-nova musicians). But in other respects he was far more suited to a leading role in U.S. jazz-bossa, because he had been playing jazz in Brazil as well as bossa nova (he was a particular admirer of U.S. guitarists George Van Epps and Barney Kessell).

Bola Sete was arguably the most important of the early wave of Brazilian musicians to the fusion of bossa nova and jazz. In *The Book of Jazz*, Leonard Feather accurately remarked that most of the bossa-nova guitarists were not jazz-oriented, and that "Bola Sete showed equal facility in every medium—electric and unamplified, Brazilian and modern jazz and every stop along the way." Though he had arrived in the U.S. in 1959, he had made few waves until Dizzy Gillespie heard him playing in the lobby of a Sheraton hotel and arranged his appearance at an afternoon concert at the Monterey Jazz Festival in September 1962, both as part of Gillespie's band and as a soloist. His mix of bossa nova and jazz duly stole the show, and led to a contract with Fantasy Records.

Despite its title, Bola Sete's album *Bossa Nova*, on which he played many of his own compositions backed by Ben Tucker on bass, Dave Bailey on drums, and the ubiquitous José de Paula and Carmen Costa, was notable for its great rhythmic variety. Cuts like "Up the Creek (To de Sinuca)" and "Samba in the Perrotoque" combined a real sense of Brazilian street rhythms (not all of them samba) with complex, flowing, glancing guitar work in which Bola Sete used jazz-derived chords and phrasings to augment a basically Brazilian style. Jazz chordings repeatedly peeked through the Brazilian texture of the wonderful "Sweet Thing (Piteuzinho)," "If You Return (Se Acaso Voce Chegasse)," and notably "Ash Wednesday," and even Sete's single-note runs had echoes of choro as well as bluesy touches.

Bola Sete teamed up with Vince Guaraldi on the quartet recording *Vince Guaraldi, Bola Sete and Friends*. This was an early example of mainstream jazz absorbing a bossa-nova beat whose most interesting cut was a long mambo/bossa-nova blend called (what else?) "Mambossa," in which both musicians explored polyrhythmic effects. Sete's next trio album under his own name, *Tour de Force*, showed a breadth of musical interest that was to intensify with time. It ended with a Bach bourrée and along the way included an interesting blues cut, "Baccara." An occasional bossa-nova percussion tick-tick merely added a little color to this piece with little other overt Brazilianisms, but "Baccara" was notable for a passage of effective and original R&B-ish blues guitar riffs, both strummed and plucked. And Bola Sete stretched the natural lyricism of "Moon River" into a virtually semi-classical rhapsody almost like one long cadenza.

Unsurprisingly, Charlie Byrd and Stan Getz were still the busiest of the American jazz-bossa stars in 1963. Byrd recorded *Once More/Charlie Byrd's Bossa Nova* for Riverside, augmenting his trio with various combinations of musicians. Some cuts added four cellos and French horn—excess baggage except in Byrd's composition "Three Note Samba," whose cello part was more interesting than most jazz-with-string backings. Like Bola Sete, Byrd's interests had always gone well beyond jazz, and his new success allowed him to explore them. A Village Gate gig recorded as *Byrd at the Gate* featured the trio with various guests, including Clark Terry, and tenor saxist Seldon Powell (whose big-band background included a stint with Lucky Millinder). The high spot of this session was a wonderful solo mini-suite, "Where Are the Hebrew Children," with influences from the blues, flamenco, and even possibly Indian music.

Stan Getz meanwhile went into the studio in March to cut an eponymous album with João Gilberto that produced not only another top-of-the-chart single but U.S. jazz-bossa's first vocal star. When Gilberto's wife Astrud recorded the English version of "The Girl from Ipanema" (Brazilian title "Garota de Ipanema"), she had supposedly never sung professionally, and indeed was in the studio mostly to translate for the Brazilian musicians involved, whose English was shaky. Her small, vibratoless voice and cool vocal style personified both the virtues and vices of the bossa nova, above all a laid-back quality that on a bad night could approach catatonia. Getz's solos meanwhile underlined just how well his style suited the relatively forthright American jazz-bossa and how effectively and even subtly he moved it into the jazz realm.

That forthrightness and subtlety were even more strongly in evidence in another album Getz recorded the same month.[6] Every track on this eponymous collaboration with Laurindo Almeida (backed by bass plus various drummers and percussionists) was a marvel, but "Minima Moça" was the jewel in the crown, gentle but quite fast, with a slightly acid edge to Getz's tenor that dispelled any hint of blandness.

The list of jazz recordings from 1963 that threw in a version of one of the big-hit bossa nova compositions would be as tiresome as it would be long. Naturally

---

[6] Though thanks to Verve's determination to milk the last drop from the Getz/Byrd collaboration, it wasn't released till 1966, when pure jazz-bossa was almost history.

enough, some worked better than others, depending on the style and sound of the musicians involved. Gerry Mulligan, for instance, was a natural for the genre—and the tone of the baritone sax singled his contributions out from the large number of mellow tenors. *Night Lights and Butterfly With Hiccups* are not his best-known albums. But most of the musicians involved—Mulligan (piano as well as baritone sax), Art Farmer (trumpet and flugelhorn), Bob Brookmeyer (valve trombone), Jim Hall (guitar), Bill Crow (bass), and Dave Bailey (drums)—had already had a certain amount of experience with Brazilian-tinged music. Both "Morning of the Carnival from *Black Orpheus*" (from *Night Lights*) and "Theme for Jobim" reflected their knowledge of this musical style.

But though fine recordings were still being made, by now the fad element in jazz-bossa seemed to many of its original enthusiasts to be taking over. Even respected jazz musicians appeared to see it as a way to a quick sales jolt, among them Duke Ellington—whose *Afro Bossa* was arguably his best recording of what was admittedly one of his bleaker periods—Coleman Hawkins, and Earl Bostic. *Afro-Bossa* was typical of Ellington in that even the title number made no pretense of having anything to do with real-world bossa nova.[7] Its opening theme was vaguely reminiscent of "Mood Indigo," and the drumming and general arrangement were in Ellington's "exotic" tradition, with echoes of everything from "Caravan" to "Black and Tan Fantasy." Ellington was, as always, being Ellington in the teeth of whatever other music was happening around him.

As *Afro Bossa* confirmed, however, even the more cynical recordings were not necessarily without merit. Coleman Hawkins's big tenor-sax ballad style, for example, fit jazz-bossa as well as Getz's cooler Lester Young-derived mellow-ness. Even though the most ebullient track on Hawkins's *Desafinado* was a jazz-samba version of "I'm Looking Over a Four Leaf Clover," he played mostly jazz-bossa classics. The backing included two American acoustic guitarists who had apparently never played jazz-bossa before but did it well; and over this backup, Hawkins was richly and splendidly Hawkins. Only (however, a big "only"!) the percussion was weak in too many places.

Earl Bostic Plays Bossa Nova was either hilarious or beneath contempt, depending on your sense of humor. But even this was quite creative in its low-brow way. Despite its title, "La Bossa" was a weird takeoff on early rock and roll. "El Choclo Bossa Nova" was really intriguing in a hallucinogenic sort of way, with a good imitation of a Brazilian rhythm (kind of generic be it said) mixed in

---

[7] According to Stanley Dance's liner notes, the band called the piece "the gutbucket bolero," which is no more accurate than the official title.

with the tango pulse and buzz-saw tenor (not forgetting the marimba imitation!). What made it all work, aside from sheer effrontery, was the quality of the rhythm section, which cheerfully mixed its genres but nowhere descended to the genteel ticking that characterized the feebler bossa-imitations.

Not all the misbegotten children of the jazz-bossa vogue were comic, crass, or commercial. One of the odder examples of Luso-marginalia came when Miles Davis—who never showed much interest in Latin jazz—recorded "Corcovado" with the Gil Evans Orchestra for the album *Quiet Nights*. The result was a ponderous arrangement taken at funereal pace, which preserved the melody but none of the sly, swift, glancing bossa-nova rhythm, stripping the piece of individuality and turning it into just another over-arranged, super-slow ballad.

By 1964, the second year of its peak, there were signs that jazz-bossa was losing steam. But this did not preclude many excellent recordings from being made, most of which reflected a maturing rather than flagging of the original genre. Moreover, though jazz-bossa formed a metaphorical 90 percent of the Brazilian-oriented jazz of the time, occasional performances gave a sense of a much wider tradition. One of the most striking came on percussionist Montego Joe's album, *Arriba! Con Montego Joe*, an outstanding early fusion recording, which included a number called "Maracatú," based on a traditional percussive carnival tradition from the strongly African northeast of Brazil.

The jazz-bossa itself was also undergoing some changes. Bola Sete's next studio recording, *Incomparable. . .,* included Paul Horn on flute—a sonic change for Bolo Sete, whose previous recordings were without any kind of wind instrument. The combination was an effective one, particularly on "Lamento de Negro," in which Bola Sete gave Horn's romantic playing a rich but discreet chorded backing—bossa nova at its gentlest. By contrast, "Sarava" was almost a demonstration of new ways to do jazz-bossa, with a jazz-flavored opening, and lots of swing-era jazz moments in Sete's guitar work. Something of the same sensibility leavened "Be-Bossa," whose blend of Brazilian and bop phrasing was remarkably subtle.

Towards the end of the year, Stan Getz played a number of live gigs with a new quartet comprising Astrud Gilberto, Gary Burton, and Kenny Burrell, that had its debut in October at the Cafe A Go Go in Greenwich Village. Given that U.S. jazz-bossa had previously been largely instrumental, a significant aspect of this collaboration was its stress on English-language vocals—ironically, a change that in the long-term would put a nail in the style's coffin. In part this was because it moved jazz-bossa dangerously nearer to pop music. But more fundamentally, it ran up against a problem inherent in the translation of song lyrics (and poetry). Language and melody are so closely intertwined that a tune that is subtle and glancing sung in Portuguese can simply sound banal in English. In addition, Astrud Gilberto's style was simply too laid back for an American ballad—and even more so for non-bossa ballads like "Only Trust Your Heart," in which she sounded at her most alienated (or perhaps simply bored). By contrast, her interpretation of the uptempo "Eu e Voce," in Portuguese, came over cool and subtle.

Though it would have taken a psychic to predict it at the time, 1965 was to be the last year of jazz-bossa's first golden age, for a number of reasons. In Brazil, as well as the United States, pop-bossa had swamped the original sound. 1965 also saw the first of the major Brazilian music festivals, which brought a new and more eclectic generation of singer-songwriters into the public eye. In addition, the previous year's military coup gave rise to a wave of protest songs and thus to a newly text-oriented approach to music. The festivals and the army were joint midwives at the birth of a new and highly eclectic idiom called "música popular brasileira," or MPB. This was singer-songwriter and vocal-oriented, and drew heavily from U.S. rock and folk as well as a range of Brazilian sources. Older musicians either adapted to MPB, or moved from hip to passé—and as a result, quite often, from Brazil to the U.S.A. A case in point was Sergio Mendes, who settled in San Francisco, formed his first U.S. group, and had something of a hit with a version of "Mais Que Nada" using English lyrics and female voices-as-instruments. Mendes had bossa-nova chops, but he was also a man prepared to adapt to the market, and his undeniably catchy work helped move the U.S. idiom away from jazz-bossa toward bubblegum pop.[8]

The movement of bossa nova into the pop field was given a further hefty boost when Astrud Gilberto left Stan Getz's group and moved (or was moved) even further into steakhouse pop. In January she recorded tracks for *The Astrud Gilberto Album* with the Marty Paich Orchestra that buried several admirable musicians in wall-to-wall strings. Another Astrud Gilberto album, *Look to the Rainbow*, which backed her with Al Cohn's big band, was more interesting. Two cuts were built on non-samba Brazilian idioms. "Frevo" was based on a fast marcha form from the northern Brazilian area Recife, and the band evoked something of the real feel of the Brazilian brass bands. "Berimbau" was named after the Congo-Angolan musical bow integral to the Afro-Brazilian martial art called capoeira. But that session was a flash in the pan. Two days before Christmas, Gilberto was back in the studio with essentially the same musicians, but this time

---

[8] Among his many hits along the way was a version of "Scarborough Fair!"

officially led by Gil Evans and using his arrangements. The result was firmly in pop ballad territory.

The movement away from jazz-bossa toward mass-pop was not, of course, universal. And, even at a time when mainstream jazz-bossa had been losing steam, the style was still evolving. When Bola Sete's trio played the 1965 Monterrey Jazz Festival with a lengthy medley of numbers from *Black Orpheus*, their performance was neither perfunctory nor predictable. The guitarist treated the standard "Samba de Orfeu" as a cooker well outside the standard jazz-bossa ethos, with Brazilian lines augmented by jazz chordings and phrases. Paulinho mixed Brazilian and jazz licks in his traps, and the core group plus a couple of added percussionists took a real shot at reproducing a street percussion batucada. In "Soul Samba," Bola Sete plays an even more full-fledged blend of Brazil and blues/jazz.

Shortly thereafter, the new trio's studio album *Autentico!* underlined Bola Sete's move away from standard jazz-bossa even more emphatically. Its references to traditional Brazilian music were rich in everything but bossa nova. "Brejeiro," for example, was a long and complex workout based on a fast baiao-like theme. "Baion Blues," driven by Paulinho's cheerfully rackety trap drumming, was similarly inspired, with a guitar line that mixed blues licks with phrases straight from Luiz Gonzaga, the king of downhome baiao.

The fall from grace of jazz-bossa as it was conceived in the early 1960s emphatically did not mean that Brazilian elements in jazz were even temporarily a thing of the past. A relatively obscure album by Dizzy Gillespie, *The Melody Lingers On*, included three Brazilian pieces. "Summer Samba," "Winter Samba," and "Portuguese Washerwoman," all moved to a strong, guitar-led, bossa nova rhythm under delicate soloing from Gillespie and lyrical flute playing from James Moody. And even later, in 1967, the most interesting cut on Cal Tjader's album *The Prophet* was "Cal's Bluedo," a jazz-bossa with agreeable flute and a nice organ solo.[9]

If the fading of jazz-bossa did not mean that Brazilian jazz was a one-wave phenomenon, nor did it signal the decline of wider Brazilian influences on mainstream jazz; both had rather moved to a second stage of absorption. Nat Adderley's composition "Jive Samba," for instance, was by now a regular part of the Cannonball Adderley Quintet's book. In the concert version preserved on the recording *Cannonball in Japan*, Adderley made no attempt to imitate Brazilian

---

[9] Though rare, this was not the first organ solo in jazz-bossa. Jimmy Rowles had played one in 1962 on an exceedingly obscure but interesting album, *Laurindo Almeida and the Bossa Nova All Stars*.

melodic patterns; and in the second theme, the bass subverted the bossa nova underpinning with heavy lines that nevertheless maintained the two-measure montuno feel. As it developed, the entire performance became ever more funk-oriented and un-Brazilian.

Approaches to the jazz-samba became increasingly intriguing as the decade wound down. Chick Corea's Bill Evans-inspired *Now He Sings, Now He Sobs*, recorded in March 1968 with Miroslav Vitous on bass and Roy Haynes on drums, included a highly impressionistic "Bossa" with minimal relationship—even rhythmic—to the original form. "Samba Yantra," after an opening montuno maintains as much in Corea's left hand as the bass, also contains no overt Brazilian rhythmic or melodic elements. By contrast, Joe Henderson's approach as reflected in "O Amor em Paz" (issued on his album, *The Kicker*), is essentially classic sax-led jazz-bossa, hardly less relaxed than the Getz/Byrd school. This is the Brazilian tinge in its now well-established role as mellowness break.

Not even the musicians most involved in the transmutation of the hard-bop/soul-jazz nexus into the next generation of funk-jazz were really abandoning jazz-bossa. But they were transmuting it. The Freddy Hubbard club date with trumpeter Lee Morgan and Big Black on congas, released as *Live at Club La Marchal*, illustrates various of the elements coalescing into a Latin-funk-jazz idiom. And if the Hubbard session was moving in this direction, tenorist Hank Mobley's *Dippin'* pretty much reached it, at least in "The Dip," which features a funk/soul-jazz horn riff, an underlying funk groove with a subtle clave two-part to it, along with pianist Harold Mabern Jr.'s Americanized-clave vamp under Mobley's soloing. This was more than embryonic Latin funk-jazz, and an intriguing pea to find in the same pod as "Recardo Bossa Nova," even though this too took a fairly hard soul-jazz approach. Mobley's sax lines were not all that different from, say, Getz's, but his tougher tone and the assertive drumming and piano under his sax gave it an entirely different esthetic from the lighter and more oblique jazz-bossa.[10]

Though it appeared in the late 1960s that jazz-bossa was a fad that had passed, in fact, pretty much the opposite was true. The Brazilian influence was beginning to mix with the other elements that would soon lead to a Latin-jazz-funk idiom:

---

[10] There was one very marked exception to the increasingly sophisticated absorption of Brazilian elements. The John Coltrane Quartet included a cut called "Brazilia" on their 1965 LP, *The John Coltrane Quartet Plays*. This had even less musical relevance to its subject than Ellington's "Latin" rhapsodies. It was as if a statement was being made: "bossa me no novas!" (unless of course the message was: "I can make this stuff over so thoroughly I'll lose you, Roberts!")

soul jazz and post-Cubop. One reason for this was the natural process of absorption. Another was the arrival, starting around 1967, of an important new Brazilian wave. The young Brazilians arriving in the U.S. late in the decade—among them singer Flora Purim, her husband, percussionist Airto Moreira, and keyboardist/composer Eumir Deodato—shared a range of ideas different from jazz-bossa. And they all hit the jazz scene fast and early. Purim and Airto began sitting in on jam sessions, with Herbie Hancock and Thelonious Monk, among others. Purim, who could sing straight bossa nova when she had to, also toured Europe with Stan Getz and performed with Duke Pearson and Gil Evans. Airto hung out with bassist Walter Booker, and jammed and scuffled. Eumir Deodato worked with Wes Montgomery, as well as Astrud Gilberto.

By the very end of the decade, these new arrivals began to make a mark on a jazz scene in which Brazilian and Cuban elements were beginning to combine Wayne Shorter's *Super Nova*, with Airto Moreira on percussion, was no mellow cocktail jazz. One of the cuts was the well-worn Jobim composition, "Dindi." But this is "Dindi" with a difference. It opens with Airto playing berimbau, and includes a 1970s-style eco/free jam including a cuica (played by Airto again). After a long free passage, Maria Booker sings in a style that crossed bossa nova with the warmer MPB, with a very simple acoustic guitar accompaniment. The free-playing (particularly Airto's instrument-rich percussion contributions), eco-babble noise-making, acid-tinged improvisation, and abrupt contrasts are all far from the jazz-bossa of only a few years earlier.

Interestingly, the impact on Latin-jazz-funk of these new arrivals may have been given extra impetus by a very different, indeed non-Brazilian element in the music of one of the leading soul-jazz exponents: Horace Silver. Silver, of course, was an important member of what had come to be called the soul-jazz school. In the notes to *Song for My Father*, Silver was quoted as saying of the title track that he was much impressed by "the real bossa nova feeling, which I've tried to incorporate into this number."

But there was more to the piece's Brazilian feeling than that. Silver's father was an immigrant from the Cape Verde Islands, former Portuguese colonies off West Africa, much of whose music has strong Portuguese elements. This makes it a natural for blending with Brazilian music, but also provides a more general empathy with Spanish-Latin forms. Moreover, Silver's father and uncles were amateur musicians who played guitar and some violin by ear, and Silver has talked about his memories of family parties with music from Cape Verde when he was growing up. Most relevant to Latin-jazz fusions, Silver's "Señor Blues" used a 6/8 time signature. Silver's *Further Explorations* album was also full of examples of Latin elements, including a Latin beat set against straight 4/4 sections.

Silver's soul-Latin mix would give another shot in the arm to the movement toward a funk-Latin-Jazz fusion. In the early '70s, this would become the leading movement in mainstream jazz.

◇ 7 ◇

Come Out Smokin'. . .

The 1960s, Part 2

The revolutionary role of the jazz-bossa was reasonably clear cut. While many of the factors that made it popular also applied to other 1960s jazz/Latin interactions, however, the journey from 1950s big-band mambo to 1970s salsa in the Latin community, and the ever-increasing familiarity of Latin music, brought about their own rather more complex evolution.

After riding high for more than a decade, Cubop in its various forms was still flourishing as the 1960s began, even if it lacked the novelty that brings press coverage. By now younger Latino musicians were thoroughly experienced in the issues raised by playing in jazz ensembles. And by the same token, many, if not most, jazz musicians were entirely comfortable playing over complex rhythms. Indeed, many of them had played with hardcore Latin groups of one kind or another. By the time trumpeter Ted Curson made the album *Fire Down Below* in December 1962, for example, he had played with both black Latin groups—Pucho and Hugo Dickens—and Latino Latin-jazz groups—the La Plata Sextet, and Pete Terrace—as well as the more mainstream bandleaders José Curbelo and Alfredito. At one point he also ran a Latin-jazz group with Palmieri trombonist Barry Rogers.

Moreover, by now the Cuboppers comprised at least two musical generations. The grand master, Dizzy Gillespie, was still active in the idiom he was so largely instrumental in creating. Despite the general takeover of small combos in jazz, he was even intermittently working in the big-band format, if only on record. In November 1960, he recorded Brazilian pianist/composer Lalo Schifrin's "Africana" with a very large, brass-dominated ensemble driven by three Latin percussionists, conga player Candido Camero, Willie Rodriguez on timbales, and Jack del Rio on bongos. In places Schifrin's arrangement made even Stan Kenton sound understated, but the authenticity and bounce of the vocals and percussion, and Gillespie's gusto in solo, gave the piece as a whole considerable authority.

The version of the Cubop standard "Manteca" that Gillespie presented at a Carnegie Hall concert in March was also a staggeringly brass-heavy ensemble with a lineup of five trumpets, four trombones and French horns, one tuba, a saxophonist doubling on flute, bass, and drums and, once more, three Latino percussionists with sharply contrasting backgrounds: the jazz-oriented Ray Barretto on congas, and two Cubans as much at ease with deep Cuban tradition as with Cubop: Julito Collazo and José Mangual on bongos. "Manteca" was an exercise in powerhouse brass bravura, but with an interesting middle section that contrasts with the prevailing blow-'em-down mood, and an excellent percussion duet between Barretto and Mangual.

On the whole, however, the Cubop of the age, like jazz in general, belonged to the small groups, whether with a full Latin rhythm section or a single drum (usually a conga) added to a basic jazz combo. By now, Ray Barretto had become many mainstream jazz groups' congacero of choice, especially for sessions like these. The list of Barretto's jazz collaborations at this time is too long to catalog. One that was particularly worth notice was Oliver Nelson's *Main Stem*, recorded by an outstanding group consisting of trumpeter Joe Newman, Nelson himself on tenor and alto, Hank Jones on piano, George Duvivier on bass, and drummer Charlie Persip. Many of the album's cuts illustrated how congas—in the hands of a man who understood jazz as well as Barretto—could amplify jazz rhythm sections. But they also illustrated the way in which jazz drummers could modify their own approach to meet the percussionist halfway without any sense of lameness or compromise. In "J&B"—a soul-jazz/blues piece in an essentially straight 4/4 rhythm with eight-to-the-bar piano touches—Barretto and drummer Persip work closely, at times trading essentially call-and-response boom-ta-chicks. In "Ho!," Barretto fills in around Persip's busy traps patterns in a collaboration as close as a good Latin percussion session. And in "Latino," where Barretto's playing is nearer to Cuban conga than elsewhere on the album, Persip's patterns run strikingly counter to the underlying flow of rhythm in ways, alien to Cuban music or earlier Cubop, that signaled a new approach to drumming. Seemingly quite un-Latin, in fact, they could not have existed without Latin rhythmic traditions.

Barretto was only one of the conga-players who specialized in playing with non-Latinos. Mongo Santamaria (and on timbales, his frequent partner, Willie Bobo), Patato Valdéz, Candido Camero, and Sabu Martínez all played on a wide range of Cubop recordings in the early 1960s. They all brought different sensibilities to the task at hand. When they worked with jazz rhythm sections that also had a grasp of the fundamentals of clave, the results could be remarkable. Largely forgotten now, guitarist Grant Green won the New Star guitar category of the *DownBeat* critics' poll in 1962. The following year he recorded an album, *The Latin Bit*, backed by a solid group that included Wendell Marshall on bass, Willie Bobo on drums, Patato Valdéz on conga, and Garvin Masseaux (who had been involved with Art Blakey's Afro-jazz experiments in the '50s) on shekere, along with pianist Johnny Acea (who had played in Gillespie's big band in 1950) on some cuts, and tenorist Ike Quebec on two numbers.

This album is a classic example of the importance of the rhythm section in Cubop. Masseaux's playing is spectacular on Parker's "My Little Blue Suede Shoes," which opens as a rumba with a fine '40s-style montuno from Acea before kicking into a straight 4/4 overlaid by a spectacular shimmering checkered pattern. "Besame Mucho" bears out the claim in the notes that Grant could personalize a melody line played almost straight, while Patato Valdéz kept the rhythm

Mongo Santamaria's Latin-jazz-soul groups of the 1960s were not only original but extraordinarily influential. This band, with tenor saxist Hubert Laws and pianist Rodgers Grant, was particularly jazz-oriented. *Frank Driggs Collection*

section well clear of the usual boleritis with a conga pattern in which the second and fourth beats were gaps filled by the bass player.

Latin jazz of whatever kind was a separate subgenre, whether within or parallel to "mainstream" jazz. Just as there had always been, there were also ways in which Latin idioms affected "straight" jazz. Some of these were rhythmic; but, at this point, there may have been a harmonic influence. By the early 1960s, some musicians were beginning to find that the harmonic emphasis of bebop could be its own kind of straitjacket, locking improvisations into a cage of chord changes. The way out that some musicians found may, consciously or unconsciously, have come from the very harmonic simplicity that other players had criticized in Cuban music.

In October 1960, the John Coltrane quartet, with its new pianist McCoy Tyner, recorded a famous version of the show tune, "My Favorite Things." In her recent book, *Saying Something*, Ingrid Monson comments of the differences between Coltrane's recording and more orthodox interpretations that: "The interludes are expanded into two-chord extendable vamps . . . soloing occurs over the vamp sections, not over the chord structure of the composition, as in a more typical jazz usage of a musical theater tune."

This was, in a nutshell, the harmonic basis of Cuban music from the rumba on. The Cuban montuno is in fact often called a vamp, though its function is far more central and positive than most vamps in non-Latin music. A montuno is a bedrock part of a very sophisticated rhythmic structure. Fundamentally, the Euro-American vamp is a device for filling time or providing a link between more important events, and the use of the word as a translation for "montuno" has less to do with accuracy than the absence of a better alternative. Coltrane's 1961 recording *Olé Coltrane* contained an 18-minute cut called "Olé," which even better exemplified the similarity. Though Tyner did not play specific patterns associated with Latin piano, they do sound inspired by Cuban music, even if at one remove. Moreover, he laid down a repetitive foundation for other rhythm instruments to build on, as Latin pianists do, and—like them also—moved away from his montuno-like repeated-pattern approach in solo. Moreover, Elvin Jones's two-measure drum patterns had a call-and-response quality reminiscent of clave, and his improvisations late in the piece worked in the same way that Latin drummers play against the montuno.

The range of Cuban-derived Latin jazz widened during the 1960s. While it is difficult to pin these things down, it seems that the flute-and-fiddle charanga vogue in Latin New York, perhaps together with the jazz-bossa movement, shared responsibility for a rise in the popularity of the flute as a solo instrument in early 1960s jazz. The most famous example, of course, was the music of Herbie Mann. Much of his early 1960s work was jazz-bossa-oriented (see Chapter 6), but he recorded a number of Cuban-inspired albums, including *Right Now* with a group that included Patato Valdéz, and *Latin Fever* with Clark Terry.

Cal Tjader, of course, had already settled into a sort of deanship of Cubop on the West Coast, but his popularity did not dampen his willingness to experiment. At the beginning of the decade, he signed a contract with Verve Records that increased his outreach without diluting his basic style—and gave him the encouragement and perhaps budget to hire a wide range of musicians for recording sessions. His first Verve record, *In a Latin Bag*, involved a new group including the great Armando Peraza (who was later to supply much of the Latin in Santana's Latin-rock) on bongos, along with Paul Horn on flute and soprano sax, Lonnie Hewitt on piano, Al McKibbon on bass, one Chonguito on congas, and Johnny Rae on traps. *In a Latin Bag* showed a range of mood and instrumentation, but few concessions to the rhythmically unhip Anglos here.

Later in the decade, Tjader's exploratory temperament led him into brushes with Eastern music, as well as more modest experiments. The 1967 *Along Comes Cal* was given an unusual sound by the addition of an organist, Derek Smith, to the basic lineup at a time when organ groups—essentially unknown in Latin jazz—were big on the Harlem soul-jazz lounge scene. "Along Comes Mary" is basically a funk/soul organ piece, with Tjader's vibes flowing nicely against the chunky organ groove. By contrast. "Los Bandidos," recorded live with a different group, has experimental piano from Al Zulaica, an unconventional rhythm, and excellent conga from Barretto.

But Tjader's most successful moment of the 1960s was the major hit he scored with "Soul Sauce," an arrangement of Gillespie's "Guachi Guaro" that he had been playing for the past decade! *Soul Sauce* (the album) also included a version of Santamaria's hit "Afro-Blue" (one of the most frequently covered numbers in the entire field) with an unusual lineup for Tjader, consisting of trumpeter Donald Byrd, tenorist Jimmy Heath, guitarist Kenny Burrell, pianist Lonnie Hewitt, bassists Bob Bushnell and Richard Davis, percussionists Armando Peraza and Alberto Valdéz, and drummer Grady Tate.

Perhaps the most adventurous of Tjader's 1960s recordings—because it matched him with the new school of New York heavies—came when he teamed up with the up-and-coming Eddie Palmieri on the LP *El Sonido Nuevo*, whose sidemen were mostly out of Palmieri's band (the main exceptions, trombonists Mark Weinstein and Julian Priester, had both jazz and Latin credits). This recording once more confirmed what Latino musicians had always known: that Tjader's

Latin-jazz chops went deeper than the lightweight pop-jazz too often ascribed to him by the jazz press. If *El Sonido Nuevo* had a fault, it was that Tjader's delicacy sometimes made the macho Latin New York trombone style seem blatting. But mostly the combination worked. The duo reunited for the equally successful Tico release *Bamboleate*. It was notable for an unusual 4/4 piece, "Resemblance," with a singularly pretty theme that was to surface again in Palmieri's "Un Día Bonito" five years later.

A musician as successful as Tjader, of course, inspired imitators and gave other vibraphonists an opening with copycat record executives (and, to be fair, a public with a taste for more of the same). Even in Latin New York, Tjader's success (and his personal appearance at dances in the Bronx) pushed wider the door already somewhat opened by Puente's early vibraphone experiments. Musicians like Pete Terrace, Louie Ramirez, and Joe Cuba, and groups like the La Plata Sextet, gave the quintet sound double authenticity in the Big Mango.

Tjader's influence, of course, also echoed through California Latin jazz. A couple of particularly interesting recordings came from a rather obscure vibes-cum-piano group, the Latin Jazz Quintet, run by a conga player called Juan Amalbert, and fronted on its debut LP by altoist Eric Dolphy. Though the vibes/piano ensemble was hardly revolutionary, Amalbert's first eponymous LP included three particularly intriguing tracks. On one level "Blues in 6/8" was jazz-with-Latin-trimmings on the old order, but the 6/8 pulse—common in Afro-Cuban religious music—gave the conga depth and provided a fresh foundation for excellent soloing by Dolphy. Other changes on the jazz/Latin meld were rung by "Spring Is Here," a mid-tempo Latin jazz ballad over a fast bolero rhythm in which Dolphy played flute, and "Sunday Go Meetin'," whose gospel-based patterns moved it into the soul-jazz-with-conga vein more common on the East Coast.

Amalbert's group, without Dolphy, released two more albums drawn from late 1960 and mid-1961 sessions (combined in a CD re-release, *Hot Sauce*). None of the musicians were "names," but they produced some solid music with two exceptionally interesting pieces. One was a version of Gene Ammons's "Red Top" that opens with a classic *rumbón* in a midtempo son-montuno rhythm that fits the theme perfectly. The arrangement features a complex piano solo with bop overtones but more chording than the classic bebop piano style, along with moments like bluesy montunos. The other outstanding arrangement is a version of Gershwin's "Summertime" as a kind of mini-suite. There is no living-is-easy here: the opening presentation, basically all-percussion except for bass at double tempo under a flowing statement of the theme by the vibes, is taken at a considerable clip before a quick *cierre* resolved into a son montuno under a vibraphone solo. Then a fine piano solo deconstructed the theme with rhythmically fragmented clave-bound chordal phrases interspersed with flashes of single-note bop before the rhythm section picked up the tempo and brought the proceedings back to a reprise of the fast thematic statement.

The one strain in 1960s jazz that did not contribute much to Latin-jazz was the idiom that has come to be called free jazz. Almost by definition, it might seem, the street-consciousness of Latin music and the no-boundaries explorations of the free jazz exponents would be mutually exclusive. In reality things were a little more complicated. In the next decade, some Latin musicians (particularly the more avant-garde Brazilians) would be sympathetic to free jazz. More fundamentally, just as James Joyce or Virginia Woolf had opened new avenues for more conventional narrative novelists, so the free-jazz improvisers eventually enriched the palette of Latin-jazz soloists.

In one case at least, jazz and Latino musicians came together to record a form of free, or at least impressionist, Latin jazz. In October 1964, keyboardist Herbie Hancock recorded an experimental album for Blue Note called *Succotash*, along with Willie Bobo, bassist Paul Chambers, and Osvaldo "Chihuahua" Martínez on congas and bongos. The result was, in some respects, paradoxical. Where Hancock played particularly free, as in "Jack Rabbit," Bobo and Martinez were hobbled by the lack of clave or other rhythmic points of reference. Indeed, the most successful piece from the point of view of the Latino players was the title track, in which Bobo defines the terms with rather raffish clave-based traps (oddly enough, not much supported by Chambers), while Hancock solos in a less expressionist, more stabbing, and more chordal style with (deliberately or out of the logic of Bobo's playing) a good deal of clave-friendly phrasing.

Another encounter of the jazz avant-garde with Cuban music was very different than Hancock's *Succotash*, and not only because its impressionism was emotional rather than technical. In the year when his aficionados were at last given the chance to hear his *Tijuana Moods* a mere half-decade after he recorded it, Charles Mingus also tried to premiere a piece called "Moods in Mambo" at a Town Hall concert as one of a number of compositions for a large ensemble. The concert ran long, and union stage hands aborted it when midnight arrived. It is not clear whether "Moods in Mambo" had been played by the time that happened, and it was only a quarter-century later that the piece saw the light of day again, when Gunther Schuller edited the relevant scores and recorded them as the *Epitaph* album.

"Moods in Mambo," a completely composed piece without solos, is more mood than mambo. It opens with a bell pattern with an ambiguous relationship to clave, and congas with a ritual rather than a dance hall mambo sound. As it develops, the percussion sounds increasingly like something that might have been written for a timpanist by a conservatory composer, rather than something influenced by Cuban drumming. Gunther Schuller, in his notes to the 1989 recording of the piece, rather implausibly compared a passage for two trumpets with "some weird atonal mariachi band," but the only consistent Latin element was the regular pulse of the cencerro.

In its own way, another work also took an emotionally impressionist approach to Latin jazz: Duke Ellington's 1968 *Latin American Suite*. Inspired by a State Department-sponsored tour of South America, this was not only the most complex but (at times) the truest to its sources of Ellington's "Latin" compositions. According to Stanley Dance's notes to the original recording, Ellington did not aim to reinterpret local music: "it reproduces musically the impressions made upon him by those countries and their people." How vivid those impressions were is an open question. The suite had recurring bossa-nova touches that would not have needed a trip to Brazil to acquire, but more frequently the Americanized tango Ellington had been using 40 years earlier.

Interestingly, the simplest part of the suite was also the most sophisticated in its use of Latin influences. Recorded a couple of years after the other sections, the Argentina-inspired "Tina" used only piano, two bassists, and drums. But Ellington's playing was so strongly influenced by authentic tango piano (an Argentinian idiom rarely heard in the U.S.) that it was almost tango piano with jazz elements. Spare though it was in its means, this was to me the most interesting section of the whole work.

The musical success of "Tina" again raises the question why so few post-1940s jazz musicians picked up on the tango—seemingly the most compatible with jazz of all Latin rhythms. For some it may have seemed by now an over-simple or over-familiar rhythm. Yet it seems odd that (the Argentinian Gato Barbieri aside) a full-blooded jazz tango should be so rare. Perhaps it was simply that the durability of Cubop and the almost overwhelming effect of the jazz-bossa *tsunami* left no room for much else in the genre.

I have come across only two other tangos from the 1960s. One was the Cannonball Adderley Sextet's "Tengo Tango," recorded live in Tokyo and issued as part of an album called *Nippon Soul*.[1] It is a classic piece of tough, but good-humored, Adderley soul-jazz. The variations in the rhythm supplied by the tango framework only heightened its effectiveness.

---

[1] Japan has always been one of the most tango-friendly of all non-Latin-American countries. I suspect that without this fact "Tengo Tango" might never has seen the light of day.

A seminal figure in the period bridging the 1960s and 1970s was Argentinian tenorist Gato Barbieri who explored jazz versions of various Latin-American traditions, including tango, at a time when it was not a fashionable activity. *Photo: David Haas*

The other 1960s tango was even more intriguing. The piece was titled "Tango Africaine," and its performer and composer was Chicago pianist Eddie Higgins.[2] Like many of the most authentic tangos themselves, this uses a variant of the classic rhythm, nearer to a straight 4/4 but with the snap on the first beat and the extreme staccato on all four beats that sums up the classic Buenos Aires accordion style. The right hand runs were a blend of bop and Art-Tatum-like late stride. The track's overall feeling moved toward the Latin funk of the era without ever losing its individuality.

If the tango was rare, Mexican music, too, was pretty much off jazz radar during the 1960s. One exception was Dave Brubeck's 1967 *Compadres* with Gerry Mulligan, recorded in April 1968 on a tour of Mexico, a solid addition to the Latin jazz canon. As you might expect given the locale and the source, the music

---

[2] It is the opening cut of Higgins' *Soulero* album for Atlantic.

was mostly Mexico-related and mellow. "Adios Mariquita Linda," for example, opens with the habanera beat that Mexican musicians had brought to New Orleans before the birth of jazz, moving into straight 4/4 after a chorus or two.[3]

Throughout the bossa nova craze, Cuban-derived Latin jazz not only continued to be played, but continued to change and develop. Specifically, it reacted to influences from the hardcore New York Latino scene, which was itself in a state of considerable flux. First, the arrival of a new Cuban dance, the pachanga, had brought with it a vogue for the flute-and-fiddle charangas that played it.[4] Second, the mambo big bands were finally faced with the same economic problems that had pretty much wiped out the big swing bands a decade earlier, complicated by the fact that the mambo sound had been around so long. Third, a new generation of musicians was about to reformulate New York's complex mix of *típico* Cuban roots with black influences, developing a local conjunto style and blending it not only with newer forms of jazz used in innovative ways, but with rhythm-and-blues.

The major names in mambo fought back by looking for ways to refresh the basic big-band sound. In part this happened perforce, when they added a solo flutist in order to play the popular pachangas. As his 1962 *El Rey Tito* showed, Puente coped just fine with the arrival of the pachanga and its attendant charanga sound, not merely adding a flute and a fiddle but adapting them to his basic big-band sound with, in for example "Malanga Con Yuca," and "Tokyo de Noche," jazz-influenced solos of fire and elegance; and in his "Oye Como Va" (as borrowed by Santana) and above all "Africa Habla," blending charanga fiddle guajeos with walls of heavy brass. A year later, *The New Sound of Machito* also contained some pachangas (and a "pachanga merengue"). But the "new sound" largely consisted in the addition of flute solos to the brass as a sop to the pachangeros. The album's best cut, "Alex Mambo," was in the now-classic vein, with hard-edged tenor solos and driving trumpet.

The New York big-band sound survived—and not only in the persons of the big three. Quixotically, perhaps, Orlando Marin formed a big band about this time, and Joe Quijano also included several big band cuts on his 1963 release, *Latin Touch*. Among them were ingenious and strongly swing-influenced

---

[3] There was also, of course, Herb Alpert's Tijuana Brass, many of whose arrangements were far better than is generally recognized. But the Tijuana Brass falls outside the scope of this book even on the most liberal interpretation of jazz.

[4] Why the chachachá, equally born of the charanga, had not not achieved equal popularity years earlier is one of the mysteries of music history. The reason may simply have been that the big mambo bands were so hot at that time.

arrangements of several mainstream hits of the time—"Maria," "April in Portugal," "Never on Sunday"—as well as a nifty "What Kind of Fool Am I?" with flute and two trumpets, and some oddities, including a boisterous mix of the twist and chachachá called "Yeah Yeah." Nevertheless, though Machito and Tito Puente held on, the sun set on the glory days of the big-band mambo on the Palladium's last night, in 1966. And indeed the symbolism was doubled in that the bands playing that final gig were Eddie Palmieri, the charanga Orquesta Broadway, and Pete Rodriguez' boogaloo band.

The pachanga/charanga wave of the early 1960s and the conjunto era that followed it both signaled a return to the *típico* as well as an economic climate in which small was better. But if the charanga appeared to signal the beginning of an eclipse for one generation of bandleaders, it also provided a launching pad for the next one. One musician who made the switch from sideman to bandleader was Ray Barretto, who formed the Charanga Moderna for a Riverside recording date. Interestingly enough, given Barretto's jazz background, *Pachanga with Barretto* was basically a version of the elegant pre-funky charanga favored by Cuba's Orquesta Aragón. Barretto would do some interesting things with the charanga format, but this first release played it strictly down the middle. On Barretto's *Latino!*, released in September, his Charanga Moderna was joined by the great Cuban trumpeter El Negro Vivar, saxist/fiddler Chombo Silva, and Willie Rodriguez. Barretto at the time described this release as "descarga," thus bidding for two hot sectors of the Latin market. In fact it was an early version of the charanga-plus-brass that Cuban bands like Van Van are still playing. *Latino!* is notable for particularly long and coherent flute lines, nearer to jazz than to the more fragmented phrasings of charanga, and for fierce soloing from Vivar and Silva. It is also full of original touches like the trio of Vivar, fiddler Stancerone, and Barretto (during "Exodus"), and a passage in "Descarga la Moderna," in which flute and/or fiddles played Cuban heads answered by jazz-oriented trumpet and sax in a cross-cultural call-and-response.

A new musician and important figure on the New York scene reacted with typical eccentricity to the charanga challenge. Rather than a flute-and-fiddle group, pianist Eddie Palmieri founded a group with a flute-and-trombone frontline that he called La Perfecta, and his older brother Charlie promptly dubbed a "trombanga." La Perfecta's first two records did not come across as particularly revolutionary (it was a measure of how far Palmieri was to travel in a decade that several cuts were versions of the danzon-cha, a mix of the nineteenth-century danzón and its descendant, the chachachá). But the third release, *Lo Que Traigo Es Sabroso*, brought him a major single hit (by the New York Latin music indus-

From the early 1960s through the 1970s, pianist Eddie Palmieri was consistently one of the most creative of New York Latino pianists, using jazz tinges (notably a McCoy Tyner influence) to expand New York salsa. In the 90s, he has turned this experience into an individual Latin-jazz sound. *Photo: David Haas*

try's rather modest standards) in the form of "Muñeca"—a number irresistible for danceability, good-humor, and lightness of touch, with a marvellous lead vocal by Palmieri's long-time singer, Ismael Quintana.

Palmieri did not originate the trombone frontline—the Puerto Rican band-leader and singer Mon Rivera had used one before him—but the adoption of the "trombone conjunto" (minus flute) as one of the hip '60s sounds of hardcore New York salsa stemmed largely from La Perfecta. Its sound was indirectly influenced by the 1950s trombone duets of J. J. Johnson and Kai Winding, because trombonist Barry Rogers, who wrote most of Palmieri's early trombone charts, idolized them as a young musician. Indeed, though the salsa trombone sound soon developed a flavor all its own, the ghostly presence of Jay and Kai hovered over both La Perfecta and its Latin New York imitators for years.

So, before long, did the phantom of a more recent jazz development: the impressionism and above all modalism of McCoy Tyner and Chick Corea, both of them major influences on Palmieri himself. They first surfaced in the title cut of Eddie Palmieri's first major hit album, *Azucar Pa'Ti*. This was notable for a long piano solo that opened with a brief, early version of Palmieri's McCoy Tyner-influenced modalism, very much in a contemporary jazz vein, that Palmieri was to extend and develop over most of the next decade. In the title cut, Palmieri kept it brief, but built on it using a guajeo rhythm pattern in the left hand that supported the right hand almost like a boogie woogie ostinato.

By the mid-1960s, Palmieri's La Perfecta was about the biggest band on the Latin New York scene, and its trombone sound was imitated by a whole generation of younger musicians. Then, in 1968, Palmieri disbanded. It was the end of an era—but far from the end of the world as some of his fans believed. The following year was to bring the first swallow of a long, hot creative summer in the form of Palmieri's album *Justicia*, the beginning of a number of extraordinarily important Palmieri releases using groups put together for the particular recording sessions.

Justicia, the most experimental of Palmieri's late 1960s recordings, was notable for an early version of his moody modal intros in "My Spiritual Indian." This piece also premiered a brief version of a solo that he was to expand for years, which set modal phrases against—or even into—montuno patterns and augmented Cuban-derived piano patterns with harmonically advanced chordings (a practice by no means confined to Palmieri alone). *Justicia's* other experimental cut was "Verdict on Judge Street," in which Palmieri again uses the ploy of a left-hand *guajeo* à la boogie bass, contrasted with chording in jazz vein in the right hand. A certain ambiguity pervades the whole piece, enhanced by quite un-Latin trap-drumming with a wash of cymbals. Unlike the jazz-top-Latin-bottom of much Latin jazz, the effect is that of a musical layer cake: jazz top and bottom, Latin filling. The tonal density just before the piece's resolution is also remarkable, with dissonant piano (including the forearm-smash tone-clusters Palmieri had borrowed from Tyner) and aggressive drumming with almost an Elvin Jones touch.[5]

Eddie Palmieri got early encouragement—and a record contract—from another seminal figure of 1960s Latin jazz, Alegre label founder Al Santiago. Santiago, a Latin-jazz enthusiast, was one of many Latinos whose musical influence was far

---

[5] *Justicia* was not the only significant Latin New York recording of 1969. Historically, its importance was at least equaled by the release of *El Malo*, the first and most jazz-influenced album by Willy Colón, the major star and most creative head of the post-bugalú generation. Colón was not directly influenced by jazz, but El Malo, along with the echoes of La Perfecta inherent in the two-trombone frontline and Colón 's own valve-trombone playing, rather unexpectedly included an instrumental track called "Jazzy" that lived up to its name.

greater than their economic success. One of his early critical successes was the 1961 album *Jazz Espagnole* with percussionist Sabu Martínez, pianist/vibraphonist Louie Ramirez, trumpeter Marty Sheller, and saxist Bobby Porcelli. But Santiago's major impact on the New York Latin scene came later that year when, inspired by a famous set of jam sessions recorded by the Cuban Panart label in the 1950s, he organized a series of recordings under the name of the Alegre All Stars that provided some of 1960s Cuban-derived Latin jazz's finest moments.

The Alegre All Stars recordings, which took place intermittently over a six-year period, were unique. The personnel varied from recording to recording, but were always phenomenal, and always built round the great Charlie Palmieri at the piano, tenorist Chombo Silva, bassist Bobby Rodriguez, and Kako on timbales. Along with this basic cadre on one or more of the All-Stars recordings were Barry Rogers; Johnny Pacheco (playing flute on the first of the series); merengue vocalist Dioris Valladares; and an amazing list of other pillars of the New York Latin scene. The repertoire included numbers created in the studio as well as Latin and jazz standards. The music was mostly classic descarga, building on fairly brief head arrangements, a great deal of soloing, and (which separated them from "mainstream" Latin jazz) excellent vocals with coro sections and all.

The splendors of this series are too many to list in detail, but they included (on the 1961 first release) a phenomenal version of "Almendra," originally a 1930s danzón, that the Alegre All Stars turns into a loose descarga startlingly different from the original, with remarkable bop-infused group vocal passages as well as fiery solo work. The group's second album includes one of the best versions of the "Peanut Vendor" ever recorded (with a remarkable vocal coro built on the dissonant trumpet section in the Stan Kenton version) among other high spots. The fourth in the series—released in 1964 before volume three, as part of an elaborate spoof about missing tapes—is notable for a searing "Manteca."

Neither the Alegre All Stars nor Santiago's other records made any kind of splash outside the hardcore Latin market, in part because Alegre was a small label with no commercial clout, but also, perhaps, because the band's approach to jazz was out of kilter with what was happening in the mainstream jazz market. The Alegre All Stars were not "cool," they were not "out," and they were far from experimental: they were joyous and unself-conscious, their solo style echoed small-band jump almost as much as bebop, and they swung like the devil, a virtue not much prized in jazz at the time.

The Alegre All Stars notwithstanding, the jazz impulse was gradually fading in the music of Latin New York throughout the 1960s. But even a relatively small market like this was not a monolith. At a time when the *típico* movement that would dominate the early 1970s was beginning to gather strength, while funk was starting to dominate in jazz and Latin soul in the barrio, a remarkable recording was issued that prefigured the music of 1970s and 1980s groups such as the Fort Apache Band in its mix of jazz with deep Afro-Cuban percussion. *Cuban Roots* by Mark Weinstein and his Cosa Nueva Orchestra, issued on the minute Musicor label, was one of the decade's most remarkable sessions. A trombonist who claimed Kai Winding, Bill Harris, J.C. Higginbotham, and John Coltrane as his influences, Weinstein had already played with a list of both Latin and jazz musicians longer than your arm. Now he put together a band including Mario Rivera on baritone sax, Chick Corea on piano, the outstanding young bassist Bobby Valentin, and a five-man percussion section comprising some of the most rootsy drummers in the city, among them Kako and Julito Collazo. The resulting cuts blended hair-raising trombone, avant-garde sax, and outer-rim piano with the deepest of Afro-Cuban rhythms, religious and secular. Until you've heard the Lennon-McCartney "Michelle" done as a rumba abierta, you haven't lived!

1966 was the Year of the Latin bugalú, New York's version of the ever-growing three-way Latin-jazz-R&B fusion that was the most fundamental contribution of the 1960s to jazz and Latin music's joint history. The bugalú —in its Latin form essentially a chachachá with a backbeat—was one of a number of amiably rowdy new Latin dance rhythms of the mid-1960s, developed by a Latino generation that had been educated in New York public schools along with soul-listening blacks and rock-enthusiast whites. Bugalú (and shingaling, which had only a moment in the sun) tended to be sung in English, jala-jala in Spanish. Later Latin soul recordings, as the label suggests, were a bit more soul- than R&B-oriented.

If Latin-jazz owed a debt to Al Santiago, so did the Latin bugalú. Santiago produced one of the first bugalú albums, *Pete Rodriguez y Su Conjunto's Latin Boogaloo*, giving it a lot of jazz elements. It was a quirky recording all round. The opening cut, "Pete's Boogaloo"—described as a "descarga boogaloo"— begins as straight conjunto before R&B-tinged subversion sets in. The piano solo opens with a Cuban sweep, then starts throwing jazz phrases in among the montunos and floreos. The intro of "Do the Boogaloo" is a blues phrase transmuted into a montuno, and a Spanish lead vocal is set against a coro in English. And so on and, very pleasingly, on.

"Pete's Boogaloo," which introduced a new generation of players, was a fairly substantial hit. But like early rock and roll, whose first chart-topper was produced by a bunch of hard-bitten veterans called Bill Haley and His Comets, the Latin soul era's first really major success was recorded by a man who had been around more than a little while. Joe Cuba's "Bang Bang," from his Tico album *Wanted*

Dead or Alive, was a disreputable classic—rowdy, jokey, double-entendre-laden—with a general air of amiable mayhem. If you listen hard, you can still hear the vibraphone that formed part of Cuba's basic sound, which was that of a Tjader-type quintet plus rabble-rousing.

The bugalú's second year in the sun also brought a number of new musicians on stage. The title track of pianist Johnny Colon's *Boogaloo Blues* was the idiom's next major hit. Colon's jaunty and quintessentially New York style showed jazz influence along with the R&B: in his blues piano at the opening of title cut, for example, and in the chordings of the opening piano guajeo in "Jumpy." A feature of the style and the period (though not of *Boogaloo Blues*) was the two-trombone front line patterned on Eddie Palmieri's La Perfecta (minus flute), with echoes of J. J. Johnson and Kai Winding, courtesy Barry Rogers's early arrangements.

Neither the black boogaloo nor the Latino bugalú had more than marginal impact on jazz. However, Dizzy Gillespie, in a relatively obscure album called *The Melody Lingers On*, covered Joe Cuba's "Bang Bang," adding his own horn comments (and verbal "ooby-doos") to Cuba's chorus and basic *guajeo*, while James Moody kicked in a tenor solo half R&B spoof and half West-African high-life in spirit.

But the mainstream jazz players were really just scratching the surface of the boogaloo. It was the not-easily classifiable dance-oriented bands that most effectively mined all the Afro-Latin-funk veins available. Willie Bobo's recording *uno dos tres* opens with "Boogaloo in Room 802," a funk-soul riff-kicker with brief ballady muted cornet and wailing R&B/jump blues tenor. Above all, its punchy dance groove set the tone for most of the other tracks. But the boogaloo-git-down ethos didn't reign at the expense of creativity. You can't—or at least I can't—fault a band that sets Lennon and McCartney's "Michelle" to a boogaloo beat.

As Latin-based fusion gradually took over from Cubop, and as non-Latinos became more adept at handling even the percussion for these non-traditional rhythm sections, the living got ever-tougher for Latino musicians working in the jazz world. Some—mostly those on the West Coast—either continued to scuffle or formed their own groups. Others literally or metaphorically took the plane East, including Ray Barretto, who signed with Fania Records and "came home" to a barrio audience that had never really been his core constituency. As he explained it to me some years later, he had spent too long trying to replicate "El Watusi" and got sidetracked.

In any event, Baretto's timing was perfect. His proven talent, after all, was for combining Latin elements with African-American, and he had a lot of soul-jazz experience. He blew Latin New York away with his first recording for Fania, *Acid*. A high spot of the title tune itself, a slow son montuno, was a muted trumpet solo with a lot of Gillespie-style half-valving and a bop approach in general. But most of the African-American elements in *Acid* were R&B rather than strictly jazz-based. The only cut with a major jazz element was the last and longest, the eight-minute-plus "Espiritu Libre." Here Barretto claimed the right to be avant-garde. It opens with free percussion, followed by fine "out" piano and free trumpet over a percussion jam held together by bass and cencerro. While the complexity of Latin rhythms has sometimes hampered jazz soloists, the free elements here are effective precisely because the underlying clave and the two rhythm instruments provide a center as much psychological as musical.

Palmieri and Barretto were major musicians and important contributors to 1960s music, Latino and non-Latino. But nobody was as important as Mongo Santamaria as a catalyst for the growth of Latin-jazz-funk, not so much in developing the music (though he stuck with it perhaps more consistently than other Latinos) but by constantly playing it for mostly black audiences. Like Barretto, Santamaria was given a grab at the brass ring of bandleaderdom by the charanga movement, and like Barretto he quickly moved from charanga-straight to jazz-influenced blends. He left Cal Tjader's band when Tjader signed with Verve, and launched out on his own by taking over an existing charanga and renaming it La Sabrosa.

Santamaria's first recording of the 1960s, however, was not a charanga. The music originally issued on the LPs *Our Man in Havana* and *Bembé*[6] was recorded in Cuba with Cuban musicians far more rootsy than what the U.S. listeners had previously heard, including the Afro-religious singer Merceditas Valdes; tres player Nino Rivera; Carlos Embales, who was associated with the percussion street rumba; and Mongo's cousin Luis Santamaria singing a couple of songs to Shango. (A "bembé" is a performance of music from the Yoruba-derived lucumí religion, and the sacred batá drums were included among the instruments—perhaps for the first time on a "mainstream" U.S. recording). Though it was not the first Afro-Cuban religious percussion released on a jazz label, it was still heady stuff.

It was also something of a diversion. Much of the music scattered over the group's following albums, *Sabroso, Mas Sabroso*, and *Arriba—La Pachanga* was in the straight charanga style. But La Sabrosa as an adventurous group staffed by Latinos entirely comfortable with jazz, including the great Cuban flute-player Rolando Lozano, José "Chombo" Silva (the violinist/tenor saxist who had been

---

[6] Reissued together on CD as *Our Man In Havana*.

part of the mid-1950s Cuban jam sessions), Machito pianist René Hernández, Willie Bobo, and Victor Venegas, one of the finest of Latino bassists.

Much of what they recorded was highly cross-cultural. "Guaguanco Mania" contained booting tenor from Silva, an Al Cohn admirer, and a fine trumpet solo in the jazz-influenced Cuban conjunto style that developed in the 1940s. In "Chombo Chavada," on which Silva played both sax and violin, his fiddle solo—though as Cuban as it was jazz-derived—was full of bluesy intonations. And as Robert Farris Thompson pointed out, Silva's jazz tenor playing meshed with the charanga-style fiddle guajeos whose smooth rhythmic drive was a fine foil for the sax (rather than just a sweetener), while their repetition acted like riffs under a swing band solo. Finally, the eight-minute "Para Tí" was another harbinger of change: a descarga (or jam) that opens with intertwining saxes and brass mambo riffs leading into a pure swing tenor solo from Silva interspersed with section brass, lovely open swing-based trumpets, and driving chase choruses. The cross-fertilization became even more heady when Silva's jazz tenor went head-to-head with purely Cuban flute.

Early in 1962, Santamaria abandoned his charanga La Sabrosa in favor of an even more Latin-jazz oriented septet, which was to produce a number of crossover hits. The first of these was "Afro Blue," whose pretty and catchy flute part and vibraphone solo were set against complex percussion with a 6/8 overlay linking it to the most Afro-Cuban of percussion. The most successful was "Watermelon Man."

Santamaria was, in fact, shifting base even before he dropped the charanga format. *Mighty Mongo* and *Viva Mongo*, mostly recorded at the Blackhawk under the name of Mongo Santamaria and His Orchestra[7] mixed straight charanga with a great deal of Latin-jazz—notably a sparkling uptempo "All the Things You Are" that effortlessly combines jazz and Latin elements. This was a classic example of what Latin jazz is about: drive, joy, and swing.

By July, when Santamaria recorded *Go Mongo* for Riverside, he had dropped the charanga format in favor of one trumpet and two saxes doubling on flute, with Chick Corea in the piano chair. It was appropriate that this LP was reissued as part of a twofer called *Skins*, since it leavened Latin jazz with some impressive Afro-Latin rhythms. The most interesting of several fine pieces (all of which essentially use strong jazz elements to augment their basic Cubanism) was "Congo Blue."[8] It featured fine sax work from new band member Pat Patrick (a

---

[7] Reissued on CD together as *Mongo Santamaria at the Blackhawk*.

[8] Not to be confused with "Afro Blue."

longtime Sun Ra sideman), and a memorable comping line from Corea that combined soul/gospel and Cuban piano—another harbinger of Latin funk.

By 1963, Santamaria was well launched on his fusion path. Three of the numbers the band played at the early fall 1963 gig preserved in the recording *Mongo at the Village Gate* were in Santamaria's developing fusion vein. "Fatback" opened with a flute duet before moving into an effectively jaunty part-Tijuana Brass, part funk-jazz riff theme, with Santamaria's congas giving what might otherwise have been amiable fluff a remarkable drive. "Mongo's Groove" had even more of a soul-jazz funk feeling, with a nice bluesy piano solo. "Creole" opened with a strange eight-to-the-bar-feel rhythm after New Orleans marching-band type traps, settled down into a soul-jazz strutter, then reverted to boogie-woogie again. And "The Jungle Bit," again more funk than Latin, included a fine bluesy piano solo with clave patterns hidden in it.

By mid-decade, Santamaria was playing a pivotal role in developing Latin-funk-jazz. On his final recording for Riverside, *Mongo Explodes*, he was joined by two soloists better known in the soul-jazz arena: reed-player Hubert Laws on piccolo, flute, and tenor sax, and—on some tracks—cornetist Nat Adderley. Perhaps the most impressive cut is "Skins." This is like a mini-suite, with an interesting head, breaking into very fast percussion with a bop theme over it, a fine piano solo based on a simple, unusual *guajeo*, and then, after a horn break like an inner coda, a percussion *rumbón* to ride the piece out. A jaunty version of "Fatback" with a fine, uncredited R&B-soul singer was R&B/funk with Latin trimmings.

Surprisingly—given that he had prefigured it since the early 1960s—Santamaria did not altogether ride the boogaloo wave, perhaps because he had moved to Columbia Records, which (as titles like *Hey Let's Party*, and *El Pussy Cat* suggest) had mass-pop aims. Still, Santamaria's eclectic approach could turn anything to reasonably good purpose. *Hey Let's Party* was a mix of then-hits ("Walk on By," "Satisfaction"), the transcendently dopey "Louie Louie," and a version of the big-band standard "In the Mood" as a son montuno spinoff. But the recording was given coherency by the developing funk/Latin mix of Santamaria's rhythm section, with its strong Cuban roots, and by consistently good soloing, notably by trumpeter Marty Sheller and saxists Hubert Laws and Bobby Capers. By contrast, Santamaria's excellent 1966 album, *El Bravo*—named for a cut that aimed at an "El Watusi" type hit (it even used the same vocalist as Barretto's original)—was mostly fairly *típico*. Even the fine jazz solos from Hubert Laws and Bobby Capers were typical of those in hardcore mambo, and much of Marty Sheller's equally fine trumpet was solidly in the new Latin tradition.

The Latin jazz spirit was also alive in the descarga movement, which continued to rumble on. Not all the recordings issued under the descarga rubric were free-for-alls. Among the best were the Salsa All-Stars sessions. Once more everybody who was anybody was playing, but Al Santiago's production and Louie Ramirez's arrangements, as tight as they were fiery, assured a killer session such as true looseness rarely produces.

The development of mainstream Latin-funk-jazz was attended by considerable irony. One of Mongo Santamaria's first really major fusion hits was "Watermelon Man." Yet the piece was Herbie Hancock's, and his original soul-jazz version was recorded by a star lineup including the great Dexter Gordon on tenor sax, Freddie Hubbard on trumpet, Butch Warren on bass, and Billy Higgins on drums.

Ironically, too, Hancock's version was already heavily Latin under a proto-jazz-funk topsoil: the horns were backed by montuno-type bass and piano, and Hancock's fine solo drifted between blues and montunos. The collective effect of the rhythm section was prophetic: its basic groove seemed to stick roughly to clave, but it gradually transmogrified into funk, largely because Higgins set up a repetitive matching groove on traps under the piano montunos, rather than improvising against them as a Latin drummer would.[9]

Hancock also got together with trumpeter Freddy Hubbard, bassist Ron Carter, and drummer Tony Williams to make "Cantaloupe Island," a sequel to "Watermelon Man." This has an even more pronounced Latin piano groove as part of its basic theme, and Carter's bass line is again essentially a montuno; but Williams's drumming is simpler, using a predominantly straight-four cymbal pattern that tilts the whole effect of the rhythmic ensemble away from Latin-jazz toward funk.

All this represented a second stage of jazz/Latin absorption, and one that explains why the 1950s get most of the credit for Latin-jazz creativity, while the mid-1960s—equally rich in a different way—have been passed over. Not only had jazz audiences come to take the whole subject for granted, but jazz musicians were making Latin elements into something new rather than incorporating them into jazz unchanged. Herbie Hancock's March 1965 "Maiden Voyage" is a case in point. Here the Latinisms in the basic rhythmic groove open out and become much lighter, and are mostly sustained on cymbals. This is not yet fully formed funk, but it has a "mainstream" jazz quality that—though it could not exist without its earlier and more Latin stages—was no longer obviously "Latin."

---

[9] Mongo Santamaria's 1963 cover of "Watermelon Man" must surely have been the only time an Afro-Cuban made it to the top of the charts with a tune written by an African-American.

One of the finest examples of mid-'60s Latin-funk jazz was recorded in May. It was a release that not only rang the changes on Latin, Caribbean, jazz, soul, and blues, but was rich in good humor in the bargain. Along with conga player Montego Joe, *Arriba! Con Montego Joe* included Leonard Goines on trumpet, Al Gibbons on tenor sax and flute, Chick Corea on piano, Edgar Gomez on bass, Milford Graves on drums and timbales, and percussionist Robert Crowder. The cheerful "Fat Man" combined an irresistible son montuno underpinning with a wonderfully crisp guiro part (very rare for Latin/jazz/soul recordings) under bluesy piano and various vocal carrying-on, a nice soul-blues riff melody, an almost R&B-styled sax solo, soul-jazz trumpet, and all the fixin's. Several cuts on the album were notably percussion heavy.

The same kind of transformation was particularly obvious in Montego Joe's LP, *Wild & Warm*. As the original notes made clear, the musicians were specifically aiming at an album with commercial appeal. And though this was a varied album (it even had some contemporary Ghanaian influence), the majority style was one or another form of Latin-jazz-funk: "Same Old Same Old," a Latin-turning-to-funk/soul-blues with a riff theme; "Give it Up," a funk blues with clave patterns and a strong Mongo Santamaria influence; and even in the good-humored foolery of the delightful soul-jazz "Ouch."

If mainstream soul-jazz was moving toward funk via various Latin tinges, so was the R&B-related style popularized by Mongo Santamaria. The title cut of Willie Bobo's *Spanish Grease* album, which rightly became a fairly major hit, mixed funk and R&B with quite classic Cuban elements. Bobo gave the ballad "Hurt So Bad" (originally a Little Anthony and the Imperials number) a strong Afro-Cuban underpinning along with lyrical bop horns and jazz-ballad, single-string guitar.

On the African-American side, much of the innovative Latin-jazz-funk fusions were made by musicians who never made major headlines. Among the most innovative was Henry Lee "Pucho" Brown, who had taken over the Joe Panama Sextet in 1959. During the very early 1960s, Pucho's band included several musicians who subsequently joined Mongo Santamaria.[10] After an unsuccessful single for Epic in 1963, Pucho made two LPs for Prestige in 1966.[11] The

---

[10] Though recordings give a false impression of stability, the interwoven New York jazz and Latin scene was like Damon Runyan's permanent floating crap game. Among the musicians who played for Pucho at one time or another were Chick Corea, who of course went on to jazz glory; saxist Bobby Capers; percussionist Steve Berrios, Jr; and bassist William Allen. Many of these were also to play not only for Mongo Santamaria, but for a range of other bands.

[11] And several more in a similar vein thereafter.

first, recorded in February, was called *Tough*, and contained something of the same mix of material as Bobo's *Spanish Grease*. The horn work was by players out of the bebop tradition, and bop touches surfaced throughout. By contrast the rhythm work, while fusion-oriented, leaned heavily on the Latin side of the mix.

Pucho demanded that his musicians be able to play jazz, funk, and Latin equally well, and it showed. Vibes playing in the Puente/Tjader lineage mixed with the Cubop horns to provide stylistic variety. A Burt Bacharach piece plus two Lennon/McCartney numbers added the hit-coverage that working dance bands have always needed to provide. Most notably, Pucho performed a sparklingly imaginative version of "Yesterday" with vibes-led melody line echoed and transmuted in places by piano montunos over a guajira-like rhythm. The second section makes the guajira conversion official with a gorgeous montuno and a classic coro vocal that totally abandons the original song. *Saffron Soul*, recorded nine months later, includes much the same mix, absent Lennon and McCartney (although it again drew on the Bacharach songbook for an okay version of "Alfie"), plus a wonderfully full-blooded version of Ellington's old pseudo-Latin "Caravan," whose pleasures include an assonant piano guajeo that gave the theme a real Latin flavor.

By decade's end, the various Latin-tinged funk sounds were increasingly taking over the mainstream jazz scene. Nat Adderley, one of the creators of the Urfunk soul-jazz sound, headed a session with tenorist Joe Henderson and pianist Joe Zawinul that illustrates this trend. Zawinul's "The Scavenger" has a heavy funk-soul groove, but the basic Latin three-two rhythm still haunts both piano and bass. Zawinul's riff is the funk equivalent of a montuno; a Latin influence, in other words.

By now, an increasing number of younger musicians were adopting various aspects of Latin-jazz-funk as at least a semi-permanent part of their arsenal. One was Joe Henderson, who played on the Adderley session and was to be a significant figure in West Coast Latin-tinged jazz. Henderson's 1967 recording, *The Kicker*, contained a fine example of early-stage funk fusion jazz of the kind that was to be mostly associated with the 1970s. Henderson's "Mamacita" had a basic clave feel, explicit in the woodblock pattern and implicit in the bass patterns. But the theme was pure hard-bop, while the horns, as well as the rhythm instruments, played essentially Latin-based funk.

Along with *The Kicker*, two recordings by young but established artists give some idea of the range of options in the new Latinized funk jazz at the end of the 1960s. In May, Herbie Hancock recorded *Power to the People* with an early version of the Herbie Hancock Sextet. The title cut itself moves to a clearly Latin-influenced beat with a 3/2 clave feel. The rhythm is interestingly transmuted, with a held third beat that shortens, syncopates, and accentuates the fourth one, creating an effect like a mix of tango, traditional clave, and the heavy final beat of the Cuban conga or Jamaican mento (and thus the fourth-beat SKA of reggae guitar). Just as significantly, drummer Jack de Johnette trampolines off Ron Carter's heavy ostinato bassline like Cuban percussion off the bass montuno. This is in strong contrast to "Afro-Centric" on the same album, which is free-jazz influenced, or "Black Narcissus," whose bass ostinatos—pretty and faintly Brazilian sounding, partly because of a repeated held note—are without any suggestion of the 3/2 clave or its Afro-Brazilian equivalents.

Trumpeter Donald Byrd's *Fancy Free*, recorded the same month, includes three cuts with clear jazz/Latin interactions, mostly in the rhythm section. The opening light riff tune of "The Uptowner" stakes out territory somewhere between soul jazz and the Tijuana Brass. The horns play straight post-bop jazz while the rhythm section sets up a funk/soul-jazz/Latin beat with inflections oddly like the held-note rhythms of which the old barrelhouse piano players like Montana Taylor were fond. "Weasil" features a similar, one-measure jazz-habanera pattern, but a duologue between the bass and electric piano and the specific ways in which the drummer keys into it hint at a two-bar process, accentuated by a horn riff under the soloing that becomes part of the rhythm section. The album's title track builds up an even more complex rhythmic sandwich in which the hi-hat plays straight 4/4, the piano a simple two-note montuno-like pattern (second note held), and the conga player a complex non-clave, single bar pattern. This is something unlikely to have developed without the Latin tinge, though not even the conga part is in itself particularly Latin.

The Latin-jazz-funk phenomenon that was to be one of the most significant jazz movements (for good and ill) of the 1970s had both deep and complex roots both in and stretching back before the 1960s. A mingling of the 1950s Cubop and soul-jazz strains, the impact of Mongo Santamaria's popularity among younger African-Americans, and the bugalú movement in Latin New York, were only some of its most important strands. But it was the 1960s that brought them all together. And they were, during the 1970s, to continue coalescing in ways that took Latin elements even further under the surface of American music. I once asked Ralph Mercado, one of Latin New York's major promoters for several decades, what was Job One. "Come out smokin' and kick ass," he said. He was talking specifically about Eddie Palmieri, but it was a good motto for the 1960s as a whole, and perhaps their most important legacy to the 1970s.

◇ **8** ◇

Got That Funky, Funky Feelin':

The 1970s

The seeming triumph of Latin-jazz-funk during the 1970s, and the healthy strain of experimentalism with which it coexisted and at times overlapped, both parts formed of a process of absorption and combination of elements that might seem on the surface mutually hostile. In particular, they enabled the Brazilian influences that had constituted a separate entity during the 1960s to become part of a greater whole without simply dissolving into some amorphous mix.

The music of Brazilian musicians Flora Purim and (in particular) Airto Moreira provides a good example of this wider movement, which at times involved the experimental use of traditional or semi-traditional material. They were an advance guard of a second, post-bossa-nova wave of musicians who came to the U.S. both because life was getting tough in Brazil politically, and because the rise of MPB ("música popular brasileira") and the singer-songwriter in Brazil (as in the U.S.) was making it harder for instrumentally oriented musicians to achieve success. Purim and Airto had long been an item (they would marry in 1972), and their careers tended to revolve around each other. In the U.S., she found her feet marginally before he did, and was working regularly while he was still sitting in on jam sessions to make connections.

As Airto tells it, his entry into the big time came when Miles Davis asked Joe Zawinul whether he knew any unusual percussionists. Zawinul, who had run across Airto in jam sessions, recommended him, and that led to Airto joining Davis for two years. The result was a revolution in percussion, which moved it from a structural role to one of providing accent and color, but at the same time opened up its potential enormously. Davis, Airto has said in an interview quoted in *The Brazilian Sound*, "really didn't want me to play rhythm all the time. He wanted me to play colors and sounds more than rhythm." And, as he told me in a conversation back in the mid-'70s: "To me percussion can be just colors in music. I relate sounds and colors a lot. You can play a dark sound and you can play a very light sound."

Airto was a small and largely uncredited contributor to Davis's music, providing a major jazz-rock-fusion experiment with a tiny Brazilian tinge. But the association opened doors. Moreover, it was his acquaintance with Zawinul that led to his playing on the first recording by Weather Report, though he refused to join the group as a regular member, partly because he was working for Miles Davis, but also (so he told me in an interview in the mid-1970s) because he found Weather Report's ambitions to be too grandiose and commercial.

In 1970 Airto also made the first recording under his own name, *Natural Feelings*, for the Buddah label. Purim shared the vocals with him, and two other old cronies and luminaries of the Brazilian jazz scene were on board, Hermeto Pascoal on keyboards and Sivuca on guitar. But *Natural Feelings* is 100 percent Airto, a quirky, creative mixture of all sorts of disparate elements both experimental and thoroughly downhome, with ample charm and variety. "Terror," its longest track, opens with bird noises, bells, and other trappings of progressive 1970s fusion, but it soon begins pulling in more traditional, or at least familiar elements—down-home acoustic guitar, Brazilian percussion, Amerindian-tinged flute, moody jazz-rock for organ and drums—before the ominous free-form overtones returned. Airto and his kindred spirits also took a fresh approach to much simpler idioms, without losing any of their intrinsic value: the attractive acoustic guitar of the samba-like "Alue"; "Xibaba"'s cuica and organ; the affably eccentric "Andei," in which Purim's vocal was set against harpsichord from Pascoal and bossa-ish rhythms; or the traditional flute and fast, light rhythmically complex melody line of "Frevo."

Airto's *Seeds on the Ground* LP for Buddah was, like its predecessor, both highly acoustic and highly (though not traditionally) Brazilian. Two Airto comments quoted on the liner notes sum up this remarkably rich recording, so fresh and yet so close to its roots: "the world of sound is very big and unlimited"; and, "I was born in a country where there is a wide variety of percussion instruments." The musicians, bassist Ron Carter aside, were drawn from the Brazilian experimental-jazz cream, notably (again) Hermeto Pascoal and Sivuca. The music included "O Sonho," by Flora Purim, sung in English to a melody both lunar and Brazil-rooted. The track was equally devoted to Purim's flights of experimental post-scat vocalizing and to solid bop keyboard solos by Pascoal. Other tracks—

notably "Uri," on which Sivuca plays accordion—lifted off from a reflective bossa-nova-like melody to become avant-garde both vocally and instrumentally, without trading coherence for freedom. But, typically enough, one of the recording's most effective cuts, "Papo Furado," was powered by an extremely traditional rhythmic approach for ostinato bass, guitar, and percussion, broken by a vehement Rio samba-school *batucada*.

Flora Purim, meanwhile, was starting to build her own career. Her background was totally different from Airto's. Born in Rio of a middle-class Jewish family, she became a jazz fan early, and her first professional experience was as a bossa-nova singer (she first met Airto when she came through Sao Paulo on tour). Although this made it easier for her to get gigs when she first arrived in the U.S., it made getting past that level a little harder. Airto's entire approach was unique, and fitted well with the currents flowing strongly in jazz at the time. On the other hand, the U.S. was bursting at the seams with female jazz singers, and singing jazz-bossa wasn't exactly the way to impress the taste-makers in the early 1970s. However, Purim had already developed a highly personal style to suit her enormous vocal range, mixing a kind of impressionist hyper-scat with everything from low-register imitations of percussion instruments to an ecstatic high-altitude shriek. The breakthrough came when she got a job with the Gil Evans band, where she met Joe Henderson, Stanley Clarke, and, above all, Chick Corea. It was when Corea formed the group Return to Forever that her career began to develop separately from Airto's, though the fact wasn't at first obvious because both of them were on the group's first album.

The partnership between Corea, Purim, and Airto was a natural, because all three had shared roots in both jazz and Latin music and a strong urge to (as Purim once put it) "create, not just perform." For Airto and Purim, *Return to Forever* was a launching pad. For Corea it was something of a change of course, but also a chance to put to use all the elements of his musical experience. His seminal *Now He Sings, Now He Sobs* album, with its strong impressionist and art-music influences, had taken him a long way from playing montunos with Mongo Santamaria. Now he was ready for another change. He said that—after more than a decade playing jazz in so many different ways—"immediately after performing as a solo pianist for a year, I decided to write some group music that would be melodic and lyrical with more traditional rhythms. It would be a music that would communicate and be felt and understood by people of all types. The compositions on the recording were the first pieces I wrote."[1]

---

[1]From the liner notes of the first *Return to Forever* album.

Three pieces on the original *Return to Forever* album showed the ways in which Corea and the rest were digesting their musical influences. The title number itself is notable for Airto's trap-drumming. In the fairly fast first section, he sets up a regular shekere-type rhythm on hi-hat, with snare-drum shots phrased to overlay a clave-like feel. Clarke meanwhile plays a subtle version of Latin-derived, two-measure funk grooves. "What Game Shall We Play Today?," a charming generically "Latin" tune that begins sounding subtly more American when Purim starts to sing in English, shows off the remarkably sunny quality that she could project so well. The most ambitious cut, the side-long "Some Time Ago—The Fiesta," mixes Latin elements with the Eurocentric impressionist strain common in 1970s jazz, opening with moments of what sounds for all the world like slightly Latinized Baroque music, leading to a Spanish-influenced melody for electric piano and bass given a flamenco tinge by its chord progression and mode, which serves as a basis for a meditative vocal by Purim. There are some startling touches, notably an unexpected flash of classic Cuban piano montuno under moody flute, and a soprano sax solo by Farrell over bass montunos on the same Spanish-sounding progression that built until, as the tempo speeded up, the piece began to spark in more familiar jazz vein.

Both Airto's involvement with Davis and Corea and his willingness to play such a wide range of gigs undoubtedly contributed to his increasing visibility in the jazz world. When you consider how many Cuban percussionists had been altering the course of jazz since Chano Pozo began the job a quarter of a century before, it is more than a touch ironic that *DownBeat* introduced a percussion category in its annual awards only in 1972. But given Airto's extraordinary influence in the early 1970s, the fact that he won it several years running was certainly not inappropriate.

Airto's own 1972 CTI album, *Free*, reflected the range of his interests at this time. It opens with a cover of "Return to Forever" that features several of the musicians from the original group, including Corea himself. It moves from very free percussion through *guajeo*-based electric piano in the familiar left-hand-montuno/right-hand-jazz vein, wordless vocals from both Airto and Purim, and fine flute from Hubert Laws. "Flora's Song," on which Airto plays wooden flute and Keith Jarrett contributes piano as impressionistic as you'd expect, mixed berimbau and strongly Spanish-influenced acoustic guitar with a generally modal approach. With all its free moments, however, the group maintained a strong sense of cohesion and even developed something of a groove. "Free" itself demonstrates both the strengths and weaknesses of unstructured improvisation. It spends far too long in the sonic rain forest, but once Airto launches into an eccentric but traditionally based vocal it unexpectedly turns into a fine track for voice and berimbau.

Free was a fine album, but it was overshadowed by the enormous success of another CTI offering led by a Brazilian musician, on which Airto also played: keyboardist Eumir Deodato's *Prelude*. Revisiting this album 25 years later is an interesting experience. The piece that turned Deodato into a seven-day wonder, "Also Sprach Zarathustra," was bizarre, in that the Strauss theme had almost no relation to what was otherwise a basic Latinate funk number with good percussion and a nice John Tropea guitar solo. Other cuts were more cohesive. "Carly & Carole" is a lyrical version of the Latin/jazz/fusion of the era, too light to be called funk, with the ghost of some departed *guajeo* hovering over Deodato's jazz-oriented electric piano. "Baubles, Bangles and Beads" opens like some Tijuana Brass guajira but develops into a cooker aided by a good John Tropea guitar solo and a strongly montuno-like bass line tightly meshed with the percussion. And then there is "September 13," very 1970s with its wawa guitar and a clave-haunted funk bass line accentuated by assertive conga playing.

While Deodato pursued a big-label career, Airto continued to rummage happily in his extraordinarily well-stocked musical grab bag. The title cut of his 1974 *Virgin Land* LP for CTI was in classic Airto vein. It opened with one of his rainforest, eco-rock intros, including a splendidly effective bull-roarer, kicked into a clave-like rhythm for a village-music, voice-and-guitar vocal, and moved through jazz-rock guitar, heavy rock drumming (Airto again), and wordless vocals playing a role often allotted to saxes. "Musikana" showed a slightly different aspect of the mix, blending pretty acoustic guitar and some more bird noises with Purim's vaguely orgasmatic vocals in free hyper-scat vein, full of glissandi and little ecstatic shrieks. But perhaps the most interesting tracks were "Peasant Dance" and "Lydian Riff," both of which had a strong Balkan feeling thanks to Milco Leviev's presence on keyboards. Throughout the album, Airto demonstrated a hundred and one ways to use cuica and berimbau to avant-garde effect without betraying the instruments' nature.

The exposure that the new Brazilian musicians were getting not only intensified in 1973, but changed its nature. In March, Airto and Purim left Return to Forever to form a group under Airto's leadership, Fingers. The band's eponymous first recording for CTI was an eclectic set with, as common factors, Airto's still largely Brazilian-based percussion and a wide range of semi-free experiments, mostly in Purim's vocals. "Wind Chant" set Purim in "out" mood against a contrasting background of repetitive Brazilian-based grooves. The most rhythmically experimental track, "Tombo in 7/4," features a vocal by Airto with a chorus and a range of percussion. "Paraná," to my mind the best track, lays a three-chord, 12-string-guitar ostinato under a free vocal from Airto, including his trademark berimbau imitations and an improvisational-sounding chorus. A pretty piano solo by Hugh Fatturoso sets off the cut's more experimental elements very effectively.

His studio recordings rarely give a sense of one of Airto's most striking qualities, a remarkable, laid back charisma. I once saw him keep the Avery Fisher Hall spellbound for almost an hour with nothing but a vendor's cart full of small percussion instruments (typically, he hadn't bothered to tell the impresario he wasn't bringing a band: after all, who needs one!). One recording that does illustrate something of this quality comes from a Felt Forum concert in which Fingers opened for Deodato, then riding high on Richard Strauss's coat-tails. New band or no new band, Airto felt no need to tailor his performance to the audience. "Branches," an example of how well he could hold an audience solo, opens with a free passage for berimbau and moves into one of his extraordinary wordless vocals, half-traditional and half eco-quirky, then migrates from something very like Congo-Angolan bardic narrative into what sounds like a Brazilian song in the Portuguese tradition, and winds up with vocal imitations of percussion. At this point Purim joined him, very pure and lyrical, and they shift back and forth between solo and duo. "Paraná" built differently from a similar opening and wordless vocal; here the band picks up on the original berimbau rhythm and turns it into a fusion groove—a very effective transformation, and evidence that Airto and Purim's gift for combining originality and what used to be called swing.

Of Airto's musical tribe, it was Purim who had to wait longest for her solo splash, but she made it in December with her first LP under her own name, Butterfly Dreams. It was typical of her literally eccentric approach that, along with the old cronies—Joe Henderson, keyboardist George Duke, guitarist David Amaro, Stanley Clarke on bass, and Airto—one Ernie Hood was featured to good effect on zither. Like most debut LPs, *Butterfly Dreams* seemed designed to show off Purim in all her personae. Among the cuts that reflected her truest musical being was "Summer Night," a piece of typical Moreira/Purim eco-fusion. The notes called her vocal "instrumental-style," but in reality, though wordless it was really very human-voice-oriented, far more so than classic scat of the order of Ella Fitzgerald. "Butterfly Dreams" itself lived up to its title with another floaty impressionistic eco-opening leading to an adventurous avant-bossa vocal, although things remained a little static until Clarke entered and organized the rhythm under a nice Henderson solo.

Flora Purim's second album, *Stories to Tell*, showed more signs of a move toward a wider audience. *Stories to Tell* is roughly half U.S.-oriented and half-Brazilian (and, on the Brazilian half, very varied as to composer and tradition). The title track opens with a powerful bass groove and moves into a tricky, clave-derived funk-jazz groove, over which Purim sings in English what from the start more resembles an improvisation on a melody than a melody itself. Throughout the album, her Brazilian roots surface in subtle ways: in her understated, fragile tone on the ballad-tempo "Search For Peace" (and even in "O Cantador," with its contrasting second section); in the beautiful "To Say Goodbye," where her vocal (echoed by Brazilian Raul De Souza's trombone) falls squarely between bossa nova and U.S. cabaret singing; and in her avant-scat on Edu Lobo's "Casa Forte," wild and pretty at once, and seemingly drawn in part from the Macumba religious cult, which blends Indian and African elements, and from *spiritismo*, with which Airto was marginally involved.

An old friend of Purim's also made his first recording as leader in 1973, this one for the excellent small Muse label. Dom Um Romao, who had come to the U.S. with Sergio Mendes in 1962 for the famous Carnegie Hall bossa-nova concert, been involved in U.S. jazz-bossa, and played with Weather Report, shared the polymathic tendency of 1970s Brazilian jazz. His eponymous release was a mixed bag whose high spots were "Family Talk," a delicious, complex samba-based piece full of elegantly spiky harpsichord from João Donato; and, "Ponteio," a true jazz-fusion piece with particularly effective trap drumming from Romao.

The efforts of Airto (and fellow-percussionists Dom Um Romao and Nana Vasconcelos) to work their way into the jazz scene during the early 1970s were helped by the fact that Brazilian elements introduced through jazz-bossa had already infiltrated the cutting edge of the post-bop jazz mainstream. In fact, the Brazilian tinge was important enough that a wide range of musicians made use of it. During the early 1970s, Argentinian tenorist Gato Barbieri made a number of important recordings on the avant-garde end of Latin jazz. His 1971 album *Fenix* had a strong Brazilian cast based on a group of musicians already working in related genres: the berimbau player Nana Vasconcelos; Gene Golden, an African-American solidly entrenched in the more rootsy end of New York's Afro-Cuban percussion scene; bassist Ron Carter; and two fusion-jazz stars of the time, Lenny White on drums and Lonnie Liston Smith on piano. In an era when expressionism dominated the experimental end of Latin-jazz, all of Barbieri's groups were remarkable for their assertiveness. In part this was because Vasconcelos' berimbau style was harder than Airto's—which gave the Brazilian-derived titles a distinctive feel—and in part it stemmed from Barbieri's abrasively macho tenor sound. But *Fenix* also stood out for Barbieri's almost single-handed creation of a jazz-tango style, notably in his version of the classic "El Día Que Me Quieras."

Barbieri maintained his interest in Brazilian music in his *Chapter Two: Hasta Siempre*, a continuation of his exploration of traditional South American forms. Two of its cuts, the two-part "Encontros"[2] and "Marissa," make use of the drummers of a Rio samba school, along with *cavaquinho*, Fender bass, traps, and the Brazilian percussionist Portinho, a relatively new addition to the U.S.-Brazilian musical community. The three other cuts include Andean *quena* flute, harp, and percussion players. It was an unusual concept at the time, though by the time Barbieri and the other studio musicians had finished, there was often so little audible of the traditional groups that their role could have been played by any adaptable performer.

Among the Brazilians themselves, Deodato continued to be the most visible, thanks in part to a new contract with MCA. His first recording under the new dispensation, *Artistry*—recorded at the 1974 Mississippi River Festival in St. Louis—pursued his established themes, notably the mix of classical (or near classical) music and jazz/funk. That aside, the set was notable for a version of "St. Louis Blues" in which the post-clave jazz-rock groove provided an unexpectedly effective cradle for the most famous of early "Latin tinge" jazz compositions (though it lost the original contrast between the habanera-bass and straight-4/4, 12-bar-blues sections).

The midpoint of the decade saw an even further deepening of the Brazilian tinge, often involving as-yet unknown musicians. Pianist Tania Maria, then living in Paris, made her first, brief appearance in the U.S. at the Newport Jazz Festival. And a poorly attended concert at New York's Town Hall theater in the fall of 1975 included an outstanding set by a Latin jazz group led by guitarist Almaury Tristao. Its members included Brazilian trumpeter Claudio Roditi, who had recently come to the U.S. to study at Boston's Berklee School of Music, a Brazilian keyboardist, Guilherme Vergueiro, tenorist Charlie Rouse, whose credits went back to the 1940s Gillespie big band via practically everybody, and that king of acoustic bass, Ron Carter. Sadly, the group didn't last long.

The Brazilian tinge was attracting more and more musicians at this juncture. This was, among other things, the era of the brilliant Keith Jarrett quintet with Dewey Redman, Charlie Haden, Paul Motian, and percussionist Guilherme Franco. But for all that, the powerhouse was still centered on Airto Moreira,

---

[2] For some reason, parts one and three were included, but not two.

Flora Purim, and the musicians, Brazilian and U.S.-born, associated with them. Purim's recording career was thrown off course in 1975 by the need to serve an 18-month sentence on a drug charge from a few years back. But Airto made a conscious effort at a career breakthrough with his *Identity* album, recorded by a new group that included Wayne Shorter on soprano and Herbie Hancock on synthesizers, as well as Egberto Gismonti (who had come to the U.S. specifically to play with Airto and Purim) on pianos and synth. As Airto told me at the time, "I've lived in the United States for almost nine years, and I never felt that I was communicating properly with the people. When I was playing concerts, 70 percent of the audience was really into it, and 30 percent was, like, 'What is this?' So now I want to communicate with that 30 percent."

Airto, however, wasn't one to produce a straightforward commercial album (whatever that may be), as the fact that Egberto Gismonti composed half the cuts clearly signaled. *Identity* was typical Airto, interweaving springing rock solos, his own Luso-jazz percussion, and endless permutations of Brazilian music into a fabric so light that its complexity was almost hidden. The piece that reached out most clearly for the mass audience was Airto's own "Flora on my Mind," with its heavy rock opening for guitar and traps and a Latin-rock beat, along with some nice, fat, plainman trombone from Raul De Souza, a relatively new arrival from Brazil.

De Souza surfaced again with guitarist Almaury Tristao and percussionists Paulo da Costa and Guilherme Franco on Azar Lawrence's *Summer Solstice* album. A Coltrane admirer who had recently come to the jazz world's attention with McCoy Tyner, Lawrence comes across as an acidly logical player longer on intelligence than soul, whose free-jazz references gained strength from the discreetly lucid Brazilian rhythmic frame as well as the contrast provided by De Souza's excellent soloing, some of his best on record.

Alas poor Lawrence, *Summer Solstice* was soon overshadowed by fellow soprano-saxist Wayne Shorter's *Native Dancer*, a milestone in the history of the Brazilian presence in the U.S. For one thing it introduced to the U.S. MPB's greatest singer songwriter, Milton Nascimento, a master of a style that draws not only on disparate Brazilian traditions, but also (more heavily than bossa nova) on U.S. influences. Nascimento's singing, while almost as eclectic as Airto's or Purim's, had fewer references unfamiliar to Americans. *Native Dancer* also combines many elements of both Brazilian and U.S. pop-funk in a beguiling but not trivial mix. Some of its simpler tracks are among the best. "Beauty and the Beast" shines simply for the quality of its acoustic soul-jazz/funk sound, from

Soprano saxist and Coltrane fan Azar Lawrence recorded a mid-1970s Brazilian-jazz-funk album with Brazilians Raul de Souza and Paulinho da Costa that prefigured by a few months Wayne Shorter's more famous *Native Dancer. Courtesy Prestige Records*

Shorter's unpretentiously admirable soprano solo to the solid groove of Hancock's gospel-meets-salsa piano backing.

It's remarkable how often the important developments in music are the work of a tiny coterie of musicians working in shifting coalitions. In 1975, fresh from his experiences in Latin New York, Cal Tjader made *Amazonas*, the most Brazilian of all his recordings. This was almost old-home-week for Airto's associates. Along with other musicians more loosely associated with him were: David Amaro guitars; George Duke (under the alias of Dawilli Gonga) on electric keyboards; Egberto Gismonti on piano and synth; Raul de Souza on trombone on one number; and Hermeto Pascoal playing flute on three pieces. Only Airto himself didn't play—and that's because he was busy producing the session.

At this remove, some of the resulting cuts sound like generic 1970s jazz rock, though given a certain freshness by being traps-oriented rather than dominated by heavy bass-guitar grooves. But many numbers were intriguing mixes of Tjader's and Airto's very different musical sensibilities. In the title cut—a João Donato composition—Tjader's marimba pegs a rather spacey '70s fusion/jazz-rock sound with a funk-jazz kick and dreamy or soaring guitars. The musicians' lyrical tendencies got most play in "Cahuenga."[3] And the most fully realized piece, "Tamanco No Samba," eschewed contemporary fusion in favor of an original approach to Brazilian music, and closed with a phenomenal three-way session of trading fours between Tjader's mellow vibes, Milanez's stabbing piano, and Amaro's fast, flowing guitar.[4]

When Airto and Purim left Return to Forever, the band's sound moved from a Brazilian to a more generically Latin-funk idiom. The more rhythm-dominated tracks on *No Mystery*—the first RTF recording after the couple's departure—had few obvious Latinisms aside from Corea's intro to "Dayride," a familiar Latin montuno. The uptempo material had moved all the way to heavily electronic jazz/rock/funk fusion, dominated by the funk rhythm section of Stanley Clarke and Lenny White. Yet, of course, this meant that a good deal of the group's rhythmic underpinning was—at a couple of removes—clave-based. Different though they were in many ways, RTF, Deodato's groups, and the jazz/rock/funk

---

[3] The CD reissue includes a longer, previously unissued version of this track, along with the originally issued short version.

[4] Another Tjader recording showing an indirect Brazilian element was *La Onda Va Bien*, his Grammy-winning first recording for the Concord Picante label. Its most interesting cut was a João Donato composition, "Sabor," in which the offhand complexities of bossa nova are transformed into something more Cuban-oriented with classic piano guajeos, flute bridging jazz and charanga, and powerful bottom-heavy conga.

wing of 1970s music were all indicative of how the Latin tinge had become so well-absorbed into these styles—just as it had been in the earliest days of jazz—that it was pretty much impossible to precipitate the Latin elements out of the overall brew.

1976 saw a number of subtle shifts of emphasis that in retrospect presaged long-term change. Airto switched labels, to Arista, and his debut album for that label, *Promises Of The Sun*, focused on the more accessible aspects of his musical universe, without distorting it. "Zuei" is typical of his percussive-scat numbers, with a strongly Brazilian melody line over a semi-samba rhythm given a haunting bass groove. "Candango" is full of zany scatting, with a rock rhythm tweaked by a little Brazilian triangle and bluesy R&B guitar from Brazilian newcomer Toninho Horta (a major influence on Pat Metheny). "Circo Maribondo" is a fast, sliding samba, characteristic in its double layer of tempi: medium-paced bass line with double-speed shuffle percussion over it. Airto's lead vocal on that number has a real Brazilian provincial sound to it. And "Ruas do Recife" is a beautiful, strongly traditional African-derived *maracatú* with a charmingly brash trombone solo from Raul de Souza, a fine popular style vocal from Novelli, and rich-toned women's choruses sung in the traditional near-unison style. Lastly, the attractive title cut mixes excellent acoustic guitar with Milton Nascimento's lead vocal, moving progressively into Airto's least commercial mood, with his strange singing, like men chanting to themselves.

Flora Purim's *Encounter*, recorded in August 1976 with several different groups of musicians, was also a further rebalancing of her "jazz" and "Brazilian" images in her avowed intention to use her "experience in all kinds of fields" to reach a wider audience. Her version of Chick Corea's "Windows" opens with a rhapsodic free intro and wordless vocal while Joe Henderson solos over a loose, held-note beat interspersed with walking bass. The title cut, which includes Urszula Dudziak among the solo vocalists, was eco-fusion with rather self-conscious free vocalisms until some fairly traditional conga nails it down a little. "Above the Rainbow," in which Purim was backed by McCoy Tyner in a sweeping, rhapsodic mood, gives a sense of Purim's vocal stylistics in a non-Brazilian setting.

One of the best Brazilian-jazz recordings of 1976 was a session released under the name of a relative newcomer, percussionist Paulinho da Costa. His *Agora*, for Pablo Records, was striking for its fairly original percussion, rich big-band sound (at a time when big-band wasn't really much happening), and its use of Brazilian elements that weren't then common currency. Two cuts were totally percussion-oriented: the voices-and-percussion number "Terra" was based on a *cafezal*, a strongly Afro-Brazilian 6/8 rhythm with a very West-African-sounding bell pattern; and "Ritmo Number One" (built of multiple overdubs by Da Costa) recreates the kind of samba-school *batucada* on which Da Costa cut his percussion teeth. But most of the record was a fairly individual take on Luso-Latin-jazz.

Paulinho Da Costa was in the studio for Pablo again the following month, this time in a more minor role playing on *Dizzy's Party*, in which Gillespie used the new fusion/funk rhythms to fair effect. Da Costa provided most of the impetus for the ten-minute title track, besides inspiring Gillespie to a mellow solo, fresher than much of his workmanlike playing elsewhere on the album. Da Costa gooses the funk-jazz groove with an implacable cencerro beat, sneaks in under Gillespie's solo with a cuica, switches to a fine Afro-Brazilian agogó pattern under the sax solo, then gave the guitar gentler support with a rattle.

Pablo Records continued to make good use of Paulo da Costa on the album *Tudo Bem*, which paired him with guitarist Joe Pass. The results were unpretentiously outstanding. Pass's gentle guitar style (single-string jazz, not the richly chorded and rhythmic approach of Gilberto or Bola Sete) was well-suited to the genre. This was no nostalgia trip, but jazz-bossa for the late '70s—less because of Pass or pianist Don Grusin, whose playing was fairly timeless, than because of the buoyant Brazilian rhythm section. Claudio Slon and bass-guitarist Octavio Bailly, both of whom thought of themselves as jazz musicians, provide a solidly swinging backing that benefits from their intimate knowledge of Brazilian music. And Da Costa provides a more varied and active percussion background than classic jazz-bossa, switching from agogó to cuica to congas and moving the other musicians with the lifting drive that is so special to Brazilian music.

One of the roles of the Brazilian influence was to induce funk to lighten up a bit. This was particularly obvious in the music of newcomer guitarist Lee Ritenour, who had worked with Sergio Mendes and Brasil '77, and later commented, "from my very first album I've always had some kind of Brazilian flavor."[5] It's tempting to draw a parallel between the heavier East coast Latin-jazz-funk sound and Ritenour's light approach to funk-fusion jazz, and the old East-Coast hard-bop/West Coast cool-jazz dichotomy.

As Brazilian references in jazz widened and moved to the more experimental reaches of the style, 1960s-style jazz-bossa did not altogether disappear into the classier reaches of easy listening. It also continued to naturalize as an alternative rhythmic underpinning to what would otherwise have been "straight" jazz, particularly in ballads, to which it often imparted a subtle effect of simultaneous move-

---

[5] From the liner notes of the CD reissue of his first album, *First Course*.

ment and relaxation. Musicians not particularly associated with "Latin jazz," let alone "jazz bossa," were by now perfectly at ease with it. In the title cut of Artie Shepp's 1975 *Mariamar* recording, both Shepp and Brazilian guitarist Iria de Paula played lines not overtly affected by the bossa-nova undercurrents of drummer Afonso Vieira; but that undercurrent lapped around their solos in ways that built a subtle rhythmic interplay. "Três Ideias" opens with an ambiguously complex rhythm, but develops into a more forthright bossa nova, rhythmic guitar chordings and all. But Shepp was able to use this rhythm simply as a platform for solos that had no need for subtext, just as he does in "Shepp's Mood," which uses the older habanera-inflected ballad bass.

The linkage of Brazilian and funk-jazz elements was, of course, not altogether new. Kenny Dorham, who composed "Blue Bossa," was a luminary of the hard bop school that was one root of funk jazz. The connection had become looser during the jazz-bossa period, but now it was tightening up again. The title cut of Freddy Hubbard's *Red Clay* album—his first for the fusion-minded CTI label, and made with Joe Henderson, Herbie Hancock, Ron Carter, and Lenny White, all musicians associated with Latin-tinged jazz of various kinds—is a good example, with its basic rhythm combining bossa nova and soul-jazz elements. Incidentally, the notes contain a revealing quote from Hubbard on his reaction to an all-star concert with a number of Latin-funk-oriented CTI musicians: "I said to myself, 'Wow! That's what it's all about! It's about feeling! Now if I can do something this exciting and still be inventive . . . I'll really have something going for me!'"[6]

A minor resurgence of the jazz-bossa old guard was also taking place by the mid-1970s. In 1976, Stan Getz and João Gilberto got together for a reunion which resulted in *The Best of Two Worlds*. This album nodded in the direction of changing times in the form of a more percussion-oriented rhythm section including a cabaça shaker, as well as an uncredited singer, Miúcha (Chico Barque's sister) who shared Astrud Gilberto's ability to perform well in English, but not her anomie.

Gilberto also appeared on an album with Herbie Mann and Antonio Carlos Jobim recorded in Rio, as well as a recording under his own name an album titled *Amoroso*, on which he sang but didn't play a note, drowned in a morass of syrupy strings. New York club-goers fared better than the record-buying public when Gilberto gave a typically introverted and brilliant solo concert at the Bottom Line in August, including a strange and wonderful "Besame Mucho."

---

[6] That a fairly eminent young jazzman was at this stage in his career only just discovering what had been the basis of all earlier jazz heavily underlines the need for a corrective in early 1970s jazz!

By the late 1970s, Brazilian music and the various tinges it inspired had become a seemingly permanent part of the jazz scene, besides exerting influence on some areas of rock. Where sambas had been a small part of many "straight" jazz albums, they might now provide the main event. Chico Freeman's *Beyond the Rain* was mostly free or straight-ahead jazz. But its major work was a complex piece nearly 15 minutes long called "Pepe's Samba." After rhythmic whistles over percussion, a Cuban conga break and idiosyncratic piano *guajeos* joined by Freeman playing somewhat mambo-style sax, this moves into a rhythm that is almost straight 4/4 but with heavy percussion from Gama Santos. Elvin Jones meantime breaks up the beat Latin-style on his ride cymbal while pianist Hilton Ruiz builds a quirky montuno. As Freeman moves into a swirling solo, heavy conga-playing and whistles reestablish themselves in a passage both free and dense. By this time, any reference to the specific samba worldview is long gone, though the rhythm is still Latinate. Here, as so often in Latin jazz, the percussion acts as balance to the soloists. But so did the arrangement, recurring mambo riffs acting like ballast on a balloon as Freeman moves between post-hard-bop and free-jazz arabesques.

At the other end of the spectrum was the first of two recordings Sarah Vaughan made in Rio for Pablo Records. *I Love Brazil*, made with a raft of well-known Brazilian musicians, offered fine music and some examples of the risks in putting a big name into an unfamiliar setting. Vaughan, of course, was one of the great ballad singers, and at her best with simple accompaniments. Backed by Milton Nascimento on acoustic guitar on his own "Vera Cruz" or on "The Face I Love," she both enriches and was enriched by a melodic tradition that perfectly suits her voice (if not the English language).

But a second Sarah Vaughan recording for Pablo was both more modest and more successful. Instead of following the 1977 *I Love Brazil*'s everybody-who's-anybody approach, *Copacabana*'s backup musicians consisted of a guitarist, Helio Delmiro, a rhythm section, and a super-soupy Brazilian vocal backup group. Many of the songs were by Jobim and the general mood was largely divided between bossa ballads, and international-Latin-cum-French ballads. Aside from being gorgeous, Vaughan's tone and style were different enough from any Brazilian singer that she created a personal vocal version of jazz-bossa. The well-known title song shines in part because of the purity and simplicity in which Vaughan excelled, as does "Gentle Rain," an inherently pretty ballad given a brilliantly simple rendering by acoustic guitar. "Dreamer (Vivo Sonhando)" is a classic example of the art that conceals art, with a nice jazz-bossa piano trio and fine electric guitar backup. And one of the least-promising songs on the album is one of the best: an English version of Ivan Lins' and Vitor Martins' pure pop "The Smiling Hour" ("Abre Alas" in the original). Its extraordinarily haunting vocal chorus contrast well with Vaughan.

Brazil also dominated a Charlie Byrd Concord Jazz Festival concert that wound up as the Concord Picante album, *Sugarloaf Suite*. This was a guitar/bass/drums trio gig, and as the title (a reference to the mountain overlooking Rio de Janeiro) suggests, it was all Brazilian-derived material, one-half of it original compositions by Charlie Byrd. Two of the other four pieces were by Jobim, and one by Dorival Caymmi. The set was tight, pretty trio jazz-bossa/samba with often hidden classical influences (appropriate to an idiom that includes Bonfá and Jobim among its major composers). The trio format—which includes some fine bass solos by Byrd's brother, Joe—keeps the tone mainstream in a way that is absolutely not pejorative: the rhythms may be less subtle than those of a João Gilberto, but their drive is entirely appropriate to the genre.

By the end of the 1970s, Brazilian influences were reflected by a wide range of musicians. John Klemmer's *Brazilia* album for ABC was something of a Barbieri imitation, pop-funk-jazz with generalized disco-Latin-pop rhythms. Seawind's A & M album, *Light the Light*, features a kind of new-wave Braziloid West Coast sound influenced by Purim, Airto, and Nascimento. Among older hands, Weather Report's *Mr. Gone* includes a track reminiscent of Airto's artier moments: "The Pursuit of the Woman With the Feathered Hat" uses percussion, chanting, and snatches of melody that, although not generically "Brazilian," stem from a Brazilian sensibility. Chick Corea's *Tap Step* album for Warner Brothers went one better, including both Airto and Purim in "Samba L.A.," a piece close to the carnival samba enredo—female chorus, whistles, and all—in which Corea's synth playing in places sounds very like a *choro* clarinet. "The Slide," another cut on the same album played by a different group, also opens with samba enredo percussion including Airtos' cuica and an agogó. The synth and bass (playing something between a groove and a solo line, over four measures!) work together more dominantly here than in "Samba L.A."

As time went on, the ways in which jazz related to Brazilian and to Afro-Cuban music began to differ. Broadly speaking, Brazilian elements became more internalized by jazz than Cuban ones, a process that was illustrated towards the end of the 1970s by the recordings of guitarist Pat Metheny. *Watercolors*, Metheny's second album for the eclectic German ECM label, is bathed in Brazilianisms. In an interview published in *Brazilian Sound*, Metheny's keyboardist Lyle Mays talked of this influence: "Under the surface the actual rhythms had a whole lot to do with Brazilian music. During the first half of the group's history, one hundred percent of the music we did had that straight-eighth rhythm, which comes from Brazilian music."

As should be clear by now, during the 1970s the Brazilian stream of Latin jazz not only consolidated and became more varied in its own right, but affected salsa, and increased its influence on Latin-fun-jazz in general. But the Cuban element in fusion jazz remained strong, Cuban-based Latin jazz continued as a genre in its own right, and all these elements tended to mix variously in individual recordings. An example was drummer Roy Haynes's LP, *Senyah*, a solid, mellow, intelligent septet recording that operates between a light-moving funk and Latin jazz. Haynes's drumming and Don Pate's bass on "Sillie Willie" are far from orthodoxly clave-based, but Haynes's playing is rich in phrasing that could have come straight from a Mongo Santamaria conga part, and Pate's bass line seem to tightrope between groove and montuno. The rhythmic underpinning of "Senyah" and "Little Titan" are straight clave-derived, two-measure funk grooves. And in general, while Haynes synthesizes a number of percussion traditions in his drumming style, the Afro-Cuban idiom is among the most dominant (though not, in the drum workout called "Brujeria con Salsa").

The Latin-funk tinge was becoming widespread by the early '70s. Stanley Turrentine's *Don't Mess With Mister T.* featured the kind of jazz-lite for which a Latin tinge had by now become indispensable. At the other end of the scale, tenorist Joe Henderson ran a Latin-funk bass under many of his recordings. His January 1973 *Multiple* used the Latin flavor lightly. In "Tress-Cun-Deo-La" a heavy montuno-type bass pegs a largely atmospheric piece. In "Turned Around," another faint reminiscence of the montuno bass is even more thoroughly absorbed. And, in "Song for Sinners," an expressionist opening with vaguely Tantric atmospheric vocalizing is kept focused by percussion with a real clave feel.

If *Multiple* is highly eclectic, Henderson's October *Canyon Lady* is more overtly Latin. Tjader sideman Mark Levine launches "All Things Considered" with pretty piano guajeos in the treble range, over percussion that does not turn Latin until Henderson's solo. The rhythmic high point of the title track is an exhilarating pattern of contrasting sections, one bass-fueled and the other more timbales-dominated.

One of 1973's more unexpected recordings was *Giant Steps*, a "what, me passé?" big-band recording by Woody Herman which included guitarist Joe Beck and Ray Barretto. This determined and reasonably successful attempt to move with the times included Chick Corea's flamenco-influenced "La Fiesta" and Leon Russell's "A Song For You," both with essentially Latin/funk bass lines over two measures. Indeed, almost every cut uses some version of the funk groove. The

Woody Herman recorded only a handful of mambos during the big-band Cubop era of the 1950s. But in early 1973, he surprised (and to be honest horrified) his old fans with an eclectic Latin-jazz-funk recording, *Giant Steps*, that involved guitarist Joe Beck and percussionist Ray Barretto. *Courtesy Fantasy Record Group*

most interesting is "Freedom Jazz Dance," with Ellington-reminiscent voicings in the ensemble writing, a remarkably contemporary soprano solo from Herman, and underneath it all a particularly clear version of the ubiquitous funk/jazz/Latin rhythmic pattern underlined by Barretto's prominent conga-playing.

Ever since the 1950s, of course, jazz musicians had been drawing from a widening cross-cultural pool. Not only did Cuban and Brazilian music have strong African elements, but players as disparate as Art Blakey and Herbie Mann had recorded with African musicians, and Randy Weston had been incorporating African and North African elements into his own piano style. In Weston's big-band recording, *Tanjah*, the two streams met. *Tanjah* included an ud player and a West African ashiko drummer as well as players with Latin experience, among them trumpeters Jon Faddis and Ernie Royal, and—above all—Cuban conga-player Candido Camero. One cut, "Hi Fly," is pretty much straight Latin after a free opening, with solid cencerro playing and Candido free-associating in Spanish. The arrangement is richer than those used by most of the mambo groups, though no richer than Chico O'Farrill liked to write. In solo, Weston opened solidly (though quite individually) jazz-oriented; but as the horns returned, he built a very convincing montuno.

Candido was also still involved, as a bandleader, in the kind of fusion band that was particularly associated with Mongo Santamaria. Candido made a recording for Blue Note in 1970 that drew from a particularly rich brew of influences. Some of the tracks are basic funk riffers drawn from among the soul hits of the time: "Tic Tac Toe" (Booker T. Jones, Steve Cropper, et al); "Hey, Western Union Man" (Gamble & Huff). But a Richie Havens piece, "I'm On My Way," opens with folky acoustic guitar and develops into a multi-level fusion, featuring punchy soul Fender bass with a clave echo, prominent Cuba-derived conga, nice soprano sax soloing, fusion-jazz horns, and strong strummed guitar with a country/rock feel. The high point of "Serenade to a Savage," besides its funk/organ-jazz crossover vein, is that classic jazz procedure, trading fours, reinvented for a dialogue between conga and bluesy guitar.

The complexity of the whole Latin jazz scene in the later 1970s was nowhere better illustrated than by George Duke, a major aficionado of Brazilian music and henchman of the Airto/Purim axis who continued his exploration of Latin-

The Bay area Escovedo dynasty—here represented by conga-player Sheila and timbalero Pete—kept West Coast Latin-jazz-funk going despite years of indifference on the national level. *Courtesy Fantasy Record Group*

The 1970s saw a great proliferation of Latin-jazz-funk styles, including a Brazilian wing whose leaders included Flora Purim and Airto Moreira. In the mid-1970s, Purim's band included (l-r) Americans keyboardist George Duke, drummer Leon "Ndugu" chancler and bassist Alphonso Johnson, and Brazilians guitarist David Amaro, poly-instrumentalist Hermeto Pascoal and Airto himself (with the optical crisis). *Courtesy Fantasy Record Group*

fusion—this time on the Afro-Cuban side—on his album, *Don't Let Go*. More than many African-American musicians working this frontier, Duke understood clave without feeling bound by it. That's one reason the cut "We Give Our Love" is rhythmically less heavy than a lot of late-1970s git-down funk. Another was the presence of congacera Sheila Escovedo, who represented the younger generation of the famous Bay Area dynasty. This, incidentally, was another in the growing number of African-American fusion-jazz recordings that featured a rootsy Cuban number: "Percussion Interlude" was a duet between Escovedo and Leon Ndugu Chancler (another African-American who understood Latin rhythmic procedures) that was almost pure Cuban street-drumming.

This was not the only strongly fusionist recording with a non-Latino leader that reverted to the Afro-Cuban *típico* source in the late 1970s. Bay-Area-based percussionist Bill Summers's *Feel the Heat*, a heavily vocal-oriented, soul-funk release, included (along with a couple of western African drummers) a cut involving Pete Escovedo and Malo veteran Ray Obiedo that was pure salsa. And Summers's *Cayenne* had a piece of space-jazz funk with far stronger salsa elements than anything that had come out of the funk-blend school before, "Latican

Charlie Palmieri, Eddie's elder brother, maintained a jazz-flavored approach to all his music, and his recordings varied from straight 4/4 to highly *típico* salsa. *Photo: David Haas*

Space Mambo." Nor were these the only examples of roots Latin elements in funk-jazz. Around the same time, in a somewhat different neck of the fusion woods, the 1977 Weather Report album, *Heavy Weather*, made use of a Cuban street-percussion sound in "Rumba Mama," besides giving a nod to the former high temple of the New York mambo in "Palladium."

This return to Latino basics brought renewed attention to the man who had as much as anybody pioneered Latin-jazz-funk, Mongo Santamaria. His end-of-the-decade *Red Hot* includes a double-handful of sessionmen including Randy Brecker, Bob James, Eric Gale, and, on some tracks, Barry Miles. But one cut, "A Mi No Me Engañas" brings a total change of pace with classic salsa piano from Charlie Palmieri, tres playing by Harry Viggiano, and a rhythm section that included bassist Sal Cuevas and Steve Berrios on timbales and drums. Significantly, or ironically, this and "Sambita," with its heavy samba enredo rhythm (cuica and all), are the standout tracks. But the rest of the LP was an implicit lesson in how much the whole Latin-jazz-funk sound owed to Santamaria.

From time to time, the fusion tendency of the late 1970s produced some unexpected, and unexpectedly successful, combinations: Paulinho da Costa, Dizzy Gillespie, and Lee Ritenour, for example, on Gillespie's Pablo recording *Free Ride*. Composed and arranged by Lalo Schifrin, one of the most firmly rooted of Brazilian jazzmen on the American scene, *Free Ride* includes some forgettable tracks. But at its best (which mostly meant the more clearly Cuban- and Brazilian-derived tracks, but included a couple of funk numbers), the mix worked, especially when it hewed to the basic bop format with its emphasis on solos. The most revealing track is "Ozone Madness," which illustrates how strong Afro-Cuban conga playing could give a fairly heavy funk beat life and spark— particularly late in the piece, when Da Costa launches into subtle variations of his basic patterns.

Free Ride showed Pablo Records trying to balance the sometimes conflicting needs of its older musicians and the perceived demands of the late 1970s market. Another 1977 Pablo recording, involving an old Gillespie associate and fellow-Cubop pioneer—Machito—was arguably more successful. Essentially a mini-suite with apparent echoes of Eddie Palmieri's "Un Día Bonito," *Macho* reached beyond Machito's usual stylistic range in either his Cubop or mambo avatars. It opens with a santería theme (a reference to Babalu Aye), then moves into expressionist electric piano over ecological noises (presumably produced by a computer). Harry Vigiani (New York salsa's favorite rock guitarist) provides some Santana-ish guitar. Then more familiar ensemble horns introduce a good, post-bop alto solo by Mario Rivera and a trumpet solo by Lou Solof, which opens with swing-period wawa effects, breaks into an unusual bop run that moved *down* rather than up the register, and then goes ballistic. In its very different way, this was as successful an experiment in updating the Cubop big-band sound as Chico O'Farrill's *Afro-Cuban Jazz Moods* from the previous year (described below).

At a time when the jazz world was increasingly open to Latin influence, the hardcore Latin New York music scene was—at least on the surface—going in the other direction. What had by now come to be called salsa was intensifying its exploration of the Cuban downhome sounds of the 1940s and 1950s. This was something incomprehensible to many jazzmen, whose reaction was summed up by a comment supposedly made by the drummer Bernard "Pretty" Purdie to the late Louie Ramirez (who told me the story). "You guys used to have an interesting Latin jazz scene going," Purdie said, "Now what you're playing is more like calypso or something."

It is ironic that the harmonic simplicity Purdie saw as simplistic was, when adopted by Miles Davis and McCoy Tyner, regarded as avant-garde. But in so far as it was true, the return to the *típico* was on one level a back-to-the-roots movement, a way of keeping Latin music Latin and of preventing it from disappearing into a fusion black hole. But there were also political and commercial factors at play. One was the presence of large new and mostly middle-aged immigrant populations, which created a demand for older Cuban sounds. The other was the rise to near-monopoly in the small northeastern U.S. Latino market of Fania Records (and the increasing number of important small labels it acquired).

In reality the Latin scene was never altogether one-dimensional, even at its most *típico*. Downhome Cuban music was a major element, but so were a wide range of experiments—and variegated outside influences, including a recurrent Brazilian undercurrent due to its success in the jazz "mainstream." And there were other complexities. The mambo by now was looking to the kids like mom and pop's music, but the old lions were still recording, though increasingly for a public moving into middle age. The ensemble brass in the big-band mambo tracks of Tito Puente's 1972 *Para Los Rumberos* is still rich in swing references. But the most jazz-related number on the LP—with a gorgeous rolling baritone sax solo and give 'em-hell brass voicings—bears the unmistakably nostalgic title of "Palladium Days."[7] Puente and Machito continued to play not only concerts

---

[7] And the Gods were laughing: *Para Los Rumberos* made no particular waves outside Latin New York despite its oomph and musicianship, but Carlos Santana made a million-selling cover version of the title track, reversing the clave in the bargain, as Puente once remarked to me ruefully.

but Saturday and Sunday "matinees" (in reality early evening sessions) at the Corso on East 86th Street for the aging but loyal fans—Latino and non-Latino—known to younger musicians as the "mamboniks" or Palladium holdovers. These may not have been the glory days, but the Corso was the major dancehall of the mid-1970s, where all the headliners played on the hipper nights (Wednesday and Friday, as the nostalgic will recall).

The truth is that no scene could be described as limited in which both Eddie Palmieri and Willie Colón were at their peak.[8] Eddie Palmieri's increasingly experimental band was almost unique in being as popular with the kids as with the cognoscenti, even though Palmieri's strength came as much from his veneration for downhome Cuban music as from his passion for McCoy Tyner and Chick Corea. Palmieri's remarkable ability to produce recordings that were among the most exploratory of his field while remaining a favorite of both the kids on the corner and the Saturday-night dancers was, of course, not the work of a single hand. The frequently phenomenal contributions of the soloists were obvious. Much less so was the role of the arrangers. As Palmieri himself once expressed it to me, he drew a sketch and his arrangers worked out the floor plan.[9]

Palmieri's street popularity also rested on two seemingly contradictory qualities: a reputation as salsa's reigning eccentric, and a devotion to classic *típico* music as strong as his urge to experiment. About half the tracks on his 1970 album *Superimposition* were rooted in classic Cuban music, including two compositions by the man regarded as the father of Cuban conjunto, Arsenio Rodriguez. Several cuts were overtly experimental. "Que Linda Eso, Eh/Isn't It Pretty," a truly gorgeous melody, opened with a conversation for impressionist piano and bowed bass, improvisatory and free. Palmieri's solo on "Chocolate Ice Cream" mixes offbeat montunos with unconventional chords, expressionism, and straight jazz, in blends different from any other jazz or Latin pianist. "17.1" is, if anything, more remarkable, with its tone clusters, complex chords, and sudden old-style Cuban *floreos*. And Palmieri himself was only part of a sound entirely

---

[8] Unlike Palmieri, Colón's relationship to jazz was indirect and accidental, stemming only from whatever influences his collaborators might have acquired along the way. But he was in his own way at least as creative as Palmieri. While Johnny Pacheco preserved the *típico* sound and Ray Barretto and Larry Harlow built on it, Colón was making salsa a music as international as it was earthy. An important part of his early sound was its use of Puerto Rican *jíbaro* mountain music. But Colón went beyond incorporating Puerto Rican parentheses into the Cuban text of salsa. His 1971 *La Gran Fuga/The Big Break* also included Brazilian rhythms as well as the first of many Panamanian-influenced numbers, along with a Ghanaian children's song, "Che Che Cole," that provided him with one of his biggest early hits.

[9] In the case of Barry Rogers, in particular, this involved not only arrangement but a great deal of unofficial, and unpaid, production work.

dependent on sidemen whose playing, if some cosmic studio engineer had dropped the piano part into sonic oblivion, would still have hovered between outstanding and stunning.

Even though the tide was running strongly in favor of the *típico* sound in 1973, the event of the year in Latin New York was the release of Palmieri's *Sentido* on the Coco label. This contains two of Palmieri's most perfectly worked-out pieces. "Adoración" was the most adventurous Palmieri cut yet. It opens with a free intro mixing Debussy-esque piano and free bass and led, via wawa guitar, to a ravishing piano passage in semi-classical/romantic-ballad vein. Next, the band kicks into a version of the same melody in hardcore salsa style leavened by touches of rock guitar, rich ensemble brass, a feisty trombone solo, rolling baritone sax riffs against ensemble brass, a stratospheric Vitin Paz trumpet solo, and a fierce montuno leavened with the occasional forearm smash from the maestro. Driving the entire cut is the remorseless swing on which Palmieri's bands had a lock.

The other major track on what many think was Palmieri's finest single recording is "Puerto Rico." This opens with a touch of rootsy tres, moved to a vocal with an achingly pretty piano obbligato, then starts toughening up by way of a *cierre* contrasting baritone sax and tres before more solos and almost anguished ensemble work interspersing equally powerful—and only superficially more conventional—vocals. Through it all, Palmieri's piano, urging and exhorting, enhanced and offset soloists and ensemble alike.

1973 also saw a reprise of the Cal Tjader/Eddie Palmieri recordings of the 1960s, this time also involving Eddie's elder brother, Charlie, and Tito Puente. *Primo*, recorded in New York for the Fantasy label, comprised not only classics like Tito Rodriguez's "Mama Guela" and Machito's "Tanga" as well as other straight mambos, but also hits from the mid-1960s bugalú movement (including Joe Cuba's "Bang Bang"), and Willie Colón's Panamanian derived hit, "La Murga." As always, Tjader remained Tjader. But he flourished in a frame more solidly salsa than the earlier collaborations, and reacted to an unusually tight, complex rhythm section by playing hotter than his usual mellow style.

The following year, Palmieri issued an album that contained his most thorough exploration of modal piano to date and perhaps ever. About half of *The Sun of Latin Music* is fairly conventional, though stunningly swinging, salsa. But two cuts are something else. About half of the ten-minute "Un Día Bonito" is a free-time prelude that combined tape sounds with the most complex version to date of the modal piano solo, which Palmieri had been developing over his last several albums. A back-to-earth percussion passage introduces the rest of the band in a jam shot through with occasional tone-clusters from Palmieri and other avant-garde trimmings, as well as a memorable vocal melody.

But "Un Día Bonito," sprawlingly ambitious as it was, is not the album's most fully realized cut. As a mini-history of Cuban music, "Una Rosa Española" achieves small-scale perfection in its recollection of past glories. A wonderful arrangement by Machito pianist René Hernández, all lace and wrought iron, makes the "gorgeous" melody (Palmieri's favorite *mot juste*) of the old Cuban salon *danzón* even more lush, before sliding into a Puerto Rican danza and from that into a modern montuno with juggernaut trombone and baritone riffs.

The elements so obviously present in *The Sun of Latin Music* also dominated Palmieri's controversial *Unfinished Masterpiece*.[10] Supported by a cast of thousands—including the phenomenal young Cuban violinist, Alfredo De La Fe—this continued his twin-track approach to recording. The A side, as usual, was entirely aimed at keeping his dance-minded fans happy. Side B was another matter. The descarga "Cobarde" opens fairly conventionally, but Palmieri's dense solo is well into jazz territory despite its adherence to the formal structures of salsa. Ronnie Cuber's soprano solo with Palmieri's tone-cluster-filled comping takes things even further out, albeit with the safety net of the classic rhythm section. And the less obviously experimental elements—a trombone solo, the chordings for both ensemble and the piano lurking under it, the montuno backing the timbales solo—are even more subversive, in that they are avant-garde salsa rather than salsa-heavy Latin-jazz. It is hard to describe the extraordinary effect of a really "out" series of solos interspersed with deconstructed traditional salsa elements and accompanied by a full Afro-Cuban rhythm section of the caliber of Palmieri's.

Even excluding Palmieri, the degree of experimentation in hardcore Latin music at this period has sometimes been underestimated by writers focusing on the effect of Fania's near but never total monopoly. Though much of this experimentation (notably Willie Colón's outstanding recordings) had nothing to do with jazz, much of it did. Many of the young musicians who were to be the leaders in the Latin-jazz of the 1980s and 1990s came together in the Conjunto Folklórico y Experimental, which in a sense formed the basis for both the Conjunto Libre and the Fort Apache Band. The basis of the group's music, and of the eponymous recording it made, was essentially a mix of the deepest Cuban percussion with jazz elements: something that had previously only been attempted by trombonist Mark Weinstein, and hinted at in a few better-known recordings.

---

[10] Controversial in that Palmieri's legendary lavishness with studio time impelled Coco Records to put the LP out before Palmieri considered it done. Thus the title, and an ensuing lawsuit.

A very different take on Latin jazz resulted in a privately produced recording organized by vibraphonist Bobby Paunetto. *Paunetto's Point* boasted an extraordinary lineup: baritonist Ronny Cuber; both Gonzalez brothers; trumpeter Tom Harrell (who had played with the Latin-rock groups Azteca and Malo as well as Horace Silver); pianist John Marrero (a student of Jaki Byard); Alfredo de la Fe; Manny Oquendo; tenor saxist Todd Anderson, late of Cold Blood and Loading Zone; saxist Bill Drewes (Jaki Byard/Gary Burton); and bassist Abraham Leboriel (Hancock and Mancini!). Paunetto himself had studied under Gary Burton at the Berklee School of Music.

Paunetto's compositions were so tightly integrated that it's easy to miss their range of reference. "A Hybrid Situation," for example, is built on a guajira rhythm under soprano sax-led ensembles and dark conservatory-based string passages out of which Todd Anderson's jazz tenor rises over rock-tinged counter-rhythms. "Fenway Funk" is a minor blues against a rock-jazz rhythm that shifts into a conga-comparsa in a move from traps to timbales, with dreamy vibes from Paunetto and punchy trombone. "Osiris" uses Afro-Cuban 6/8 shaker pulsations in a piece based on modal contrapuntal lines with no debt either to salsa or earlier Latin jazz. Even the most *típico* track, "Heavy on Dee Bacon," blends brisk strutting rhythm and classic Cuban piano with cool-jazz tonalities.

Out of the ordinary though they were, both these albums seem quite mainstream beside the 1974 *Maquina de Tiempo/Time Machine*. Rafael Cortijo, one of the finest Puerto Rican percussionists, had introduced the Afro-Rican bomba into salsa a decade or so before and worked extensively with the plena, a Puerto Rican form loosely parallel to the calypso. But those were dance-band recordings. Now, in the middle of the Cuban-*típico* boom, on a small Latin label sold hardly at all outside the *barrio*, there appeared under his name a recording that must have been fully understood by maybe a dozen people all told—most of whom were playing on it.

Maquina de Tiempo/Time Machine combined elements of traditional Puerto Rican music totally unfamiliar to the jazz world, with 1970s jazz elements and various Brazilian touches (including some cuica friction-drum!). The musicians were a mix of non-Latinos with one foot in jazz and one in salsa, and Latinos who (Cortijo and saxist Mario Rivera aside) were unfamiliar even to most New York salsa fans. With its spiky contemporary jazz sax solos, its ultra-authentic percussion, and its rhythmic structures beloved of Puerto Ricans and unknown to pretty much anybody else, *Time Machine* gave new meaning to the term quixotic. But it was one of the finest Latin-jazz recordings of its decade and possibly the most genuinely experimental recording issued in Latin New York during the 1970s.

Among the other adventurous recordings of the early to mid-1970s was one that, by falling smartly between two commercial stools, illustrated the importance of marketing in the music business. The Latino scene, which had so rapidly adopted the boogaloo and soul influences in the 1960s, did not provide any economic warmth for the funk that was doing so well in the Anglo world. But it did produce an interesting though commercially unsuccessful funk fringe. Vibraphonist/pianist Chico Mendoza chose this seemingly very unpropitious moment to form a band called Ocho, based on a mostly African-American group that had been playing Latin jazz for non-Latin audiences throughout the 1960s.

From 1972 to 1976, Ocho made four recordings that mixed the Latin-jazz vibraphone quintet sound with funk and Cuban music. The group had an all-sax frontline (with two players doubling on flute), and included vocals seen by its record company as essential in the *típico* atmosphere of the time. Ocho made few waves in the four years of its existence, though it helped keep alive the concept of a complex jazz-influenced Latin idiom at a time when *típico* reigned. Listening to a recent reissue of the band's work it seems clear that its biggest mistake—a costly one, perhaps—simply was not gunning for the Anglo market.

All this suggested that, though more clearly marked than it had been for two decades, the frontier between jazz and hardcore salsa was still far from impermeable. And, a number of young musicians with jazz as well as salsa chops were beginning to make an independent mark about this time. The Gonzalez brothers in particular, trumpeter/conga-player Jerry and bassist Andy, both worked consistently with jazz as well as Latin groups, and both were to become pivotal names in Latin jazz in the 1980s.

Both were also, in 1973, involved in one of the most surprising and least-known (because it was not released until 1996!) Latin-jazz albums of the early 1970s. Tenorist Houston Person's *Island Episode* was recorded for Prestige with Hank Jones on piano and Jimmy Ponder on guitar. The rest of the musicians were all Latinos: besides the Gonzalez brothers, Victor (Vitin) Paz was on trumpet and Nicky Marrero on timbales.[11] A couple of the cuts were straight jazz-ballads, but others were something essentially unique for the time: jazz soloing along with a backing far more *típico* than any of the earlier Latin jazz, as if Dizzy Gillespie had recorded with Arsenio Rodriguez. Most unusual of all was the cut "Montuno Merengue," which fused jazz with a mix of Cuban and Dominican rhythms far more overtly than had yet been attempted.

---

[11] There was also some remarkable *tres*-like playing, which I doubt was guitar and double-doubt was Ponder's handiwork, so somebody may have gone uncredited.

Three years later, the spirit that had led to the formation of the Grupo Folklórico y Experimental bore what was to prove permanent fruit, in the form of the first LP by the group Libre, *Con Salsa. . . Con Ritmo. . .* Co-led by percussionist Manny Oquendo and bassist Andy Gonzalez, Libre preserved the familiar trombone sound, but it was particularly significant as a precursor of the major groups of 1980s Latin jazz. Libre's first recording was a particularly rich mix of jazz styles and older Cuban elements. One cut, "Saoco," made use of the sacred batá drums. But the most striking aspect of the album, aside from the quality of the soloing, was the spirit of experiment symbolized as well as anything by the band's reworking of Charlie Parker's "Donna Lee" as a danzón.

By 1976, the major labels' rediscovery of Latin jazz, largely a fruit of the relative commercial success scored by the idiom's funk wing, began to impinge on Latin New York. That year, Ray Barretto—whose musical interests had always ranged beyond *típico* salsa—formed a concert-oriented group with the aim of "exploring extensions of salsa with jazz and rock" as he put it to me at the time. In August, Barretto's new group played New York's Bottom Line nightclub, and Atlantic Records—which had originally signed a deal with Barretto for one studio recording—were enthusiastic enough to release a live recording of the date in advance of the scheduled studio album. The double-album *Tomorrow: Barretto Live* mixes new arrangements of many of Barretto's earlier hits—including a version of "Que Viva La Musica" which fills up an entire side—with new fusion-minded numbers: the rock-flavored "Vaya," whose brass riffs draw equally from salsa, R&B, and jazz; and a two-part suite. The suite consists of a cool-jazz mood-piece, "Night Flowers," and a loping, Latin-jazz number, "Slo Flo," with Archie-Sheppish tenor solo by Dick Mesa, and marvelous half-Cuban, half-jazz flute from Artie Webb. "Slo Flo" also features John Blair playing a combination of jazz violin and gully-low black breakdown on an instrument he called a "vitar," embedded in shouting Latin brass.

The following year, the major labels made their most adventurous sortie yet into hard-core salsa, releasing recordings by the two salsa stars best known outside the Latino market: Ray Barretto and Eddie Palmieri. Barretto's first studio recording for Atlantic, *Eye of the Beholder*, aimed at funk crossover using musicians drawn from both the New York Latino and the funk worlds, including the Crusaders' Joe Sample and Willie Colón trombonist Reynaldo Jorge (the album was officially a Crusaders production). The result was a tight, intelligent, punchy album that swings between jazz, funk, and Latin sounds with subtly intriguing touches: the title cut, for instance, had a melody played on the bass. "Salsa Con-Fusion" (based on elements of one of Barretto's recent salsa-market hits,

"Guarare") segues from a kind of hard rock with a fast rumba effect into to a more solidly hard-rock feel, before winding up with another fast rumba. "Tumbao Africano" comes nearest to Palmieri's more ambitious moments with its synth opening leading to heavy percussion, including batá drums, and its mambo-inflected horns. The rest of the album is tightly melded Latin funk, very much of its period.

It is hard to believe that CBS knew what it was getting into when it signed a deal for an album by Eddie Palmieri. Unlike Barretto, whose attitude to marketing issues has always been down-to-earth, Palmieri apparently saw his album, *Lucumi, Macumba, Voodoo*, as a chance to strut his most experimental stuff on a larger stage. A couple of tracks presumably pleased Columbia's marketing types. "Highest Good" set Harlem River Drive-type music to a crossover funk beat. And "Spirit of Love" was presumably seen by Columbia as the hit-radio single with its fusion-jazz beat, wordless female chorus, and disco-era, soft-soul lead vocal. But "Spirit of Love"'s pop potential was subverted by one of Palmieri's gathering-storm modal solos (treble raindrops, chordal thunder on the horizon).

From the viewpoint of the mass-marketing mind, the rest of the album was even more problematic. The title track mixes Afro-Latin vocals and percussion (with prominent Brazilian cuica) with densely menacing bebop-influenced brass and reed ensembles, fairly prominent rock guitar, a fine baritone sax solo by Ronnie Cuber, R&B bass-guitar breaks . . . well, you get the idea: Top 40 it wasn't. And then there is "Mi Congo Te Llama," almost 13 minutes long. This opens with very authentic religious vocalists, chorus, and percussion, and moves via a cello passage to Palmieri in his most expressionist mood. A slightly pretentious string-section passage leads to and lurks under an uptempo mambo section with brass and coro that carve a path of reason through general "out" carryings on. A free ensemble framed more rock guitar before more coro with Cuban trumpet, a classic conga solo supported by Palmieri with one of the basic montunos he did so well, and a splendid final jam. *Lucumi, Macumba, Voodoo* wasn't Palmieri's best album, but it was well up there for experimentalism.

By now, even Fania Records was taking some notice of the shifts in the market. The overall effect of *Time*, the first album by Ricardo Marrero and The Group (a band then ten years old), was not of "crossover" so much as of a exceptional variety. "The Taste of Latin" (an instrumental) was notable for strongly jazz-inflected flute playing by David Valentin and tumbling piano by Marrero, more jazz than Latin, over a rhythm that blends bomba, bossa nova, and a mambo-cum-funk bass line. "Sin Tí," after a free piano opening, had a highly unusual vocal by Nancy O'Neil that mixes Brazilian and Cuban styles. "Sentido" (no relation to the Palmieri piece) is even more Brazilian, with flowing, glancing singing by O'Neil. "Land of the Third Eye" is rooted in 1970s expressionist jazz, with a free percussion opening, modal melody, and spiky soprano sax solo by John Figueroa.

While Barretto, Palmieri, and Fania boss Jerry Masucci aimed their different visions at the big time, less well-known groups continued to make adventurous recordings. Though essentially Latin jazz, Bobby Paunetto's second self-pro-duced album, *Commit to Memory*, goes well beyond Latin-percussion-with-solos-on-top formulae. "Spanish Maiden" floats flamenco harmonies and moods on top of a mid-tempo blend of Cuban rhythms; in "Taz," the piano shifts between Latin and jazz comping under sax solos that balances free jazz and more formal styles. The jazz waltz "El Catalan" is a warm, straight-ahead piece with just enough bite to stop it going sugary; it segues directly into "Dragon Breath," a blend of cool jazz tonality and funk rhythms. "Delta" mixed conservatory and jazz techniques, with an intro in canon form before an improvised contrapuntal ensemble-solo section. The Keith Jarrett composition, "Cora," has a highly unusual frontline of flute, clarinet, and bass clarinet, and a warm J. J. Johnson-style trombone solo. And "Good Bucks," an unorthodox 12-bar blues, is braced between the sacred batá drums and some remarkable Latin-blues piano playing.

The blurring of lines between Latin and fusion styles that marked the late 1970s was symbolized by an attempt made by Fania Records to move in on the (largely illusory) fusion-as-quick-buck-market. They issued an album called *Spanish Fever*, which added Maynard Ferguson, Hubert Laws, David Sanborn, Eric Gale, and Jay Berliner—all jazz players with Latin experience—to the Fania All Stars, itself a salsa equivalent of Jazz at the Philharmonic. *Spanish Fever* mostly veered between okay salsa and dull disco-funk, but in retrospect at least a couple of tracks rose above the ruck. "Que Pasa?" a strutting son montuno, has a rare Miami-style two-language coro, urban jazz-rock guitar from Gale, post-bop sax from Sanborn, a touch of bugalú, and a lick of reggae. "Sin Tu Cariño" with Ruben Blades includes fine jazz/Cuban piano (uncredited) from Papo Lucca, leader of Puerto Rico's Sonora Ponceña and one of a number of salsa pianists capable of excellent Latin jazz. These are not move-the-earth cuts, but they aren't dreck either.

While the Brazilian stream and the increasingly varied Latin-jazz-funk wave were important aspects of 1970s Latin jazz, the more straightforward descendants of Cubop were also flourishing. Gato Barbieri's *Chapter Three: Viva Emiliano Zapata*, recorded in June 1974, was as adventurous as anything the period had to offer. To record an album of thorough-paced jazz tangos in the mid-1970s was as revolutionary as poking around the edge of the politically correct Third World, because the tango, in so far as it was remembered at all, evoked an image both antiquated and comic. Even in Argentina, only Astor Piazzolla's campaign to turn it into a wing of art music got any respect, and Piazzolla was as yet unknown in the U.S. To hire Chico O'Farrill to write the charts was equally revolutionary. Though O'Farrill is one of the great big-band arrangers, both big bands and O'Farrill himself were as far from being hip in 1974 as the tango itself.

And *Viva Emiliano Zapata* was no nostalgia trip. The opening cut, "Milonga Sentimental," was indissolubly attached to the name of the greatest of tango singers, Carlos Gardel. But Barbieri and O'Farrill kept no part of the original except the introduction and elements of the rhythm. Barbieri had always been somewhat limited in his playing, but O'Farrill's arrangements and the tango rhythm freed him to give rein to a macho lyricism at which he only hinted else-where. All in all, not least thanks to an honor roll of outstanding jazz and Latin musicians, *Viva Emiliano Zapata* was Barbieri's best and most genuinely revolutionary recording.

Given that the tango was at the time so far out of fashion as to be somewhere in left field of Betelgeuse, it's an odd coincidence that another saxist was involved in a very different jazz-tango venture. *Summit*, which Gerry Mulligan and *nuevo tango* luminary Astor Piazzolla recorded for an Italian label, was more interesting than successful. The contrast of baritone sax and bandoneon, which could have been marvelous, was diluted by Piazzolla's lush orchestral arrangements, and Piazzolla's art-music orientation ironically left him sounding as much French as Argentinian in solo. It would have been wonderful to hear one of the classic bandoneon players, with their astounding punch and snap, in similar circumstances.

One of the pleasures of the mid-1970s was the return to Latin jazz of Chico O'Farrill, who had spent the last decade—his album for Gato Barbieri aside—working mostly for Count Basie. With his old colleague Dizzy Gillespie, O'Farrill picked up a major and seemingly dead form of the 1950s, the Latin-jazz suite. In June 1975, they recorded for Pablo Records two works for large orchestra, released under the title *Afro-Cuban Jazz Moods*. The first was "Oro, Incienso y Mirra," first played in public at a concert at New York's St. Patrick's Cathedral. In his notes to the album, O'Farrill describes this as:

> a hybrid from a structural point of view. Even though it tends to the rhapsodic.
> It is really a loose set of variations on . . . three firm thematic statements . . .
> the harmonic language is eclectic (polytonality, tone clusters, occasionally a

dash of serial writing juxtaposed to clearcut diatonic melodies and so forth), as it was not my intention to adhere to a rigid harmonic concept. . . . However, the most important melodic statements have a flavor of unmistakable Cuban origin and this is a key ingredient, aside from the rhythmic element, in establishing the Afro-Cuban ambiance of the music.

O'Farrill had been reworking the other composition, "Three Afro-Cuban Jazz Moods" ("Calidoscopico," "Pensativo," and "Exuberante"), ever since its original version was played by Clark Terry at the 1970 Montreux Jazz Festival. In Gillespie's 1975 recorded version, it was a splendidly ambitious work whose harmonic writing ranges from early big-band section punch to occasional tone clusters. Rather than base each movement on a different rhythm, O'Farrill alternates rhythms for contrast and progression within each section, setting a traditional Cuban guaguancó against a syncopated 6/8, moving from a building brass break into a light piano montuno. Above it all, Gillespie soars and capers like a man 20 years younger than his age, never making obvious concessions to the context but chopping across or floating freely over the percussion patterns with the ease of someone who has been soaking himself in Latin music for nearly 40 years.

As always, not all the interesting happenings of the period were in either prevailing styles or avant-garde mode. One of the freshest individual Latin-jazz releases of the year came from a bunch of old hands playing what were by now Afro-Cuban and Brazilian standards. This was a live recording, *Tokyo Debut*, featuring altoist Art Pepper with his basic group, plus percussionist Poncho Sanchez, then a Tjader sideman, and on some tracks Tjader himself and his guitarist Bob Redfeld. What mainstream musicians could do with mainstream numbers is graphically illustrated by the group's version of the bebop classic, "Cherokee." After a few choruses in familiar vein, matters take an unexpected turn when the drummer launches into a Latin-like lick between side drum and cymbals, Sanchez kicks in, and a heavy driving rhythm section impels Pepper onward, changing the whole dynamic of the piece.

An even more integrated Latin tinge opens Los Angeles-based alto saxist Arthur Blythe's first major-label recording, *Lenox Avenue Breakdown*. The opening number, "Down San Diego Way," features a curious but effective mix of elements. Cecil McBee opens it with a fine Cuban-style bass montuno, samba-type cuica and whistles courtesy of Guilherme de Franco, Jack de Johnette (doing a fabulous imitation of timbales on his traps), and Blythe in duet with flutist James Newton. Then each in turn solos on a somewhat calypsonian melody. Except for a faintly mariachi-ish touch in some of the ensemble playing, you wouldn't know

San Diego was a hop and a skip from Mexico, but this is a splendid number with a lot of love for the *típico* and even more for Anglo-Caribbean music.

This ease in playing both Brazilian and Cuban-derived pieces as aspects of a wider Latin-jazz vocabulary was an important, if not particularly ostentatious, part of the 1970s jazz scene as a whole. Many Anglo musicians had considerable experience in both genres. Some, indeed, played music mixed enough that their main distinction from late 1970s funk was a disdain for electronic instruments. And even here there were exceptions, like Clare Fischer. Fischer's music could only with the wildest stretch of the imagination be called funk, but unlike many musicians of his age, he was far from hostile to synthesizers and other electronic instruments. As he explained[12], he discovered synthesizers in 1970 when they were young, clunky, and expensive to move, and fell in love with them. He settled for the Rhodes electric piano because it combined portability with the ability to sustain notes far longer than the acoustic piano.

Fischer's skill at blending bop runs and Latin elements whether Cuban or Brazilian, was second to none, like his ability as an arranger/composer to use musical complexity as a road to freshness rather than obfuscation. His 1978 album *Salsa Picante* shows the sophistication of his vision. "Guarabe" started as what Fischer called "a kind of 6/4 mambo" and moved into a guajira with a harmonic bass tumbao. "Descarga-Yema Ya" was based on a lucumí percussion pattern and chant suggested by Sanchez.

As you'd expect from a man who once named a pet poodle Bachiana in honor of composer Heitor Villa-Lobos, the Brazilian influence on *Salsa Picante* was also strong. Ary Barroso's *samba cançao.* "Inquietaçao" is played without a bass to evoke the range a Brazilian guitarist uses. Fischer's own "Minor Sights" is an uptempo jazz-bossa with a long melody line and time changes that once again come over fresh rather than fancy.

The transactions by which jazz and Latin elements intermingled could by now be fearsomely complex. In the 1960s, Charles Mingus's work had not revealed any serious understanding of Latin music. But during the 1970s he produced two remarkable and highly personal examples of Latin-influenced music. His 1974 *Changes Two* album, recorded with a band that included transcultural pianist Don Pullen and the young trumpeter Jack Walrath, showed Latin influences in at least three cuts. Two of these were straightforward. "Duke Ellington's Sound of Love" is based on rhythms that, though basically straight 4/4, retain something of the Americanized habanera that was Ellington's main tool when he wanted to sound

---

[12] In the notes to his 1978 album *Salsa Picante*.

Latin. And another Ellington related piece, "For Harry Carney" includes a gorgeous bass riff that, without setting up a clave feeling, has a displaced second-phrase accent typical of much Cuban bass playing.

The Walrath composition "Black Bats and Poles" (originally, and since, called "Rats and Moles") was another kettle of fish. Walrath had spent some years of consistent Latin playing, both in the Bay Area and New York City. Aside from a strong montuno opening, "Black Bats and Poles" does not contain much overtly Latin material. But Walrath says he originally wrote it for a salsa group with which he was playing: "As he [Mingus] did it we just started playing it fast and it became a kind of jazz-rock piece. I originally wrote it for a Latin band because I like that [montuno] where the bass goes di-di-KOONG. . . . It was my only real conscious attempt to do an actual Latin arrangement, but it's something completely different on the record!"

Even more remarkable was Mingus's composition "Cumbia and Jazz Fusion," released on an album of the same name. According to Walrath, this was inspired by tapes of Colombian mountain cumbia Mingus heard while on tour in South America. The resulting piece was recorded by an orchestra that added to his regular lineup several extra horn players, Panamanian flutist Mauricio Smith, no less than four conga players—among them Candido Camero and Ray Mantilla—and sundry other percussionists. The 28-minute result was essentially a suite in one complex movement. It opens with field recordings of mountain cumbia. Soon Mingus lays a powerful bass montuno under the brass and double-reed on the original tape, with added studio percussion. This gives way to rich big-band walls of sound and a fine Walrath solo. The remarkable rhythmic drive generated by bass, percussion, and brass no longer has anything much to do with the cumbia, but it is heavily, if generically, Latin.[13]

Around halfway in, Mingus drops the montuno altogether in favor of straight 4/4, opening up the space for a more conventional sax-plus-rhythm sound succeeded by more rich, vaguely Kentonian brass and an impressionistic piano solo. Then comes a new, more vamp-like bass pattern and percussion in a humorous mock-rural passage; growly fun and games with the lower brass instruments; moments of swing and lyricism; a rumbón for drums and congas; and a section combining cumbia-like piccolo with a takeoff of "Shortnin Bread." The idea of blending South American traditional music and jazz was not entirely new, but

---

[13] The cumbia, which is a major dance form in Colombia, spread to Mexico and to a lesser extent the Spanish-speaking southwestern U.S. It also surfaced from time to time in New York salsa, but it is very rare in jazz. One of the few jazz-cumbias I know was composed by baritone saxist Ronnie Cuber, who was a regular sideman for Eddie Palmieri during the 1970s.

Cumbia and Jazz Fusion was one of the most adventurous Latin-jazz experiments of its period.

Mingus was not the only musician of the period to produce highly experimental jazz with a Latin edge. One group, in fact, signaled the beginnings of the wider multicultural influence that was eventually to be marketed under the label of World Music or worldbeat. The group Codona brought together two Brazilians—multi-instrumentalist Egberto Gismonti and percussionist Nana Vasconcelos—with African-American tabla player Colin Walcott, and trumpeter Don Cherry. Codona played a mix of Amerindian, Afro- and Euro-Brazilian, jazz, and "free" eclectic elements on which Vasconcelos sang and played berimbau, cuica, and percussion.

Nor was Codona the only group of the period to mix Indian and Brazilian elements with jazz. Former Mingus saxist John Handy formed a group called Rainbow with Bola Sete that included the great north Indian sarod player, Ali Akbar Khan, and the Carnatic violinist, L. Subramaniam. Too predictably, Rainbow was met by the record companies with a roar of silence, though it did give a few concerts in California.

Another, even more important and much less noticed prediction of the coming Latin-jazz movement, was the appearance of a new group called the Latin Percussion Jazz Ensemble which opened for Dizzy Gillespie at the Bottom Line. This first performance was a little disorganized despite the caliber of the players: Tito Puente, the leader; violinist Alfredo de la Fe, saxist Mario Rivera, pianist Eddie Martinez; conga-player Patato Valdéz; Johnny Rodriguez on bongos; and bassist Sal Cuevas.

The same year also provided one of Latin jazz's best-kept secrets, a recording on the tiny American Clave label that brought together most of the members of the future Fort Apache Band along with pianist Hilton Ruiz and a number of New York's most important non-"name" percussionists. With a couple of exceptions, the pieces the group play could have been in almost any enterprising Latin jazz group's repertoire: Wayne Shorter's "Nefertiti," Thelonius Monk's "Evidence," and Duke Ellington's "Caravan." It also pokes fun at the other side of the Latin-hyphenated ocean in a version of "The Lucy Theme" with all the deep percussion that I doubt Desi Arnaz had ever heard, let alone thought of trying to play. This was that rarity, a music fusing Afro-Cuban/salsa and hardcore jazz by a group of musicians with real experience in, and a real passion for, both.

A third event that forecast the Latin-jazz boom of the 1980s was the Newport Jazz Festival's belated recognition of the Latin element in jazz. This bore fruit in a number of special concerts, among them a "Schlitz Salute to Jazz Latino" fea-

Salsa bandleader Johnny Pacheco and percussionist John "Dandy" Rodriguez (son of "Johnny La Vaca") were regulars on the hardcore 1970s scene, but they both also contributed to Latin-jazz recordings from a basis of strong Latin roots. *Photo: John Storm Roberts*

1979 saw a turning point in Latin-jazz when the Cuban super-group Irakere appeared unannounced at a Carnegie Hall concert in June. They were joined on stage then by Americans Stan Getz and Maynard Ferguson (center). Reedman Paquito D'Rivera and trumpeter Arturo Sandoval (face obscured here) were to become important part of the subsequent Latin-jazz revival. *Photo: arnold jay smith*

turing the Machito orchestra and Tito Puente's concert band (with Dizzy Gillespie for several numbers), as well as Mongo Santamaria with Cal Tjader, and a "Brazilian Night" at Carnegie Hall, with João Gilberto, Stan Getz, and Charlie Byrd. But the high point of the festival went almost unnoticed: the appearance of the Cuban Latin-jazz group Irakere, which played its first U.S. gig unannounced on the same night as one featuring Airto and Flora Purim, which meant that most people who would have been interested missed them. Columbia Records, however, was on the ball, organizing a "live" recording session a week or so later that gave weight to Irakere's avant-*típico* aspects as well as their jazz leanings.[14] It was the perfect curtain-raiser for the Latin-jazz revival of the 1980s.

---

[14] Unfortunately the resulting double album stressed only the jazz and avant-Afro-Cuban sides of Irakere's music, an imbalance corrected only two years later by a Milestone release, *Chekeré Son*, recorded in Havana in 1979, and including all the *típico*-based numbers Columbia recorded but then left off its release.

❖ 9 ❖

But It Ain't Necessarily So. . .:

The 1980s

As the 1970s tiptoed into the 1980s, it seemed that fusion had become the predominant jazz style, and that funk rhythm sections drawing from soul-jazz, gospel, Cuban, and Brazilian sources were taking over from both "straight" or shuffle 4/4. Therefore, Latin jazz, as it had been understood, had served its purpose and was being subsumed into a larger whole. As usual, there was some truth in these misconceptions; but, as the old song says, it ain't necessarily so.

One joker that has always prevented critics from seeing what was really in the cards is the arrival of new musicians on the scene who move music in unpredicted ways. Among the players from overseas who were significant influences (whether or not they were capital-N Names) were ex-Irakere reedsman Paquito d'Rivera who by 1983 was running a band that contained two other relatively new names, neither of them Cuban: Brazilian trumpeter Claudio Roditi and Dominican pianist Michel Camilo.[1] And adding to the impact of Brazilian jazz were not one but two women pianists: Tania Maria from the beginning of the decade; and Eliane Elias, who arrived near its close.

Three very different recordings summed up the state of Brazilian music as the U.S. slid into the 1980s. Laurindo Almeida and Charlie Byrd's *Brazilian Soul* was a perfect example of the subtle and rich simplicity achieved by men who do not need to do too much. Byrd's composition "Stone Flower" and a fine version

---

[1] Camilo's first mark on the U.S. was made the same year when the retro vocal group Manhattan Transfer won a Grammy with his song "Why Not?". But he also scored Latin-jazz points early, playing piano on a couple of 1985 cuts for Patato Valdes's album *Masterpiece*.

of "Don't Cry for Me, Argentina" aside, the repertoire was oriented to earlier styles, including choro and even a waltz, and earlier or less-familiar Brazilian compositions: "Carioca"—mostly Almeida here—by Ernesto Nazareth, who died in 1934; and "Naquele Tempo," by one of the creators of samba, Pixinguinha, which is a delicious evocation of an older style of Brazilian melody and guitar work. Byrd's "Stone Flower" falls on the jazz-bossa side, a very quirky arrangement with bluesy chordings and bendings from Byrd as well as some fine bass playing.

At the other end of the jazz/Brazilian continuum, jazz/funkster George Duke spent three weeks in Rio to record *Brazilian Love Affair*. As he described it in his notes, his aim was to "get some cross-talk going on. . . . to bring a little bit of the fire that I had doing my funk stuff and jazz stuff, into that music without losing the essence of either one." The notion that Brazilian music lacks fire is a little bizarre, and most of the tracks fall between two stools. But at its best, notably "Up From the Sea it Arose and Ate Rio in One Bite," it works. The percussion (cuica and all) had all the drive and fire needed to mesh with Duke's funk sensibility, and the younger generation of Brazilian musicians were already eclectic enough to mesh with him pretty much seamlessly.

The third album was the first U.S. recording of a Paris-based musician with a totally new approach to jazz/Brazilian fusion, singer/pianist Tania Maria Correa Reis, known professionally as Tania Maria. Though she started out studying classical music and disliked playing in clubs, Tania Maria developed an unpretentiously individual style of both playing and singing that was evident from her first U.S. album, *Piquant*, released in late 1980 and produced by Cal Tjader. As she announces with a bang in her very first cut, "Yatra-Tá," her singing—like Flora Purim's, though to very different effect—combines a personal approach to jazz scat with a Brazilian equivalent that seems almost self-invented. Like Purim, too, she often scats in unison or octave with a piano line. But while Purim is all etheriality and spaciness, Tania Maria exudes earthy warmth. So does her piano playing, built from a personal mix of jazz chordings and semi-jazz phrasings with both Cuban and Brazilian *guajeos*, jazz-oriented bridges (not really bop, because they were far more chordal), and a personal version of the common salsa/Cuban trick of creating cross-rhythms by setting one hand against the other.

Tania Maria's own composition, "Super Happy," has a strong jazz-bossa underlay. The piano's jazz-oriented lines were tied into amplifications of the basic samba chord patterns, married to jazz voicings and progressions. But more often the jazz and Brazilian elements (whether vocal or instrumental) are both more equal and harder to disentangle. "It's Not For Me To Say," a jazz-bluesy vocal, has echoes of both Sarah Vaughan and Billy Holiday (a neat trick!). Her version of Jobim's "Triste" opens with a ballad accompaniment over a bossa-nova rhythm, first inferred then stated by the bass and guitar, before being picked up by the drummer. With the piano playing what—with a different rhythm under it—would be pure bebop-tinged, mainstream jazz-balladry, while the rhythm changes subtly from bossa nova to bossa-tinged jazz as the piece develops, the relationship of jazz to bossa nova becomes ever clearer. Tania Maria takes a different approach to "Chiclete Com Banana," a piece by Jackson do Pandeiro from the urban Northeast of Brazil. She gives it a bluesy piano part under rhythmic scatting that then turns as quirkily bluesy as her piano, before mixing highly rhythmic phrasing with flashes of Ella Fitzgerald. And "Vem P'ra Roda," a piece very much in Tania Maria's uptempo jazz style and a permanent part of her repertoire in the 1980s, is notable for a mellow, single-string jazz-guitar solo overtaken by her characteristic bop rephrasing of Brazilian melody lines.

Tania Maria's second album, *Taurus*, confirmed her stature as a musician with an approach as original as it is attractive and unpretentious. She also revealed the capability to handle a wide range of material. Many of the cuts were her compositions, with the best perhaps being "Que Vengan los Toros," which features some of the most complex and varied playing on the disc, and showed Maria's love of abrupt rhythm changes as a basis for her arrangements. In this piece, an intricate piano part with a pasedoble echo and hints of her conservatory background gave way to a jaunty bop-based solo. Then, there was an abrupt drop into ballad tempo that introduced a ballady scat vocal, before another abrupt return to the opening tempo. "Bandeira do Lero" contains a wonderful passage in which Tania Maria toughens her voice and sings a vocal riff paralleled by an archetypal bass groove. Then, the rhythm changes and the percussion heightens *batucada*-like while she drops her voice into the mix to close out the track. A striking aspect of *Taurus* is a seven-minute version of "Cry Me a River," so indissolubly associated with Peggy Lee. It's fascinating to hear how subtly Tania Maria shapes the melody and makes it her own over a shifting rhythmic pattern led by Rob Fisher's bass, before leaving it behind completely during scat choruses of remarkable rhythmic subtlety, playing around the beat to wonderful emotional effect.

Tania Maria next recorded one of her best-selling albums, *Love Explosion*, issued in 1984. This broke away from her trio format, adding a slew of hornmen (notably Justo Almario on alto) and, in a less felicitous attempt at fusion crossover, then-popular vocalist Jon Lucien on the title cut and a sweet-funk girl group. Tania Maria had enough originality and musical intelligence that it mostly worked. "Deep Cove View," for example, builds on a funk groove laid down by musicians who understood both jazz and Latin music, and created patterns that suited Tania Maria's typical chorded style. The same is even truer of the album's most successful cut, "Bela Be Bela," on which hit-hunting ambitions were forgotten. Tania Maria digs in, working all her usual elements of jazz, blues, and Brazilian jive into her solo amid plenty of the break-the-flow *cierres* she loved, supported by another powerful and appropriate bass-guitar funk groove, this one augmented with a definitely Brazilian-based rhythm.

The determination to make Tania Maria a big-S Star was resumed by Capitol Records later in the decade. Her 1988 release, *Forbidden Colors*, has all the usual elements of a bid for market share: synthesizers; English lyrics and studio musicians (in this case drummer Steve Gadd); and a downplaying of instrumental work in favor of vocals. That it worked better than many such "crossover" attempts was due to several elements. First, the group was small and coherent. Second, it included Airto Moreira, a good bridge between the real and the surreal. Third, the synth was limited to three tracks. Finally, Tania Maria's melodies were adaptable to English lyrics, and her vocal prowess was such that she could enliven even the dullest language. Both vocally and instrumentally, "O Bom É" was classic TM.

Live, Tania Maria remained less crossover-minded, as the recording of a sextet gig at the Great American Music Hall, San Francisco makes clear.[2] This recording also shows how she varied her standard repertoire over time. By now her unofficial signature tune "Yatra-Tá," for example, is if anything more jazz-oriented, though her scatting still has strong echoes of the Brazilian jazz style shared by singers like Elis Regina. The best passages have first bassist John Peña and then John Purcell matching her vocal line—a very effective tonal contrast. By contrast, the new numbers not only show the most change in her basic approach, but if anything take it further in the direction of Brazil than before: from "Fiz a Cama Na Varanda," which combines a pretty ballad in MPB vein with a rhythm that integrated *batucada* and fusion-jazz through "Come With Me," with its funk-jazz kick in the bass line contrasted with an unusually ethereal Luso-scat vocal to "Sangria" with strong *batucada* feeling in the percussion and opening ensemble, a fast samba throb in the guitar work, and voice and soprano sax mingling in some very Luso-jazz vocalizing.

While Tania Maria's approach to jazz-samba remained very Brazilian, the "straight" jazz musicians had by now transmuted the basic samba rhythm.

---

[2] It was called (perhaps as a comment on her previous effort) *The Real Tania Maria: Wild!*

Vibraphonist Bobby Hutcherson's 1984 *Good Bait*, with Branford Marsalis playing soprano sax, pianist George Cables, bassist Ray Drummond, and the veteran drummer Philly Joe Jones included a version of McCoy Tyner's "Love Samba" with a jagged, heavy pulse light years from the flow and bounce of the Rio Thing or even the choppy swing of enredo. Herbie Hancock's heavily electronic *Sound System* includes a piece called "Hard Rock," with a drum machine as light and swinging as Godzilla in a snit, but percussion like the fast choppy drumming of samba enredo. As the presence of three African drummers on *Sound System* symbolized, at this point the electronic-eclectic fusion movement among musicians like Hancock seemed to be straining conventional definitions of jazz, Latin, or other musical styles.

As if things weren't confusing enough already, by the mid-1980s the crossover between "world fusion," (often referred to as "world beat"), jazz, New Age, and Latin music was causing headaches effectively (though agreeably) summed up by the guitar duo Strunz & Farah. Their album *Frontera* includes cuts that are essentially Iranian/Spanish, and the flamenco influence is strong throughout. Yet "Quetzal," with Alex Acuna on drums and percussion and Miguel Cruz on congas and bongos, shows a Latin/jazz mix along with the Spanish music references of which the duo was so fond. In this piece, the fast, faintly new-agey guitars (with, in Farah's case, a fair amount of jazz phrasing) are carried by a definite montuno bass line at first, then—after a break that was essentially flamenco—a percussion/bass pattern that is semi-montuno/semi-groove.

Tania Maria's playing, soaked as it was in both jazz and Brazilian music of all kinds, was both individual and populist. And it may be no coincidence that while she was at her peak, there was a recrudescence of that older populist Brazilian jazz style, jazz-bossa. Just as older New York Latino musicians who had seemed on the edge of retirement in the mid-1970s were swept into the Latin-jazz limelight in the 1980s, so some of the stars of early 1960s jazz-bossa kept the torch burning. Among them was the man who probably introduced the style to the U.S., guitarist Charlie Byrd. At a week-long gig at Charlie's Georgetown, in Washington, D.C., Byrd celebrated the classic jazz-bossa sound with alto saxophonist Bud Shank, co-creator of an even older style, the 1950s jazz-baiao. Baiao or bossa, the mellow but acid-edged alto and cleanly rich guitar seemed as fresh as ever. Typically of the genre, only one number—Jobim's "Insensatez"—was a jazz-bossa perennial. The standout was the version of Jerome Kern's "Yesterdays," one of those ballads that make you suspect the bossa nova was somehow in the collective unconscious long before it manifested itself, so fine a fit they form. Byrd launched it with a lyrical solo guitar in the original spirit of the song, to which Shank acceded with gorgeous sax, rich and simple. Then the band kicked into a mid-tempo samba and got down to cooking with an unusual amount of jazz phrasing in Shank's solo, perfectly blended with Byrd's and his backup musicians' Brazilianisms.

Perhaps the ultimate indication that jazz-bossa was back in favor in the jazz mainstream was the fact that Ella Fitzgerald added Jobim to her ongoing "Ella Sings. . ." series. Her Pablo double-album, *Ella Abraça Jobím*, involved a mess of fine musicians, spread over a couple of three-day sessions several months apart. Like Sarah Vaughan, Fitzgerald basically sang the slow numbers in the way she would sing any ballad and was most creative in more up-tempo numbers, even managing to inject some freshness into "The Girl from Ipanema," singing it— and, after a Zoot Sims solo, scatting it—in pure Ella style. Because the backings combined the two genres, the results were essentially a personal take on jazz-bossa, though backed by a more solid rhythm section, including cuica, than the 1960s versions of the style.

The overtly Brazilian wing in 1980s jazz was given another lift by the arrival of a second woman pianist with eclectic tastes: pianist Eliane Elias. Born in São Paulo in 1960, by the time she was 12 she was playing Bud Powell, Art Tatum, and Bill Evans material. When she was 17, she joined MPB luminaries Vinicius de Moraes and Toquinho for three years. She moved to Paris in 1981, met Eddie Gomez, and moved to New York to play with his fusion band, Steps Ahead. She married saxist Randy Brecker and in 1985 they made an album together, *Amanda*. Then, in 1987, she recorded her own first album, *Illusions*, a mix of bop, ballads, and choro, backed by Eddie Gomez, Al Foster, Stanley Clarke, Lenny White, and Toots Thielmans.

The infusion of new Brazilians and the general spread in awareness naturally created another generation of Brazilian-minded American jazz musicians, who were starting to make a mark toward the end of the decade. One of these was guitarist Jeff Linsky, who played a smaller Latin-American guitar called a requinto on his first album, *Up Late*, which features a group of other young musicians with various kinds of Latin-jazz background. The centerpiece to *Up Late* is an eight-minute-plus version of one of Latin music's finest ballads, "Besame Mucho." Linsky gives it a good deal of flamenco influence, then moves to an almost classical approach subverted by bluesy bends before the percussion picks up a samba beat and flutist Steve Kujala takes off with a bluesy, bop-influenced flute solo with almost shakuhachi-like touches. The rest of the CD is strongly Brazilian-influenced, most originally in a version of the Rogers and Hart piece "I didn't Know What Time It Was" played as a flute-dominated samba.

The return of the Brazilian-jazz mainstream was matched by a certain Brazilian tinge in more experimental jazz groups. A prime example was the Pat Metheny group, which moved somewhat to the Latin-jazz-fusion center in the early 1980s, hardening its sound slightly by recruiting percussionist/vocalist Nana Vasconcelos—a logical move, given Metheny's earlier interest in Brazilian rhythms. Vasconcelos first appeared with the group in 1982, at a series of concerts in Germany documented on the ECM double-album *Travels*. Analyzing his influence reveals the complexities involved in tracing an element as pervasive as the Brazilianisms in *Travels*. At times, as with the group Codona, Metheny's band ranged very far afield. "Are You Going With Me?," for example, contained many Brazilian touches but also something of the held-note post-habanera ballad beat that U.S. country music inherited from Mexico via the southwestern U.S.; more eclectic yet, the opening held note hinted of a Scottish drone, and there were even similarities to some Arab drumming (all of which would have been available to Metheny on record by the early 1980s). "Straight on Red," a particularly fine track whose ethereal guitar floated above an earthy layer of percussion, was a clearer case of Brazilian influence, with drumming and a bass line like almost straight samba enredo. "Goodbye" had an equally obvious but very different Brazilian inflection, with Vasconcelos (buried in the mix) singing a theme with clear Portuguese-Brazilian aspects haunted by the ghost of Indo-African religious chants. Its pulse was as near as anything to a mix of bossa nova and bolero. "Song for Bilbao," too, was clearly Latin in its percussion and rhythm section, and Mays's keyboard playing, bluesy in the right hand, had phrasings in the left that fall in or close to montuno patterns. The Brazilian edge was an integral part of Metheny's work throughout the 1980s, and it moved progressively toward the popular Brazilian center, notably when the band lost Nana Vasconcelos and gained percussionist Armando Marçal, a grandson of one of the founders of urban samba.

The Brazilian presence in Latin-influenced jazz of all kinds also increased. Several cuts of Milt Jackson's *Big Mouth* draw much of their individuality from their Brazilian elements. "Bag's Groove," a version of Jackson's best-known composition (here transformed from a 12-bar to 6-bar frame) is paced by Carlos Vega's heavy-on-the-offbeat funk drumming. Paulinho da Costa, who opens the piece with a Cuban-style cencerro beat, later got into complex Brazilian patterns on woodblock. And even more improbably (but successfully), Jackson's ballad-like vibraphone playing on "The Days of Wine and Roses" is supported by a rhythm whose funk surface had a definite *batucada* undertow.

The use of a jazz-bossa rhythm with non-Brazilian ballads, which had started early in the original jazz-bossa period as part of the so-called "dilution" process, was becoming ever more standard practice. When Milt Jackson went back into the studio to record the remaining cuts of his *Big Mouth* album, he too turned ballad material—including the classic "I'm Getting Sentimental Over You"—into jazz-bossa. Jackson maintained the basic ballad feel despite a good deal of double-tempo in his own runs, while guitarist Oscar Castro-Neves confirmed and amplified the Brazilianisms. Ray Brown's bass under Neve's fine solo was also fascinating: It was Latinized in its montuno-like quality, but in the details of its phrasing very much jazz. In "I Owes Ya," it was Castro-Neves's guitar that establishes the boss-nova ambience, playing strongly rhythmic chordal passages before a three-way jam for piano, guitar, and bass in which the guitar's bossa nova chording also shades the piano's basically ballad approach.

Meanwhile, some of the earliest Brazilian-jazz-fusion luminaries were still in the mix. Though Wayne Shorter's *Phantom Navigator* wasn't nearly as Brazilian as *Native Dancer*, several of its tracks are colored by Brazilian-influenced funk. "Remote Control" combines a very heavy backbeat with ancillary percussion fills to create a by-now familiar funk rhythm that sounds like a well-sublimated samba enredo pattern. The Latin gene in "Forbidden Plan-iT" is more recessive, but it is still there, as forms a bridge, including what sounds a little like a pandeireta. And though "Yamanja" (the Yoruba goddess of water, spelt Brazilian-style) is dominated by a heavy backbeat, the percussion includes an agogó.

By now, the use of Brazilian elements in various forms by every sort of jazz musician was almost commonplace, and the ways in which it was done became ever more varied. Among the "hardcore" jazz examples, one of the most striking was *Ming's Samba*, saxist David Murray's first major-label release. Murray's powerful soloing made no concessions to Rio, but his accompaniment was another matter. Among his sidemen was drummer Ed Blackwell, born in 1927 in New Orleans and well-known there in the 1940s before he got involved with Ornette Coleman in the 1950s. Blackwell opens "Ming's Samba" with a drum solo reminiscent of the old big-band swing drummers, and later alternates a clave/samba cowbell pattern with a faster version that takes on the quality of a straight-jazz cymbal lick from early bebop. Like so many jazz pianists by this time, John Hicks had a solid grasp of Latin fundamentals, and made effective use of montuno patterns before moving into more mainstream comping under Murray's soloing.

While the Brazilian presence in Latin jazz was consistently strengthening throughout the decade, there were also major changes for the New York-based Latino bands. While the jazz world was becoming much more aware of hardcore Afro-Cuban music, the New York salsa scene was going through enormous change. Fania Records, so dominant during the 1970s, was in decline, and with it the near-stranglehold (never total, be it said) of the big names and the *típico* sound. They were replaced by a new and extraordinarily ebullient generation of merengue bands from the Dominican Republic, and the rise of so-called *salsa romantica*, a more or less salsa-flavored pop-idiom. During the 1970s, thanks to Fania's heavy promotion of already proven stars, new bands and young musicians had had a tough time getting established, especially if they did not fit into one of a few stylistic bags. Despite the commercial dominance of merengue and salsa romantica, the early 1980s saw both the rise of new groups playing one or another kind of Latin jazz and the revival of several older musicians' apparently fading careers. Two 1982 recording dates symbolized both aspects of this situation neatly. One was the debut recording on the new Concord Picante label of the Latin-jazz group led by Tito Puente, which had first appeared at New York's Bottom Line in 1979 and launched Puente on a new international career, scoring a smashing success at the Montreux Jazz Festival. The other was the first recording of Jerry Gonzalez' Fort Apache Band. It was also significant that there was a great deal of overlap between the two groups.

Puente's Latin Ensemble added to its leader's mambo flair two generations of musicians as familiar with jazz as with Afro-Cuban music, among them Jorge Dalto on piano; violinist Alfredo de la Fe; Mario Rivera on saxes and flute; and Jerry Gonzalez on congas and flugelhorn. The group mixed Afro-Cuban and jazz tunes, but tended toward jazz themes. The band's early repertoire was preserved on the LP *On Broadway* (not a live album despite the disingenuous title): "T.P.'s Especial" is a straight mix: a bop theme with mambo rhythm. "Sophisticated Lady" is notable for a solo by violinist De La Fé faintly reminiscent of Eddie South and a piano solo in which Dalto made no attempt to sound Ellingtonian but created a mood of post-bop lushness that fit the melody perfectly. "Bluesette" gets a funkish send-off with a heavy clave-based ensemble riff, moving into a mambo-like rhythm behind a terrific Rivera tenor solo. Typical of the subtlety of the band is the way Dalto flicked into a montuno pattern under the bop bridge on this piece. The eight-minute "On Broadway" is guitarist Edgardo Miranda's bicultural day out. First he played a nifty, mostly single-string, jazz guitar solo with bluesy piano accompaniment by Dalto. Then he takes up a cuatro and cooks, first montuno-style and then in semi-jazz vein but with a sonority very different from guitar, over a masterly bass montuno from Andy González.

Like its predecessor, Puente's second Concord Picante recording (this one by a bigger group), *El Rey*, contained a mix of new mambos, Puente classics (on this set, "Oye Como Va" and "Ran Kan Kan"), and jazz-associated numbers. Perhaps

Jerry González and the Fort Apache band brought young musicians with long Latin jazz and salsa experience together with players more associated with jazz. It was to become one of the most significant ensembles of the '80s and '90s. Clockwise from left, Jerry González, Larry Willis, Andy González, John Stubblefield, Steve Berrios, Joe Ford. *Courtesy Milestone Records*

the finest track, and certainly my favorite, was an obscure Eddie Heywood number called "Rainfall" with a haunting descending montuno which I assume is part of the original arrangement, lovely Jorge Dalto piano, and effective vibes playing by Puente, who turned the instrument into an extension of the rhythm section to an extent that I've rarely heard elsewhere. Equally intriguing is a big-band version of Coltrane's "Giant Steps." A Coltrane tune is a special challenge for any sax player of course—those were mighty big shoes—but Mario Rivera seemed undaunted, playing a semi-out solo mixed low in the section work. An effective passage of fast-bop ensemble work came next, leading to a tumbling piano solo that combines bop and montuno styles.

Jerry Gonzalez's Fort Apache Band included many of the young musicians working with Puente, among them both Gonzalez brothers, Miranda and Dalto, along with a roster of avant-roots musicians. The group's debut recording, *River Is Deep*, based its Latin jazz on deep Cuban roots, including three straight performances of Afro-Cuban percussion music: an invocation to the Yoruba god Elegua; "Guiro Apache," an unusual number for three shekeres and a cencerro;

and "Rio Está Hondo," a guaguancó for percussion and bass. Even the more conventional Latin-jazz numbers were based on rhythms closer to Africa than most "Afro-Cuban" jazz. The 11-minute "Bebop," which included a heavy comparsa rumbón with traps participating, was typical. The effect was much denser than the forward-moving Cuban dancehall rhythms, not just because of the large number of percussionists but the nature of the comparsa itself, a kind of drum cantata under the horns.

Though the Fort Apache Band was to be the best known of the Latin-jazz groups involving the younger generation of Latin musicians, it was not the only one. Among its peers was a band that included two of the foremost young percussionists combining jazz and Latin experience, leader Ray Mantilla and Steve Berrios (a trap-drummer as well as percussionist). In January 1984, The Ray Mantilla Space Station recorded an album, *Hands of Fire*.[3] Aside from a predictable stress on Afro-Cuban percussion forms, Space Station grooved off fairly avant-garde jazz styles. *Hands of Fire*'s major cuts are "Mantilla's Blues" and "Mariposa." The former opens with striking chachachá-type guiro (an instrument not much used by Latin-jazz groups) over which pianist Eddie Martinez, a veteran of Barbieri and Barretto among many others, moves, in a mere four bars, between montunos and bluesy jazz runs. The nine-minute "Mariposa" opens with two minutes of solo conga picked up by a minute's-worth of traps. A pause: Then both drummers lead into an urgent, fairly "out" theme interspersed by drum breaks and underpinned by a bass half-montuno/half-groove, before a soprano solo with Wayne Shorter echoes. The basic rhythm, which continues to be mixed though strongly clave-based, is given effective added juice from a steady cencerro-like cymbal stroke.

Yet another potential leader of the new Latin jazz generation was Jorge Dalto, who in 1985, after years of contributing to other people's bands, made the first recording with one of his own. Jorge Dalto & the Interamerican Band's *Urban Oasis* drew on at least a couple of generations of major musicians, most from the New York school, but two of them Brazilian. Benny Golson's "Killer Joe" was the album's grabber, heavy on the percussion and notable for a bluesy bop solo from Dalto, leading into a simple montuno behind percussionists José Mangual Sr. and Patato Valdéz, and culminating in single-chord riffs in clave rhythm for the ride out.

It was emblematic of the direction that Latin jazz was taking that the Brazilian presence was also felt in *Urban Oasis*. Over half the cuts are Brazilian-derived,

---

[3] Issued on the Red label from Italy.

Steve Berrios is typical of a generation of Latino virtuosi at much at home with jazz of all kinds as with salsa and the deeper forms of Cuban and Cuban-derived music. *Courtesy Milestone Records*

several with fusion-jazz overtones. Brazilian guitarist José Neto's "Sentido de Sete," for which most of the percussionists sat out, is Brazil-tinged fusion jazz, and "Ease My Pain" with Neto on guitar and Brazilian bassist Sergio Brandao on bass includes an agreeable fusion-jazz vocal by Dalto's wife Adela, given extra bite by the underlying samba rhythm. "Samba All Day Long," is sparked by excellent jazz-style flute from Artie Webb, driven by a samba rhythm with an unusually hard edge. And Freddy Hubbard's "Skydive" gets an appropriately fusion-jazz underpinning anchored by solid Latin percussion and enlivened by a good solo from Webb, straddling charanga and jazz. Dalto's untimely death in 1985 deprived the Latin-jazz world of a man who looked like he was becoming one of the new generation of significant bandleaders.

Cuban-born New York pianist Sonny Bravo, long one of New York's finest salsa pianists, came into Tito Puente's Latin Jazz Ensemble in Dalto's place. The

Argentinian Dalto had been highly adept at Cuban-style montunos, but to Bravo they were mother's milk. No rhythm section with Puente in it would be anything but tight; Bravo made it tighter yet and bound it more indissolubly to the front line. Any question about his impact was resolved by the second cut on the group's third album for Concord, *Mambo Diablo*. Bravo launches the familiar "Take Five" with an extraordinarily powerful version of the tune's defining opening piano pattern and never looked back, mixing the basic riff with a series of *guajeos* that kick an already smoking band into overdrive in what may be one of the finest single performances in Latin jazz. If ever there was a demonstration of what the piano means to this kind of ensemble, this is it! Mario Rivera's solo, far more gully-low than Paul Desmond's in the original, also works like a dream.

The fragmentation of the Latin market and the move of former mambo and salsa musicians into Latin jazz aimed at a more general jazz audience was not a phenomenon of the East Coast alone. As the decade started, the main news from the Bay Area was the rise of the Concord record label, with its specialist Latin-jazz sublabel, Concord Picante. Concord came out of the gate at top speed: Tania Maria was one of its artists, Tito Puente was to be another, and Cal Tjader was a very important third. Tjader, like Puente, was the sort of musician who gives a young label instant credibility, but more of a star in Concord's California home territory.

Musically, Tjader's *Gozame! Pero Ya. . .* broke no new ground. But it was a reminder that it's perfectly possible, even in jazz, to refresh (rather than merely recycle) a style established a quarter of a century before. That freshness was thanks in no small measure to long-term pianist Mark Levine and conga-player Poncho Sanchez, who provided an authenticity without which the band might have moved past mellow to lightweight. Though the subtleties tend to pass most listeners (and dancers) by, a pianist's contribution is relatively obvious. Levine's opening to his own "Shoshana" is characteristic: basically a montuno, but very "out" chordally by Latin standards. But he could also spark a piece like "Bye Bye Blues," backing rhapsodic flute with balladish piano before leading the rhythm section into a midpace stomper with a great montuno. Levine's comping, like most Latin-jazz piano, typically blends bop runs and Cuban-style rhythmic patterns. But under the percussion solo he plays a lengthy unchanging one-chord montuno, standard for salsa pianists but whose function only the best Latin-jazz pianists really grasp.

The conga's role is less obvious than the piano's. It doesn't peg the rhythm section: that's the job of the bass. It is no longer the only spokesperson and improvising voice: salsa percussion sections are more democratic than African

Conga-player Poncho Sanchez moved from Cal Tjader's band to become the California Bay Area's most important Latin bandleader, with equal footing in classic salsa and Latin-jazz. *Remo Percussion, courtesy Berkeley Agency*

and neo-African drum corps. But it is the deepest of the drums and it gives the rhythm the metaphorical as well as literal depth and that edge of gravity which (like the sadness under the surface in all great New Orleans jazz) makes it more than party-party music. At the time, Sanchez was not a star conga player like Aguabella or Santamaria, but he provided Tjader's group with a depth and steadiness to which his growing solo skills were gravy.

The effect of the growing confluence of disparate styles in Latin jazz was becoming ever more marked, though many groups were still separating out Brazilian-based and Cuban-based idioms in separate numbers. Nevertheless, Brazil, Cuba, and the U.S. were converging in individual pieces. Because producers often meddle in record sessions whereas live gigs are at the behest of the bandleader, a Cal Tjader gig at the Great American Music Hall in San Francisco in August was particularly revealing.[4] Pianist Mark Levine's "Santo Domingo" is based on a Brazilian carnival piece, but many of its elements—including Levine's piano montunos and in-clave comping chords—are Cuban-inspired, while Gary Foster's flute solo is essentially jazz-based, without any significant Brazilian or charanga elements.

---

[4] Captured on a recording called *A Fuego Vivo.*

The course of West Coast Latin jazz was altered not long after this session, when Tjader died of a heart attack while on tour in the Far East. It was a major loss. Playing a style most jazz writers did not understand, and in an age when the old European Romantic concept of the suffering artist had to some extent infected jazz, the modest, decent, talented, and agreeable Tjader did not get the critical respect he deserved. But whether you think jazz is about creating honest and complex music or expressing the deepest aspects of the artist's own personality (another Euro-Romantic concept, of course), Tjader's work should rank high, even if he was fortunate enough to have a temperament and a life that weren't the stuff of dramatic anecdotes.

After Tjader's death, conga-player Poncho Sanchez formed a group based in the San Francisco Bay area that was to become one of the most consistent Latin jazz groups of the decade, partly because it was so stable. Two members of the rhythm section, the Banda brothers, had been childhood friends of Sanchez in Texas. Like Sanchez's live performances, *Sonando* operated within a kind of Cubop-gone-*típico* ethos. The mambo-style "A Night in Tunisia" brings the piece home to the central Afro-Cuban canon in a total fusion of Cuban percussion and jazz soloing. "Con Tres Tambores Bata Un Quinto y Un Tumbador" opens with a splendidly mellow trombone solo before switching to a 6/8 rhythm that originated in the Afro-Cuban religious ceremonies, for a voices-and-percussion jam supported by piano. The title cut is a fine semi-*típico* chachachá with classic duet vocal and strutting rhythm. The group stakes its claim to the whole *típico* turf with a bow to tradition in the form of a flute-led performance of the classic danzón, "Almendra."

Bien Sabroso, Poncho Sanchez's second album and a Grammy nominee, confirmed the group as a solid, mainstream band based on good solos, good arrangements, and exciting playing in general, getting much of their job satisfaction from audience response and a full dance floor. It also continued what was becoming a band tradition of recording at least one Cubop classic per album, in this case Kenny Dorham's "Una Mas." "Keeper of the Flame" in particular takes a pleasingly fresh look at tested ingredients. An original piece, it has an ensemble arrangement that goes beyond the usual bop heads (it reminds me faintly of the Gerry Mulligan-Miles Davis Nonet) and a fast piano montuno that, while it stuck to clave, is neither bop nor any of the familiar Cuban-derived *guajeos*.

By the standards of a pretty stable unit, Poncho Sanchez's band underwent a major personnel overhaul for its 1985 recording, *El Conguero*. However, the changes—a new trumpeter and trombonist—adjusted rather than revamped the band's sound. Sanchez amplified his usual format by including three standard (or at least semi-standard) numbers by three very different musicians: "Shiny Stockings," by Basie alumnus Frank Foster; Joe Loco's "Yumbambe," a mambo from the 1950s; and the Gillespie/Pozo mega-classic "Tin Tin Deo," for which the group pulls out the Afro stop with chekeres and batá drums in the percussion. A 6/8 opening rhythm pattern performed by that percussion is reiterated through-out the statement of the piece, often set against 4/4 phrases to suit contrasting thematic elements.

Sanchez's success on the West Coast scene was something of an anomaly. Despite a large Cuban/Puerto Rican component in California's Latino population, there was still no hardcore salsa recording industry on the West Coast, and the salsa-oriented dance halls tended to book headliners from the East. Even the Escovedo dynasty—timbalero Coke, conguero Pete, and Pete's better-known, conga-playing daughter, Sheila—were in a semi-permanent state of struggle. They worked pretty steadily on other people's records, including various Latin-rock bands: Coke was with Santana for nearly a year, and Pete was involved with the excellent, though less-successful, Latin-rock group, Azteca. But recordings under their own name were oddly rare, given their experience and originality. One they did make, Pete Escovedo's *Yesterday's Memories, Tomorrow's Dreams*, with a band that included former Azteca guitarist Ray Obiedo, was as percussion-oriented as you might expect. But it also touched on South American idioms that only Gato Barbieri had explored in a jazz context. "Zina's Zamba," based on an Argentinian folk form, is the most strikingly unusual track, opening with a strummed intro from the small Andean charango guitar and changing into a full-blooded, *batucada*-like rhythm over contrastingly smooth horns. Equally arrest-ing in a different way is a long, powerful big-band approach to Eddie Palmieri's "Revolt," with a fast mambo opening, a substantial *rumbón*, and a powerful Sheila Escovedo conga solo.

Throughout the 1980s, the strengthening of the Brazilian wing, the move toward Anglo markets of New York Latino musicians, and the continuing activity of the funk-jazz fusion wing also brought about an ever more common three-way balance of "straight" jazz, Afro-Cubanisms of various kinds, and a Brazilian tinge. Pretty much any cut of George Duke and Stanley Clarke's album, *The Clarke/Duke Project*, illustrate the way post-Latin funk rhythms work. The piano opening of "Touch and Go" is essentially a montuno. And "Let's Get Started" is an excellent example of the basic fact that—like all Afrocentric styles, notably the Afro-Cuban rhythm section as well as traditional West African music itself—the complexities of funk rhythm sections were built from an interplay of patterns that taken individually were quite simple. On its own, the backbeat here would sound like a heavy approach to classic 4/4, but the two-measure bass-guitar groove adds more than a ghost of the clave responsorial effect even without clave's particular offbeat pattern.

Four out of nine pieces on Stanley Clarke's *If This Bass Could Only Talk* also rang changes on Latin-based fusion grooves. Charles Mingus's "Goodbye Pork Pie Hat," in which Clarke plays a bass lead, is supported by a fusionized version of the old loping habanera-ballad rhythm. "I Want to Play For Ya," on which Clarke plays everything except drums, is intriguingly ambiguous. Each measure has a two-phrase, call-and-response pattern that seems descended from Latin-derived funk grooves. But these have no vestigial clave feel, and the persistent held notes of the bass line also lacked a montuno feeling. The highly fusion-minded "Funny How Time Flies," on which Paulinho da Costa played largely undetectable percussion, is a clear example of the habanera-ballad, one-measure, clave-bass. Intriguingly, instead of a bass montuno contrasting or jigsawing with it, Clarke essentially plays the clave itself, or a partial version that interlocks with the drummer to complete the phrase.

Needless to say, by no means all of the interesting music was being made by the Big Names. One of the most interesting fusion recordings of 1980 was made for Latin Percussion, the country's best-known manufacturer of Latin rhythm instruments. Latin Percussion issued a handful of recordings, including an LP/booklet set demonstrating the complexities of the Latin rhythm section, mostly aimed at percussion wannabes. Their most interesting release involved the outstanding young Cuban violinist Alfredo de la Fe, whose credits included work with Eddie Palmieri (in concert and on record) and a stint with Tipica 73, one of New York's finest charangas. Driven by the montunos of the veteran bassist Sal Cuevas, *Alfredo* mixed charanga, rock, and funk with twists. "Hot to Trot" is a Cuban/disco/Brazilian jam of a kind that had been done before, but not often so well. "Canto del Corazon" is avant-charanga that mixes impressionist piano à la Jarrett or Corea, Star Trek synth, earthy percussion, vocals both charanga-style and disco, and fiddle shifting in and out of wawa enhancement over a funk backbeat. And the most intriguing cut of all is an extraordinary version of "My Favorite Things" arranged by a Colombian conservatory composer named Francisco Zumbeque. It moves from free eco-jazz twanglings and synth—Mary Poppins meets Mr. Spock—to a burnished, glowing string version of the melody with strong nineteenth-century overtones and a solo from de la Fe that moves from 3/4 to a faster 6/8 rhythm, with its Afro-Cuban religious overtones.

The three-way Brazilian-Cuban-funk nexus also provided 1980s jazz with some of its more popular newer artists. Like other jazz-fusion musicians with a

Latin bent who tarnished their reputation by achieving a certain amount of popular success, acoustic guitarist Earl Klugh, who claimed Laurindo Almeida as one of his major influences, has tended to be dismissed as a purveyor of jazz-lite. But his work with keyboardist Bob James provided a fresh and somewhat lighter take on Latin-jazz-funk that was to prove to be one of the subtexts of the 1980s Latin tinge. While acoustic guitar was, of course, basic to bossa nova itself and much jazz-bossa, an equal partnership of acoustic guitar and piano had been rare in jazz and its cousins since the great piano/guitar Chicago blues duos of the 1930s. Klugh's guitar work was clean and lyrical, with both a Spanish and a classical edge—an effective contrast to James's agreably bluesy acoustic piano.

Five out of the six numbers on the Klugh/James recording *Two of a Kind* were in some way Latin-influenced. The most notable is "The Falcon," which, after a long rhapsodic opening, kicks into a rhythm that is clearly Latin-derived though quite far from Cuba or Latin New York. This is modified under James's piano, then changed again into something close to a *son* montuno driven by percussionist Sammy Figueroa's classic, straight-ahead cencerro, before developing an underlying pulse reminiscent of street rumba, but offset by a Brazilian shaker. In its way, the backing to "Wes" is even more intriguing, with the crisp snap of classic tango but an added bounce (created largely by Figueroa's conga, both in line and sonority) that is far from tango in spirit.

Meanwhile, Klugh's inspiration, Almeida, was back in the studio with Charlie Byrd to record an album that reflected the opening up of categories during the 1980s. Despite the fact that Almeida by now was tarred with a jazz-bossa brush, it drew on music from all over Latin-America. *Latin Odyssey* was, in fact—with an exception or two—not a Latin-jazz album. It moved between "national" (localized conservatory) music and the more upmarket reaches of popular music (Lecuona's "Gitanerias," the waltz "Turbilhao de Besos," a pretty version of Manuel Ponce's habanera "Estrellita" and a ravishing one of his "Intermezzo Malincolico," and Piazzolla's "Zum and Resureccion del Angel"). And despite jazz-based brushwork from drummer Chuck Redd, the undoubted swing of "El Gavilan" stems from its own history: It started life as a Venezuelan joropo and was arranged by its composer into something that comes close to capturing the fire of a Mexican huapango.

I commented earlier on one of the major ironies of jazz: the fact that of all the Latin-American idioms that have led to specific Latin jazz genres, the habanero/tango—so influential on jazz at its inception and so adaptable to small-group jazz styles (with its one-measure rhythmic pattern and, in the case of the tango, the remarkable snap of its small combo version)—had so little post-bebop impact. In the 1980s, that began to change (even aside from the continuing work of Gato Barbieri). Paul Bley, Gary Burton, and David Murray were three jazz musicians who rediscovered the tango as a jazz idiom.

Bley, who formed a stylistic movement of one, was working largely in Europe. The title track of his 1983 solo album *Tango Palace*[5] was not only a rarity but way out in jazz left field—an elegant piece more classical even than Piazzolla's more art-music-minded efforts. It was almost a tango as Chopin might have written one! Burton made an interesting tango album with pioneer Astor Piazzolla's group (see below). The most exhilarating of all these jazz-tangos was David Murray's "Spooning," which Ed Blackwell opens and closes with sublime eccentricity by playing New Orleans-style parade drumming! Murray's theme fits the tango rhythm and ethos perfectly, without in any sense sounding imitative of the Argentinian originals.

Perhaps thanks to the success of the Nonesuch "Tango Project" recordings, the flurry of jazz interest in the style increased mid-decade. In 1985, Laurindo Almeida and Charlie Byrd recorded *Tango*, an album full of non-tango references of all kinds, and yet one that came off as totally integrated. (In Argentina itself, the guitar duet has been around in tango for ever, from Carlos Gardel to conservatory-oriented art-tango players). As an ensemble, and when Almeida played lead, the album was largely in the style of the art-tango. But Byrd throws into his solos—in particular on "La Rosita" and "The Moon Was Yellow"—jazz-oriented runs and bluesy bent notes that turn some numbers into tango-jazz of a high order. (As further evidence of these men's musical intelligence, they resurrected that brilliantly generic, greatly under-rated composition, "Hernando's Hideaway.")

These rare jazz-tango initiatives also produced one of 1986's most interesting Latin-jazz events. Gary Burton's Montreux appearance with Astor Piazzolla's quintet, recorded by Atlantic as *The New Tango*, comes nearer than anything I have heard to a true jazz tango, in part because it is a sextet recording without the strings that marred Gerry Mulligan's collaboration with Piazzolla a generation before. Given Piazzolla's predilections, it still has a very strong art-music cast, notably in the violin playing of Fernando Suarez Paz. Burton's vibraphone matches Piazzolla's usual music more closely than Mulligan's sax both in tone and style (which could be seen either as an advantage or not). But when the group develops the whiplash snap of the classic tango (as in "Vibraphonissimo"), the potential for a true tango-jazz starts to emerge.

---

[5] Released on the Italian Soul Note label.

Meanwhile, the country's most famous and influential congacero—Mongo Santamaria—was also back in a jazz setting with Dizzy Gillespie and a group that included a drummer/timbalero, Steve Berrios, who was to become one of the big names in 1980s Latin jazz. *Summertime* comprises four long numbers. "Mambo Mongo," perhaps the peak, is a strong workout for Santamaria with a classic piano and bass montuno backing him up, and outish soprano sax (not credited!) making a very nice contrast with the downhome sound below it. The other high spot is a particularly good 14-minute version of Santamaria's own "Afro-Blue," which the mellowness of late-period Gillespie suits especially well, as does the unusual rich, baritone-led sound of the opening—a splendid foil for the standard flute part as well as for the powerful way in which Santamaria drove it. Despite the provenance of the title track (which has been surpassed by other Latin-jazz versions of the tune) and the typical Latin-soul à la Mongo of the opening to "Virtue," *Summertime* was surprisingly *típico* for a Gillespie-led group.

Santamaria's own 1987 album, *Soy Yo*, documented his consistent tendency to create Latin-jazz-funk versions of recent pop numbers, in this case, Anita Baker's "Sweet Love" and Sade's "Smooth Operator." As always, Santamaria kept his sound fresh by using young musicians. "Sweet Love," in an arrangement that contrived to be both tight and lush, is a vehicle for quite powerful sax playing by Sam Furnace. The title track is a reminder that Santamaria was one of the creators of the whole idiom. It opens with a very heavy funk offbeat, develops into a samba enredo with cuica and other Brazilian percussion under an attractive tenor solo, and gains variety from a nice impressionist post-bop piano solo. Even more interesting is "La Manzana," which opens with an essentially eight-to-the-bar rhythmic pattern, then moves via a bass montuno break into a 6/8 piece as if progressing from Black to Latino New York. Among these modern players, guest artist Charlie Palmieri's work on "Mayeya" provides an almost startling and extremely effective contrast: the kind of lush older Cuban style that many younger pianists have forgotten or never known.

Mongo Santamaria's *Soca Me Nice* was notable for a substantial Brazilian edge along with its Afro-Cubanisms. "Tropical Breeze" and "Cookie" are both light sambast, the latter with a flute duet. Even "Soca Me Nice" itself, a piece with far more punch than the real soca bands both in the rhythm section and the horns (including a tremendous tenor solo from Mitch Frohman), contains a strongly Brazilian percussion jam. The rest of the album uses jazz, soul, and Afro-Cuban elements in the way Santamaria has made so familiar over the years. It contains one brilliant track: a version of the Beatles' "Day Tripper" done as a guajira in which the Cuban rhythm fits the melody like a glove.

By now, Latin jazz was coming in pretty much all imaginable forms, but the full-blooded first-generation cross was still important, both in its own right and as a role model. The engine room of all Afro-Latin music is the rhythm section. And again, the support that salsa rhythm sections of any caliber give the front line is incomparably greater than its equivalent in non-Latino Latin-jazz. Even when all the musicians in a Latin-jazz rhythm section are outstanding, they rarely approach the power and cohesion of a piano-and-rhythm group all of whose members share the same reverence for the tradition and its roots.

The album of choice for devotees of the real thing in Latin piano and Afro-cuban music was undoubtedly Charlie Palmieri's *A Giant Step*. This is as fine an example as you'll find of full-scale, Cuban-derived piano quintet music, backed by a rhythm section whose members are major musicians in their own right. Some of the cuts are Palmieri's own compositions; others are older standards like the venerable Puerto Rican danza, "Bajo las Sombras de un Pino"—modified habanera rhythm and all—and the delicious, 1940s-redolent "Rumba Rhapsody." One track was a version of younger brother Eddie's "Muñeca" with enough brotherly love to refrain from outshining its composer but every indication that the job could have been done. All were extraordinary. Though he was always modest about his jazz capabilities, Charlie Palmieri could outplay most pianists in jazz, let alone in salsa or Latin jazz. And his talent for balancing freshness, and reverence for tradition was if anything finer than Eddie's. He launches "Fiesta a la King," for example, in classic Cuban vein, moves into a session of trading fours (a purely jazz format) with bassist Bobby Rodriguez, then lays out the theme in the right hand supported with bop chords before moving into very "out" *guajeos*. His own "Start the World I Want to Get On" (a title that reflects his attitude as well as his humor) opens with an enhanced montuno using advanced chordings, moves into bop, single-note runs, then switches to more classic Cuban piano before picking up the original "Stop the World. . ." theme as a montuno under the percussion jam.

A different kind of heavily *típico* Latin jazz came from the minute Cayman label. You don't get much more quality and variety than are on the Cayman All-Stars' album *Super All-Star*. The personnel is a roll of honor, the titles are classics, and the style has one foot in Latin jazz and the other in Cuban *típico*: superb charanga-style flute from ex-Irakere star Paquito D'Rivera and conjunto trumpet from Chocolate Armenteros; but also solid jazz-based solos from saxist Hector Rivera and trombonist Steve Turre. The musicianship and unselfconscious joy generated by recordings like this defies description or categorization.

An interesting feature of the 1980s was the number of older jazz musicians who had begun including Latin-jazz numbers in their regular repertoire without feeling the need to add Latin percussion. Many of these were jazz-bossa numbers that had, so to speak, grown along with the musicians, neither influenced by the 1970s avant-Brazilian musicians, nor simply retro in spirit. Alto saxist Frank Morgan, whose career had been distorted by a long-term gig in the California prison system, included a couple of Latin-flavored numbers on his album *Lament*, with Cedar Walton on piano, Buster Williams on bass, and Billy Higgins on drums—all of whose Latin-jazz experience went way back. "Ceora" and "Ana Maria" both use a subdued bossa-nova pulse carried without guitar to enliven mid-tempo ballads. The overt Brazilianism isn't much more than a tinge, but a tinge that subtly modifies both the bass line and Walton's piano phrasings, even though neither was obviously Brazilian.

At the other end of the spectrum, Morgan also showed up on vibraphonist Terry Gibbs's *The Latin Connection*, along with Sonny Bravo on piano, Tito Puente playing timbales on some tracks, and a heavy New-York-Latino rhythm section. The group plays all jazz (rather than Latin) standards, most of them from the bebop era. Most of the soloing is from Gibbs, but Morgan gets in some admirable bebop. There was too little Sonny Bravo (though when he does solo, his match of jazz to the underlying clave rhythm is spiffing), but he is constantly there with montunos honed to an edge that Latin-jazz pianists rarely achieve.

As the decade faded, releases by musicians not usually associated with Latin jazz continued to underline the increasingly indissoluble jazz/Latin interdependence. Unlike some of his earlier recordings, the McCoy Tyner Big Band's *Uptown/Downtown*, on which that Latin-jazz veteran Steve Turre played trombone, contained no ostensibly Latin-jazz material; but one track, "Love Surrounds Us," was built on an interesting rhythm pattern spread over two measures, clearly though unidentifiably Latin-derived. Similarly, keyboardist Buddy Montgomery's recording, *So Why Not?* (with former Tania Maria conga player Willie T. Colón in the rhythm section) included a couple of pieces with fusion-jazz grooves that at times seem to have samba echoes: the title cut and "My Sentiments Exactly." Colón adds depth to the lyrical "Waterfall" with a traditional Cuban conga triplet pattern on the fourth beat as well as more conventional bolero-like fills.

What one might call "straight" Latin jazz (to distinguish it from the various funk-oriented idioms that had developed, while recognizing the degree of overlap that makes all labels iffy) was far from being the purview of the older musicians alone. Three important arrivals from the Caribbean kept mainline, mostly Cuban-based, Latin jazz fresh. The more creative end of Latin jazz got a powerful boost during the mid-1980s thanks to various former members of the Cuban Latin-jazz group, Irakere. Most notably, saxist/clarinetist Paquito D'Rivera had been leading a band for a couple of years before he recorded *Manhattan Burn* for Columbia. This product of several sessions showed a fusionist sensibility, besides including several excellent straight-4/4 cuts to establish D'Rivera's unhyphenated status. Like any good jazz recording, this one was full of pleasing surprises, like the use of the familiar "Night in Tunisia" montuno as an intro to "All the Things You Are." But aside from such evidences of innate musicianship, two things made this, like many other D'Rivera sessions, important. One was D'Rivera's liking for older and unfamiliar Latin American idioms from countries usually ignored, here indulged in a charming clarinet/acoustic guitar duo rendering of two Venezuelan waltzes. The other was his penchant for the clarinet itself, an instrument virtually extinct in post-bebop jazz. In "Paquito's Samba" he again sets clarinet against Haque's acoustic guitar, backed by a Brazilian-augmented rhythm section which gave a very Rio-carnival feel under Claudio Roditi's admirable trumpet solo. These tracks, not the fusion efforts, are the ones that still sound fresh more than a decade later.

1988 saw the first recording led by an important new pianist, Michel Camilo. Born in the Dominican Republic of a partly Cuban family, Camilo came to the U.S. in the early 1980s and went solo in 1985 after working with Tito Puente (with whom he appeared at the Montreal Jazz Festival), Paquito D'Rivera, and others. Camilo has claimed influences ranging from Beethoven through Ernesto Lecuona to Art Tatum and Erroll Garner, and unlike some Latino "straight" jazz players, he is open about these influences. As he commented in the notes to his eponymous first album, "the Caribbean cultural heritage is part of my style. You can hear it in my playing. One tries to extract that percussive touch from the piano, which is also a percussion instrument." At the same time, he used an acoustic trio "because it's the traditional jazz format. It is important to follow the jazz line to prevent anyone from saying that we can only play Latin music. . . ."

Six out of the nine numbers on *Michel Camilo*, recorded in February 1988 with Mongo Santamaria on one cut ("Blue Bossa"), were indeed "straight" jazz. One of the others, "Para Voce (for Tania Maria)" was quite elusive. The bass and drums played a quirky jazz-with-a-little-cryptic-samba pattern, over which Camilo's phrasings (themselves not overtly Brazilian) combine to intensify a real but almost subliminal samba/bossa feel that anyone not knowing Brazilian music well would likely miss. Unsurprisingly, given Santamaria's presence as well as the nature of the by-now-classic theme, "Blue Bossa" was more extroverted, but it was no less original. After an amusingly grandiose Lecuona-esque opening, Santamaria came in alone. Camilo's solo opened with a Brazilian clave-based theme, which he moved to his left hand while playing fairly fast bop on top. Then he threw in a couple of *guajeos* that may have been a sign to Santamaria that a break was coming up, and began scattering more overt Cuban references. Santamaria's playing throughout was as effective and brisk as you'd expect, but in all honesty Camilo's piano was so absorbing that you didn't really notice the conga much.

Though the 1980s was perhaps most notable for the amazingly complex and complete absorption of Brazilian, Cuban, and other Latin elements into what seemed an ever-more Latinized jazz mainstream, there were other activities that were to prove just as important. One was the increasing mix of jazz with deep, often religious-derived Cuban percussion. There had already been a handful of examples in earlier decades, but during the 1980s the impetus increased. Among the musicians moving out of the specifically Latino music scene, the Fort Apache Band was particularly wedded to this concept. But there were other musicians who, whether or not they became names, were to show themselves important innovators.

One example of this trend was a short-lived new Latin jazz group, Bakateo, who made an appearance back in 1980 at one of New York's last jazz lofts. The

Pianist Michele Rosewoman represents the most consistently interesting wing of Latin-jazz within the general jazz world. An outstanding soloist she has also worked since the early 1980s with the big band, New Yor-Uba. *Photo: Ron Campbell*

New Yor-Uba, inspired by the Afro-Cuban religious tradition and powered by a percussion section of the Yoruba batá drums that are crucial to the ceremonies of lucumí or santería. L–r: Orlando "Puntilla" Rios, Rosewoman, Gene Jackson, Gene Golden, Eddie Bobe, Abraham Rodriguez. *Photo: Ron Campbell*

group's repertoire consisted of bop-oriented numbers built on rumba-columbia, comparsa, bakoso, and other extremely roots-Afro-Cuban rhythm, a formula that was to become more common as the decade wore on. The group included a remarkable young pianist, Michele Rosewoman, who emerged as an outstanding musician. "Using none of the montunos that provide Latin references in most jazz fusions," I wrote at the time, "she welds broken, tumbling melodic phrases, fiercely chopping full-hand chords, Bud Powell runs, and a constant Afro-Cuban rhythmic undertow into a totally coherent whole—the first purely jazz playing I've ever heard that meshed with Latin rhythms instead of riding above them."[6] Rosewoman has remained one of Latin jazz's best pianists and, alas, best-kept secrets.

This roots-end activity continued throughout the decade. One of the most powerful Latin-oriented albums of 1987 was *Arawe*, recorded by Cuban con-gacero Daniel Ponce. This is a remarkable recording on a number of levels. Though it is extremely percussion heavy, the horn arrangements are almost as powerful as the drumming, as was some of the soloing: notably by Steve Turre on

---

[6] In a review for *The Village Voice*.

"Orimi"; Tito Puente playing marimba on "Holiday"; and cuatro player Yomo Toro on a couple of tracks.

Ponce made use—for his own particular purposes—of a facet of Cuban music far more rural and far more Afrocentric than any of the earlier dance styles. It was an endeavor that had begun with Dizzy Gillespie's short-lived and inchoate collaboration with Chano Pozo four decades earlier (see Chapter 4). Now in the 1980s, Fort Apache, Ponce, Rosewoman, and many others were finding ways of realizing a vision that had, however dimly, been one of the greatest of Gillespie's many crucial contributions to Latin jazz. It was a vision that was to carry forward strongly into the 1990s, which was to reinterpret its legacy from the 1980s in so many rich and often surprising ways.

◈ 10 ◈

Everything is Everything:

The 1990s

For Latin jazz, the 1990s has been a decade of great richness and also of confusion, which can be summed up by an Eddie Palmieri title, "Everything Is Everything." All the various strands that went into the ever-more complex scene of the previous decades were proliferating, and at the heart of this proliferation was an audience, or audiences, with greater understanding of more root styles than had perhaps ever existed before.

It was a sign of the times that in 1990 Mongo Santamaria, the man who as much as anybody was responsible for the Latin-jazz/funk sound, played a gig at Seattle's Jazz Alley using largely *típico* material, notably in the rhythm section. The music was far from pure salsa.[1] The solos were mostly solidly Latin-jazz oriented, and often original: on the opening track, "Home," pianist Bob Quaranta plays a nice line in montuno rhythm created from soul riffs (his piano on the soul-jazz chachachá "Bonita" is also magnificent). But most of the underlying rhythms are Afro-Cuban, and (though he played bebop elsewhere) Ray Vega's beautiful solo on "Bonita" draws heavily from the Cuban, rather than the jazz, trumpet style. This isn't to say that the band couldn't do the soul-jazz strut, as "Philadelphia" proves. But even here the rhythm section has largely abandoned semi-funk grooves in favor of something more completely Cuban.

The rapid growth in the new wave of Cuban influence on jazz during the early 1990s stemmed in large part from two émigré ex-members of Irakere: reedsman Paquito D'Rivera and trumpeter Arturo Sandoval. The Messidor recording

---

[1] It was released on the CD *Live at Jazz Alley*.

Reunion brought them back together along with a near-sensational group. This may not be the best recording by either artist, but it was certainly my favorite for swing, joy, and chutzpah. I have heard few interpretations of a classic more compelling than their version of Mario Bauza's "Tanga":[2] from Danilo Perez's blues-drenched piano through Fareed Haque's single-string guitar, Sandoval's Gillespie-reminiscent muted trumpet and tearing wall-of-sound open solo, D'Rivera remaking the alto sax with a nod to everybody who had remade it before him, and a bass line moving easily between montunos and straight 4/4. D'Rivera was particularly fine in solos that were fresh and original while evoking Charlie Parker at every turn of phrase. I'd hate to do a Latin-jazz Quality Top 40, but *Reunion* would be a strong contender if I was forced.

Paquito D'Rivera's contributions to the 1990s Latin jazz scene have been many and varied. He has recorded for Columbia, and for the tiny Cayman label. He has played booting sax on jazz numbers and liquid clarinet on a Venezuelan waltz. In 1996 he organized a big band for a CD called *Portraits of Cuba* that continued the on-and-off tradition of Latin-jazz suites. The suite's arranger, Carlos Franzetti, drew on a century's worth of compositions stretching from "Tu," the most famous nineteenth-century habanera, to the theme from "I Love Lucy" (!), taking in along the way such classics as the Ignacio Piñeiro *son* "Echale Salsita" and the more or less inevitable "Peanut Vendor." Franzetti commented that he tried to make the relationship of the soloists to the ensemble that of the concerto grosso (i.e., divided between solo and ensemble sections). Despite recognizing the pivotal role of Cuban percussion, he aimed to create the rhythmic pulse out of the wind sections as well as the percussion, as a counterpoint. Chico O'Farrill aside, I can't think of anybody who is currently even attempting this scale of work in either jazz or Latin music.

D'Rivera and Sandoval were not the only Cuban musicians kindling interest in the island's newer sounds. Not only was the founder of Irakere, Chucho Valdez, still working in Havana, but another young Cuba-based pianist, Gonzalo Rubalcaba, was beginning to make a splash in Europe and earning a reputation among U.S. jazz audiences who couldn't hear the man himself. In July 1990, bassist Charlie Haden and drummer Paul Motian, of Liberation Orchestra renown, appeared at the Montreux Festival with the phenomenal young player.[3] Much of the concert was straight jazz. But at times (notably in his own composition "Prologo Comienzo"), Rubalcaba mixed rich post-bop piano, sometimes built on

---

[2] Incorrectly attributed to Gillespie in the notes.

[3] A meeting captured on the Blue Note recording *Discovery*, issued under Rubalcaba's name.

snatches of Cuban themes, with overtly Cuban elements ranging from the elegantly decorated style of the older virtuoso musicians to almost-familiar montunos. But much of the time his fusion was more unconscious and more complete: the work of a man equally at ease in jazz, Cuban idioms, and classical music.

A more eclectic session with Rubalcaba and a varied collection of other Cuban musicians was organized in Cuba by Canadian flutist Jane Bunnett. Bunnett has said that her aim in recording *Spirits of Havana* was not primarily to make a Latin-jazz-fusion recording; however, that's what she was inevitably going to get, with Gonzalo Rubalcaba and Hilario Duran among the musicians and "Epistrophy" among the titles. At the same time, with traditionalist singer Merceditas Valdes and vocal/percussion group Grupo Yoruba Andabo on board, there was plenty of both Deep Afro and *típico* Cuba in the mix. Bunnett's session was, in fact, a version of the approach taken by avant-traditionalist groups like the Fort Apache Band. That it was so different from their work reflects the richness of the Latin-jazz tradition as it has evolved as well as the distinctions among individual musicians.

The core Latino scene that had for so long fueled other idioms had changed almost unrecognizably by the beginning of the decade. Throughout the 1980s, New York had steadily lost its dominance in international Latino markets, and New York salsa had lost most of the young Spanish-speaking audience to various forms of Latino rap and to international Hispanic pop.[4] By 1990, pretty much all the major New York Latino musicians had moved into (in the case of some of the older musicians, back into) the wider jazz field. And they had done so with considerable success.

The growth of the Latin-jazz market was particularly freeing for Ray Barretto, whose early career had, after all, been built on bridging jazz and Latin music. *Handprints*, Barretto's first recording with a new Latin-jazz septet, was one of his most intriguing recordings in the genre. Much of the credit for this was due to Barretto's new pianist, Colombian Hector Martignon, who announces his presence from bar one with a stunning montuno on "Tercer Ojo" strongly reminiscent of Ellington's 1936 "Echoes of Harlem" in clave rhythm. But there was also a remarkable power and tightness about the band, and a freshness about almost all the arrangements. One of the best cuts, the Barretto composition "Brandy," begins as a mid-tempo jazz-bossa, guitar and all, and gains added oomph from a gorgeous soprano sax solo and a percussion section both light and assertive. Just

---

[4] As well, of course, as to African-American and other Anglo idioms, which had been appealing to U.S. Latinos since the 1940s.

as fine in its very different way is "Triangle," with horn charts that give off a whiff of Haitian jazz and a series of competitive mini-solos that create the kind of extroverted joy in which salsa has long had such an edge on jazz.

The revival of older styles and of the Old Guard reached back beyond Barretto—and even Tito Puente—to Mario Bauzá, the man largely behind the musical innovations of Machito's Afro-Cubans back in the 1940s. Bauzá had split with Machito in the 1980s and formed his own group, but it was in the '90s that his big band started making serious waves. In 1991, he recorded a suite in five movements based on his own '40s composition "Tanga," which was arranged by Suitemeister Chico O'Farrill.[5] Like all of O'Farrill's writing, this combines rich ensemble sonorities with a rhythmic range from classic mambo and creamy bolero to Afro-Cuban religious 6/8 and secular *rumba abierta*—a journey back into the music's roots that inverted the common progression of such works. Several of the other cuts were arranged by another Machito veteran, Ray Santos, in total contrast to O'Farrill's style. Some are jazz-mambo inclined, some *típico*. All were driving, fierce, and filled with tearaway brass and sax solos. Yet another contrast was given by the remaining number, dedicated to Cuban pianist Chucho Valdes by his ex-colleague Paquito D'Rivera. This is a crisp chachachá with an ultra-crisp alto solo from D'Rivera himself along with ensembles of splendid punch and clarity.

The 1990s career revival of men who were by this time essentially icons did not fundamentally alter their playing styles, but it did—because this was essentially a jazz-audience phenomenon—give them a tilt that was often less a matter of arranging style than of the choice of musicians. As a 1992 Birdland gig preserved on a British CD, *Brazilian Sunset*, makes clear, Mongo Santamaria was still hewing to the general Latin-jazz-soul sound. But from the opening bars of "Bonita," which pianist Ricardo Gonzalez launched with an intro that is a mix of montuno, soul riff, and quotes from classical music, the band makes clear that it is in the business of creating timeless, not retro, music. Much of Santamaria's style, of course, had always come from his soloists; much of the rest, from an approach to rhythm both fresh and downhome. Latin jazz groups have set "Summertime" to a variety of rhythms, for example; Santamaria's version is a mid-tempo chachachá whose brisk rhythm (and Jimmy Crozier's alto solo) take it well away from the asleep-by-the-riverbank atmosphere of the original. Equally fresh, and entirely appropriate, is the New Orleans parade-style drumming that launched Marty Sheller's "Gumbo Man," thrown into relief by a basic

[5] A shorter, four-movement version of this suite was premiered in a Harlem church in 1989.

rhythmic line that you could trace from Jelly Roll Morton to Fats Domino, the Neville Brothers, and beyond. New Orleans also haunts the title cut, a samba with a ride-out that Jerry González's Fort Apache Band, reveals how even the most avant-garde Latin musicians tend to have a much greater reverence for tradition than jazzmen, at least on the practical level. The band's use of both jazz and Cuban elements is best illustrated by a near-12-minute mini-suite version of Miles Davis's "81" that moves from a chachachá into a guaguancó with passages of straight 4/4, all built on particularly fine bass from Andy Gonzalez. Overall, the heads and solos here (with the exception of a long percussion *rumbón*) are straightahead post-bop, most notably Jerry Gonzalez's trumpet playing, which builds on elements of many of his predecessors—Dizzy Gillespie's unparalleled way with ballads, the cool fire of early Freddy Hubbard—and makes them entirely his own.

Not all the artists associated with the big salsa groups switched altogether to Latin jazz. For over a decade Papo Lucca, pianist/leader of the salsa group Sonora Ponceña—which was based in Puerto Rico and popular throughout the Spanish-speaking countries of the Caribbean basin—had been playing an impressive Afro-Cuban style with strong jazz elements. In 1993 he went public with a compact disc called *Latin Jazz*, leading a nine-piece group with a front line of flugelhorn and soprano sax. Both Lucca in his accompanying role and his rhythm section take an almost entirely salsa-based approach to their work, though Lucca's solos are more rooted in jazz than his comping. The result is a classic illustration of both the advantages and the limitations of the tight Afro-Cuban rhythmic structure: the soloists are borne up and cradled in rhythm, but also to some extent swaddled in it, without the chances for idiosyncrasy that the deeper percussion forms offered groups like the Fort Apache Band, let alone the far looser bonds of traditional jazz 4/4.

Papo Lucca's Latin-jazz recording was a one-shot experiment, probably because he was the leader of a band that still had a big following in the Latin market, while both he and his record label were unknown to the jazz world. Overall, the move of the Latinos into Latin jazz was symbolically capped when Eddie Palmieri put together a three-horn front line, and in 1993 went into the studio to record Palmas, which he claimed as his first entirely instrumental session (in fact there's a vocal chorus on "Mare Nostrum," though no classic *sonerismo*). This characteristically tight recording could be seen as the archetype of no-frills, Afro-Cuban Latin jazz, with jazz horn solos, an extremely tight Cuban-based rhythm section, and Palmieri mediating between the two with his familiar mix of fiercely traditional montunos and modal jazz-inspired passages.

If Palmieri's band continued to be notable for the intensity of its swing, Tito Puente and Mario Bauzá kept alive the power of the big band—a power always due to arrangement as much as execution. Puente's 1993 *Royal T* is striking less for the solo work, fine though much of it was, than for the sheer gusto of its six-member front line. The breadth of approach that allows Puente to include the Mingus composition "Moanin'" on the same CD as the swing-era classic "Stompin' At the Savoy" rest about equally on the arrangements and the soloists. Several numbers ride on the contrast between Sam Burtis's warm and humane trombone and Bobby Porcelli's darkly sinewy baritone sax. *Special T* also offers an unusually good window on the arranger's art because its ten numbers feature no less than eight arrangers, of three musical generations, including Puente him-self, a master of big band style. To hear the enormously different use each made of essentially the same sonic palette is a musical education in its own right.

There is some remarkable writing, too, on Mario Bauzá's second Messidor release, *My Time Is Now*, including the first really fresh approach to "El Manisero," the number that started it all, since Stan Kenton's mid-1940s record-ing. Built on a rhythm with a strong 6/8 feel very different from Moises Simons's original composition, it stands in stunning contrast to the elegant danzón that fol-lowed it, "Memories" (which features lovely clarinet and solid alto from guest Paquito D'Rivera, who also composed and arranged it).

While the established musicians of two generations were taking over the Latin jazz heights, the recrudescence of the genre continued to give more local bands a shot at the recording studio and equally important, at a return match. The Luis Bonilla Latin Jazz All Stars was a mix of student musicians and more experi-enced players (Bonilla himself is a young trombonist with an obvious liking for J.J. Johnson). The group's 1991 *Pasos Gigantes* consists mostly of musicians with a purely local California name, but stiffened them with three old hands, reedman Justo Almario, bassist Abraham Laboriel, and drummer Alex Acuña. The repertoire is a mix of jazz standards—the title track is John Coltrane's "Giant Steps"—and more *típico* material. The solo work was mostly fairly straightfor-ward bebop, but Acuña and Laboriel's rhythmic approach is quite individual, with drumming and sometimes bass lines that fit neither the Afro-Cuban nor the Latin-jazz-funk norms.

Three years after his own first album, Bonilla showed up again, together with trumpeter Tony Lujan, on a recording led by another of those family-affair rhythm sections in which California seems to specialize: The Garcia Brothers' *Jazz Con Sabor Latino*. Bonilla appears on most of the CD, playing more richly and warmly than three years before. Despite an apparent mentor relationship, the

Garcia brothers' music is less weighted on the *típico* side than Poncho Sanchez's, but the similarities are considerable—especially the tightness of the rhythm sections and the un-flashy solidity of the soloists, notably Bonilla and tenor saxist Rob Lockhart. This is far from experimentalist playing, but there is no sense of regression or jazz lite.

While the more jazz-oriented record labels were picking up increasingly on Latin jazz in its varying avatars, the Latin record industry itself has remained fragmented since the demise of Fania, for both good and ill. The bigger labels in Colombia, Mexico, Miami, and New York focus on potential best sellers, with occasional reissues of classics (real and perceived). This has created a vacuum which many musicians filled with self-issued recordings. Trumpeter Junior Vega took a sizeable group he called Latin Jazz Today into the studio to record a CD, *Images of Music*, that would have been tough to make with record-company accountants looking over his shoulder. On one level *Images of Music* evokes a classic mambo orchestra sound, but it also has a strong experimental tinge expressed in a piece called "Comparsa de Samba," which blends two seemingly disparate Cuban and Brazilian carnival rhythms under a remarkably rich big band sound.

In 1994, some less-known southern Californian Latin-jazz groups started to get attention with the first releases of the tiny Dos Coronas label. These CDs featured bands well-known in the Los Angeles area but unknown beyond. One of them was Chevere, led by Rudy Regalado, a Venezuelan singer/percussionist with credits in Latin rock and jazz going back to the early 1970s. The band's *La Gloria* album was mostly straight salsa, but two cuts mixed salsa and Latin jazz in sometimes iconoclastic ways.

If the West Coast was by now open to music with solid traditional Latin roots, much of the credit goes to Poncho Sánchez, whose mix of Latin jazz and more *típico* numbers had become something of an institution in northern California. Sánchez's success, and the ensuing recognition that a California Latin-jazz scene existed, was beginning to lead to recordings by other local bands, most of them with more chops than fame.

The renaissance of California as a Latin jazz center was mostly due to the long-term activity of the Fantasy group of labels. But the newer Concord Picante label also contributed—and not just on a regional level, given that its main star was Tito Puente. Puente's 1991 *Out of this World* album fell between his big band and the small Latin Jazz Ensemble. But on the whole the sound is that of the more Latin-oriented orchestra, not only in the fierce mambo-style ensembles that flank the solos in the opening "Descarga," but in a very mellow arrangement of

Bud Powell's "In Walked Bud." The solos are another matter. Pianist Sonny Bravo's work on Puente's "Amanecer Guajira," theoretically one of the most *típico* numbers in the set, is far out, as is Mario Rivera's playing—fierce and flowing on tenor, elegant on flute. *Out of this World* is also exceptional in its playlist. I don't know who thought of Latinizing "Sweet Georgia Brown," but it is an inspiration only enhanced by Michael Turre's baritone sax and Rivera's wonderful flute (check the triple tonguing!).

Puente's 1995 release, *Tito's Idea*, continued the move toward ever richer arrangements that was a feature of the 1990s.[6] The writing was particularly subtle in the complex title tune, a genuine 3/4 composition without the crutch of Afro-Cuban derived 6/8. The band takes a flyer into even more adventurous realms in Puente's "Asia Mood," on which trombonist Steve Turre plays a solo on conch shell. As if to remind us of how much his sound has changed over the years, Puente includes a splendid piece in his 1950s Palladium vein, "Mambo Sentimental," followed by a full-throated version of Clifford Brown's "Joy Spring," and then perhaps the best of the jazz-oriented arrangements, a version of Horace Silver's "Yeah" by pianist Sonny Bravo that claimed it for classic big-band bebop (an enterprise aided by Sam Burtis's humane and far-ranging trombone solo).

An important element in the consolidation of Latin jazz was the increasing clout of individual Latin musicians within jazz, coupled with their willingness to be identified with Latin music rather than moving away from it as they got better known. Three out of the nine pieces on Michel Camilo's *On the Other Hand* have a strong Latin component. The title cut opens with gospel sounding piano, then cuts into a fifty-fifty Latin-funk beat, with Sammy Figueroa keeping things in line on conga aided and abetted by a titiboom cowbell pattern that belongs equally to jazz and salsa. The general mood is too boisterous for bebop, with horn punctuations that seem to draw equally from bop, soul, and mambo, while Camilo moves from blues-gospel to buoyant jazz piano. "Suite Sandrine Part Three," a basic building block of Camilo's permanent repertoire, opens with distant trumpet somewhere between taps and "Thus Spake Zarathustra" and moves through a remarkable series of jazz and funk avatars into a powerful and traditional descarga with superb Cuban-style piano shot through with jazz moments.

After years of struggle, California's Pete Escovedo began to appear more regularly on record with various permutations of what he specifically called a

---

[6] These may have stemmed from either or both of two influences. One was the prestige of Chico O'Farrill, whose ensemble writing has always been very rich. The other was the internationally popular *salsa romántica*, which applied the lush orchestrations the mambo bands had reserved for boleros to more uptempo material.

Latin-fusion band built around about a dozen musicians, including his daughter, Sheila E; guitarist Ray Obiedo—once of the Latin-rock group Azteca and long an Escovedo henchman—and that old fusion hand, George Duke. Duke is in particularly excellent jazz-oriented form in a solo on "All this Love" (no fusion nostalgia here). All in all this is a powerful recording, thanks largely to a tight family rhythm section paced by aggressive timbales from the leader. It also proves that there is still life in some of the fusion elements of the 1970s. The vocal on the Earl Klugh composition, "Cabo Frio," is pure '70s-lite, but it works surprisingly well over a mid-paced rhythm that mixed the old jazz habanera with something of a son-montuno feel. And one might do worse for retro-disco than the Brazilian-influenced "Tiemblas," which keeps well clear of jazz-bossa cliche.

Escovedo's new releases were among various straws in the wind suggesting that elegance and even prettiness might no longer be a total no-no even at the non-Brazilian end of Latin jazz, as was shown by Steven Berrios's *And Then Some* CD. There are few things more beguiling than the opening chorus of this recording, with its soft two-voice coro, jovial trombones (Escovedo sideman Wayne Wallace, overdubbed), and bustling percussion. And it doesn't get much prettier than George Mraz's double-bass opening to "Blues for Sarka."

Nor was California the only area beginning to produce more Latin jazz recordings. The well-established bilingual Miami Latin scene tended to various Caribbean/Latin/soul mixes, but it did have a Latin-jazz wing. Among the Latin-jazz oriented pianists making first recordings as solo artists around this time was Michael Orta. Orta had played fairly regularly with Paquito D'Rivera in the 1980s. His solo debut, *Freedom Tower*, was split between straight jazz and Latin-jazz cuts, with D'Rivera playing alto and clarinet on the Latin-leaning cuts, notably Orta's own "Latin What?" (a reaction to vague audience requests. "Lots of times you get asked to play Latin—that can mean samba, salsa, merengue, songo—what?," as Orta explained), in which D'Rivera plays bop alto with occasional Cuban melodic quotes while Orta provides a solid version of a common Latin jazz solo pattern, nifty montunos interknit with bop runs.

An intriguing example of Floridian Latin-jazz-funk is a version of the Sonny Rollins tune "Mambo Bounce" recorded by a group called The Chartbusters built around organist Lonnie Smith—a former Lou Donaldson sidekick—and drummer Idris Muhammad. Muhammad opened the piece, which was included on the album *Mating Call*, with a series of drum breaks on clave before a shift into Latin-funk territory reaffirmed by a classic jazz-funk organ solo in which Smith reminded the world that jazz-organ riffs were often clave-inspired.

The young Miami-based pianist Michael Orta draws from a bicultural zone that is more familiar in the pop music of Gloria Estefan than in jazz. But it is a bedrock part of the Miami musical experience, and one that is likely to become the future of Latin-jazz in general. *Courtesy Contemporary Records*

Lonnie Smith also showed up on *Soul Mates*, a release by Terry Myers, a Florida saxist with a well-deserved local reputation and a lot of swing who fit right in with Smith's fat organ sound. One cut, "Samba de Jolari," is a classic jazz samba with the prominent guitar and mellow sax soloing that has become standard for the genre. Most of the rest is ostensibly straight 4/4, but with plenty of Latin-tinge rhythms: the rocking post-habanera lilt of the bluesy "Opal's Smile," for one, and the clave-haunted funk-jazz groove of "Gotcha."

Particularly in New York, Latin jazz was still a big tent, and the deeper roots of Cuban music—including its Afro-religious tradition—continued to be an important part of it throughout the 1990s. Like the recordings of the Libre/Fort Apache continuum (see below), drummer/percussionist Bobby Sanabria's *New York City Aché* covers a range from Yoruba-based religious percussion to Cubop. But with no crossover in the musicians themselves, the sound is very different (and consistently gorgeous: listen to Gene Jefferson's flute on the charanga sections of "Brindando el Son—que Rico Es!"). Perhaps the most intriguing cut of all was "El Saxofon y el Guaguancó," a dialogue for alto and rumba group. But then again, there is also "Blue Monk" performed as a wonderfully bluesy son montuno with a rich jazz violin solo from Lewis Kahn, a veteran of Larry Harlow's 1970s hardcore New York salsa group.

Different in so many ways though they were, most of these bands continued to take their Latin tinge from Cuba and/or Brazil—but not quite all of them. In 1993, Dominican reedman Mario Rivera invited another undervalued saxist, George Coleman (with whose jazz octet he had been playing for years), as a guest on his *El Comandante* CD, a fine and offbeat recording. The overarching concept of this set (though not of all its tracks) is its use of the Dominican merengue as the Latin element in a Latin jazz experiment. Why the merengue, like the tango, should not have been used more in Latin jazz is a mystery. You would think its mix of a 2/4 rhythm with the very distinctive five-beat throb of the small *tambora* drum would be a natural as both a bridge between straight 4/4 and clave-based patterns and a change of rhythmic pace. "Frank's Tune," a merengue version of a piece associated with Coleman's octet, is a splendid example of the possibilities for a jazz-merengue marriage. Taken in isolation, Walter Booker's bass line is a mid-tempo straight 4/4, but embedded within it, and within the tilt that the tambora part gave it, was the sense of a much faster merengue 2/4. Things get even more complex in "Pretty Blues," in which a slight shift in phrasing virtually reverses the merengue pulse—an effect that pianist Hilton Ruiz used both powerfully and subtly in a comping passage early on, by placing a stabbing chord where the stressed last beat of the *tambora* pattern would normally be.

It's a measure of New York City's decline as a Latin recording center, and the ever-increasing importance of the countries on the Caribbean's southern rim, that the entire rhythm section of Ray Barretto's group New World Spirit (a refinement of the band that had made *Handprints*) had a Colombian connection. Pianist Hector Martignon and bassist Jairo Moreno are both Colombians by birth, and drummer Satoshi Takeishi, though Japanese, spent six years studying in Colombia. Once known only as the source of the cumbia and of an accordion-led quartet style almost as jovially manic as Dominican merengue, Colombia has become a major center of Latin-Caribbean music. Twenty or even 15 years ago, the notion that one might have a hardcore Latin-jazz rhythm section without any Cubans would have seemed a little off the wall; to staff one exclusively with Colombians would have been unthinkable.

Like Cal Tjader, Ray Barretto is not an avant-gardist but an experienced and intelligent musician with excellent taste on both sides of the aisle, and a particular talent for picking young players. Trumpeter Ray Vega's arrangement of Nat Adderley's "Work Song" for New World Spirit's first CD, Taboo, with its effective recasting of the basic theme and its solid soloing, renews what always was an unflashy and populist theme while remaining entirely true to it. The whole album is full of good things, among them Martignon's piano on two of his own compositions—"Guaji-Rita" and the *cinema-vérité* "99 MacDougal Street"—as well as the Latin-funk overtones and midtempo kick of Barretto's own "Montuno Blue." Another particularly beguiling CD by Ray Barretto's New World Spirit, *My Summertime*, includes an intriguing "Autumn Leaves" with Gillespie-like muted trumpet. However, the best track is Barretto's extraordinarily effective arrangement of "Summertime" as a guajira, complete with his own touchingly human bilingual vocal.

By the mid-1990s, the Fort Apache band was one of the country's leading Latin jazz groups; it was also one of the oldest established. It had started life with the advantage of remarkable group musicianship, built on it with a longevity that went back to regular early 1980s workshops in New York City, and created the kind of self-confidence that makes for the ability to be quite adventurous without sounding strained. The band's *Crossroads* album illustrates all of these qualities. The group's remarkably strong grounding in Afro-Cuban percussion, which lent it a great deal of its authenticity, is once more evident in several percussion *rumbones*. The remarkable mellowness that cushions the band's more experimental solos in jazz warmth is expressed particularly strongly in "Thelingus," a tribute to Thelonious Monk, Duke Ellington, and Charles Mingus. Though arrangements like Larry Willis's reworking of "Ezekiel Saw the Wheel" went well beyond the simpler type of bebop head, this was still a group of soloists, but one that long playing together had given the cohesiveness that Duke Ellington claimed came from knowing how his sidemen played cards—*plus* greater collective freedom than Ellington ever permitted.

Manny Oquendo's Libre was historically an uncle of the Fort Apache Band (Andy Gonzalez plays bass for both groups). But the bedrock of the band's persona is the New York trombone frontline perfected during the 1960s through the offices of men like Barry Rogers and now in its second generation in the person of musicians like Papo Vasquez and Jimmy Bosch, who grew up with it as kids. Moreover, though Oquendo is one of the great roots percussionists and a mentor to many of the members of the Fort Apache Band, his sense of tradition is more closely bound than theirs to earlier dance forms and to popular music in general. "Tu No Me Quieres" on Libre's 1994 *Mejor Que Nunca/Better Than Ever*, for example, was a danzón-cha of the sort that appeared on Eddie Palmieri's first La Perfecta release (on which Oquendo played). Intriguingly, there was yet another version here of the Weill/Nash "Speak Low." The jazz elements in Libre are strong: pianist Willie Rodriguez in particular is a master of the solo who slides between jazz and salsa. But all in all, while Fort Apache has taken classic Latin jazz to a peak, Libre is rooted in the great days of New York salsa. The band's *On The Move/Muevete* CD reflects this background as well as its members' jazz chops, along with the added warmth that often comes from recorded club dates. But though Libre's musical roots are varied, its basic sound is firmly on the *típico* end of the jazz/Latin spectrum. Most of *On the Move*'s material was Cuban-focused salsa, including a couple of classics (notably Bobby Capo's chachachá "Piel Canela"). But the gutsy, macho trombone sound was pure Latin New York.

Another particularly intriguing manifestation of the New York Latino jazz congeries was the Afro-Blue Band. The group's *Impressions* CD includes percussionist Steve Berrios, reedsman Mario Rivera, and the like, but also Hilton Ruiz on piano, and African-American former Basie-ite trumpeter Melton Mustafa. There is even a violinist to provide the Latin-funk title track with both charanga and jazz fiddle touches. Ruiz's work on this track is very jazz-oriented, quite "out" in places, as if the support of a Latin-aware group playing straight jazz allowed him to cut loose even on a clave-based number. This was an imaginative recording all around, not least in a version of "Afro Blue" far denser and tougher than the original.

The same year, Steve Berrios made his own debut recording for Milestone, *First World*, with his group Son Bacheche. In general terms, this recapitulated the considerable range of traditions with which he is at home. There were straight bop tributes to Art Blakey, Philly Joe Jones, Elvin Jones, and Max Roach (of whose percussion group, M'Boom, Berrios has long been a member). Several tracks drew from Afro-Cuban secular percussion styles. Two feature Berrios solos, playing more or less complex layers of overdubbed percussion. "Uranus" moved between straight-4/4 and montuno-based rhythms under jazz soloing that was—as on all the jazz-oriented cuts—notably smooth and urbane. On a couple of cuts, all these elements came together, most notably in a fusion of a traditional

Melton Mustafa, an alumnus of the Count Basie band has often worked with Latin-jazz sounds, both with his own big band and with groups like the Afro-Blue Band. *Courtesy Contemporary Records*

Cuban piece with Ornette Coleman's "Lonely Woman" that went beyond almost all the experiments of Berrios's contemporaries.

Trumpeter Charlie Sepulveda was also exploring an updated version of the fusionist spirit with his trumpet/tenor frontline group, The Turnaround. Like many fusionist recordings, their 1996 CD *Watermelon Man* was augmented by a raft of guest artists. At times the results work better in theory than in practice. The rappers who provided a rhythmic contrast to the conventional *coro* on "The

Watermelon Man" would have been more effective if they had been used less marginally. But the best cuts illustrate the ability to blend tradition and new ideas with originality that so much of the best Latin jazz and salsa have possessed. Sepúlveda's composition "Alicia," with its elegant danza rhythm and lyrical flute (Dave Valentin on form yet again); the contrasting "Mr B.B.," with its emphatic percussion, nimble bop head, and rhythmically adventurous piano; and the magnificently eerie "Childhood Nightmare;" all suggested a musician with plenty of road in front of him and a good map.

Despite its growing popularity in the U.S., some of the most interesting 1990s Latin jazz appeared on foreign labels, notably the German label, Messidor. Messidor released a number of notable albums, including a remarkable session under the name of the great Cuban pianist Bebo Valdez (father of Chucho), Mario Bauzá's big band, and percussionist Giovanni Hidalgo's recording *Villa Hidalgo*, with saxist David Sánchez, one of the new stars of Latin jazz. Dizzy Gillespie played a pleasant muted solo on the title track of Hidalgo's CD; however, the strongest moment is Eric Figueroa's remarkable tumbling piano patterns like some manic double-montuno backing Hidalgo's conga toward the end of the track. Paquito D'Rivera's guest role on "Bahia San Juan" is also impressive, giving the piece more life than any other cut on the record.

By no means all the self-produced or teeny-label recordings were by Latino artists alone. One of the more unexpected experiments of the mid-1990s was a CD on the Hip Bop Essence label that brought several survivors of the 1970s jazz-fusion era together with younger New York Latin-jazz luminaries. A lineup of Gato Barbieri, Bob James, vibist Mike Mainieri, drummer (and here also percussionist) Lenny White, bassist Andy Gonzalez, and percussionist Steve Berrios might sound like a horse designed by a committee. Yet perhaps because nobody here had anything to lose, there was no grandstanding, no gotta-get-over fusion licks, no pseudo-macho competitiveness. Even Barbieri is somewhat subdued and so, by no coincidence, gives one of his best recorded performances. And underneath it all lay the prerequisite for this kind of performance: a phenomenal rhythm section, in which Gonzalez, Berrios, and Lenny White interweave the sort of support and encouragement only musicians long past showboating can give.

The acceptance of Latin jazz in the U.S. during the 1990s was arguably also helped by feedback from the less-rigid European jazz scene. Not only were European record companies unaffected by the U.S. embargo on Cuba, they were also more ready to take both commercial and artistic risks. Moreover, groups forced to scuffle in the U.S. appeared regularly at European jazz festivals. As just one example, The Jazz Tribe, of whom the best-known members were ex-Mingus trumpeter Jack Walrath and Latino conga player Ray Mantilla, played at Italy's La Spezia Jazz Festival, a gig recorded for Italy's Red label. Though Walrath was a member of one of Charles Mingus's more exploratory bands, neither he nor the rest of the soloists was self-consciously "out," let alone truly outré. Backed by a fine rhythm section in which pianist Walter Bishop, Jr. played more of a jazz than a Cuban role and Ray Mantilla on congas kept the Afro-Cuban faith, this was a perfect example of the difference between trendy and fresh. That this was not picked up by a U.S. label is a depressing comment on the American record industry. So is the fact that Walrath's 1995 recording with his group, The Masters of Suspense, was also released in Europe rather than in the United States. *HipGnosis* draws from Walrath's wide musical background, which included many R&B and Latin gigs, and reflected a breadth of musical interest that led him to use reconstructed Aztec modes in two compositions. But *HipGnosis* is not a rerun of the wilder shores of 1960s free jazz, but accessible music from a tight group with a strong stress on (admittedly far from pop-style) vocals.

Another fish out of the placid 1990s waters did find a (tiny) U.S. label to release his work. Alto/soprano saxist Jorge Sylvester's *MusiCollage*, on the Postcards label, was a prime example of how much variety can be got out of a small and fairly standard combo. Though two of the musicians—trumpeter Claudio Roditi and percussionist Bobby Sanabria—were familiar, they were almost unrecognizable in surroundings like "Resolution 88." Its percussion was eerily personal rather than anchored to some Brazilian or Cuban tradition, and the arrangement, in so far as it existed, was so loose that Sylvester as soloist was less supported than framed.

So, yes, the new orthodoxies are inimical to some excellent musicians. But then again, so was the avant-gardist orthodoxy that saw the past uniquely as something to reject (a view more common among critics and fans than among musicians, be it said). And the new historicism has also had beneficial effects. One of these is a rehabilitation of the big-band sound (which was surviving only in the hands of a very few, very well-established groups like Puente's) that has allowed at least one or two groups to emerge (if only in the recording studio). One recording group was organized by Melton Mustafa, who had played trumpet at various times with the Count Basie band, Duke Ellington, Lionel Hampton, and Jaco Pastorius (!). On his CD *Boiling Point*, Mustafa's band performs original charts, many of them with strong Latin elements (big-band Cubop rather than mambo). "Bridging the Gap," for example, opens with a trombone montuno pattern with trumpet punctuations. "The Gift of Knowledge (El Don del Conocimiento)" is a merengue—very unusual for Latin-minded jazz groups—with

Cubop horn arrangements, montuno-based piano, a flute solo that is definitely jazz rather than charanga, and a tearaway trumpet solo by Mustafa.

Another by-now classic Latin jazz style that had never lost an audience but had essentially gone underground was the vibes-centered quintet. Until his death, Cal Tjader had remained its main (and, as far as most people were concerned, only) exponent. But at the level of local clubs it lived on in the music of groups like the Estrada Brothers, who had been playing in and around the Oxnard area for a mere 40 years when Milestone issued their album *Get Out of My Way* in 1996. Much of the brothers' repertoire was standard—"Tin Tin Deo," "Blue Bossa," Mongo Santamaria's "Mi Guaguancó"—but their approach was not. While Ruben Estrada's vibes playing was reminiscent of Tjader, alto saxist Henry Estrada was a contrarian who turned bop influences into something elegantly elegiac. Yet his flute playing on "Blue Moon" (taken as a midtempo mambo) is far more assertive than most jazz flute. And given their almost guaracha-like interpretation of "Blue Bossa," the go-for-broke joviality of the bugalú "Get Out of My Way," and the remarkably revisionist opening to their version of "Besame Mucho," it would be hard to claim that the brothers haven't staked out their own territory.

Another recording in something of the same vibraphone quintet genre was made the same year by vibraphonist Emil Richards. Richards formed part of a short-lived group run by the great Cuban conga-player Francisco Aguabella back in 1962 (as did the daddy of Cubop bassists, Al McKibbon), but has spent most of his career as a successful studio musician. All three showed up together again on Richards's *Luntana,* along with a number of other old hands. Richards is a hotter mallet-player than Tjader was, with more use of marimba, a shorter decay time, and more powerful and often more rootsy percussion (as, for example, in "Well I didn't" and the impressive Miles Davis's "All Blues"). All in all, *Luntana* is further evidence of the reality that the vibes/piano Latin sound is a format of considerable flexibility and zest.

The vibraphone quintet sound also resurfaced on the East Coast when New Jersey produced a second Ocho, a young group called Carabali whose major influence seems to be Joe Cuba's popular bugalú group of the mid-1960s, change-of-pace English-language songs and all. However, Carabali's playing was no mere nostalgia trip. The excellent vibraphonist Valerie Naranjo worked off Oscar Hernandez's piano as if the pair of them had just thought of the idea—one of the signs of a genuine revival as opposed to a camp-retro fad.

The Brazilian jazz scene meanwhile was flourishing and becoming ever more integrated as one very important element in a wider jazz world along with its

The Latin-jazz revival has led to the "discovery" of bands like the southern-California-based Estrada Brothers, who have been locally popular for a mere three decades. *Photo: Steve Maruita, courtesy Milestone Records*

Cuban and New York derived cousins. On the one hand, the old jazz-bossa was continuing its comeback a generation after its first impact. After several adventurous recordings, Charlie Byrd returned to home base in a quartet recording, *The Bossa Nova Years*. Together with saxist/clarinetist Ken Peplowski, he ruminated on a set of bossa nova's best-known compositions, many of which he had played untold times in the previous 30 years. The effect is part reminiscence about old companions, part summary of a life's relationship. Byrd's warm reflectiveness is enhanced by Peplowski's performance, on both clarinet—an instrument rare in bossa nova but basic to instrumental *choro*—and unusually gentle sax.

Laurindo Almeida was also keeping busy. In October 1991 he appeared in trio at the Jazz Note in Pacific Beach, California. Though the gig was issued by Concord Picante as *Outra Vez* ("Once More"), there was nothing retro about its tour de force, a phenomenal duet consisting of Almeida performing Beethoven's "Moonlight Sonata" while bassist Bob Magnusson played Thelonius Monk's "Round Midnight." The rest of the performance moved between the U.S. and Brazilian ends of trio jazz-bossa, both highly skilled and mellow. It's a measure of how close the two wings were that a version of Irving Berlin's "Blue Skies" was quite as Brazilian in feeling as the Brazilian compositions themselves.

Though Byrd and Almeida were both part of the bossa nova's fundamental association with the guitar, most of the more impressive new Brazilian jazz exponents were pianists. The best of the new players, in fact, took their Brazilian influences and made them over with piano playing of remarkable breadth. Compared with almost any pianists since the bebop revolution, Don Pullen's performances on his 1991 Blue Note recording with the African-Brazilian Connection were rich, subtle, accessible, and (shh!) swinging. From Guilherme Franco's berimbau opening to "Capoeira," the message is deep Brazil, and you can hardly get more enchantingly lilting than the opening chorus of "Listen to the People (Bonnie's Bossa Nova)," with its fusion-jazz vocal and Pullen's history-haunted, post-bop, Luso-stride solo. Nor was Brazil the only influence here: there are two cuts by Sahelian vocalist/percussionist Mor Thiam, out of the African tradition that is probably most influential on the blues; and a piece by Pullen called "Doo-Wop Daze."

Pullen wasn't alone in remaking Brazilian jazz in his own image. Pianist JoAnne Brackeen had been recording with her own groups, mostly trios, since the 1970s, and in the late '70s she spent time with Stan Getz. But her 1991 *Breath of Brazil* was her first specifically Brazilian jazz outing, with a rhythm section of two Brazilians and Eddie Gomez (who you will recall, first brought Tania Maria to the U.S.). The most interesting cuts on the CD are her own compositions, because they blend their Brazilianisms with a harmonic approach that cuts across the customary jazz-bossa pieties.

Brazilian pianist Eliane Elias was also increasing her Brazilian content, as well as both consolidating her position in New York and establishing a personal vocal style. Without straying into Flora Purim territory, Elias's singing on her album *A Long Story* is more lyrical than Tania Maria's, as is her piano work, which draws from both jazz and the richly chorded acoustic guitar of classic Brazilian bossa nova. Her 1993 album, *Paulistana*, is more Brazilian-minded than some of her earlier recordings, and features an impressive roster of Brazilian guest musicians (including Ivan Lins singing his own "Iluminados"). Given a basic rhythm section that includes bassist Eddie Gómez and drummer Jack DeJohnette, as well as her own long history as a jazz-oriented player, the strong jazz components here come as no surprise. But Elias's jazz playing in the title cut is no bebop rerun. The rich chordal and rhythmic interplay between her two hands transcend simple descriptions, as does the driving Brazilian barrelhouse of "Carioca Nights." And her low-key approach to the old warhorses of the *Black Orpheus* stable—at once ornamented in detail and true to the simplicity of the originals—was a quiet *tour de force*.

Though they share moments of similarity, the difference between Elias and Tania Maria is partly a function of the difference between a pianist and a vocalist-cum-pianist, but more particularly a matter of temperament. Elias is cooler, Tania Maria more down-home; Elias is rhythmically more urban-samba-oriented, Tania Maria more *batucada*-inspired; Elias is from São Paulo, Tania Maria from Rio; Elias uses rhythm to give bite to her harmonic byplay, Tania Maria uses harmony to add kick to her rhythmic playing (and singing). These two artists present an extraordinarily complex pattern of similarity and diversity in what might seem a pretty limited field.

The work of Manfred Fest was an example of the complex crosscurrents involved in 1990s Brazilian jazz. Fest is a Brazilian jazz musician and, along with his wife Lili, a composer. Its Brazilian roots aside, his piano style is strongly bop-oriented, with a fair amount of Cuban influence. Fest's *Oferenda* album, recorded in New York, mixes U.S. and Brazilian musicians, and draws stylistically from many sources. Even a Jobim number like "Passarim" is transmuted with (a pianistic bow to Debussy aside) strongly Cuban-influenced. "Smoke Gets in Your Eyes" is given an effective underlying samba pulse; "Guararapes" is based largely on a *maracatú* rhythm from the Afro-Brazilian northeast, move well into more familiar territory by a wordless vocal of a kind familiar to Americans since Flora Purim's arrival. The remaining tracks show a similar diversity.

Purim and her husband Airto Moreira, meanwhile, continued to pursue their personal musical obsessions. Their quartet Fourth World predictably paid as much attention to roots as to experimentalism. An appearance at London's Ronnie Scott's Club was typical in its mix. José Neto played acoustic guitar in cavaquinho style on a samba in which Purim sings her trademark Luso-scat, often in unison with his guitar. Then he builds a solo partly out of quotes from her vocalisms and partly on takeoffs of various traditional cavaquinho patterns. This is improvisation in depth, yet with a lightness that makes it, if anything, more impressive.

Mellow, of course, has always been Brazilian turf. But at its best, that mellow is joined by glow and zest. Witness *Brazil from the Inside*, a recording by the Trio da Paz, consisting of guitarist Romero Lubambo, bassist Nilson Matta, and drummer Duduka da Fonseca, all three of whom have been responsible for much of the glow on recordings by other musicians (some of whom are on hand here). Playing alone, as in "Aquarela do Brasil," the trio gives new meaning to an instrumental bossa-nova style warmer and less reflective than Gilberto's. Joined by Claudio Roditi, Herbie Mann, and pianist JoAnne Brackeen, they provide the Latin half of a Brazilian jazz poised equally between both sides of its equation.

While many Brazilian musicians in the U.S. remained identifiably Brazilian in style, they all also thought of themselves as jazz musicians. And not a few played both sides of the fence with equal ease and frequency. Trumpeter Claudio Roditi worked equally fluently in straight bebop, Cuban-derived Latin jazz, and on both sides of the line between jazz-samba and samba-jazz (that is, between the U.S. and the Brazilian version of the hybrid). The first and last cuts on his 1993 *Jazz turns Samba* are his own compositions. One piece, Bobby Timmons's "Moanin'" was gospel-oriented, soul-jazz with a beat that adapted neatly to the samba. A couple more were semi-standards, including Kurt Weill's 1943 "Speak Low" (a remarkably popular piece with Latin jazz groups of the '90s). The rest were jazz pieces, including the bebop classics "Birk's Works." "Donna Lee," and John Coltrane's "Giant Steps," and the less-familiar "Moment's Notice" (perhaps not incidentally, both early enough to have a lot of hard bop in them). Most of the soloing, including Roditi's own, is very bebop-oriented, as was much of the drumming. There are in fact no Brazilians in the rhythm section—Ignacio Berroa is the only Latino—and though the basic pulse of the samba and bossa nova are still present, the overall sense of the rhythm is more Cuban: harder, and—as Carlos Santana once put it to me—driving down rather than lifting and buoyant like the Brazilian originals.

Roditi followed this with the CD *Samba Manhattan Style*.[7] Though the group was balanced between Brazilians and U.S. musicians, with a Brazilian pianist (Helio Alves) and drummer (Duduka da Fonseca), this was emphatically a jazz record. Yet, just as the ghosts of Kansas City hovered behind the sax of Charlie Parker, so the souls of Brazilians past peered over Fonseca's and Alves's shoulders. Roditi himself is quoted in the unusually good notes as tracing the style back to the 1960s, when a samba jazz was developing in parallel with the more vocal and guitar-oriented bossa nova, by a procedure he described as "you think

---

[7] Released on the small Reservoir label.

jazz but play Brazilian rhythms." Here, though, there were also a jazz-born intensity and Cuban-inspired drive-'em-down quality to the rhythm section.

In their different ways, Elias, Tania Maria, and Roditi were all working within a group tradition that was, by birth, their own. American musicians, who came to Brazilian music attracted by love rather than birth, provided a further enrichment to the mix, in part because theirs was an individual rather than a group experience. The more personal nature of pianist Don Pullen's Afro-Brazilian fusion showed its strength in a concert with the African Brazilian Connection at the 1993 Montreux Jazz Festival.[8] Although he lacked traditional instruments like Guilherme Franco's berimbau which had been featured on the group's studio recording, Pullen made up for it by varying his performance. For instance, in "Capoeira," he made his piano theme—which in the studio recording came as a powerful contrast to the ethereal-earthy quality of the berimbau—lighter and more Brazilian in feel. Overall, a comparison of the numbers that appear on both sessions shows a group that is both improvisationally strong and stylistically consistent, though the mood at Montreux was more subdued, set by the long, lyrical "Ah George, We Hardly Knew Ya," dedicated to Pullen's longterm partner George Addams, who had recently died.

By the mid-1990s, Brazilian-jazz groups were everywhere and Brazilian-jazz recordings, once rare, formed an ever-increasing percentage of all jazz releases. Back in the '60s, Leonard Feather remarked that the bossa nova had brought about a revival of the guitar in jazz. Three decades later, much of jazz guitar was strongly Brazilian influenced. A player who had worked mostly as an accompanist in the Los Angeles area, Joe Pisano, recorded a series of largely jazz-bossa-inspired duets with a wide range of guitarists of three generations, from Joe Pass through Lee Ritenour to Ron Affif.

Pisano, however, had been around a while. The new generation of Brazil-oriented guitarists saw things differently. Like so much 1990s Brazilian jazz, Jeff Linsky's second album for Concord Picante, *Angel's Serenade*, avoided the bossa-nova standards. Most of its pieces were Linsky's own compositions, with the exceptions of Kurt Weill's 1943 "Speak Low" and Victor Young's "Beautiful Love." Linsky's approach falls somewhere between jazz-bossa and bossa nova itself, with Linsky's warmly elegant solos matched by elegantly warm flute.

By the mid-1990s, the children of the original jazz-bossa fans had grown up, and the pure guitar-and-voice-based bossa nova returned as something fresh and new in recordings like the release *Bossa Nova* by Ana Caram. Her versions of

---

[8] Issued on CD as *Live . . . Again.*

such classics/warhorses as "Chega de Saudade" (the song that launched the bossa nova in Brazil in 1958) have the freshness of rediscovery (it helped that the rhythm section included drummer Duduka de Fonseca and, crucially, guitarist Romero Lubambo). Caram's retelling of these old tales has the softness that goes with the territory without the alienation that Astrud Gilberto had brought to it.

Another artist with a very different take on acoustic Brazilian turf is Badi Assad, the female, and most jazz-oriented, member of a remarkable trio of guitar-playing siblings. She represents on the one hand the pure Brazilian end of a full spectrum of styles, and on the other the taste for experiment that had been upper-most in the work of predecessors like Airto and Flora Purim. A recording Assad made in New York City in June 1995 under the name *Rhythms* contains examples of both ends of her range, in the instrumental "Choro de Juliana" on the one hand and on the other in the remarkable "Moods," with its strikingly eerie use of a cop-per pipe as a kind of sopranino didjeridu, and hocketing singing borrowed from Pygmy vocalism.

All this time, of course, the Brazilian, Cuban, and by now you-name-it ele-ments were fusing in a thousand different ways. The title cut of Adela Dalto's *Papa Boco* is a doctored merengue that opens with such a staggeringly catchy melody and rhythm, it's hard to believe that it didn't end up in some top ten or other. Taken as a whole her album has a definite Brazilian tinge. Dalto is a singer with a second-generation Latin fusion voice, neither Brazilian- nor Cuban-derived (though leaning more to Rio than to Havana), and both jazz- and pop-ori-ented in a way that has been rare to nonexistent in straight jazz since the decline of the big-band singers. Since her husband Jorge's death, she had been working with a number of mostly Cuban-oriented Latin jazz groups, but her co-producer and music director here was a Brazilian pianist, Aloisio Aguiar, a high school buddy of Claudio Roditi. Roditi played on the recording, along with a phenome-nal collection of familiar Brazilian and Latin-jazz musicians, including Brazilian guitarist Romero Lubambo, Puerto Rican cuatro player Yomo Toro, and New York percussionist Milton Cardona.

Another of the late 1990s' best recordings reflected this pan-Latin quality with Brazil strong in the mix: the first CD as leader from Hector Martignon, Ray Barretto's pianist. Though he is himself Colombian, he used his album, *Retrato em Branco e Preto*, to explore a largely Brazilian landscape (the title itself comes from a Jobim/Buarque composition). That something special is at hand becomes clear barely a minute into the first number, when Martignon set up a right hand ostinato like some Latino-Scottish jig. This is an impressive record in general, and several tracks stand out: the Colombian "Coqueteos," which comes over as a

Adela Dalto, widow of pianist Jorge Dalto, has gone on to make her own mark in Latin-jazz with a vocal style that mixes Cuban, Brazilian, and jazz singing in a '90s blend that transcends its constituent parts. *Courtesy Milestone Records*

delicious Colombian response to the Brazilian classic "Tico Tico No Fubá"; a couple of cumbia-based compositions by Martignon, "La Candelaria" and "Noviembre, Susurro y Cumbia"; and "She Said She Was From Sarajevo," which mixes a subdued bossa-nova feeling with a Balkan 7/4.

In the past, "straight" jazz players of Latino background often seemed to regard Latin gigs as peripheral to their main concerns; now it was becomingly increasingly acceptable—if not expected—that these artists play music that reflected their heritage. Pianist Hilton Ruiz is a good example. Though Ruiz is New-York based, Puerto-Rican born, and worked with various Latin-soul groups in his early teens, he spent most of his professional life in the "straight" jazz field, even though he almost always played something with a Latin tinge on his gigs. During the 1990s Ruiz came home, so to speak, in a series of concerts and recordings. His 1992 sextet concert at New York City's Birdland showed Ruiz to be completely at home on both sides of the aisle. Despite a two-tenor-sax lineup (rare outside the quirky combinations producer Norman Granz used to favor), the performance here could have happened any time over the last 30 years. But the urbanely swinging performances—split between Latin and "straight" jazz—confirmed once more that a classic style is infinitely fresh. In large part this was due to the rhythm section of Andy Gonzalez, Steve Berrios, and Giovanni Hidalgo, who combined individual chops with the effortless tightness that comes from much playing together. But whether as jazzman or montunero, Ruiz himself plays as though he'd just got religion, and much of the time his solo work slides between the two idioms as if they had always been one stylistic continuum.

Ruiz also appeared on a 1994 recording with a new Tito Puente group, the Golden Latin Jazz All Stars. He outdoes himself (twice!) on Kenny Dorham's standard "Un Poco Mas," first in a tumbling post-bop solo and then in the marvelously subtle hesitation that transformed his apparently simple two-chord montuno under Puente's timbales solo. The whole recording, in fact, was remarkable. The 6/8 underlay to Marty Sheller's composition "In a Heart Beat," with its classic haunting conga *toque*, may seem effortless, but it's superb. Mario Rivera's tenor soloing here is as good as anywhere, which is saying something indeed. And flutist Dave Valentin, sometimes dismissed as a lightweight by jazz critics, consistently proves that the problem is not his playing so much as some of its past contexts.

Ruiz was so busy in 1995 that he seemed to have cloned himself. He surfaces on a couple of tracks of Mongo Santamaria's recording *Mongo Returns*: Ary Barroso's "Bahia," and his own "Free World Mambo." "Bahia" is transformed both by Ruiz's solo and by Eddie Allen's splendidly raunchy wawa trumpet, which preceded it. "Free World Mambo" ties together street percussion with jazz soloing in a way that other groups—notably the Fort Apache Band—have taken further, but which Santamaria's musicians have been doing since the early 1960s. Once more, the contrast between more than somewhat wild trumpet and piano of controlled fire and elegance made for real creative tension.

Ruiz's own recording the same year, *Hands On Percussion*, drew from some of the best young soloists of the 1990s, notably tenorist David Sánchez and a rhythm section of Andy Gonzalez, Steve Berrios, and Ignacio Berroa, along with Tito Puente on timbales on a few tracks. Puente appeared in a convincing remake of the Charlie Parker classic, "Ornithology," and was showcased on "Vibes Mambo," a classic of clave-based, montuno-rooted vibraphone playing. Once more, David Valentin's flute playing disposes of any theory that he is a light-weight: In "Blues for 'Cos'," he shines particularly in contrast with José d'Leon's tenor and a blues-rich Ruiz solo. "Ornithology" aside, the standout here, and not just for chutzpah, is their version of Ellington's "Cottontail," which features more fine work from David Sánchez.

Dominican pianist Michel Camilo offers a particularly impressive blend of Latin and jazz elements on his second CD, *One More Once*. The title cut is a 12-bar strutter whose opening ensemble and sax solo combines soul-jazz and *pa'lante* Afro-Cuban elements, with the traps supplying a classic cencerro-type, straight-note kick on woodblock. Camilo's own solo bursts with a joyous barrel-house feel in and around its rippling single-note runs, but as the piece develops he embeds his playing in as crisp a band sound as anybody's feet could desire. The process in "Why Not?" was the reverse, with a feisty conga line that com-bined with a solid traps backbeat to hint at the crisp 2/4 of the Dominican merengue. In "Suite Sandrine" Camilo's range and subtlety echoes in a progres-sion from near-free jazz to kicking, percussion-propelled Latin jazz, as if from self-questioning to certainty. And the deceptively bluesy piano opening to the remake of "Caribe" led to a dazzling conflation of a couple of generations of Latin-Caribbean music, percussion-driven but given depth by a minor-feeling piano montuno edged with melancholy, before a flaring single-note solo flashed kingfisher-like between bop and wrought-iron-and-lace Cuban piano.

At all times, of course, the existing mainstream jazz styles are fed by ideas from musicians too original to gain easy and general acceptance. Some, like the various musicians associated with the Fort Apache Band, eventually come into their own. Others, perhaps too original or drawing from too many unfamiliar sources, have had a particularly hard struggle. One such is the pianist Michele Rosewoman.[9] But the apparent growth in the branch of Latin jazz that melds advanced jazz with particularly Afrocentric Cuban percussion seems to have ben-

---

[9] Like Walrath, Rosewoman has been taken far more seriously by European labels notable for encouraging experimental musicians and idioms—Italy's Black Saint, and Germany's Enja—though Blue Note did finally "discover" her.

Some career! Half a century after his emergence as a leader in the New York mambo sound, Tito Puente is a leader in the Latin-jazz revival of the 1990s. *Photo by David Labarsk, courtesy Berkeley Agency*

efited her during the past decade—at least to the extent of getting some recognition from the U.S. record industry.

Rosewoman's position may have been somewhat more isolated because most of the Afrocentric Latin jazz has come from groups emerging from the Latin rather than the jazz side of the Latin-jazz equation, such as Fort Apache.[10] Her

---

[10] The individual musicians in all the bands have been a mix of Latino and non-Latino. The issue is more one of market segmentation than of musical style, but it is nonetheless a real part of the musicians' world.

technical chops are considerable, and her range of influences even more so. While showing obvious signs of the usual post-bop enthusiasms (Thelonious Monk of course, but also touches of more expressionist players like McCoy Tyner), she is heavily influenced melodically and harmonically by Billy Strayhorn. But from the start she has integrated into her work both Afro-Cuban elements and the African elements from which they derive, most notably with her (at time of writing) un-recorded big band, New Yor-Uba.

Rosewoman brings these influences together on her 1993 quintet recording, *Harvest*, most notably in "Warriors (Guerreros)," a composition usually played by New Yor-Uba. This blends a bop-derived Latin-jazz head with Yoruba-lan-guage vocals and extends post-bop piano playing. If one can generalize at all about a notably rich style, Rosewoman seems to like working outward from a beguiling theme, and is *not* interested in building a jazz/Latin synthesis by the very common method of mixing Cuban and jazz elements in a solo. When she did start building an ostinato in "Warriors," it was closer to a bass than a piano montuno, and even closer to some of the insistent, deep-voiced drum calls of both western African and deep-Cuban percussion.

Rosewoman's dual dedication to Afro/Latin roots and the more exploratory zones of jazz is mirrored in a very different way by a Puerto Rico-based band that has also been renewing the deeper reaches of Afrocentric Latin music. Led by multi-percussionist Raúl Berrios, Clave Tres' self-produced recording *From Africa To the Caribbean*, is a mix of many familiar elements, including: some delicious flute playing given extra tonal delicacy by prominent tres guitar; fla-menco; Cuban *septeto* trumpet; soprano sax that is both out and mellow; and touches of African mbira and percussion. But Clave Tres has abandoned the 16-pulse (that is, essentially, four-bar) building block of most Latin (and a great deal of other western) music for a 12-pulse pattern common in West African music. Except on Afrocentric musico-ideological grounds this might not seem like a big deal, but when added to the other complexities of Afro-Latin rhythms it creates both a different set of rhythmic possibilities, and also melody lines that fall out-side the most familiar popular music patterns. The band's second recording, *Kónkolo Salsero*, uses the same basic pattern in a series of remarkably fine ver-sions of such standards as "Caravan" and "Summertime," to all of which the move from a 16- to a 12-beat pulse imparted extraordinary freshness.

As the 1990s draw to a close, what now? Is Latin jazz, as one musician pre-dicted, "the next big thing?" Given that Latin music of one sort or another has played such an important role in jazz from the very beginning, and that Latin jazz in all its forms has so steadily enlarged its turf for the past half-century, it seems unlikely that it will go away any time soon. On the other hand, it may well meet increasing competition from influences further afield. The incorporation into jazz of music from other, non-Latin, cultures has also been building since the 1950s, albeit on an even smaller plane than Latin-jazz influences. Until recently, these world music styles have received very little critical attention, perhaps because these new overseas influences are so disparate and have only recently been subsumed together under the label of World music (and partly because most jazz aficionados and writers know even less about them than about Latin idioms). Critics have long taken note of the work of Afrocentric musicians like Yusuf Lateef and Cecil Taylor, though without any real understanding of the African component in their work. But the degree to which Indian and other Asian music has affected jazz since Coltrane—which in the 1990s includes an entire U.S. Asian-jazz movement—has gone almost totally unremarked, as has the presence of a non-Latin Caribbean strain stretching back at least to the 1920s (and, in the case of Haiti, to the very origins of New Orleans jazz).

As the U.S. discovers that it is a part of the larger world, Latin-jazz will move from being the only non-U.S. fusion of significance to a role as the dean among many others. Its boosters have always called jazz an international music. Until recently that merely meant that it had fans all over the world (it was far less influential on other styles than Cuban music). Now the old boast looks like its becoming reality.

Glossary

Agogó   A two-note clapperless double-bell, joined by a curved piece of metal and struck by a stick. It is used in the African-derived religions of Brazil, and both name and instrument are of West African origin. The agogó was brought to the U.S. by Brazilian musicians during the 1970s.

Baiao   Based on one of many rhythms from Northeastern Brazil, the modern baiao developed in the mid-1940s and became popular in Rio de Janeiro a few years later as a reaction against the era's relatively bland pop popular music. Its most famous performer (some say creator), accordionist Luis Gonzaga, became and remained a national star.

Barrio, El   The districts of Latin American towns are called barrios, so when Latinos moved into New York's East Harlem, it became The District. The word is often used metaphorically as a special application of some such concept as "the street," as in "word in the *barrio* is that. . . ."

Batá Drums   Religious drums of Nigerian origin and sacred to Yoruba-derived religions in Nigeria and Cuba. They look like an hourglass with one chamber larger than the other. A single drum-head is stretched across the top. Unconsecrated batá have long been used in Cuban dance music: just how long, nobody has yet established.

Berimbau   A large Brazilian musical bow some versions of which are called *irucungu*. The player holds an open gourd resonater against the chest and taps the string with a stick. The berimbau is of African inspiration: there are hundreds of types in Africa, and dozens in the Congo/Angolan area that was a major source of Afro-Brazilian culture. Whether the present form is native to Brazil is still argued and is largely a matter of semantics. The berimbau moved out of Afro-Brazilian culture into popular music in the 1970s.

Bolero   The Cuban bolero was originally a medium-tempo form played mostly by guitar trios, and that's the instrumentation that suits it best. As it moved into Cuban dance music and then international-Latin pop, it got slower and more sentimental. It was and is the most common rhythm played by mambo and salsa groups to satisfy the cheek-to-cheek set, and in my unshakable (though not very widely shared) opinion is unsuited to the salsa rhythm section.

Bomba   An Afro-Rican three-drum dance whose percussion form still shows its African ancestry clearly. The bomba is still performed in its original form in the village of Loiza Aldea, birthplace of the man who introduced it to the dance floor, Rafael Cortijo. Except performed by folk-festival groups, the rural bomba appears to be dead, but it has become a permanent, though minor, element in Latin dance music.

Bossa Nova A mix of various Brazilian rhythms, particularly the samba, with mostly West Coast jazz influences. Both the term and the sound surfaced in Brazil around 1958, depending on definitions. The core style is generally considered as being the kind of laid back, vocally oriented music with richly chorded guitar and oblique rhythms epitomized by João Gilberto. U.S. music buffs were exposed to only a fraction of the musicians and styles that soon developed. The bossa nova became a pop style just as quickly in Brazil as in the U.S.; Brazilian writers distinguish between bossa nova and samba-jazz.

Boogaloo A rhythm-and-blues offshoot whose origin is mysterious, boogaloo seems to have originated in Chicago in 1965. Some say that Wilson Pickett's "Mustang Sally" and "In the Midnight Hour" were boogaloos. The only number with the word in the title to hit the Top 40 was "Boogaloo Down Broadway" by Fantastic Johnny C. As a musical style, the boogaloo is almost impossible to tie down: it is probably best seen as a dance done to any music that fits at the time.

Bugalú, Latin The Latin bugalú was a mid-1960s New York Latin style inspired by the African-American boogaloo, which almost immediately became its own thing. The beat has been described both as a simplified and sharply accented mambo and as chachachá with a backbeat. The lyrics were usually in English, the singing moved between Cuban and black inflections, and solos were jazz- or R&B-influenced. The shingaling and the Puerto Rican jala jala were subsets of bugalú. The Latin style was often spelt the same as the African-American; I use the Latinized version for clarity.

Cencerro A cowbell, hand-held and played with a stick, to produce a two-note rhythm. In salsa, the bongo player usually switches to cencerro to drive the band through the instrumental sections after the main vocals.

Chachachá The chachachá, inspired by one of the sections of the old danzón or a mambo step depending on your source, emerged in Cuba in the early 1950s. As always, there is dispute about its creator, though the most likely candidate is the bandleader Chepin. It is essentially a charanga form, and a flute-and-fiddle chachachá with the snap and crack of a good timbalero would make a dead snake strut. New York dancers sometimes called it a double mambo, because of its resemblance to a mambo with a double step between bars. Pet peeve: It is NOT a chacha or any two-syllable variation thereof: What gives it its very name is a triple step!

Charanga Originally a "charanga francesa" or French orchestra, the charanga consists of flute backed by fiddles, with timbales prominent in the rhythm section, and a distinctive duet singing style. Charangas have ranged from pure white-gloves-and-potted-palms ensembles to something that would sear steak. As time went on charanga fiddle solos started to be influenced by jazz, though the hottest charanga violinists are hotter than any of their jazz equivalents. A charanga with added brass is one of the most popular forms of contemporary group in Cuba itself, Los Van Van being perhaps the best-known example.

Cierre A break, but used more extensively than in jazz. A cierre can ranges from a two-note bongo phrase to a complicated pattern for a full band more like a bridge-passage. Used a lot or a little, good cierres are fundamental to salsa structure, but they are so varied and used in so many ways that closer definition would be misleading. Unlike jazz breaks, cierres are rarely for a solo instrument.

Clave An offbeat 3/2 or 2/3 rhythmic pattern over two bars, clave is the basis of all Cuban music, and every element of arrangement and improvisation should fit into it. The same type of pulse also underlies most other Afro-Latin musics without being such a big deal. Clave will drive you crazy until you get used to it, though it isn't really all that arcane. The guaguancó, for example, is in 2/3 reverse clave—except when it isn't—and the same is true for pretty much all the common rhythms. Another way of categorizing clave is in two slight variants, "*son*" clave and "guaguancó/rumba" clave, both of which can be 3/2 or 2/3. Clave is a simplification, under Euro-Latin influence, of a common West African organizing concept that consists of a regular total number of sounds *and silences*, usually carried on a bell. The concept is a musical one; very few of even the best dancers, let alone most ordinary salsa fans, know the word.

Clave, in The requisite state of playing according to the dictates of a piece's basic clave pattern (see above).

Clave, out of To play out of clave, or to cross clave, is the Cuban-music equivalent to mortal sin. In musician-speak it is the ultimate putdown. One jazz musician of my acquaintance concluded after several years' experience with salsa groups that the concept is partly mythical, certainly as far as front-line playing is concerned. But another non-Latino with much salsa experience once told me that if a band gets out of clave the dance floor will gradually empty. In other words, though dancers don't know what clave is, when things go awry they sense it.

Claves Twin strikers of resonant wood used frequently in Cuban groups up to the 1940s. Their player spelled out the basic clave pattern (q.v.), which in groups without claves remained implied. Claves have made a modest comeback in the 1990s under the influence of Cuban revivalist *son* groups. Many variants of the clave sticks exist throughout Latin America and anywhere African-derived music is played.

Comping Basically an abbreviation of "accompanying," comping became the bebop and post-bebop term for what the pianist does during somebody else's solo, and more specifically for goosing a soloist with staccato chords, often harmonically advanced. I have seen it used (or misused) as a kind of bebop equivalent of vamping.

Conga Rhythm The Cuban conga was originally a carnival dance-march from Santiago de Cuba, with a heavy-fourth-beat, the rhythm common to carnival music in many parts of the New World. The conga is more easily simplified than most Cuban rhythms and was a natural for 1940s nightclub floorshows. Contrary to his own belief, it was not introduced to the U.S. by Desi Arnaz, but filtered in around 1935.

Conga Drum A major instrument in the salsa rhythm section, the conga is literally the "Congolese drum," and it began life in the Afro-Cuban cults. Arsenio Rodriguez is said to have introduced it to the conjuntos on a regular basis, and Machito's Afro-Cubans were the first to use it on New York bandstands. There are several types of conga, including the small *quinto*, a solo improvising instrument; the mid-sized *conga*; and the large *tumbadora*. Played by an expert, the conga is capable of a great variety of sound and tone, not only from the different ways of striking or rubbing the head, but through raising the instrument's rim off the ground by holding it between the knees. A conga-player is called a *conguero* or *congacero*.

Conjunto (English: "combo") Cuban conjuntos developed during the 1940s either from the carnival marching bands or from an amplification of the earlier *septeto* depending on whom you believe (I lean to the latter as a more direct link), and combined voices, trumpets, piano, bass, conga, and bongo. Its most obvious feature is a two- or three-trumpet front-line. Arsenio Rodriguez ran a seminal Cuban conjunto that used the smoky tone of the *tres* guitar to offset the brass. During the 1970s, conjuntos with a trombone rather than a trumpet front-line became the dominant sound in the U.S. The word is used in other styles and countries to mean groups of totally different instrumentations, often accordion-led.

Coro Literally, "chorus." In salsa and its Cuban antecedents, it refers to the two or three-voice refrains of two or four bars sung during montunos. The lead singer improvises against the refrains, and to the people who sing them. Coros are used in various ways in arrangements; as reprises or, by an alteration of the refrain, to establish a change of mood. In Miami and to a lesser extent in New York, a bilingual *coro* has been used to powerful effect, with an English-language R&B phrase answered by a classic Cuban-Spanish one or vice-versa.

Cuarteto See **Septeto**.

Cuatro The Puerto Rican cuatro used to have four courses of two strings each (hence the name) but these days normally has a fifth course, giving it ten strings in all. In Venezuela and Trinidad, it has four strings and is somewhere between a guitar and a ukulele in size. The Puerto Rican cuatro is the dominant melodic instrument in Puerto Rican *jibaro* country music. Players like Toñito Ferrer, Yomo Toro, and Nieves Quintero expanded its sound with bluesy and jazz-influenced runs. Willie Colón helped bring it into salsa by hiring Yomo Toro back in the 1970s.

Cuica A small Brazilian friction drum crucial to the carnival samba sound. It is made of metal and has a tube fastened to the inside of the drumhead, which is rubbed to produce a squeaky noise (using the same principle as a wetted finger and a window pane, but with a much more flexible sound). In Brazilian samba school use, the cuica has an ambiguous role somewhere between a lead drum and a manic vocalist. The instrument's origin is also ambiguous. The name seems to come from a Congo-Angolan name for a similar instrument, *kwita*, and the instrument is also probably West African derived (while the cuica is metal and most African equivalents are not, there is one metal version in Dahomey—though this could conceivably have been a reverse import). On the other hand, there is a traditional Spanish equivalent called the *zambomba*, and Portugal may well have had something similar, so we may have here a case of two traditions reinforcing each other. Why the cuica developed in Brazil and not in Spanish-speaking Latin countries is one of the questions that makes studying musical cultures so intriguing.

Danzón A Cuban ballroom dance developed from the contradanza in the late 1870s. It was played by clarinet-and French-horn *típicas* until the late 1920s, and flute-and-fiddle charangas until the early 1950s. The danzón bears the mark of Europe and its first section was usually a promenade, but its charm is not merely nostalgic. Its melodies echo from time to time in modern salsa, especially in combinations like the danzón-cha, two of which were on Eddie Palmieri's first recording.

Descarga The word means "discharge" (as in firing a gun) and is a Latin musician's slang term for a jam session. Descargas occupy a position midway between salsa and Latin-jazz, because they tend to preserve the Cuban vocals and structures yet contain far more jazz soloing than does salsa.

Groove Groove has various meanings in jazz, none of them too precise. The sense in which I use it in this book is that of a repeated pattern in the rhythm section, usually over two measures, that is common in funk jazz and which I believe to be clave-derived.

Guaguancó The mid-paced guaguancó, a form of street rumba, has African roots. It was originally a drum form related to the street-rumba. Though often played 4/4, it has a strong 6/8 feel. The basic rhythm is traditionally carried by three congas and usually includes a good deal of solo drumming. The theme of a modern guaguancó is a somewhat loose melody line. It is usually but not always played with a 2/3 reverse clave. A contemporary guaguancó group, Los Muñequitos de Matanzas, has gained a certain amount of international fame.

Guajeo A riff in charanga style, especially for violin. Guajeos tie the melodic and rhythmic elements of a number together, acting as a sort of trampoline for flute and other solos. They are melodic patterns based on the basic clave and tumbao. The clave-based patterns that are the basic building blocks of a piano montuno are also often called guajeos. What they should not be called is "vamps."

Guajira The slow guajira played by salsa groups comes from the Spanish wing of Cuban music. Its lyrics frequently deal with rural nostalgia. The montunos used in contemporary guajiras still derive much of their flavor from the old guitar patterns of the rural musicians. The guajira is somewhat like the slow *son* montuno but is more delicate and less driving: where the *son* montuno is implacable, the guajira would break your heart.

Guaracha Originally a Cuban topical song form for chorus and solo voice, with improvisation in the solo, the guaracha developed a second section full of improvisation, as did the *son* and the *son* montuno. In the 1930s it was written off as a dying breed, but by the mid-1940s it was a major dance-band rhythm and seems to have been a major root of the dance-band mambo. The guaracha is uptempo, and its most famous exponent today is Celia Cruz.

Güiro. The güiro is a scraper much used in rural music, and also in *típico*-oriented dance music, but rare in Latin jazz. The Cuban and Puerto Rican version is made from a notched gourd and played with a stick. The instrument played in the

Dominican Republic is metal, and in rural merengue sometimes takes over the lead-instrument role. Poor players produce a steady ratchet-like sound. Both versions came into the dance bands at various times; in the 1970s, Johnny Pacheco didn't leave home without it, and the metal version was crucial to the 1980s merengue revival.

Habanera Properly called a *danza habanera*, this Cuban dance was the first major Latin influence on U.S. popular music in general and jazz in particular. It also provided the rhythmic basis of the modern tango, which makes the two influences hard to untangle.

Inspiracion ("Inspiration") An improvised phrase by a lead vocalist or instrument, particularly in the dance-hall rumba. The first set of *inspiraciones* on record is said to be the trumpet part of Don Azpiazú's "The Peanut Vendor."

Jíbaro Music The music of the *jíbaro* mountain farmers of Puerto Rico is strongly Spanish in origin. Mostly string-based, one of its most important vocal structures is the décima verses that a good singer must be able to improvise. The small cuatro guitar is the emblematic *jíbaro* instrument, though the accordion has been important since the late nineteenth century and other instruments have come and gone as fashions change. As far as most urban Puerto Ricans are concerned, *jíbaro* music is hicky till Christmas time, when it becomes roots.

Latin Rhythms The basic meter of salsa is 4/4, organized by the two-bar clave pattern. The individual forms, of which the most common are listed separately, are not simply "rhythms" that can be tapped on a tabletop, but complex combinations of rhythmic pulse, melodic phrasing, speed, and song form. Brazilian music and older Cuban music are mostly 2/4, and the move to 4/4 seems to be a U.S. influence. Many Latin rhythms, wherever they come from, derive from complicated fusions of African, Iberian, and, far enough back, North African Berber elements.

Lucumí Cuba's most widespread African-derived religion, also called *santería*, particularly by Puerto Ricans. Its theology is based on the faith of the Nigerian and Dahomeyan Yoruba people, and Yoruba is the liturgical language of Cuban lucumí. Lucumí is one of many African-derived faiths, and is widespread in Puerto Rico (and the Latin U.S.) under the general name of "santería." Lucumí gave an important Yoruba basis to Cuban rhythms and various rhythmic and instrumental elements to salsa. Many modern salsa musicians, not all of them Latino, are adherents of lucumi, or *santería*, and the sacred batá drums are ever more widely used in secular music.

Mambo An Afro-Cuban form generally thought to have come out of the Congolese religious cults. Several important Cuban musicians including Arsenio Rodriguez, Israel "Cachao" López, and Damaso Pérez Prado have been credited with introducing the mambo to the 1940s dance band conjunto. The U.S. big band mambo of the 1940s and 1950s had very strong jazz influences, particularly in the section writing and horn soloing.

Mambo Section A section of contrasting riffs for salsa frontline instruments, setting trumpets against saxes or trombones, for example, sometimes under an instrumental solo. The section was said to derive from the so-called *estribillo* of the *son montuno*, a faster improvised instrumental second section, which was greatly expanded for big band mambo purposes.

Maracas   A tuned pair of rattles made from gourds filled with pebbles or seeds, one of a wide range of Amerindian-derived rattles. Vegas chorus girls in silly costumes waving maracas around have given the instrument a bad image, but a skilled maraca player like Machito plays a subtle role in the polyrhythmic counterpoint.

Marimba   A rural Central and South American xylophone featuring wooden slats mounted over resonators. The name is African and the instrument probably is also, but the Latin-American marimbas are mostly Amerindian except in western Colombia (where the playing style is still very African), in parts of Mexico, and, in particular, Guatemala. Marimba groups—notably the various ensembles run by the Hurtado brothers of Guatemala—were popular in the U.S. during the 1920s, which explains why Xavier Cugat had one in his first rumba band.

Marimbula   A wooden box with prongs of metal fastened to it, tuned to play a series of bass notes. The marimbula was common in Cuba and the Dominican Republic, as well as in several non-Latin Caribbean islands (in Jamaica it was known as a rumba-box). Though it is a whole lot larger—the player sits on it while performing—its origin is the almost omnipresent finger-pianos of Sub-Saharan Africa.

Maxixe   A Brazilian dance derived from an earlier local ballroom dance called the lundú and heavily influenced by the early twentieth-century tango. It was briefly popular in the U.S. around the First World War, but was basically too much like a faster tango to catch on for long. Some old photos suggest that the original Lindy hop may have borrowed a couple of breakaways from the U.S. version of the maxixe.

Merengue   There are dances called merengue in other countries, which don't necessarily have the same rhythm. But the only merengue that concerns us is from the Dominican Republic, where it dates back at least to the early nineteenth century. The Dominican merengue has a notably brisk and snappy 2/4 rhythm with a flavor very different from the more complex Cuban and Puerto Rican rhythmic patterns, sort of like a subversive polka. In the 1980s a hip big-band version of the dance took Latin New York by storm. More recently there's been a swing back to the old country forms, for accordion, tambora drum, metal scraper, and voice, which in the 1970s were strictly Hicksville in the eyes of Dominican city folk. Both accordion players and the big merengue bands of the 1950s and 1960s, like Johnny Ventura's and Felix del Rosario's, were considerably jazz-influenced.

Montuno   A basic clave-based rhythmic vehicle in Cuban and salsa numbers, based on a two or three-chord pattern repeated ad-lib under the instrumental or vocal improvisations. The term was originally applied to a drum or bass-line made up of repeated *tumbaos*, but is also applied to the piano equivalent. In no case should the montuno be thought of as vamping! In jazz or your neighborhood piano bar, a vamp is a holding pattern played while the pianist thinks of something more interesting to do. A montuno is a positive and integral link between soloists and rhythm section or an ostinato backing to a percussion solo, and at all times a crucial aspect of the Cuban and Cuban-derived rhythmic fundamentals.

MPB (Música Popular Brasileira) MPB refers to the text-oriented, highly eclectic, singer-guitarist style that grew up in the late 1960s and 1970s, of whom the most famous exponents include Gal Costa, Milton Nascimento, and Gilberto Gil. MPB has more varied and a greater number of U.S. elements in it than did the bossa nova. A crucial early recording, *Tropicalia*, carried its Beatlemania as far as the design of the cover. Perhaps because it was born during a military regime, its lyrics tend to be more specifically political than earlier social-comment styles. But it is not as limited lyrically as the various "protest song" genres, nor as limited musically as most Spanish-language *mueva trova* or *nueva canción*.

Pachanga A dance of the 1960s, born in Cuba but popular for a while in Latin New York. It started as a charanga form and brought about a fairly long-lasting charanga revival in New York, but was also taken over by the remaining big bands. The pachanga didn't last as long as most major Latin dances, supposedly because dancers found it too fast.

Plena An Afro-Puerto Rican urban topical song form often compared to the Trianidad calypso (by me among others). It is said to have grown up in the town of Ponce during World War I. The plena has four- or six-line verses, with a refrain. Lyrical content is social comment, satire, or humor. Instrumentation has ranged from percussion through accordion or guitar-led groups to various dance-band formats. The large, rattle-less tambourine called a *pandereta* is an essential part of the plena's original rhythm section. It has had various moments in the urban dance sun, and more recently a number of semi-traditionalist plena groups have grown up in New York and Puerto Rico. Though it has fairly strong African elements, it is a typical creole idiom that could not exist without both Spain and Africa.

Rumba/Rhumba Most of what the United States calls rumbas were forms of the *son* which swept Cuba in the 1920s. The original Cuban rumba was a secular drum form with many variants, including the guaguancó and the columbia, though modern musicians tend to regard all these as separate. Its descendent variations can be heard in New York parks any summer weekend played by groups called rumbas or rumbones. By analogy, a percussion passage in a salsa number, or a percussion-only jam session, is sometimes called a rumba or rumbón. The dance-band form—and the intrusive "h" that is common though not universal in U.S. spelling—has more complex and unexplored roots than the usual attribution to *yanqui* ignorance. There is some evidence that the word was also applied to dance-band versions of *sones* in late 1920s Cuba.

Salsa Hot, up-tempo, creative Latin music, and in particular the U.S. mix of (mostly) Cuban with Puerto Rican, Panamanian, and jazz elements. The dictionary sense is just what your supermarket means by it. Originally, it was applied to music as a description such as "swinging" or "hot," or as an injunction to musicians: "Sauce it up a bit," so to speak. The origins of the current usage are obscure, but it began to circulate in the late 1960s and early 1970s. Bandleader Willy Rosario once told me he had first heard it used in its modern sense in Venezuela around 1964. There is a persistent myth that "salsa" is just a marketing term to disguise the rip off of Cuban music. However, although New York salsa is largely based on Cuban foundations, its essence is its accretion of Panamanian, Puerto Rican, jazz, and R&B elements.

Samba   An Afro-Brazilian dance with untold variations in different parts of Brazil. The best-known are the urban sambas, which swept Rio in the 1920s and are said to derive from the Brazilian maxixe and the highly percussive sambas of the carnival "schools" of Rio. The name itself is clearly of African derivation, which is not very helpful since in various spellings (zamba, semba) it described very different music in other parts of Latin America. The samba is NOT coterminous with Carmen Miranda, but she was in fact a fine samba singer and her group the Banda da Lua was excellent when you could hear it under all those studio musicians in the movies.

Septeto or Sexteto   The Cuban septetos and sextetos of the 1930s were trumpet-led string groups, usually with tres, guitar, maracas, bass, and bongo, playing mostly *sones* and boleros. They essentially developed from tacking a trumpet onto a string-and-percussion *cuarteto*. Famous groups included the Septeto Nacional and the Sexteto Habanero. The music they played fell somewhere between the guajiro string groups and the brassier conjuntos. Septeto trumpet style is singularly lyrical, moving between nineteenth-century brass-band cornet and jazz in its inspiration. The septeto style as a whole is subtle, crisp, and utterly beguiling.

Shekere   An African-derived rattle made of a large gourd with beads held by a string net on the outside. It is one version of a rattle common in Africa and Afro-Latin America and works on the opposite principle from maracas. In Spanish it is spelt "chekere," and in Brazil it is called an afôxe. Both the instrument and the name come from Nigeria.

Son   The *son* is perhaps the oldest and certainly the classic creolized-Cuban form, an almost perfect balance of African and Hispanic elements. Originating in Oriente province, it surfaced in Havana before World War I and became a popular urban music played by string-and-percussion quartets and septets. Almost all the numbers Americans called rumbas were, in fact, *sones*. "El Manicers" ("The Peanut Vendor") was a form of *son* derived from the street cries of Havana and called a pregon. The rhythm of the *son* is strongly syncopated, with a basic chicka-CHUNG pulse.

Son Montuno   A normally reverse clave (2/3) form, with a pronounced CHUNG-chicka feel. The *son* montuno, which spun off from the general *son* tradition, was one of the first forms to include a second, improvised section, the montuno. Though it is not fast, the Afro-Cuban *son* montuno has an intense, almost relentless quality.

Sonero   Strictly a man who sings or plays the Afro-Cuban *son*, but also the improvising lead singer in various Cuban and salsa styles. A good sonero improvises rhythmically, melodically, and verbally against the backdrop of the coro's refrain. A bad one often makes a fortune in salsa romántica (known derisively as "salsa monga" as in salsa needing Viagra).

Straight 4/4/Straight 2/4   The kind of basic jazz rhythm section pulse that used to be standard. Four (or two) more or less steady beats to the bar without patterns of held notes. This is not a standard jazz term but it's handy in comparing Latin and "straight" jazz.

Tambora   A double-headed drum basic to the rural Dominican merengue. It is slung over the shoulder and played with a single stick, while the other head is damped by hand to give a remarkable range of tonal variety. If the tambora player sits down and tucks his instrument between his legs, he's about to play a 6/8 *mangulina*, for which he uses his hands only, like a conga drummer.

Tango   Probably the world's best-known dance after the waltz, the modern tango developed in Argentina at the beginning of the twentieth century, from late nineteenth-century roots. It took its rhythm from the Cuban habanera and the Argentinian milonga, and in its very early stage had an unquantifiable amount of African influence. The origin of the word itself is much debated but appears also to be African-derived. Though the tango started as a largely guitar music—and flutes and even Indian harps were used—the classic tango instrument is a type of accordion called a bandoneon. By the 1920's three styles had developed: Argentinian, American, and European or Continental.

Timbales   A percussion setup consisting of two small metal drums on a stand, with two tuned cowbells, often a cymbal, and other additions. A Cuban version of the U.S. trap-drums, the timbales descended from small military dance and concert bands. They were originally confined to the charangas and orquestas *típicas*, which they gave a crisply jaunty snap, but during the 1940s they came into wider use. The timbales are played with sticks, and a good timbalero will use the sides as well as the bead and rim of the drums. A standard timbales beat, the *abanico*, is a rimshot-roll-rimshot combination.

Típico   A vague but very important concept in Latin music of all kinds. Literally it means "typical" or "characteristic," but it is used to identify down-home, popular styles whether urban or rural. The Cuban *típico* music that became so important in New York in the 1960s and 1970s was basically conjunto- and charanga-based. But septetos or Tex-Mex accordion groups or street-samba bands are also *típico*.

Toque   A "beat," but in Cuban music and its derivatives a standard rhythmic phrase for percussion. Many toques derive from African religious drumming, in which particular rhythmic patterns were used to summon individual gods. A Latin percussionist is judged not so much by his energy level, but by his knowledge and use of standard toques and variations in his improvisations and in support of the band. Traditionalists hold that if you don't know the toques you're not a conga-player, just somebody knockin' on a drum.

Tres   In Cuba and contemporary salsa, a six-string Cuban guitar with three double courses, a mainstay of guajiro music and of the Afro-Cuban septetos. The *tres* was established as an important part of the Cuban conjunto by Arsenio Rodriguez and came into New York salsa during the Cuban *típico* revival of the late 1960s and early

1970s. There are a zillion related instruments in Latin America, which long preserved all the varieties of guitar that died out in Europe, besides developing a slew of its own.

Tumbao A repeated rhythmic pattern, originally for an ancestor of the conga drum called a tumba (hence the name), but also applied to the double-bass and increasingly also to the piano equivalents. Based on the fundamental clave, the bassist's and/or pianist's tumbaos provide the framework for the percussion's rhythmic interplay.

Select Discography

Note: The dates given are of recording, when known; otherwise of original copyright. All catalog numbers are for CD releases or reissues, unless otherwise indicated.

Compilations

Early Music of the North Caribbean 1916-1920
    (Harlequin HQCD67)
Afro-Cuba: A Musical Anthology (Rounder 1088)
Boogie-Woogie Special (Topaz Jazz)
Best of Latin Jazz, The (Verve 314 517 956)
Brazil Samba Roots (Rounder 5045)
Cuban Big Bands (Harlequin HQCD63)   1940–42
Culture Clash in New York City: Experiments in Latin Music
    (Soul Jazz SJR29)   1970–77
More Than Mambo (Verve 314 527 903)   1949–67
Original Mambo Kings, The (Verve 314 513 876)   1948–54
60s Gold (Fania SP53)   1960s
Montuno Sessions, The (Mr Bongo MRBCD004)   1986–89
Jammin' in the Bronx (Tropijazz RMD 82044)   1995
Brazil: A Century of Song (Blue Jackel BJ5000) 4 CDs/Bklt

Individual Artists and Bands

ADDERLEY, CANNONBALL QUINTET
Cannonball in Japan (Capitol 93560)   1966
Country Preacher (Capitol 30452)   1969
Inside Straight (Original Jazz OJCCD7502)   1973

AFRO BLUE BAND
Impressions (Milestone MCD9237)   1994

AGUABELLA, FRANCISCO/BENNY VELARDE Orchestras
Ay Que Rico! (Fantasy FCD24731)   1962

AIRTO
See also PURIM, FLORA & AIRTO
Natural Feelings (Buddah)   1970
Seeds on the Ground (Buddah; reissue One Way 30006)   1971
Free (CBS ZK40927)   1972
Virgin Land (CTI)   1974
Promises of the Sun (Arista)   1975
Identity (Arista AL4068)   1975

—— / DEODATO
In Concert (CTI 6041)   1973

—— / FLORA PURIM / JOE FARRELL
Three Way Mirror (Reference RR24)   1985

ALEGRE ALL STARS
Vol. 1 (Alegre 8100)   1961
Vol. 2 *El Manicero* (Alegre 8340)   1963
VOL. 3 *Lost and Found* (Alegre 8430)   1966
Te Invita (Alegre 6028)   1961–76

ALMEIDA, LAURINDO
Outra Vez (Concord Picante CCD4497)   1991

—— / CHARLIE BYRD
Brazilian Soul (Concord Picante CCD 4150)   1980
Latin Odyssey (Concord Picante 4211)   1982
Tango (Concord Picante 4290)   1985

—— / BUD SHANK
Brazilliance Vol.1 (World Pacific 96339)   1953
Brazilliance Vol.2 (World Pacific 96102)   1957

—— / CARLOS BARBOSA-LIMA / CHARLIE BYRD
Music of the Brazilian Masters (Concord Picante CCD4389)   1989

—— & THE BOSSA NOVA ALL-STARS
Viva Bossa Nova (Capitol ST1759; LP)   1962

AMALBERT, JUAN LATIN JAZZ QUINTET
Hot Sauce (Prestige PRCD24128)   1960–61

ANDERSON, CLIFTON
Landmarks (Milestone MCD9266)   1995

ASSAD, BADI
Rhythms (Chesky JD137)   1995

AUSTIN, LOVIE
1924–1926 (Classics 756)   1924–26

AZPIAZU, DON AND HIS HAVANA CASINO ORCHESTRA
(Harlequin HQCD10)

BAILEY, BENNY Quintet
Peruvian Nights (TCB Records TCB96102) CD   1984

BARBIERI, GATO
The Third World (Flying Dutchman AYL1-3815) LP   1969
Fenix   1971
Under Fire (Flying Dutchman)   1973
Chapter One: Latin America (ABC/Impulse; CD reissue: MCA Impulse 39124) 1973
Chapter Two: Hesta Siempre   1974
Chapter Three: Viva Emiliano Zapata (ABC/Impulse; CD reissue:
     GRP Impulse 111).   1975
Caliente (A&M SP4597; CD reissue A&M 3247)   1976
Para Los Amigos (CBS Special Products)   1981
Afro-Cuban Chant (Hip Bop Essence HIBD8009)   1995
Afro-Cubano Chant (Hip Bop Essence 8009)   1995

BARNET, CHARLIE & His Orchestra
1941 (Circle CCD65)   1941

BARRETTO, RAY
Carnaval (Fantasy FCD24713)   1961
Acid (Fania SLP346)   1972
Tomorrow: Barretto Live (Atlantic SD2-509)   1976
Que Viva La Musica (Atlantic SD2-510)   1976
Eye of the Beholder (Atlantic SD19140)   1977
Handprints (Concord Picante CCD4473)   1991

——, AND NEW WORLD SPIRIT
Ancestral Messages (Concord Picante 4549)   1993
Carnaval (Fantasy 24713)   1993
Taboo (Concord Picante CCD4601)   1994

BAUZA, MARIO & HIS AFRO-CUBAN JAZZ ORCHESTRA
(Messidor 15819)   1992
My Time Is Now (Messidor 15824)   1993
944 Columbus (Messidor 15828)   1993

BERRIOS, STEVE & SON BACHECHÉ
First World (Milestone MCD9234)   1994
And Then Some! (Milestone MCD9255)   1996

BLAKE, EUBIE
The Eighty-Six Years Of. . . (Columbia C2S 847; Original 2-LP set)   1969
Concert (Stash ST130) LP   1973

BLAKEY, ART
Holiday for Skins (Blue Note BST84004/5)   1958

—— / SABU
Duets (Blue Note 81520) CD   1953

——, & HIS JAZZ MESSENGERS / SABU
Cu-Bop (Fresh Sounds Records FSRCD95) CD   1957

——, & THE NEW JAZZ MESSENGERS
Buttercorn Lady (Mercury LP LML4021)   1966

BLEY, PAUL
Tango Palace (Soul Note 121090)   1983

BLYTHE, ARTHUR
Lenox Avenue Breakdown (Columbia 35638)   1979

BOBO, WILLIE
Do That Thing/Guajira (Tico SLP1108)   1963
Spanish Grease/uno dos tres (Verve 314 521 664)   1965–66

BOLA SETE
See also GUARALDI, VINCE/BOLA SETE
Bossa Nova (Fantasy 8349; CD reissue OJC 286)   1962
Tour de Force (Fantasy 8358)   1963
Incomparable (Fantasy 3364; CD reissue OJC 288)
Solo Guitar (Fantasy 3369 LP)   1965
Monterrey Jazz Festival (Fantasy 8689)   1966
Autentico! (Fantasy 8417; CD reissue 890)   1971
Goin' To Rio (Columbia 32375 LP)   1973

BONFÁ, LUIS
Non Stop to Brazil (Chesky JD29)   1989

BONILLA, LUIS LATIN JAZZ ALL STARS
Pasos Gigantes (Candid CCD79507)

BOSTIC, EARL
Plays Bossa Nova (King 827)   1963

BRACKEEN, JOANNE
Breath of Brazil (Concord Picante CCD 4479)   1991

BROWN, PUCHO
Tough (Prestige)   1966
Saffron Soul (Prestige)   1967

BRUBECK, DAVE QUARTET
Bossa Nova U.S.A. (Columbia CL1998) LP   1963

BULLOCK, HIRAM
Carrasco (Fantasy FCD9679)   1997

BUNNETT, JANE
Spirits of Havana (Messidor 15825)   1991

BURTON, GARY and ASTOR PIAZOLLA'S QUARTET
The New Tango (Atlantic 81823-2)   1986

BYRD, CHARLIE
See also SHANK, BUD with CHARLIE BYRD

Bossa Nova Pelos Passaros (OJCCD107)	1962–3
Byrd at the Gate (OJCCD262)	1963

——/ LAURINDO ALMEIDA

Brazilian Soul (Concord Picante CCD 4150)	1980
Latin Odyssey (Concord Picante 4211)	1982
Tango (Concord Picante 4290)	1985

—— TRIO

Sugarloaf Suite (Concord Picante CCD4114)	1979
The Bossa Nova Years (Concord Picante CCD4468)	1991

BYRD, DONALD

Fuego (Blue Note CDP746534) CD	1959
Fancy Free (Blue Note CDP89796)	1969

CALLOWAY, CAB

Jumpin' Jive (Jazz Archives ZET732 CD	1938–46
1940 (Classics 614) CD ("Rhapsody in Rhumba"/"Yo Eta Cansa")	
1941–1942 (Classics 682) CD ("Conchita")	

CAMERO, CANDIDO

Beautiful (Blue Note Japan 84357)	1970
Brujeas de Candido (Tico TSLP1142)	1971

CAMILO, MICHEL

Camilo (CBS/Portrait RK44482)	1988
On Fire (Epic EK45295)	1989
On The Other Hand (Epic EK46236)	1990
One More Once (Columbia CK66204)	1994

CAMPBELL, GARY

Intersection (Milestone MCD9236)	1993

CAMPO, PUPI

Rumbas and Mambos (Tumbao TCD007)	1948–51

CANO, Eddie

Deep in a Drum (RCA Tropical 4321)	1957

CARABALI

(Mango 539888)	1992

CARAM, ANA

Bossa Nova (Chesky JD129)	1995

CARDONA, MILTON

Bembe! (American Clave) CD: AMCL1004	1987

CARTER, RON

Blues Farm (CBS ZK40691)	1973

CARTER, JOE, QUARTET
Um Abraço No Rio (Empathy E1008)   1992

CAYMAN ALL STARS
Super All Star! (Cayman CLP902)   1984

CESTA ALL-STARS
Salsa Festival (MP Productions 3125)

CHARTBUSTERS, THE
Mating Call (Prestige PRCD11002)   1995

CLARKE, STANLEY
I Wanna Play For You (Epic EK64295)   1978–79
If This Bass Could Only Talk (Portrait PK 40923)   1988

CLARKE / DUKE PROJECT
(Epic EK36918)   1985

CLAVE TRES
From Africa to the Caribbean (FDAM001)   1995
Kónkolo Salsero (FDAM002)   1997

COLON, JOHNNY
Boogaloo Blues (Cotique 1004)   1967

COLTRANE, JOHN
Bahia (Prestige PCD415)   1958
Olé (Atlantic 1373)   1961
. . . Quartet Plays. . . (Impulse MCAD3310)   1965

COREA, CHICK
Inner Space (Atlantic Jazz 2305)   1966
Now He Sings, Now He Sobs (Blue Note 90055)   1968
Tap Step (Warner Bros; reissue Stretch STD-1109)   1979–80

CORTIJO, RAFAEL y Su Combo
Time Machine/Maquina de Tiempo (Coco Records/MP Productions)   1974

CUBAN JAM SESSION
Vol.1 (Panart 1A501-00410)   1956
Vol.2 (Panart 1A501-00415)   1956

CULTURE CLASH IN NEW YORK CITY
(Soul Jazz Records SJRCD29)   1970–77

CURSON, TED
Plays Fire Down Below (OJCCD1744)   1962

DA COSTA, PAULINHO
Tudo Bem (Pablo 2310-824)   1978
Happy People (OJC783)   1976
Agora (OJC630)   1979

DALTO, ADELA
Papa Boco (Milestone 9235)   1995

DALTO, JORGE
Listen Up! (Gaia 2009)   1980
——— & The INTERAMERICAN BAND
Urban Oasis (Concord Picante CCD4275)   1985

DAVIS, EDDIE "LOCKJAW"
Afro-Jaws (Riverside OJCCD403)   1961

DAVIS, MILES
Miles Ahead (Columbia CK 53225)   1957
Quiet Nights (Columbia PCT-08906)   1962–63

DEODATO
See Also AIRTO/DEODATO
Prelude (CBS ZK40695)   1972
2 (CBS ZK40930)   1973
Artistry (MCA)   1974

DODDS, BABY, TRIO
Jazz à la creole (GHB Records GHB50) LP   1946

DONALDSON, LOU
Blues Walk (Blue Note 46525)   1958

DORHAM, Kenny
Afro-Cuban (Blue Note 46815) CD   1955

D'RIVERA, PAQUITO
Manhattan Burn (Columbia CK 40583)   1986
Celebration (Columbia CK 44077)   1987
Tico! Tico! (Chesky JD34)   1989
Havana Café (Chesky JD60)   1991
Reunion (Messidor 15805)   1992
Who's Smoking? (Candid CCD 79523)   1992
Portraits of Cuba (Chesky JD145)   1994
Caribbean Jazz Project (Heads UP HUCD-0333)   1995

DUKE, GEORGE
See CLARKE/DUKE PROJECT
Don't Let Go (Epic EK35366)   197?
A Brazilian Love Affair (Epic/Legacy EK53032)   1979

EDWARDS, TEDDY
Nothin' But the Truth (Prestige OJCCD813)   1966

ELIAS, ELIANE
Illusions (Blue Note 46994) LP   1986
A Long Story (Manhattan 95476)   1991
Paulistana (Blue Note 89544)   1993

ELLINGTON, DUKE
Early Ellington (Decca GRD3-640) — 1926–31
Duke Ellington 1938 (Columbia Special Products P2-13367) 2LPs — 1938
Carnegie Hall Concerts (Prestige 34004) 2 CDs — 1943
Afro-Bossa (Reprise R6069) — 1962–63
Latin American Suite (Fantasy 8419) OJCCD469 — 1968

ESCOVEDO, PETE
The Island (EsGo EG001) — 1983
Yesterday's Memories, Tomorrow's Dreams (Crossover 45002) — 1985

ESCOVEDO, PETE & SHEILA
Solo Two/Happy Together (Fantasy FCD24747) — 1997

ESTRADA BROTHERS
Get Out of My Way (Milestone MCD9260) — 1996

EUROPE, Lieut. JIM's 369th "Hellfighters" Band
Complete Recordings (Memphis Archives) — 1919

FAJARDO ALLSTARS
Cuban Jam Session Vol III (Panart 501-00415)

FELDMAN, VICTOR
Venezuelan Joropo, The (Pacific Jazz ST20128) LP — 1967

FERNANDEZ, ENRIQUE
The Enriquillo Latin Jazz Winds (Mapleshade 04632) — 1997

FEST, MANFREDO
Oferenda (Concord Picante CCD4539) — 1992

FISCHER, CLARE
Salsa Picante (Discovery DS 817) — 1978

FITZGERALD, ELLA
Ella Abraça Jobím (Pablo) — 1980–81

FLANAGAN TOMMY / GERRY MULLIGAN
Jeru Columbia CS8732 (LP)

FORT APACHE BAND
The River Is Deep (Enja ENJ-79609-2) — 1990
Earthdance (Sunnyside SSC1050D) — 1991
Obatatá (Enja ENJ-79609-2) — 1992
Crossroads (Milestone MCD9225) — 1994

FREEMAN, CHICO
Beyond the Rain (Contemporary/OJCCD479) — 1977
Destiny's Dance (Contemporary 799) — 1981

GARCIA BROTHERS
Jazz Con Sabor Latino (Tres Coronas DDC9406) — 1993

GARLAND, RED TRIO
Manteca (Prestige/OJCCD428) — 1958
Rojo (Prestige/OJCCD772) — 1958
Rediscovered Masters Vol.1 (Prestige/OJCCD768) — 1958

GARNER, ERROLL
Mambo Moves. . . (MG20055) — 1954

GETZ, STAN
Big Band Bossa Nova (Verve 825771-2) — 1962
Bossa Nova (Verve 314 529 904) — 1962–67

——— / LAURINDO ALMEIDA
Getz/Almeida (Verve 823149-2)

——— / CHARLIE BYRD
Jazz Samba (Verve 810061-2)

——— / JOAO GILBERTO
Getz/Gilberto (Verve 810048-2) — 1963
Getz/Gilberto #2 (Verve 314-19800-2) — 1964
The Best of Two Worlds (Columbia CK33703) — 1976

——— / DIZZY GILLESPIE
Diz & Getz (Verve 833 559) — 1953–54
Jazz Masters (Verve 314 521 852) — 1953–57

———WITH NEW QUARTET, FEATURING ASTRUD GILBERTO
Getz au Go Go (Verve 821725)

GIBBS, TERRY
The Latin Connection (Contemporary C14022) — 1986

GILBERTO, ASTRUD
Jazz Masters 9 (Verve 314 519 824) — 1964–66
The Astro Gilberto Album (Verve 823451-2) — 1965
Look to the Rainbow (Verve 821556-2) — 1966
With Stanley Turrentine (CBS ZK44168) — 1971

GILBERTO, JOAO
Live in Montreux (Elektra Musician 60760) — 1986

GILLESPIE, DIZZY
"Afro-Cuban Bop" at the Royal Roost (Jazz Live BLJ8028) LP — 1948
Pleyel Concerts (French Vogue DP18) 2 LPs — 1948 & 1953
Dizzy's Diamonds (Verve 314 513 875) 4 CDs/Bklt — 1955–64
Dizzy on the Riviera (Philips 200-048) — 1962
The Melody Lingers On (Limelight 82042) — 1966
Bahiana (Pablo 2625-708) 2 LPs — 1975
Dizzy's Party (Pablo OJCCD823) — 1976
Free Ride (Pablo OJCCD784) — 1977

—— / **MACHITO**
Afro-Cuban Jazz Moods (Pablo OJCCD447)   1975

—— / **ARTURO SANDOVAL**
To a Finland Station (OJCCD733)   1982

GISMONTI, EGBERTO
Sol do Meio Dia (ECM)   1978

GONZALEZ, JERRY
See also FORT APACHE BAND, THE
Ya Yo Me Curé (American Clave 1001)   1979

GORDON, DEXTER
Gettin' Around (Blue Note CDP46681)   1965

GREEN, BENNIE
Blows His Horn (Prestige/OJCCD1728Z)   1955

GREEN, GRANT
The Latin Bit (Blue Note 37645)   1962

GUARALDI, VINCE TRIO
Cast Your Fate to the Wind (Fantasy OJCCD437)   1962

GUARALDI, VINCE / BOLA SETE
and Friends (Fantasy 8356)   1963
From All Sides (Fanstasy 3362)   1964
En El Matador (Fantasy 3371)   1968

GUZMAN, PABLO'S JIBARO JAZZ
Live At The Blue Note (rodven RVVD3125)   1995

HALL, JIM
. . .Where Would I Be? (OJCCD649)   1971

HANCOCK, HERBIE
Cantaloupe Island (Blue Note 29331)   1963–65
Sound System (Columbia CK-39478)   1984

—— / **WILLIE BOBO**
Succotash (Blue Note LP BNLA152)   1964

HARGROVE, ROY'S CRISOL
Habana (Verve 314 537 563)   1997

HAWKINS, COLEMAN Sextet
Desafinado (Impulse A28)   1962

HAYNES, ROY
Senya   1973

HENDERSON, EDDIE
Dark Shadows (Milestone MCD9254)   1995

HENDERSON, JOE
The Kicker (Fantasy/OJC 465)   1967
The Milestone Years (Milestone MCD4413 8-CD set)   1968–1975

Multiple (Milestone)	1973
Canyon Lady (Milestone)	1973

HERMAN, WOODY
In Disco Order, Vol. 31 (Ajazz 424)	1953–54
Giant Steps (Fantasy OJCCD344)	1973

HIDALGO, GIOVANNI
Villa Hidalgo (Messidor 15817)	1992

HIGGINS, EDDIE
Soulero (Atlantic 1446)	1965

HOLLOWAY, RON
Struttin' (Milestone MCD9238)	1995

HUBBARD, FREDDIE
The Night of the Cookers (Blue Note 28882)	1965
Red Clay (CBS ZK40809)	1970

HUTCHERSON, BOBBY
Good Bait (Landmark LCD 1501-2)	1984

IRAKERE
Misa Negra (Messidor 15972)	1986
Live At Ronnie Scott's (World Pacific) CD: CDP80598	

JACKSON, MILT
Big Mouth (Pablo/OJCCD865)	1981

JOHNSON James P.
1921–1928 (Melodie Classics 658)	1921–28
1944 (Melodie Classics 835)	1944
Original Folkways Recordings (Smithsonian/Folkways 40812)	1942–45

JOHNSON JAY JAY
The Eminent Jay Jay Johnson Vol.2 (Blue Note 81506) CD	1954–55

JOPLIN, SCOTT
The Red Back Book (N.E.Consrvatory Ragtime Ensemble) (Angel 36060) LP	

KENTON, STAN
Retrospective (Capitol Jazz CDP 7 97350) 4 CDs/Bklt	1941–42
The Formative Years (Creative World ST1061)	1941–42
23 Degrees North, 82 Degrees West (Viper's Nest VN1007)	1952–53
Cuban Fire (Capitol Jazz B21Y-96260)	1956, 1960
Milestones (Creative World ST1047) ("The Peanut Vendor")	

KEPPARD, FREDDIE
The Legend (Topaz (1052)	1926–27

KIRBY, JOHN & His Orchestra
Loch Lomond (Circle CCD47)	1940–41
(Circle CCD14)	1941–42

KLEMMER, JOHN
Brazilia MCAD 5864   1979

KLUGH, EARL and BOB JAMES
Two of a Kind (Manhattan B21S-99191)   1982

LATIN JAZZ QUINTET + ERIC DOLPHY
Caribé (Prestige OJCCZD819)   1960

LAWRENCE, AZAR
Summer Solstice   1975

LIBRE
Con Salsa . . . Con Ritmo   1976
Mejor Que Nunca (Milestone MCD9226)   1994
On the Move/Muevete! (Milestone MCD9263)   1996

LIGHTHOUSE ALL-STARS
Mexican Passport (Contemporary CCD14077)   1952–56

LINSKY, JEFF
Up Late (Concord Picante CCD4363)   1988
Angel's Serenade (Concord Picante CCD4611)   1994

LLOYD, CHARLES QUARTET
A Night in Copenhagen (Blue Note 85104)   1983

LOCO, JOE
Mambo Loco (RCD049)   1951–53
Loco Motion (Fantasy FCD25733)   1960–61

LONGHAIR, PROFESSOR
The Lost Sessions (Rounder 2057)   1971–72

LUCCA, PAPO
Latin Jazz (Fania JM669)   1993

MACHITO & HIS AFRO-CUBANS
 (Harlequin HQCD87)   1949-50
Tea for Two (Saludos Amigos CD62045)
Cubop City (Tumbao TCD012)   1949–50
Latin Soul Plus Jazz (Fania FA74) CD   1948–49
The New Sound of. . . Tico (TRSLP1084)   1963
Mucho Macho (Pablo PACD 2625-712) CD   1977

MANN, HERBIE
Jazz Masters 56 (Verve 314 529 901)   1957–60
Right Now (Atlantic 1384)   1964
Latin Fever (Atlantic 1422)   1964

—— / JOAO GILBERTO W. ANTONIO CARLOS JOBIM
 (Atlantic 8105)   1962–63

MANN, HERBIE / MACHITO & HIS AFRO-CUBANS
Super Mann (Trip TLP5031; LP reissue)   1958

MANTILLA, RAY SPACE STATION
Hands of Fire (Red RR123174)   1984

MARIA, TANIA
Piquant (Concord 4151)   1980
Taurus (Concord 4175)   1981
Come with Me (Concord 4200)   1982
Love Explosion (Concord 4230)   1983
Wild! (Concord 4264)   1984
Forbidden Colors (Capitol 90966)   1988
Outrageous (Concord 4563)   1993
No Comment (TKM 5001)   1995

MARRERO, RICARDO
Time (VayaJMVS64) Original LP   1977

MARTIGNON, HECTOR
Retarto em Branco e Preto (Candid CCD79727)   1996

MARTINEZ, SABU
Palo Congo (Blue Note Japan TOCJ1561) CD   1957

MARTINEZ SABU / ART BLAKEY
Duets (Blue Note 81520) CD   1953

——& HIS JAZZ MESSENGERS
Cu-Bop (Fresh Sounds FSRCD95) CD   1957

MATOS, BOBBY
Sessions (CuBop CBCD011)   Anthology

METHENY, PAT
Watercolors (ECM1097)   1977
Travels (ECM 78118-21252-2)   1982

MINGUS, CHARLES
New Tijuana Moods (Reissue of Tijuana Moods with additional material;
    Bluebird (5644-2-RB)   1957–62
Epitaph (Columbia C2K454289)   1962&1987
Changes Two (Rhino RK41404)   1974–75
Cumbia & Jazz Fusion (Rhino RK41404)   1977–78

MOBLEY, HANK
Dippin' (Blue Note CDP46511)   1965

MONTEGO JOE
Arriba! Con. . . (Prestige 24139)   1964–65

MONTGOMERY, BUDDY
So Why Not? (Landmark LCD-1518)   1988

MORALES, NORO
"Live" Broadcasts & Transcriptions (Harlequin HQCD78) CD   1942–1948
Rumba Rhapsody (Tumbao TCD036)   1945–51
Campanitas de Cristal (RCA Tropical 3357RL)   1953–55

MORGAN, FRANK
Lament   1986

MORTON, FERDINAND "JELLY ROLL"
Anamule Dance (Rounder CD1092) CD   1938
Winin' Boy Blues (Rounder CD1094) CD   1938
The Quintessence (Fremeaux FA203) 2 CDs

MULLIGAN, GERRY
Night Lights (Phillips 818271-2)   1963
Butterfly With Hiccups (Limelight LM82004)   1963

MULLIGAN, GERRY / ASTOR PIAZZOLLA
Summit (Music Hall MH100051)   1974

MURRAY, DAVID
Ming's Samba (Epic/Portrait RK44432)   1988

MUSTAFA, MELTON
Boiling Point (Contemporary CCD14075)   1995
St. Louis Blues (Contemporary CCD14085)   1997

MYERS, TERRY
Soul Mates (Contemporary CCD14078)   1995

NELSON, OLIVER w. JOE NEWMAN
Main Stem (Prestige OJCCD1803)   1961

O'FARRILL, CHICO
Cuban Blues (Verve 314 533 256)   1950–54
Pure Emotion (Milestone MCD9239)   1995

OCHO
The Best Of. . . (Universal Sound USCD4)   1972–1976

ORTA, MICHAEL
Freedom Tower   1995

PALMIERI, CHARLIE
Hay Que Estar en Algo (Alegre 8580)   1966
A Giant Step (Tropical Budda TBLP003)   1984

PALMIERI, EDDIE
Azucar Pa'Ti (Tico 1122)   1965
Mozambique (Tico SLP1126)   1965
Justice/Justicia (Tico SLP1188)   1969
Super-Imposition (Tico 1194)   1970

Santido (Coco)	1973
Sun of Latin Music (Coco/MP Productions 3109)	1973
Unfinished Masterpiece (Coco CLP120) Original LP	1975
Lucumi, Macumba, Voodoo (Sony Tropical CDL81530)	1978
Salsa-Jazz-Descarga "Exploration" (MP Productions)	Compilation
Palmas (Nonesuch American Explorer 961649)	1993

PARKER, CHARLIE
Anthology (Accord 500122)	1946–1947
Broadcasts (Richelieu AX120)	
The Bird Returns (Savoy SV0155)	1948–1949
South of the Border (Verve 314 527 779)	1949–52

PASS, JOE & PAULINHO DA COSTA
Tudo Bem (Pablo 2310-824; CD reissue OJC 685)	1978

PASTORIUS, JACO
Live in Italy (Epic EK33949)	1976

PATTON, JOHN
Boogaloo (Blue Note 3187)	1968

PAUNETTO, BOBBY
Commit to Memory/Paunetto's Point (Tonga TNGCD8305/2)	1976&1973

PAZ, TRIO DA
Brasil from the Inside (Concord Picante 4524)	1992

PEPPER, ART
Tokyo Debut (Galaxy 4201)	1977

PEREZ PRADO, DAMASIANO
Kuba-Mambo (Tumbao TCD006)	1947–1949
Concierto Para Bongo (UA Latino 3489) LP	
The Mambo King Vol.1 (RCA Latino 3495RL)	1957

PERSON, HOUSTON
Island Episode (Prestige PRCD11007)	1973

PETERSON, OSCAR
Tristeza on Piano (Pausa 7124) LP	1982

PETERSON, OSCAR TRIO
Soul Español (Limelight LS86044) LP	1966

PISANO, JOHN
Among Friends (Pablo PACD2310 956)	1994

PONCE, DANIEL
Arawe (Island ISL1159)	1987

POWELL, BUD
The Amazing Vol.1 (Blue Note CDP81503)	1949–51

PUCHO AND THE LATIN SOUL BROTHERS
Tough! (Prestige 24138)   1966
Yaina (Cubop CBCD007)   1977

PUENTE, TITO
Mambos With. . . (Tumbao TCD011)   1948–51
Cuando Suenan Los Tambores (RCA Tropical 3226RL)   1949–51
Best of, The, Vol.1 (RCA Tropical 3369RL)   1950–60
Cuban Carnival (RCA Tropical 2349RL)   1955–56
Tambó (RCA Tropical 73470RL)   1950–60
Dance Mania (RCA Tropical 2467RL)   1950–60
Best of Vol.1 (RCA Tropical 3369RL)   1950–60
Top Percussion (RCA Latino 3264RL)   1957
Yambeque (RCA Tropical 4321RL)   1960
Now! (GNP Crescendo 2048)   1961
Para Los Rumberos   1972
On Broadway (Concord Picante CCD4207)   1983
El Rey (Concord CCD4250)   1984
Mambo Diablo (Concord CCD4283)   1985
Un Poco Loco (Concord Picante CCD4329)   1987
Out of this World (Concord Picante CCD4448)   1990
Mambo of the Times (Concord Picante CCD4499)   1991
Royal T (Concord CCD4553)   1993
Tito's Idea (Tropijazz CDZ81571)   1995

—— & WOODY HERMAN
Herman's Heat & Puente's Beat (Palladium PCD 5156)   1958

—— / GOLDEN LATIN JAZZ ALL STARS
In Session (Tropijazz CDZ81208)   1994

PULLEN, DON and the African Brazilian Connection
Kele Mou Bana (Blue Note 98166)   1991
Live. . . Again (Blue Note 30271)   1993

PURIM, FLORA
Butterfly Dreams (Milestone OJCCD619)   1973
Stories to Tell (Milestone OJCCD619)   1974
Encounter (Milestone OJCCD798)   1976
—— & AIRTO
Humble People (Concord Records GW3007)   1985

QUIJANO, Joe
Leyendas (Sony Tropical 81531)   1968

RAMIREZ, LOUIE Y Sus Amigos...
(Cotique 1096)   1978

REGALADO, RUDY y CHEVERE
La Gloria (Dos Coronas DDC9407)   1994

RETURN TO FOREVER
Return to Forever (ECM 78118-21022-2)   1973
No Mystery (Polydor PD6512)   1975

RICHARDS, EMIL
Luntana (Interworld)   1994
Afro-Cuban Jazz (Interworld 923)   1996

RITENOUR, LEE
First Course (Epic/Legacy 46114)   1976
Captain Fingers (Epic EK34426)   1977

RIVERA, MARIO
El Comandante (Groovin' High 1011)   1993

ROBERTS LUCKEY / WILLIE "THE LION" SMITH
Harlem Piano (Good time Jazz OJCCD10035)   1958

ROBERTS, TOM
Night Cap (Solo Art SACD121)

RODITI, CLAUDIO
Gemini Man (Milestone MCD9158)   1988
Slow Fire (Milestone MCD9175)   1989
Jazz Turns Samba (Groovin' High 1012)   1993
Manhattan Samba (Reservoir RSR139)   1995

RODRIGUEZ, TITO
Mambo Mona (Tumbao TCD014)   1949–51
Mambo Gee Gee (Palladium PCD021)   1950–51
Best of, Vol.2 (RCA Tropical 4321-15944)   1953–55

RODRIGUEZ, PETE
Latin Boogaloo (Tico SLP8520)   1966

ROGERS, SHORTY
Manteca/Afro-Cuban Influence (RCA Tropical 3449)   1958

ROLLINS, SONNY
Nucleus (Milestone M9064)   1975

ROMAO, DOM UM
Don Um Romao (Muse 5013)   1973
Hotmosphere (Original Jazz Classics OJCCD977)   1976

ROSEWOMAN, Michele
Harvest (Enja ENJ7069)   1992

RUBALACABA, GONZALO
Giraldilla (Messidor 15801)   1989
Discovery (Blue Note 95478))   1990

RUIZ, HILTON
Live at Birdland (Candid CCD79532) — 1992
Hands On Percussion (Tropijazz CDZ81483) — 1995

RUMBA CLUB
Desde La Capital (Palmetto PN2013) — 1993

SACASAS, ANSELMO
Sol Tropical (Tumbao TCD079) — 1945–49

SANABRIA, BOBBY & ASCENSIÓN
New York City Aché (Flying Fish FF70630) — 1993

SANCHEZ, PONCHO
Sonando (Concord Picante CCD4201) — 1983
Bien Sabroso (Concord Picante CCD4239) — 1984
El Conguero (Concord Picante CCD4286) — 1985
Papa Gato (Concord Picante CCD4310) — 1987
Fuerte! (Concord Picante CCD4369) — 1988
Familia (Concord Picante CCD4369) — 1989
Live At Kimballs East (Concord Picante CCD4472) — 1990
Cambios (Concord Picante CCD4439) — 1990
Soul Sauce (Concord Picante CCD4662) — 1995

SANDOVAL, ARTURO
No Problem (Jazz House JACD014) — 1988
Tumbaito (Messidor 15974) — 1986

SANTAMARIA, MONGO
Yambu (Fantasy 8012; reissue OJC 276) — 1958
Afro-Roots (Prestige PRCD24018) — 1958–59
Our Man in Havana (Fantasy FCD24729) — 1960
Sabroso (Fantasy OJCCD281) — 1960
Arriba! La Pachanga (LP) (Fantasy 3324)
At The Black Hawk (Fantasy FCD24734) — 1962
Skins (Milestone 47038) Orig albums Go Mongo! and Mongo Explodes — 1962–64
Introduces La Lupe (Milestone 9210) — 1963
At the Village Gate (OJCCD490) — 1963
Stone Soul (Columbia CS9780) Orig. LP — 1969
Red Hot (Columbia 35696) Orig. LP — 1979
El Bravo! (Columbia 9211) Orig. LP — 1966
Soy Yo (Concord CCD4327) — 1987
Soca Me Nice (Concord Picante CCD4362) — 1988
Olé Ola (Concord Picante CCD4387) — 1989
Live at Jazz Alley (Concord Picante CCD4422) — 1990
Brazilian Sunset (Candid CCD79703) — 1992

Mambo Mongo (Chesky JD100)	1993
Mongo Returns (Milestone MCD9245)	1995

SEAWIND
Light the Light (A&M)   1979

SEIS DEL SOLAR

Decision (Messidor 15821)	1992
Alternate Roots (Messidor 15831)	1995

SEPULVEDA, CHARLIE, and THE TURNAROUND
Watermelon Man (Tropijazz RMD82010)   1996

SHANK, BUD
See also ALMEIDA, LAURINDO/CHARLIE BYRD
Tomorrow's Rainbow (Contemporary 14048)   1988

—— **w. CHARLIE BYRD TRIO**
Brazilville (Concord Picante CCD4173)   1981

SHEARING, GEORGE

Jazz Masters 57 (Verve 314 529 900) CD	1951–53
Latin Escapade (Capitol SM11454) LP	1956
Latin Lace (Capitol ST1082) LP	
Latin Affair (Capitol ST1275) LP	1963
—— and the MONTGOMERY BROTHERS (Jazzland @DMC:OJCCD040)	1961

SHEPP, ARCHIE
Mariamar (Horo HZ01)   1975

SHORTER, WAYNE

Super Nova (Blue Note 84332)	1969
Native Dancer (Columbia PC33418) Original LP	1975
Phantom Navigator (Columbia CK40373)	1987

SILVER, HORACE

Song for My Father (Blue Note 84185)	1963–64
Pencil Packin' Papa (Columbia CK64210)	1994
——/J.J. JOHNSON Cape Verdean Blues (Blue Note 84220)	1965
—— & the Silver Brass Ensemble It's Got To Be Funky (Columbia CK53812)	1993

SIMS, ZOOT
Art 'n' Zoot (Pablo 2310-957)   1981

STEPS AHEAD
(Elektra Musician 60168) LP   1983

STITT, SONNY
Kaleidoscope (Prestige OJCCD060)   1952

STRUNZ & FARAH
Frontera (Milestone MCD9123)   1984

SUMMERS, BILL
Feel the Heat (Prestige P10102)   1977
Cayenne   1978

SYLVESTER, JORGE
MusicCollage (Postcards 1011)   1996

TAYLOR, BILLY
Cross Section (Original Jazz Classics OJCCD1830)   1953
With Four Flutes (Riverside OJCCD1830)   1959

TJADER, CAL
Mambo With. . . (Fantasy OJCCD271)   1954
Plays Mambo (Fantasy OJCCD 274)   1954
Los Ritmos Calientes (Fanasty 24712)   1955
Latin Kick (Fantasy OJCCD642)   1956
Black Orchid (Fantasy FCD24730)   1956–59
Latin Concert (Fantasy OJCCD643)   1958
Sentimental Moods (Fantasy FCD24762)   Late 1950s
Jazz Masters 39 (Verve 314 521 858)   1961–67
Soul Sauce (Verve 314 521 668)   1964
"Latin + Jazz" (DCC Jazz DJZ604)   1968
Descarga (Fantasy FCD24737)   1971–72
Amazonas (Fantasy OJCCD840)   1975
La Onda Va Bien (Concord Picante 4113)   1979
Los Ritmos Calientes (Fantasy FCD24712)
Gozame! Pero Ya. . . (Concord Picante 4133)   1980

—— / **CHARLIE PALMIERI / TITO PUENTE**
Primo (Fantasy OJCCD762)   1973

—— / **EDDIE PALMIERI**
El Sonido Nuevo (Verve 314 519 812)   1966

—— / **STAN GETZ**
Ginza Blues (Fantasy OJCCD275)   1963

TURRE, STEVE
 (Verve 314 537 133)   1997

TURRENTINE, STANLEY
Don't Mess With Mr T. (CBS ZK44174)   1973

—— / **MILT JACKSON**
Cherry (CBS ZK40936)   1972

TYNER, McCOY
Uptown/Downtown (Milestone 9167-2)   1988
Blue Bossa (CDC9033)   1991

VALDES, BEBO
Bebo Rides Again (Messidor 15834)   1994

VALDES, MIGUELITO
Mambo Dance Session (Caribe Classics) CD   1949

VALDÉZ, PATATO
Masterpiece (Messidor 15827)   1984

VAUGHAN, SARAH
I Love Brazil! (Pablo 2312-101)   1977
Copacabana (Pablo 2312-125)   1979

VAZQUEZ, PAPO
Breakout (Timeless SJP311)   1991–92

VEGA, JUNIOR / LATIN JAZZ TODAY
Images of Music (Junior Vega JV002)   1995

VELARDE, BENNY / FRANCISCO AGUABELLA Orchestras
Ay Que Rico! (Fantasy FCD24731)   1962

WALRATH, JACK / MASTERS OF SUSPENSE
HipGnosis (TCB Records)   1995

WEATHER REPORT
Heavy Weather (Columbia CK-47481)   1977
Mr. Gone (Columbia CK-46869)   1978

WESTON, RANDY
Tanjah (Verve 214 527 778)   1973

WILLIAMS, SPENCER / King Oliver
The Immortal King Oliver (Milestone MLP2006)   1928

WINTER, PAUL w. Carlos Lyra
The Sound of Ipanema (Columbia CL2722) Orig. LP   1962
———Sextet
Jazz Meets the Bossa Nova (Columbia CL1925) Orig. LP   1962

Select Bibliography

"Caught in the Act: Cal Tjader," by John Tynan, *DownBeat*, June 27, 1956, quoted in *West Coast Jazz* p.104).

"Yancey Special: Variationen Über einen Bass," by Karl Gert zur Heide, *Hot Jazz*, June 1969.

Austerlitz, Paul. Merengue: *Dominican Music and Dominican Identity*. Philadelphia: Temple University Press, 1996.

Badger, Reid. *A Life in Ragtime: A Biography of James Reese Europe*. New York: Oxford University Press, 1995.

Berendt, Joachim E. *The Jazz Book*, 4th ed. Chicago, Lawrence Hill Books.

Berliner, Paul F. *Thinking in Jazz: The Infinite Art of Improvisation*. Chicago: University of Chicago Press, 1994

Blesh, Rudi. *Combo USA*. New York: DaCapo Press, 1979.

Blesh, Rudi, and Harriet Janis. *They All Played Ragtime*, 4th ed. New York: Oak Publications.

Calloway, Cab, and Bryant Rollins. *Of Minnie the Moocher & Me*. New York: Crowell, 1976.

Carner, Gary. *The Miles Davis Companion*. New York: Schirmer Books, 1996.

Cheatham, Adolphus "Doc." *I Guess I'll Get the Papers and Go Home*. London: Cassell, 1996.

Collier, Simon, Artemis Cooper, Maria S. Azzi, and Richard Martin. *Tango!* New York: Thames & Hudson, 1997.

Daniel, Yvonne. *Rumba: Dance and Social Change in Contemporary Cuba*. Bloomington, IN: Indiana University Press, 1995.

Deffaa, Chip. *Voices of the Jazz Age*. Carbondale, IL: University of Illinois Press, 1992.

Descarga Newsletter, passim.

Díaz Ayala, Cristóbal. *Musica Cubana del Areyto a la Nueva Trova* (Ed. Cubanacan).

Díaz Ayala, Cristóbal. *Discograpfía de la Musica Cubana Vol.1* (Fundación Musicalia).

Ellington, Edward "Duke." *Music is My Mistress*. New York: Da Capo Press, 1988.

Feather, Leonard. *Encyclopedia of Jazz*. New York: Da Capo Press, 1988.

———. *Encyclopedia of Jazz in the 60s*. New York: Da Capo Press, 1988.

———. *Encyclopedia of Jazz Yearbooks*. New York: Da Capo Press, 1993.

———, and Ira Gitler. *Encyclopedia of Jazz in the 70s*. New York: Da Capo Press, 1988.

Gandy, Joan W. and Thomas H. *The Mississippi Steamboat Era, 1870-1920*. New York: Dover Books, 1989.

Gillespie, Dizzy, and Al Fraser. *To Be Or Not To Bop*. New York: Da Capo Press, 1985.

Gioia, Ted. *West Coast Jazz: Modern Jazz in California 1945-1960*. New York: Oxford University Press, 1992.

Gitler, Ira. *Swing to Bo: An Oral History of the Transition in Jazz in the 1940s*. New York: Oxford University Press, 1987.

Glasser, Ruth. *My Music Is My Flag: Puerto Rican Musicians and Their New York Communities, 1917-1940*. Berkeley, CA: University California Press, 1997.

Handy, W.C. *Father of the Blues*. New York: Da Capo Press, 1991.

Haskins, James. Scott Joplin: *The Man Who Made Ragtime* (Stein & Day), 1980.

Hasse, John Edward. *Beyond Category: The Life and Genius of Duke Ellington*. New York: Da Capo Press, 1995.

Hazzard-Gordon, Katrina. *Jookin': The Rise of Social Dance Formations in African-American Culture*. Philadelphia: Temple University Press, 1992.

Herman, Woody, and Stuart Troup. *The Woodchopper's Ball*. New York: Limelight, 1994.

Carr, Ian, Digby Fairweather, and Brian Priestley. *Jazz: The Rough Guide*. London: Rough Guides/Penguin, 1995.

Jasen, David A., and Trebor Jay Tichenor. *Rags and Ragtime*. Mineola, NY: Dover Books, 1989.

Gerard, Charley, with Marty Sheller. *Salsa Rhythm of Latin Music*. Tempe, AZ: White Cliffs Media Co., 1988.

Jewell, Derek. Duke: *A Portrait of Duke Ellington*. New York: W. W. Norton, 1980.

Klinkowitz, Jerome. *Listen: Gerry Mulligan*. New York: Schirmer Books, 1991.

Korall, Burt. *Drummin' Man: The Swing Years*. New York: Schirmer Books, 1992.

Linares, María Teresa. *La Música Popular* (Havana, Instituto del Libro)

Lis, Eduardo, "Creating a New Tradition: The Brazilian Jazz Experience in North America." York University, Ontario, Canada, unpublished Master's thesis.

Lomax, Alan. *Mr. Jelly Roll*. Berkeley: University of California Press, 1993.

Maggin, Donald L. *Stan Getz: A Life in Jazz*. New York: Morrow, 1996.

Malone, Jacqui. *Steppin' On the Blues: The Visible Rhythms of African-American Dance*. Carbondale, IL: University of Illinois Press, 1996.

Marquis, Donald. *In Search of Buddy Bolden*. New York: Da Capo Press, 1993.

Mattfeld, Julius. *Variety Music Cavalcade, 1620-1969: A Chronology of Vocal and Instrumental Music Popular in the U.S.* Englewood-Cliffs, NJ: Prentice-Hall, 1973.

Mauleón, Rebeca. *Salsa Guidebook for Piano and Ensemble*. Petaluma, CA: Sher Music Co, 1993.

McGowan, Chris, and Ricardo Pessinha. *The Brazilian Sound: Samba, Bossa Nova, and the Popular Music of Brazil*, 2nd ed. Philadelphia: Temple University Press, 1998.

Monson, Ingrid. *Saying Something: Jazz Improvisation and Interaction*. Chicago: University of Chicago Press, 1996.

Nisenson, Eric. *Around About Midnight: A Portrait of Miles Davis*. Rev. ed. New York: Da Capo Press, 1996.

Oliver, Paul. *Songsters and Saints*. New York: Cambridge University Press, 1984.

Owens, Thomas. *Bebop: The Music and Its Players.* New York: Oxford University Press, 1996.

Patiño, Manny, and Jorge Moreno. *Afro-Cuban Keyboard Grooves* Book/CD set. E. Rutherford, NJ: Warner Bros Publications, 1997.

Patiño, Manny, and Jorge Moreno. *Afro-Cuban Bass Grooves* Book/CD set. E. Rutherford, NJ: Warner Bros Publications, 1997.

Perrone, Charles. *Masters of Contemporary Brazilian Song: MPB, 1965-1985.* Austin, TX: University Texas Press, 1989.

Priestley, Brian. *Mingus: A Critical Biography.* New York: Da Capo Press, 1988.

Reisner, Robert. *Bird: The legend of Charlie Parker.* New York: Da Capo Press, 1988.

Riis, Thomas L. *Just Before Jazz: Black Musical Theater in New York, 1890 to 1915.* Washington, DC: Smithsonian Institution Press, 1989.

Roldon, Cesar Miguel. *Salsa* (Caracas, Oscar Todtmann Editores).

Rose, Al, and Edmond Souchon. *New Orleans Jazz: A Family Album.* Baton Rouge, LA: Louisiana State University Press, 1967.

Rosenthal, David H. *Hard Bop: Jazz & Black Music 1955-1965.* New York: Oxford University Press, 1992.

Russell, Ross. *Bird Lives!* New York: Da Capo Press, 1996.

Castro, Ruy. *Chega de Saudade, A História e as Histórias de Bossa Nova.* (Sao Paulo, Companhia das Letras).

Salas, Horacio. *El Tango.* (Buenos Aires, Planeta).

Salinas Rodriguez, José Luis. *Jazz, Flamenco, Tango: Las orillas de un ancho río.* (Editorial Catriel).

Schuller, Gunther. *Early Jazz.* New York: Oxford University Press, 1986.

Schafer, William J., and Johannes Riedel. *The Art of Ragtime: Form and Meaning of an Original Black American Art.* Baton Rouge, LA: Louisiana State University Press, 1973.

Schafer, William J. *Brass Bands & New Orleans Jazz.* Baton Rouge, LA: Louisiana State University Press, 1977.

Sher, Chuck, ed. *The Latin Real Book.* Petaluma, CA: Sher Music Co., 1997.

Silvester, Peter J. *A Left Hand Like God: A History of Boogie-Woogie Piano.* New York: Da Capo Press, 1989.

Singler, Barry. *Black and Blue: The Life and Lyrics of Andy Razaf.* New York: Schirmer Books, 1993.

Southern, Eileen. *Biographical Dictionary of Afro-American and African Musicians.* Westport, CT: Greenwood Press, 1982.

————. *The Music of Black Americans.* 3rd ed. New York: Norton, 1997.

Spellman, A.B. *Four Lives in the Bebop Business.* New York: Da Capo Press, 1985.

Spottswood, Richard. *Ethnic Music on Records: A Discography of Ethnic Records Produced in the United States, 1893-1942.* Carbondale, Ill: University of Illinois Press, 1990.

Stearns, Marshall W. *The Story of Jazz.* New York: Oxford University Press, 1956.

Stewart, Jack. "The Mexican Band Legend." *Jazz Archivist* Vol. VI, 2 (December 1991) and Vol. IX, 1.

Thomas, J.C. *Chasin' the Trane: The Music and Mystique of John Coltrane*. New York: Da Capo Press, 1988.

Tucker, Mark. *Ellington: The Early Years*. New York: Oxford University Press, 1991.

———, ed. *Duke Ellington Reader*. New York: Oxford University Press, 1993.

Views on Black American Music: Proceedings of the 14th, 15th & 16th Annual Black Musicians' Conferences. University of Massachusetts, Amherst

Waller, Maurice, and Anthony Calabrese. *Fats Waller*. New York: Schirmer Books, 1977.

Williams, Martin. *Jazz Masters of New Orleans*. New York: Macmillan, 1979.

Woll, Allen. *Black Musical Theatre: From Coon Town to Dream Girls*. New York: Da Capo, 1991.

Wynn, Ron, ed. *All Music Guide to Jazz*. San Francisco, CA: Miller Freeman Books, 1994.

Index

SAINT CATHERINE OF SIENA

Mons. LODOVICO FERRETTI o. p.

SAINT CATHERINE
OF SIENA

EDIZIONI CANTAGALLI

Traduzione dall'italiano di Sonia di Centa

Imprimatur:
† GAETANO BONICELLI
Arcivescovo Metropolita
Siena, 8 luglio 1996

INDICE

SAINT CATHERINE

On the Feast of the Annunciation, which in that year, 1347, coincided with Palm Sunday, twin girls were born to Giacomo Benincasa, a dyer of the Fontebranda section of the Goose district in Siena, and his wife Lappa di Nuccio Piangenti. These two little girls, Giovanna and Catherine, joined an already rather large family of 22 other brothers and sisters: Giovanna died, however, immediately after her baptism, while Catherine survived in order to love and suffer for the next thirty-three years.

The Benincasa family, well-known for its Christian faith and piety, was bound by a deep and reverent affection to the Dominican Fathers of Camporeggio, and their imposing church which still dominates the hill overlooking Fontebranda and affords an excellent view of the entire city, was assidously frequented by all its members. Catherine's family, unusually large even by the standards of the late middle ages including in-laws and cousins, was permeated naturally, by the teachings of Christianity thanks above all to Giacomo, a gentle, patient soul, and Lapa, a much more nervous even querellous type of person. They were honest hard-working parents though and they provided for their children not only the material necessities of life, but also an atmosphere of stability and peace. When Catherine was only a year old the Black Death had already begun its gruesome work of eliminating one third of Europe's population; among those so cruelly eliminated were the parents of a ten-year old boy named Tommaso della Fonte who, shortly afterwards was adopted by the Benincasa family thanks to the efforts of one of Catherine's elder sisters, Niccoluccia, whose husband, Palmiere della Fonte, was the boy's uncle. Little Thomas had already felt a strong attraction towards the Dominican Order and he enjoyed learning about its brief, but fascinating history and talking about it to everyone in his new family. As Catherine was growing up, she was especially impressed by Tommaso's stories, even to the point of piously kissing the foot- prints of any Dominican priest who happened to pass in front of her house.

Catherine was evidently a very devout little girl and when she was about six years of age the most decisive event of her whole life occurred. One day, as she was walking with one of her brothers, Stefano - perhaps they were returning home on having completed an errand for their mother - Catherine stopped and looked up at the majestic church of Saint Dominic dominating the hill of Camporeggio and at that very instant had a vision of Jesus Christ seated on a splendid throne dressed and crowned as a pope, and flanked by the Apostles, Peter, Paul and John. Catherine remained immovable for what seemed to be a very long time and felt an inexpressible joy when Jesus smiled and, raising his right hand, blessed her. Stefano, who had continued walking all this time, noticed Catherine's absence, waited a few seconds for her to emerge from her trance and then yelled to her impatiently. At that moment her attention snapped and she lowered her eyes in order to see where her brother was, but when she looked up at the church again, the vision had vanished. Catherine immediatly felt a sharp pang of sorrow and burst into childish tears. Shortly after this episode, her adopted brother Tommaso decided to become a Dominican and entered the novitiate in the Priory of San Domenico and inspired by his example and by the stories she had heard from his lips about the holy martyrs, the virgins and the fathers of the desert, Catherine also decided that she wanted to go to the desert in order to love and serve God. Why should she not, she reasoned accept the evangelical inviation to abandon everything - father, mother, brothers, sisters, home - and go to live in a cave, the better to be alone with God and talk to Him? Even though she had never before dared to wander beyond the city walls, Catherine resolved to carry out her intention. One morning, having supplied herself with a piece of bread she quietly slipped out of the house and walked towards the gate of San Sano on the outskirts of Siena. Thinking to find a cave within short distance, she boldly continued walking for a good while until she finally saw some of them dotting the hills of the surrounding countryside; she chose one, entered it, knelt down and began praying with all the ardour of her infant spirit. Catherine spent almost the entire day in this precocious exctasy until the bells of San Do-

menico announced the approach of evening. She returned to her senses and, with a childlike intuition
of God's will, retraced her steps back to the gate
of San Sano and arrived safely home without arou-
sing the suspicion of the others who presumed that
she had simply paid an unusually long visit to one
of her elder married sisters. Catherine understood -
or thought she did - what God wanted of her: to
leave the world behind, live in solitude and listen
to him speaking to her in the depths of her heart.
From that moment on, Catherine began to feel a
hunger and a thirst for the things of Heaven and,
gradually, to weigh the value of earthly joys, human
affections and her own life in relation to the Eternal
Goodness that had been revealed to her. She reali-
sed that only God was the Highest Good and that
everything else was utterly empty and insignificant
compared to Him; and this elementary truth became
so clear and fixed in her mind that, raising herself
above all wordly concerns she understood that only
God could fill her heart and make her happy. Catherine thus felt transformed and sharply separated
in her thoughts, desires and aspirations from everyone else in her own family who were so intent
on pursuing the things of this life and hoping to
find happiness in them. She knew that only God in
His infinite Goodness was worthy of all her love
and felt acute anguish in the fact that her little heart
was incapable of containing Him. Catherine's prayers
had nothing in common with those which other
small children habitually recited; they really welled

up from her mind and heart and even her body seemed to participate in the fervour of her soul.

Notwithstanding her tender age, Catherine knew that she prayed best when she was alone. During these moments of solitude she perceived more clearly the voice of God speaking to her and she even tried to find little hideouts all around the house where she could prolongue her devotions. She would conceal herself for hours in these beloved retreats conversing with the Lord who flooded her soul with light, grace and joy.

All these spiritual activities did not distract her, though, from normal family life. Catherine was cheerful and courteous with her brothers and sisters, and she always showed particular respect and affection towards her parents and, even though she had formed a rather peculiar habit of reciting the Hail Mary on her knees for every step of the stairs, she would immediately bounce to her feet and fly up and down those same stairs in obedience to the slightest request from her siblings or parents.

There was only one thing she could not habituate herself to: the hearty nourishing meals enjoyed so much by the others. The amount of food their mother prepared seemed excessive to Catherine; she preferred to subsist on bread and a few herbs, and she never drank wine. Whenever she was given meat, she slipped it onto Stefano's plate and, in this way, Catherine trained herself to eat what was only strictly necessary in order to obtain complete self-mastery and grew in her desire to live in union with God.

MOTHER LAPA

Catherine's mother was a restless, keen-witted, no-nonsense woman who did not see much to admire in the way of life her small daughter was creating for herself. Lapa felt an especial affection for Catherine, the only one of her numerous brood she had been able to breast feed because of her continual pregnancies, and she had the satisfaction of seeing her become a robust, attractive child; but she also looked with a wary eye on all those long prayers, retreats, abstinences, vigils, and certain other mortifications that Catherine was not able to keep secret and which began to visibly weaken her. And she became quite alarmed when she discovered that her favourite daughter had made a habit of leaving her bed almost every night in order to sleep on the rough tiles of the floor. Lapa shrewdly concluded that Catherine needed a husband and that the duties of married life would be the most efficient means of distracting her from all those incomprehensible austerities. In the late middle ages, Siennese city life was (as it still is today) marked by many popular civil festivities which were considered as an excellent occasions by mothers or elder sisters for presenting their young, pretty, well dressed marriageable girls to public gaze. Lapa found a prompt and able ally in her married daughter Bonaventura, of whom Catherine was very fond, and who finally convinced her younger sister to pay more attention to her appearance and to make herself more attractive like most girls of the time (as now) were wont to do. Catherine at first resisted their suggestions but finally, to avoid further arguments, gave in to their importunities; she had already completed her fifteenth year of age, was rather pretty and radiated a certain graciousness and innocence which could easily have won her a husband. She had already made, however, some years previously, a vow of absolute virginity to God and she showed herself in public just a few times only in order to pacify her mother and sister while maintaining always her firm intention not to be contaminated by worldly vanities. In that same year, 1362, Bonaventura died during childbirth and Catherine, seized by sharp pains of remorse for having followed her advice about making herself more physically attractive, renounced forever all such earthly concerns and pleasures, and resolved to return to her former penitent way of life. Catherine had agreed to make her debut in Siena social life only to please her sister and, even though her confessor, the learned Raymond di Capua, assured her later on that Bonaventura's death was not her fault, she never forgot the unhappy episode nor forgave herself for what she considered to be a grave sin on her part. Catherine's conscience may have been a bit too delicate and even laughable compared to our hard bitten twentieth-century ones, but it was undoubtedly more admirable. Tommaso della Fonte, meanwhile had already been ordained a priest in the Dominican Order and, thanks to his precocious reputation for sanctity, Catherine had chosen him to be her spiritual director. Giacomo and Lapa were quite pleased with this development, thinking that Tommaso was just the man to prevail upon their daugher to abandon her abnormal religious practices; and he accepted the challenge. Catherine disclosed to him the secrets of her soul, above all the absolute resolution that Jesus would be the only love of her life. She had already given her entire heart to Him and had no more love to spare for a merely human husband. Catherine spoke with such fervour and certitutde that Tommaso not only ceased to doubt her, but told her that if her decision was really so radical and irrevocable, to take a pair of scissors and without wasting any more time cut off totally, or almost, her lovely long- flowing hair. So she did it; and, in order to hide her rather clumsy barbering efforts, began going around with a white veil on her head. When Lapa discovered her daughter's new unsual hairdo, she was for a moment - but only for one moment assuredly - speechless with shock before reacting with shrieks of rage and pain against Catherine in front of the entire family; only Giacomo managed to keep a cool head and not to rashly condemn his insubordinate daughter. An unassuming, easy-going man in all situations, Giacomo was unable to restrain his wife from punishing Catherine physically, even acquiescing in her decision to deprive Catherine of her own little bedroom and forcing her to share one with her brother Stefano. Thanks to this rough experience Catherine learned one of the great truths of the Christian life: even when it is not possible to live in external solitude, one can always retire into oneself, or more precisely, into the interior cell of the heart. And one can live in this latter solitude at all times and in all places, even in the thick of routine duties and the press of human transactions, listening to God's voice and working with Him for the salvation of souls. Catherine persevered in her prayers while sharing Stefano's bedroom without complaining about the harsh treatment she was receiving and, one day, the Lord decided to confirm her progress in sanctity in a special way. One morning, as Catherine was alone in the room praying on her knees, Giacomo was passing by, and, stopping for a moment, he peered at her through a crack in the wooden door and saw a snow-white dove nestled upon her head. He immediately called for Lapa, but by the time she arrived the dove had disappeared. From that day on, Catherine's parents began to understand that she was destined for higher things than the world could offer and that God was guiding her according to His own designs. It was useless to fight against Him.

MANTELLATE

Catherine thus, got her old room back, bare and unattractive as it was, but dear to her, and continued her prayers and penitences. Lapa, however had not completely surrendered and she still tried to think of other ways to distract her daughter from her spiritual fixations. She conceived the idea of taking Catherine to some hot springs at Vignone, a small town in the Tuscan countryside of Val d'Orcia, which were famous for their health-restoring waters. Catherine, upon obtaining permission to bathe alone, turned the cure into a torture by positioning herself right under the spray of boiling hot water and, with astonishing resistance, survived the treatment by thinking of the pains of Purgatory. The desire to suffer had become second nature to her and she dreamt of offering her whole life as a holocaust of love to God. Upon returning home Catherine heard about the existence of the Third Order of Penance which the great Founder of the Dominican Order, Saint Dominic, had created with the noble intention of giving lay people the opportunity of collaborating in the work of spreading the faith, defending the rights of the Church and sanctifying themselves in the process. A small group of these devoted men and women already existed in Siena and, among them was a good number of widows who, under the direction

of one of the Dominican Fathers led an almost totally cloistered life, each one in her own home. The
people of Siena called them the Mantellate because
they all wore a black "mantello" or cape over a
simple white tunic fastened tightly to their bodies
by a black leather belt and their religious garb was
topped with a white veil upon their heads. These
pious ladies were not nuns in the modern sense of
the word, nor were they juridically tied to the Dominican Order by the vows of poverty, chastity and
obedience or by any particular monastic rule. They
assiduously frequented the Church of San Dominico
for their religious practices usually in the so-called
Chapel of the Vaults, famous today thanks to Saint
Catherine. There was, however, only one obstacle in
the way of Catherine's desire to join this congrega-
tion; she was too young, still only a teen-ager. And,
though Catherine begged her mother to intercede on
her behalf with the Prioress, Lapa was quite happy
to discover that such an impediment existed and
absolutly delighted when the Prioress explicitly declared that her daughter was too young and pretty
to join their group.Divine providence, however had
- as usual - an ace up Its sleeve, and facilitated
Catherine's entry into the Mantellate by allowing her
to come down with smallpox. Her whole body was
ravaged with blisters and consumed with a burning
fever and she warned an anxious Lapa that she
would not recover unless she could join the Mantellate. The Prioress agreed to visit Catherine at her
home with some of the other sisters and they were
so favourably impressed by Catherine's angelic words

and demeanour that even though her girlish beauty returned after the bout with disease, her virtues were judged to be solid enough for admittance to the Mantellate. So Catherine entered the Third Order of Saint Dominic and became during her brief life its greatest member and honour, personifying and extending its activities for the good of souls, the support of the weak, the comfort of the helpless and the defense of the Church. And those same sisters who once hesitated to welcome her into their group soon learned to love and revere her as Mother and Guide. But for the moment, nobody could or would have predicted that God had planned such an illustrious career for this humble, illiterate girl. Catherine herself was content to know her place in this new family and, in the meantime, her only preoccupation was to nourish the love for God she felt in her heart. For the next three years she lived in rigorous retirement and almost continuous silence, stepping outside her house only when it was necessary to go up to San Domenico and participate at Mass and the Divine Office, which she listened attentively to the other Mantellate recite since she didn't know how to read, and to receive spiritual direction from her confessor, Tommaso della Fonte. While at home, she lived in her austere little room taking just enough food and drink to survive, conversing familiarly with her Lord, the blessed Virgin and the Angels and Saints and, gradually, winning the respect and admiration of everyone. Only God, of course, knew what was happening in Catherine's soul during the long nights she passed in solitude watching and praying until the bells of San Domenico summoned the friars to their pre-dawn devotions. And as the silence of the night was being so rudely interrupted by the tolling of those bells, Catherine used to say: "Behold, O Lord, your servants, my brothers, have been sleeping until now and I have remained awake in your Presence. Shortly, they shall praise your name: protect them and increase your grace in them and grant me now a little sleep." Then, she dropped off at once but never, literally, for more than a couple of hours. She would wake up to greet the dawn of a new day with the praises of God on her lips.

BRIDE OF CHRIST

The good Lord especially loves those souls who prefer to consecrate their hearts and their lives to Him in love rather than to earthly pleasures and He uses such people, purified and sanctified by His grace, as precious instruments to extend the benefits of salvation to all mankind. These people in general and, holy women in particular, become intimate associates in the work of redemption and the Redeemer Himself calls them His brides. Their lamps are always shining brightly thanks to the oil of faith, hope and charity and the gospel of Matthew shows their readiness to respond to the invitation of their spouse. Among all the elected souls in the history of Christianity, Catherine certainly earned the right to be called the Bride of Christ more, perhaps, than any other woman. Her first and most famous biographer, Raymond of Capua, enjoyed recounting the different ways in which Christ visibly confirmed Catherine's supernatural mission: the wedding ring, the crown of thorns, the exchange of hearts and the wounds in her hands, feet and side. In 1367, on the last Thursday before Lent, while all Siena was in the midst of its usual merry-making, Catherine was alone at home praying more intensely than ever. The world no longer existed for her, she felt completely separated from other people and had no desire to see or share their trivial and even sinful pursuits. She felt so close to God and her heart was so brim-full with His love that other things had simply ceased to count. Catherine was already entering the highest stages of contemplation in which she heard the Lord speaking to her the words He had spoken to the ancient Israelites through the prophet Hosea "I will betroth you in faithfulness". Upon hearing these words Catherine experienced in the depths of her soul the first sublime episode of her mystical life. She saw the Lord Jesus Himself, holding in His hand a brilliant golden ring, accompanied by the blessed Virign Mary, Saint John the Evangelist, Saint Paul, Saint Dominic and David who was sweetly playing a harp. Our Lady then took Catherine's hand and placed it in that of her Divine Son as He slipped the wedding ring on Catherine's finger, exhorting her with heavenly words to work courageously for the glory of God, armed with the faith. When the vision vanished, Catherine knew that she had reached the end of her retired life. She was twenty years old and after having tasted the joys of the purely contemplative life, felt irresistably called to the active apostolic life, not knowing exactly, however, where or how to begin. But she trusted fully in God to guide her and, in order to make Catherine undestand that she must go out into the world, He no longer manifested Himself to Her in her tiny room, but outside the door commanding her to come out. Even the habit she wore proclaimed her to be the daugher of an Order called to action and apostolic work for the salvation of souls and the honour of being the bride of Christ stimulated her to work for the glory of her Spouse and inflame the entire world with His love.

ANGEL OF CHARITY

Catherine's first field of action was, obviously her own home. God had given her the power to speak in His name and she used it well when she convinced two nieces, the daughter of her sister-in-law Lisa, who was also a member of the Mantellate in San Dominic, to embrace the religious life; the two little girls listened to the voice of the Lord, and thanks to Catherine became cloistered nuns at the Convent in Montepulciano, forty-four miles southeast of Siena by rail, already famous because of the Holy Dominican Virgin, Saint Agnes of the same town, who had lived there fifty years before Catherine's birth. All the members of her family, Lapa a bit less than the others, now listened to Catherine's words with respect, even awe; particularly when those words, normally so sweet and humble, became fiery and imperious in asserting the honour of God and threatening woe to anyone who tried to oppose them. Even the good Friars of San Domenico venerated by Catherine as though angels from heaven, sometimes hesitated to openly contradict the dyer's daughter. Quite often they stumbled upon her as she was praying in ecstasy in their church and observed her closely; her face was pale, her eyes full of tears, a celestial radiance seemed to emanate from her whole person. And everyone, priests, religious and lay people testified that Catherine with her words and deeds always encouraged them to lead holier lives. Catherine showered all her love on her vast spiritual family, especially the poor, who were her dearest friends; real, visible personifications in flesh and blood of Jesus who said "Whatever you did for the least of my brothers, you did for me". And once, Christ Himself really appeared to her as a poor man begging to be fed and clothed. After having received permission from her parents to succour the needy with some of their household goods, Catherine's generosity knew no limits. She would often go to the local hospital, just across the street facing the Cathedral, appearing like an angel of mercy to the sick, the hungry, and tired pilgrims. And none of the other members of the Mantellate of San Domenico who served as nurses in the hospital could hold a candle to Catherine when it came to consoling the patients in their material and spiritual necessities. "Nobody has ever spoken to us like this woman" they used to declare; and just seeing her and listening to her brought them much inner tranquillity. Catherine even volunteered to take care of lepers and showed no fear of contracting their highly contagious, piteous disease. The city fathers had established a special house for them well outside the walls called Saint Lazzarus, a good half hour walk from Fontebranda and Catherine went to visit them almost every day. And if she met any who refused her charitable ministrations she doubled her visits and efforts to overcome their loneliness and bitterness of heart and, often, with her prayers obtain a complete cure in body and mind for them. Even the gaols opened their doors to Catherine. She entered and exited them quite freely bringing the soothing power of her words to alleviate the miserable existence of the inmates, many of whom were perfectly innocent of any serious wrongdoing and were in prison only because they had happened to be on the losing side in the frequent and unedifying political struggles of the day. Catherine's brief presence filled their unhappy lives with light and many of them followed her exhortations to bear their misfortunes with patience and hope and many, perhaps for the first time in their lives acquired some real peace of soul as they more or less cooperated with God's grace. Catherine's words were particularly efficacious when it came to advising patients suffering from terminal disease to look realistically at their situation and prepare for the solemn moment of death and, as usual, her admonitions penetrated not only the ears but also the hearts of even the most unpromising candidates, particularly the notorious criminal Andrea dei Bellanti whom she accompanied to the gallows after he had repented and confessed his sins.

CATHERINE'S FATHER

Rising loftily above the steep narrow road on Via del Costone which leads from the opposite side of Siena into the Fontebranda district, the impressive church of Saint Dominic towers high above the valley like some austere impregnable fortress crowning the hill of Camporegio. This name, which means "the regal field" or "the King's camp" was probably given to the hill when Henry, King of the Romans used it as his base of operations during the seige he led against Siena in 1186. The construction of Saint Dominic's was begun in 1225 and completed in 1262 but it consisted only of the nave or vertical part; the transept, or horizontal part, was begun a few years later, and in order to support its weight an elegant crypt was first built underneath consisting of robust columns, magnificent vaults and a low ceiling, all characterised by a noble simplicity. This crypt was at first called the Church of the Deceased, because many members of noble families and of the Third Order, along with other friends and benefactors of the Dominican Fathers, often asked to be buried within its hallowed walls; and the good Fathers, just as often granted their permission for the fulfillment of these pious requests and prayed daily for the eternal rest of all those hopeful souls. On August 22, 1368 Catherine's father died and the

Dominicans most willingly accorded him an honourable resting place in their crypt; and, shortly afterwards they reserved a special burial vault for the entire Benincasa family. Many relatives and acquaintances joined in the funeral procession from Fontebranda to Camporegio, trying to console poor Lapa who was totally distraught with grief. Only Catherine managed to maintain internally and externally a certain composure and tranquillity. She alone had prepared her father's corpse for the coffin and arranged all the necessary details for the funeral ceremony and without wasting a single tear, even helped the graveyard diggers as they lowered Giacomo into the ground. To those who were surprised and reproachful towards Catherine for her apparent coldness and lack of filial piety, she replied: "May it please the Lord to send all of us a similar death!" She had assisted her father during his last illness, had reminded him that the solemn moment of death was nearing closer, had prayed for his eternal salvation as he humbly resigned himself to the divine will and had watched him die in peace. Catherine never doubted for a moment that he had gone straight to heaven and tried to communicate to the members of her family this comforting conviction. Catherine interceded for her father's salvation with sighs, prayers and tears and obtained it on one condition; her heavenly Spouse made her bear the pains that would have been inflicted on Giacomo in Purgatory in expiation for his sins. The good Lord granted Catherine's desires because her one and only preoccupation during her life, as becomes a true Dominican, was the salvation of souls and the supernatural consolation she experienced in knowing that her father was enjoying the happiness of heaven allowed her to take such an apparently unemotional view of his death. Even the above-mentioned pains that she lovingly endured for the rest of her life were sweet to Catherine and useful for the purification of her own soul. All the members of the Benincasa Family eventually came to rest in that special burial vault in the crypt of Saint Dominic and, of course, an honoured place was reserved for Lapa next to her beloved husband. In 1619 the remains of the entire family were transferred to the upper church under the marble altar of the little chapel which contains that priceless treasure of Siena, the Sacred Head of Saint Catherine.

THE TWO CROWNS

There were, are, and always will be people who find everything laughable, who scorn what they cannot comprehend, who attempt to measure all things accrding to their own limited viewpoints and during her short life Catherine was one of the favourite targets of the scoffers. They considered her way of life to be suitable only for a madwoman and her mystical visions and experiences as the fruit of an overheated imagination; and the fame that already surrounded her name everywhere was looked upon simply as the effect of a subtle cleverness or a studied vainglory. The marvelous wonders that Divine Love produced in Catherine's soul, making her feel as if it had been shot forth from her body into eternity, were misunderstood and judged maliciously; and her followers who witnessed these extraordinary events were taken for dreamers or dupes. Other people, who were more generously inclined, concluded that Catherine's tenor of life was smply exaggerated, not very helpful for growth in the virtues, especially prudence and the duty of keeping oneself in reasonably good health, temperance; and they openly abhorred that continuous privation of food and sleep, which was causing Catherine such evident pain and taking heavy toll on the robust constitution nature had endowed her with. As her fame spread from her Fontebranda neighbourhood over all Siena, Catherine must have heard about the uncharitable things her detractors were saying about her. She, however, took a typically charitable attitude towards her enemies, calling them friends and benefactors. My defects are so numerous, she used to say, they haven't even begun to list them all. Not that the doubts and unjustified suspicions which many people entertained did not cause Catherine great inward pain, particularly when they existed in the minds of priests and religious consecrated to God. But rather than judge them harshly, Catherine took advantage of their murmurings to ruthlessly examine her own character just in case there was a grain of truth in what her critics said. She thus felt even more inspired to humble herself and grow in perfection. After every self- examination she experienced great peace of soul and she resolved to persevere in doing all the good that God called her to do. And, one day, her celestial Spouse gave her a visible sign of His infinite predilection for her. He appeared to Catherine holding in His sacred hands two crowns: one was made of pure gold studded with precious brilliant jewels, the other was made of hard piercing thorns. Jesus spoke saying: "Take the one you prefer". And Catherine, without hesitating for an instant, chose the crown of thorns. The choice simply confirmed what she already understood; that she must bravely bear acute sufferings during this life, especially when they consisted of the above- mentioned cruel accusations, murmurings, suspicions and condemnations which were constantly launched against her way of life. And when Catherine discovered that all these things had reached the ears of the Master-General of the Domincian Order, Father Elia da Tolouse, she sent him the following note: "This is my glory, that others may speak evilly of me for the rest of my life. This is what I desire. I do not feel sorry for myself, but for them." By lovingly and patiently wearing the crown of thorns, Catherine won the right to wear the crown of gold and jewels for all eternity.

MOTHER AND GUIDE - THE LETTERS

During this time Catherine's soul was undergoing a continual process of transformation that rendered it holier and lifted it above all the worries and commotions of earthly life. Whoever attentively observed her could not fail to notice that she was by now totally dominated and led by a superior will or divine grace which without destroying her rich natural talents, brought them to the peak of their perfection in her looks, in her words, in her exterior actions, in her whole life. Affable towards everybody, but maintaining a certain independence in her relationships, Catherine gradually acquired a self-possession and an imperturbability that quite astonished many who came into contact with her. She no longer looked at men, women, and life itself from a merely human viewpoint. This mysterious process of spiritual transformation reached its supreme consummation in July 1370 when Catherine had a vision of Jesus, Who, placing His hands in her chest, extracted her heart of flesh and replaced it with His own Heart aflame with Divine Love, which burned away all the dross of Catherine's old nature and at the same time, purified her and changed her into a completely new creature. She immediately recognized with even greater clearness what her mission was; to save souls at any cost. But she had to seek them out, even leave her native city and go wherever God called her, ignoring all other voices. It was really as if God Himself whispered words to her ears, words so full of flaming love that they could have proceeded only from Him. As a group of loyal, devoted friends, men and women, began to form itself around her, Catherine used them almost as personal secretaries in order to extend her message outside the confines of Siena. They looked upon her as and began to call her their mother and teacher and Catherine began dictating her first letters "in the name of Christ Crucified and sweet Mary"; these letters were essentially invitations to conversion, exhortations to strive for greater sanctity, trenchant rebukes to people of all ranks who gloried in their vices. And while condemning the wicked acts of others and inciting them to perform the opposite works of goodness, Catherine's humility and genuine self-forgetfulness shone in the vibrant phrases she used in order to wake up the spiritually asleep, arouse their consciences, and frighten the evildoers. The vigorous intelligence that nature had given her and that the light of truth always so well illumined, the tender heart always open to all the refinements of love and, thanks to the grace of God, able to embrace great and noble desires, are all revealed in the many letters Catherine dictated to her disciples and sent to men and women high and low, in all walks of life. All her letters are amazing feats of literacy, worthy of the most accomplished correspondents of any time or place, especially when one remembers that Catherine was a typically unschooled girl who had not yet learned to read and write. She acquired her literary talents directly from the Lord Himself and she exploited them to the full, tirelessly urging her readers to cultivate the virtues of love, peacefulness, generosity towards neighbours, absolute trust in God and sweet suffering with Christ. Catherine's missives display a masterly and harmonious blend of urbanity, eloquence, strength, and humility; intransigent with herself, but clement towards others, she invariably blamed herself when the others failed to live up to her high standards of Christian morality and apostolic work. She wrote, literally, to everyone: the near and the far, the poor and the rich, the low and the powerful, not excluding Kings and Popes and, especially towards folks in these last two categories she could use frighteningly energetic language. This epistolary apostolate of the Virgin of Siena lasted for more than ten years and the brilliance and intensity of its flame was extinguished only at the instant Catherine died. But this is not true; thanks to the loving efforts of her disciples the spiritual motherhood of Catherine displayed in her letters has lasted and produced fruits of holiness for more than six centuries. Her letters are a priceless and essential component of the spiritual and intellectual heritage of humanity, required reading for anyone who wishes not only to understand Catherine's message in a purely theoretical way, but to be purified and sanctified by it and, thus, reach eternal salvation.

THE PLAGUE

Catherine was born right at the beginning of the infamous Black Death, which according to the best historians wiped out one-third of Europe's population; a similar plague that broke out in 1374 was less murderous, but nevertheless quite frightful. Like its more merciless predecessor it was no respecter of persons: the young and the old, the strong and the weak, the high and the low were all unwilling victims of the unwelcome and devastating visitation. Once a person was struck, death was only a matter of a few hours. In Catherine's own family eleven members were cruelly cut down by the plague's scythe: two brothers, one sister and eight among her nieces and nephews. And finding herself in the midst of such atrocious suffering, Catherine rose to the occasion. She rallied the other Mantellate around her and they did their best to console the sick and the dying. A certain Matthew Cenni, the head of the Hospital of Mercy gave Catherine a hand in these charitable works until he was brought down by the horrible disease and forced to take to his bed; when Catherine went to visit him she cried out: "Matthew, Matthew, this is no time to be lazy". And he immediately arose, completely healed. Many people who had fallen into total despair because of the miserable situation gave themselves unreservedly to the moment, snatching at even the basest fleeting pleasures to make their lives more tolerable; but when Catherine fired her rebukes like arrows at them, they repented and began to think more seriously about this life and the next. Blessed Raymond of Capua, Fra Barthlomew Dominici and the hermit Fra Santi were Catherine's usual companions as they trudged up and down the sometimes torturous, winding, narrow streets of hilly Siena, entering the most lurid tenaments and the overcrowded hospitals in order to at least save the souls of those whose bodies were beyond repair. Catherine's white habit alone was a joyous vision for her fellow-citizens who were desolated by the troubles of the times and she lavished on them her expertise in the art of spiritual consolation. In such moments she wielded a truly supernatural power conferred by God and many by her touch and her words were restored to perfect health. The plague eventually ceased; and Catherine, who had managed to remain uncontaminated during its entire course fell gravely ill. Her only desire was to leave this world and fly straight to heaven, but our Lady appeared to her and showed her the many, many souls whose salvation depended upon her and Catherine realized that her work had only just begun.

AT MONTEPULCIANO

In the autumn of 1374 Catherine conceived an unalterable desire to visit the hill-town of Montepulciano, less than fifty miles south of Siena, where the glorious Dominican Saint Agnes had died in 1317, leaving her nuns a treasury of edifying memories and an attractive example of heroic virtues. The fame of her sanctity and news of the miracles which took place through contact with her sacred corpse spread quickly throughout the whole Tuscan region; when Agnes died even the small children ran up and down the streets of the town crying: "The Saint is dead!". Her blessed body, which is still incorrupt, had been left by the other nuns in their church for public veneration and fifty-seven years later it was still resting on the same catafalque, surrounded by golden votive offerings and its head was covered with a simple white drape. Catherine went to Montepulciano with two other Mantellate and, the following day, Fra Tommaso della Fonte arrived there in the company of Blessed Raymond of Capua who had already lived at the monastery as the nuns' confessor for three years and had been recently nominated as their direct Superior by the Dominican Order. When they reached the convent the nuns lost no time in telling them about a charming wonder that had occurred on the previous day: Catherine had bowed low in order to affectionately and reverently kiss one of Agnes' feet and, at that very instant, the latter courteously raised her foot and met the former's lips in mid air! Catherine visited the monastery in Montepulciano many other times during her life: the second visit was made in the company of the two nieces who became nuns there. They were the daughters of her brother, Bartholomew, and their mother, Lisa, accompanied them on that important day. On this visit Catherine did almost the same thing as on the first one: she bowed low to venerate Agnes, placing her head next to that of the saint and prayed intensely for a few minutes, then she raised her head and said to the onlookers: "Do you not see the gift that the Lord has sent you from heaven?" As Catherine was pronouncing the last word, the bystanders looked up and beheld a light rain of dew falling all around them. Catherine was always generous towards the sisters in Montepulciano; she did her best to sustain them in their material necessities, especially when their monastery fell upon hard times, and she wrote some lovely letters to her nieces, full of Christian wisdom. She urged them to live like true daughters of Saint Agnes and to imitate, most of all, that humility which had gained such great glory for her. To a certain Sister Eugenia who from her tenderest years had faithfully preserved the fresh flower of her baptismal innocence for Jesus, Catherine wrote advising her to keep in mind and to follow "the ways" of their glorious Saint and to dedicate herself to prayer, solitude and union with God. The Lord Himself had already revealed to Catherine that she would attain the same grade of glory in paradise as Saint Agnes and that they would be inseparable companions for all eternity. This is the only happiness worth striving for, which Jesus offers to His loyal disciples, a happiness that will always seem incomprehensible to those who give their hearts to the riches, honours and pleasures of this world.

BLESSED RAYMOND DELLE VIGNE

While Catherine was ministering at the bedside of Matthew Cenni as he hovered between life and death, she met for the first time the saintly Dominican priest Raymond of Capua who came from a noble family descended from from a certain Pier delle Vigne, chancellor of the Holy Roman Emporer Frederick II. Catherine had glimpsed him more than once in the Church of Saint Dominic as he went about his pastoral duties in the company of Fra Tommaso dell Fonte and Fra Bartholomew Dominici; it just so happened that she was seeking someone of his moral and intellectual stature to be her confessor and spiritual director and, after having asked Our Lady in prayer for guidance in the matter, chose him. Blessed Raymond was at that moment forty-seven years old and, as we have seen had already been living in Montepulciano as the official confesso of the Dominican nuns there. Catherine made a wise decision in entrusting her soul to Raymond. He greatly assisted her in those works of charity she performed during the plague of 1374 and he was her travelling companion and primary colloborator in her efforts to convince Pope Gregory XI to leave Avignon and return to Rome. Raymond, for his part, was a highly intelligent man who immediately recognized what was in front of him; the person he was dealing with was such an extraordinary vessel of grace that he gladly humbled himself before her and considered himself to be her most unworthy disciple. Even though he was older than she, he entrusted himself to her as to a most tender mother and whenever she spoke to him about the mysteries of the faith, of grace, of the joys that God grants to His elect on earth and in heaven, he, undoubtedly found in her a most enlightening teacher. Catherine was an almost inexhaustable source of comfort for Raymond during their brief partnership. She healed him of his various physical illnesses and strengthened him in his spiritual trials, stimulating him by her own example to persevere in scaling the heights of Christian perfection. The letters Catherine wrote show how delicately she tried to guide him and how tactfully she humbled herself before him, asking his pardon for the impulsiveness of her heart in urging him to persevere in the ways of the Lord. Catherine wanted to see him perfected in faith and ardent in love; and she wanted Raymond not simply to work untiringly for the church, but to literally shed his blood for it. Catherine was already preparing some of her best disciples for Raymond when in a few years time he should become the Master-General of the Dominican Order and promote its reform: two women, heroines of holiness, the Blessed Maria Mancini and Blessed Chiara Gambacorta, who were attracted to the Dominican life by Catherine's example and on being sent to the famous monastery in Pisa reawakened in the other nuns a real desire for the contemplative life which spread throughout the Order; and many men such as the Blessed Giovanni Dominici who became Raymond's right hand in the work of the renewal expecially in Florence and Fiesole. Blessed Raymond who, when Catherine was still living, defended her many times and even favoured her unusual and eyebrow-raising habit of receiving Holy Comunion every day became after her death her most celebrated and loyal biographer to the joy of her other followers. His life of Catherine is lucid, eminently readable and full of Christian wisdom; he tells the straightforward truth and his book, after Catherine's own letters, is the most polished and brightest mirror of her life.

PISA

In 1370, a certain gentleman named Piero Gambacorta became the head of the Pisan government and until his tragic death twenty years later guided it with great wisdom. He had a daughter, a delightful flower of beauty and goodness whose name was Tora, an abreviation of Theodora and who, at the rather tender age of twelve was married off to a rich youth named Simon Massa. The glowing reports of Catherine's fame had reached the ears of the Gambacorta family and they invited her to their city. She arrived in February of 1375 accompanied, as always, by Blessed Raymond, her spiritual daughters, and other priests for hearing the confessions of converts. The little group was greeted at the entrance to the city not only by Gambacorta himself and his family, but even by the Archbishop and goodly number of other civil and ecclesiastical dignataries. Among these illustrious folk was Theodora or Tora, as she was affectionately nicknamed, Gambacorta's favourite daughter, a sweet, gentle girl who was so impressed by Catherine that she immediately joined the group of disciples. During her stay in Pisa, Catherine and her daughters lived as guests in the home of a local nobleman, a certin Gherardo di Buoncorte, whose house was situated near the Church of Saint Christine, in the famous district called Cinica, on the left bank of the Arno river, not far from the lovely Church of Holy Mary of the Thorn. One of Piero Gambacorta's motives for drawing Catherine to Pisa was his hope that her presence and her words would not only bring spiritual benefits to all, but also serve as a salutary invitation to the many rival political factions to put aside their ferocious hatreds and lay down their arms. And we shall shortly see how in that city Catherine received from her Divine Spouse one of the most sublime manifestations of His love which powerfully encouraged her to persevere in her admirable mission for the church and civil society. One of her followers, the Blessed Giovanni Dominici, in a letter written to her mother who was staying in Venice, has left us a precious description of how whole-heartedly Catherine threw herself into the work of peace-making: "At Pisa I heard her speak to certain sinners; and her sermons were deep, fiery and powerful." And there is no doubt that Catherine's arrival in the important seaport and that the desires she expressed in her private talks with Gambacorta, Buoncorte and other Pisan nobles, inspired them to magnanimously adhere to and help with financial contributions, the "holy passage" as she liked to nickname the Crusade against the heathens. Catherine also did her best to make her distinguished hosts understand that success in such a complicated project depended above all on their refusal to join Florence and Milan in the newly created anti-papal League; and, thanks to Catherine's persuasive words, the Pisans - at least, for a while - remained loyal to the Pope, Gregory XI.

Power politics however was, quite rightly, very low on Catherine's list of priorities. She had more important things to think about, real flesh and blood people, especially Gambacorta's daughter, Tora who possessed a generosity and an ardour second only to Catherine's own. She listened attentively to and meditated seriously on the irresistable words of the Virgin of Siena and, little by little, began to disattach her heart from the things of this world; and when, only three years later, her husband's death made her a widow, she ignored all new invitations to marriage and consecrated herself totally to God. Tora kept before her mind's eye the incisive phrases Catherine used in order to depict the miserable efforts of those who try to serve the world: "When God cuts away the branch on which they were sitting, they immediately find another one, with the danger of losing God forever... Since God has loosened you from the world, I want you to tie yourself to Him and to marry Christ Crucified with the wedding ring of the holy faith." The voice of Catherine penetrated that large soul with such force, that not only did Tora bravely resist earthly attractions and enthusiastically embrace the cross of Christ, but also took the Dominican habit and the name Chiara (Clare) becoming like Catherine mother and guide to a slew of holy virgins and promoter in Italy of a fervent return to the ancient discipline in the Dominican Order. After 1380, when Catherine's heavy mantle fell on Tora's physically slender but morally capable shoulders, she made firm friendships with Blessed Raymond of Capua, Blessed Giovanni Dominici and other disciples of Catherine, and worked indefatigably to realize the great saint's desires. Tora was particularly observant of religious poverty and even refused to accept a tempting, substantial economic contribution from her father for the building of new monastery, preferring to trust only in Providence. Tora died in 1419 and was later officially declared "blessed" by Pius VIII.

THE STIGMATA

In the small Romanesque Church of Saint Christine in Pisa, then as now lapped by the current of the Arno, a certain Crucifix, painted by Giunto Pisano, was venerated by all. Catherine liked to pray before it and often, in the fervour of contemplation, was completely caught up in God, remaining for hours in ecstasy. On April 1, 1375, as she was communing in prayer with her Divine Spouse, Catherine received one of the most sublime communications of Divine Love possible to anyone. Blessed Raymond who was present describes the scene in the following words: "After having celebrated Mass and given her communion, she remained insensible for quite some time. And as I was waiting for her to return to her senses, in order to receive, as often happened, some spiritual consolation from her, in an instant her tiny body, which had been prostrate, little by little, was raised up and, as she was on her knees, she stretched out her arms and hands remaining rigidly for some time in that position with her eyes closed; finally, as if she had been mortally wounded, she suddenly collapsed and shortly after, regained consciousness. Then she called for me and said, "You must know, Father, that by the mercy of our Lord Jesus, I already bear in my body his stigmata... I saw the Crucified Lord coming down towards me enveloped in a blinding light; and by the force of my desire to meet my Creator, my body was made to elevate itself. Then from the scars of His most sacred wounds I saw descending upon me five blood-stained rays, which touched my hands, my feet, and my heart... And I immediately felt such pains in all these parts of my body, especially in my side, that if the Lord had not performed another miracle I don't think that I could have survived such a trial"". Accompanined by Blessed Raymond, Catherine just managed to reach Buonconte's house where she was guest and, once again, collapsed as if she were dying. By this time almost all her disciples had heard the news and were gathered anxiously around her weeping for fear of losing her. When she came to herself she repeated to Raymond that if the Lord had not sustained her she would have died instantly. All her followers began praying for their mother and with tears streaming down their faces said: "We well know that you wish to be with your Spouse Jesus; but your reward is already guaranteed; rather, have mercy on us for we are too weak yet to continue by ourselves in the storms of life!" Catherine had to stay in her bed the whole week; and the following Saturday she spoke once again to Blessed Raymond saying: "Father, it seems as if the Lord has condescended to grant your prayers: you shall have what you requested". In fact, on Sunday, upon receiving Holy Communion from the hands of Raymond, Catherine went into ecstasy and felt new strength being infused into her. When she retuned to her normal state, she seemed so robust that everybody felt certain their prayers had been answered. Blessed Raymond asked: "Are those wounds imprinted in you body still causing you pain, Mother?" And Catherine: "The Lord has listened to me. Considering the sorrow I feel in my soul, the wounds I have received do not bother but rather comfort me; and where there was affliction, now there is respite: I truly feel it... " Catherine had also obtained another favour from her celestial spouse, that the stigmata should remain visible.

THE CARTHUSIANS OF CALCI

After having received the supernatural gift of the holy stigmata, which certainly helped to increase the interior fire of charity, and zeal and, even, her bodily strength, Catherine committed herself as never before to her superhuman mission for the good of the Church and society. And she went forward in her arduous tasks without losing any of her natural tact and sweetness, but rather growing in humility almost to the total forgetting of herself: it seemed as if she had completely disappeared in order to make room for Jesus Christ whose word of life she was bringing to others with all the fiery, uncontrollable love He had infused into her virginal heart, and she also carried upon her body the miraculous signs of His passion which gave her so much more vigour. Catherine accomplished so much in such a brief span; from the spiritual direction of other common girls like herself who became her first inseparable companions, to the guidance of men, lay and religious, humble and noble, even those who were older and reputed wiser than she, an illiterate girl; from the absorbing work of reforming the religious Orders, to the delicate prodding of powerful princes to their duties; from the same prodding of the clergy, to the reconciliation of warring Tuscan cities among themselves and to the great mission to all

Italy and the entire Church; even winning the respectful attention of the Pope himself who showed a certain docility to the voice of this loving daughter as though it were the oracle of God. We may thus say without fear of exaggerating that God Himself wanted this great Saint to dedicte her life to the improvement of the Church and society of the times; and everyone could see that she really made the needs of others her own and that she worked and suffered, offering herself as a victim-soul to God in order to satisfy them. After the episode of the sacred stigmata, Catherine's zeal was directed particularly towards the conservation and the increase of fervour in the religious Orders. After her own Dominican Order, which she so richly loved and tirelessly tried to bring back to its antique splendour, Catherine's predilections went to the Carthusians who were already well-known to her, since they had two monasteries only three miles from Siena. Her journey to Pisa gave Catherine the opportunity to know them better and to lavish upon them her affectionate care. On the fertile plains surrounding Pisa, about six mils from the city, there still stands in a place called the Dark Valley, the splendid Carthusian monastery of Calci. This monastery was still under construction during Catherine's time thanks to the offerings of a certain Prete Nino Pucci of Spazzavento and a Pisan merchant known simply as Mirante Virginis; and it was further embellished thanks to the contributions of other Pisan noblemen such as Piero Gambacorta. Catherine visited Calci a number of times during her sojourn at Pisa in 1375 and once on her return from Avignon. She enjoyed the edifying conversations of the monks and nourished a sincere love for them and oriented one of her closest disciples to the Carthusian way of life, Stefano Maconi who became the first prior of the Carthusian monastery at Pavia and was, after his death, beatified. Though Catherine's life was as full of apostolic action as anyone else's, she loved to taste the joys of the contemplative life, the complete separation from people and things, acquiring from the fullness of prayer and penance renewed energy for her projects. And even in the midst of these happy moments of devout retirement she continued her apostolatic mission for others with humility and simplicity, igniting in the hearts of her hosts the fire of divine love. Catherine maintained contact with the prior Don Giovanni Lipezzinghi of Calcinaia and some other monks of the establishment by letter and persuaded the Pope, Gregory XI to contribute something to its upkeep. There are still some traces of Catherine's presence in the monastery even today: the Chapel of the Colloquies where she spoke to the monks of heavenly realities, and the precious relic of her finger, jealously guarded by Stefano Maconi and taken by him to the Carthusian monastery at Pontignano near Siena and then to the one at Pavia.

TO THE ISLAND OF GORGONA

In that summer of 1375, Catherine received yet another invitation to visit another place of interest. It came from Don Barthlomew Serafini di Ravenna, prior of the Carthusian monastery recently built on the small island Gorgora, just thirty miles from the Italian mainland. Naturally, Catherine accepted the inviation, and escorted by about twenty followers, including Raymond and some other friars, set sail from Pisa. It was the first time she had ever seen the sea. One call well imagine that mysterious feeling of peace and tranquillity that descended into her soul when, by slow degrees, almost imperceptibly, the coast vanished from her sight and she found herself surrounded by vast expanse of sea and sky. The rocky island, still far away appeared like a huge solitary fortress lost in that vastitude; but, in fact, it was a refuge, a spiritual oasis for Christian souls aspiring to higher things. They arrived very late and had to spend the first night at a small inn about a mile away from the monastery. The next day, the Prior himself with some of his monks came to welcome Catherine and he immediately beseeched her to make an edifying discourse for them. Catherine, as usual, rose to the occasion and spoke with much sweetness, meekness and goodness. After the impromptu speech-making Catherine went up the rocky, winding path that led to the monastery on high.

It was truly the house of God and she was at once enamoured of it during those few days she spent there. She spoke a second time, to the whole community and Don Bartholomew, who was the monk's official confessor, later testified to Blessed Raymond, that each monk received from Catherine exactly that advice or those admonitions that he needed. She came away from Gorgona with a most pleasant remembrance of the place and its inhabitants; and afterwards, whenever she chanced to meet some pious soul desiring to flee from the world and live in holy contemplation and solitude, Catherine always urged him to go to Gorgona. To the Prior of the monastery, the same Don Bartholomew, Catherine left a precious souvenir, her own black mantle or cape which he later brought to the Carthusian monastery in Pavia. In a couple of her letters Catherine refers to him as a "mirror of virtue" and to his community of monks as "good and holy". The monks at Gorgona had their own boat and some of them insisted on escorting Catherine back to Pisa. The return voyage was brief and smooth and as Catherine was disembarking she gave the monks her blessing and said: "If anything should happen during your return trip to Gorgora, do not fear: the Lord is with you". And on the way back, as the little boat was drawing near to the island a furious storm began and after being tossed around here and there by the wind and waves, the little boat was almost smashed to bits on some rocks but, as Catherine had assured them, the storm suddenly ended, a total shipwreck was gratefully avoided and the monks got safely home.

TO LUCCA

Catherine had hardly set foot in Siena after her trip to Pisa when Pope Gregory XI, who had heard so much about her virtues and the power of her words and was so worried about the rebellion of the Florentines who were drumming up support among other Italian city-states, let her know of his desire that she should travel to another Tuscan city, Lucca, in order to persuade its inhabitants to hold fast in their obedience to the Papacy. She had already once written to the magistrates of Lucca, called the Elders, exhorting them to refuse any alliance with Florence and to remain steadfast in their loyalty to the Pope; but in September 1375 she decided to make a personal appearance in Lucca with some of her disciples, including a well-known local minor poet, Ranieri (Neri) di Landoccio. Catherine was received with all due honours and lodged in the house of a certain Bartholomew Balbani.

Her motive, though, was more spiritual than political. Lucca possessed an inestimable treasure: a stupendous Crucifix called "the Holy Visage". The splendid octagonal chapel of the Civitali had not yet been built in the Cathedral of Lucca, but this venerated work of art had been in the city since the eighth century, brought there (so it was believed) from Palestine; and even after the Cathedral had been enlarged the famous Crucifix remained in its original place, attracting the devoutful respect and love of all visitors. Catherine also wished to make a pilgrimage to the "Holy Visage"; and on September 14, the Feast of the Holy Cross, she paid homage to the sacred image, as she was swept along by a crowd of the faithful. The Sienese Virgin was always moved by the remembrance of the sacred relic and when she wrote to some friends in Lucca afterwards she urged them to be full of holy love for God by contemplating that "most sweet and venerable Crucifix". Lucca was famous also for its statue-making, especially statues of the Child Jesus. Catherine had formed friendships with other families in Lucca besides the Balbani, in particular with a certain Giovanni Perotti, a dealer in leather goods, and his wife Monna Lippa; and they made a gift to her of one of these statues of the Child Jesus realistically clothed with some lovely colored drapes of their own production. They in turn received a most welcome gift from Catherine; a letter still extant in which she, taking a cue from their statues, speaks about Christ Crucified being our vestment according to the words of St. Paul: "Clothe yourselves with our Lord Jesus Christ"; and she also speaks about the wedding garment mentioned in the Gospels which, covering our nakedness, protects us from the coldness of sin and warms us with that priceless and delectable charity which will bring us to the nuptials of eternal life with God which was manifested to us by the wood of the most Holy Cross.

Catherine also fixed her attention on one of Perotti's daughters who demonstrated an aptitude for the religious life and wrote to him saying: "Bless my little girl for I want her to become a bride of Christ, consecrated only to Him".

MESSENGER OF THE PEACE

Many times during her short life Catherine was chosen by God to calm ferocious hatreds, help others put aside old grudges and to bring the olive branch of peace in the midst of warring factions. She would have preferred to do all this in the solitude of her cell but the Lord preferred that she should do her peace-making in public where everyone could see her. In fact, nobody was more skilled than Catherine in eliminating discord and rooting out hate from human hearts. And hate existed, unfortunately, in frightening abundance in fourteenth-century Tuscany: between entire families who transmitted it to their posterity along with material goods,often solemnly conferming it with oaths even at the moment of death; and between different cities whose citizens delighted in wicked revenge and in horribly bloody feuds. The same people who blithely forgot or ignored the Christian law of mutual forgiveness, nevertheless had the nerve to enter churches and pray before the altars to the God of love and peace.

More often than not, it was the wives, the daughters and the mothers who ran to Catherine in these trying situations; such as Angela Salimbeni, wife to Pietro Belforti, who begged her to reconcile their two grown sons, Benuccio and Bernardo. Sometimes Catherine's disciples acted as go-betweens for the rival factions: such as the celebrated English hermit William Flete who sent her that ferocious fellow Vanni di Ser Vanni who had stubbornly sworn never to sign a peace treaty unless she could do so with the blood of his enemies. But God's love in Catherine conquered all especially when it shone in her eyes as she lifted them up to heaven in prayer and, thanks to the potent words of that Bride of Christ, hearts of ice melted and tears streamed down the manly chests covered with thick armour of those who had been erstwhile enemies.

Catherine's sorrow was even more acute and her prayers more heartfelt when she discovered such hatred among the ministers of God. A certain Pietro da Semignano, for example, absolutely loathed one of his confreres in the priesthood. Catherine wrote a letter reminding him that he had been elected to administer the fire of divine charity, the Holy Eucharist; that God had made him a minister of His word which was the word of charity, that he had fashioned him into an angel on earth by virtue of the Sacrament of Holy Order; and she pleaded with him "to strip away from your heart and mind all miseries and especially hate...Oh how unpleasant it is to see two priests separated by such mortal hate! It is only a miracle that God does not command the earth to open and swallow you both!".

In her capacity as the angel of peace Catherine had to visit many times various towns that dotted the Sienese countryside such as Montepulicano,

Asciano and Montalcino and numerous castles of powerful noble families in constant conflict with one another that dominated the austere hilltops. Her irenic mission brought her into contact with some real experts in power politics when she preached peace to the rulers of Florence, exhorting them to make war on the infedels rather than on their fellow Catholics. It must have been an impressive spectacle to watch this humble young woman of the people go boldly up the celebrated inner staircase of the Palazzo Vecchio in Florence and listen to her heart-piercing harangue demanding that the Florentines cease their rebellion against the Pope and become once again his obedient sons. A couple of years later, as we shall see, Catherine was almost murdered for using such unladylike language. A group of angry Florentines who had been arbitrarily excluded from public office burst into the courtyard of the house where she was staying accusing her of meddling too much in politics and threatening to kill her right then and there. Catherine, with great presence of mind and a calm voice, replied that a bloody martyrdom would be the most welcome and gratifying type of death in the world for herself, so long as her disciples should be spared. The would-be assassins were completely and literally disarmed by Catherine's dignified, imperturbable bearing and quietly went away. She was, however, deeply disappointed about being denied a martyr's death. Nobody who spoke words of peach in those violent times did so quite so loudly and constantly as Catherine because nobody loved God as much as she did. Whenever she saw her efforts crowned with success her heart rejoiced greatly and sung for the victory of the olive branch and in some letters to her followers she even enclosed some pieces of it.

FOR ROME AND CHRIST'S TOMB

Nothing surprises a modern reader of the life of Catherine quite so much as the union and harmony that she managed to achieve between her impetuous heart and her shrewd, native intelligence. Along with her grandiose vision of the situation and the problems of her times she united a sure instinctive grasp of the means necessary to correct them which astonished almost everyone. This was absolutely not due to any book-reading or long experience in practical, hard-headed affairs; Catherine saw things from a higher vantage-point and judged them with a superior certainty thanks to the vigour of her faith and the ardour of her charity which inspired the words pronounced by her lips and, thus, she could say: God wills it, such has been revealed to me by my heavenly Spouse. Mere human expediency and mundane craftiness were weak and useless in dealing with this strong-willed young woman. This was embarassingly evident - for some people - when Catherine, in her letters and talks with men and women who held the reins of government in their hands, explained her views on sundry matters summing them up in two unalterable propositions which dominated her thoughts. She wanted to see all Christendom united as one family around one centre, the Pope whom she called "the sweet Christ on earth", and she wanted him to retun to his natural place of residence, Rome, which she compared sometimes to a homicidal playground, or to a devastated and sterile garden, that she hoped might be transformed into an oasis of peace and a bower full of flowers and fruits.

The main cause of those murderous struggles and of Rome's other problems was the prolonged absence of the Pope. From 1305, Rome had been deprived of its spiritual and political Father. A most unwise decision had moved Clement V to establish his residence in Avignon, a city in southeastern France about sixty-six miles by road from Marseilles. The five Popes who succeeded Clement were, like him, all Frenchmen; but the last of them, Gregory XI, who ruled from 1370-1378 was, in theory, the most unlikely of them all to be energetic and steadfast in his resolution to return to Rome. Elected Pope at only forty years of age, timorous and irritatingly indecisive by nature, he deserved Catherine's stern rebuke: "Act like a man!". Gregory's wishy-washy character was not the only obstacle that impeded him from returning to Rome; the powerful French king did all he could to keep that precious hostage in his own hands and from their strongholds in Italy the various papal representatives were only too glad to cooperate with him. These papal legates were all too often utterly unworthy men who, because of their harsh methods of governing and total lack of loyalty to the Pope, provoked many Italian cities - already much too fanatically jealous of their independence - to open rebellion against the papacy.

And when these rebellions exceeded certain reaso nable limits, as in the case of Florence, a papal inderdict was inevitable; which, in its turn only served to inflame even further the raw sensibilities of the local populations.

Another running sore of Italian political and social life was the existence of angry factions which divided almost every city and town, and ancient rivalries which were never completely extinguished. In many cases, for childish reasons and in private matters, little armies were formed and little local wars were fought; and, by sad necessity there arose the so-called "companies of adventure", headed by fierce men-at-arms whose cunning in directing thousands of other men and cruelty in massacring their enemies and innocent folk, earned them reputations as valiant warriors.

Catherine was painfully aware of all this and her heart was deeply touched by the helplessness and anguish of so many good humble souls, of the disinherited, of the many widows and orphans; and she understood perfectly how much damage was being done to the Church which for too long had had to abandon the idea of promoting a Crusade as the price for allowing itself to get a bit too involved in power struggles which sapped its strength and tarnished its prestige. There was no time to lose and Catherine did her best, according to her lights, to correct the unhappy situation by offering the most efficacious remedies she knew and asking God's help in her prayers to actuate them: the return of the Pope to Rome and a Holy Crusade.

In any case, Catherine wanted a Crusade not only to win back from the sacrilegious hands of the heathens the Holy Sepulchre of Christ, but also to rid Italy of its foulest plague: the legions of mercenaries that stained the flower of her face with the purple testament of bleeding war. The Sienese virgin hoped that these men, mostly foreigners and all hardbitten professionals who, externally at least shared the same Catholic faith, would enthusiastically gather around the banner of the Cross fired by the ideal of trouncing the pagans and, thus, mercifully liberate Italy of their presence. United, they would be invincible against a common enemy and such a holy victory would surely slake their thirst for military glory. Catherine understood the irresistable appeal of a great and simple idea whose moment has arrived and it immensely pleased her to immagine the Vicar of Christ himself restored to his official seat in Rome issuing the magnificent invitation to all Christian princes and their subjects.

Catherine struggled and literally worked herself to death for these two projects and she had to go to an early grave bitterly disappointed by the knowledge that her efforts had never been fully successful.

THE COUNT

Among the leaders of the mercenary armies during Catherine's time, none was more celebrated and feared than the Englishman John Hawkwood, nicknamed by the Italians as "the Falcon of the Forest". He was the captain of an awesome host of several thousand soldiers, called the Free-Lancers; and he offered, for the right amount of gold, military assistance to any and all of the Tuscan cities who needed it in their terrible internal wars. Wherever they went they left behind wastelands marked by ravaged fields and devastated homes. They earned their living by armed robbery, spreading terror and death everywhere, not sparing even women and children. Cities had to shell out enormous amounts of money in order to save themselves. On June 21, 1375, Florence had to shell out some 130,000 florins in order to get rid of Hawkwood; he then decided to invade Pisa, but the Pisans persuaded him to attack somebody else by paying him 30,500 florins in three installments and so, on July 8 of that same year he made amost unwelcome visit to the Republic of Siena. Fortunately, for Siena that is, St. Catherine sent the powerful warlord a celebrated letter. Pope Gregory XI had already inaugurated a new Crusade by writing two Bulls; one to the superiors of the Dominican and Franciscan Orders and the other privately to Blessed Raymond of Capua. They were ordered to drum up support all over Italy for the sacred Crusade and to encourage everyone to particpate in it. Catherine was delighted.

She immediately perceived, however, that such a grand undertaking would never get off the drawing boards and become a reality unless those mercenary armies that were causing such bloody devastation all over Italy with their internecine wars were stopped and their energies diverted to higher things. With this idea in mind Catherine tried to win over Hawkwood.

She knew that ten years previously, during the reign of Urban V, he had promised to help that Pope in a similar situation by lending his army against the infidels and she wanted to remind him of that promise. Catherine never forgot that often, even in the worst men, there was pinch of generosity which could become the fountain of good actions and that even they still have a conscience which could bearoused to a salutary remorse. Hawkood moreover was, externally, a believing Christian, and he just might have gloried in the thought of becoming a true soldier of Christ and atoning for his sins.

While he was encamped near Siena, Blessed Raymond and a companion arrived at his tent and asked permission to speak to him. They were carrying a letter from Catherine who, "in the name of Jesus Crucified and of sweet Mary", had a message for him and his men. The burning desire of the holy virgin was that they should place themselves and their weapons in the service of Christ. "If in order to serve the devil, you have until now endured hardships and worries", she said, "from this moment on, I want you to change your ways and take up the cause and the cross of Christ Crucified, become the Company of Christ and go fight those heathen dogs, who possess our Holy Land, where the sweet first Truth Himself lived and underwent pain and death for us". She repeated the Pope's appeal and reminded Hawkwood of his own promise made many years ago. "You who are so fond of wars and combat, stop afflicting poor Christians, for it is an offence against God, and go fight against those others! It is simply horrible the way we Christians who are members of the body of Holy Church persecute one another! Thus, you will show yourself to be a true and manly knight". And knowing full well that the shortness of earthly life is a powerful stimulus to generosity and the performance of good works, Catherine concluded: "I beseech you, dearest brother, remember how brief your time is in this life".

The fame of this Sienese mantellata who conversed with God and spoke to others in His name, had already reached the ears of John Hawkwood; and he was touched by her letter. The voice of his conscience rebuked him for not having kept his former promise to the Pope and he wondered how Catherine knew about it. He treated the two religious quite affably and in unison with his soldiers swore an oath to join the Crusade as soon as it was definitely organised, saying as much to Catherine in a letter entrusted to Raymond bearing his own seal. The new Crusade was greeted with great enthusiasm everywhere. Catherine was her usual restless self, sending fiery letters to princes and cities and obtaining promises of help for the holy project. And hoping for an early start of what she called the "holy passage" wrote: "I can smell the odour of the flower which is beginning to open!" Unfortunately the pious hopes of so many like Catherine never became reality because of disagreement among the Christian princes and the absence of the Pope from Italy. It is a fact, however, that from that moment on Hawkwood became much less ferocious and even showed a certain meekness on occasion. He died in Florence in 1394 and was given a sumptuous funeral in the Cathedral of Santa Maria del Fiore and afterwards, a giant frescoe of him on horseback was painted by the artist Paolo Uccello.

Catherine had already died fourteen years previously and undoubtedly her prayers obtained forgiveness for the cruel soldier whom she had once called "her sweet brother in Christ".

AMBASSADOR FOR FLORENCE

The celebrated trial of strength between the Florentine Republic and the Pontiff became, according to the designs of divine providence, the means by which Catherine was able to bring about one of the greatest victories in the history of the Church.

The obstinate rebellion of the Florentines who with their Milanese allies tried to win over to their side the other Tuscan republics, began to weigh heavily upon them. Florence was basically a Guelph city and wished to remain loyal to the Pope, but it had good reason to complain about the haughty and overbearing Papal legates who were suspected of trying to destroy its liberty, and the citizens were beginning to feel the unpleasant effects of the recently imposed Papal interdict. The Florentines slowly realized that their suspicions about the Pope's alleged intentions to invade Tuscany with his armies and become its sole master were totally unfounded, and that their vain attempts to oppose him with violence and to draw other Italian cities to their side were bound to end in failure.

As soon as Catherine heard about what was happening, she tried to calm the agitated spirits and exhorted everyone to work for peace; she especially desired the Pope to be merciful, urging him to conquer the hearts of his rebellious and ungrateful sons with love, and she sent Neri di Landoccio, one of her closest and most trusted disciples, to Avignon with a letter for the Pontiff. In this remarkable letter Catherine expresses her deepest desire in the following words: Peace for the love of God! If you wish to mete out justice or take revenge, take it out on me, your miserable subject, and inflict on me whatever pain or torment pleases you, even unto death! She also begged the Pope to send his answer verbally to her by means of the trustworthy Neri. And, as if all this wasn't enough she wrote a letter to two Italian Cardinals, Giacomo Orsini and Pietro da Ostia asking them to intercede with the Pope on behalf of the Florentines adding that even if the original troublemakers deserved to be punished, the severe effects of the interdict were doing far more harm to the innocent majority that venerated the Pope as a father.

Unfortunately, many influential people in Florence were becoming more hardened in their obstinacy to Catherine's great sorrow and the Pope's great idignation; and the latter's anger was fanned to a white heat when the Florentine legates, headed by Donato Barbadori, came to Avignon full of arrogance and accusations against him rather than humility and respect.

Gregory XI, therefore, as an extreme remedy, launched his interdict against the rebellious city. When news of the Pope's decision reached Florence, it had a terrible effect on the entire city, not only because of the spiritual, but also because of the material and financial damage it caused, especially to merchants. The common folk were deeply distressed by the folly of their leaders; and the whole populace was convinced that only Catherine, known to be highly influential with the Pontiff and armed with supernatural power and who had already pleaded their cause by letter, could usefully intercede for them. Thus, while still in Siena, she received a written mandate from Niccolò Soderini, head of the Florentine government, to go to Avignon as the official Ambassadress of Florence.

Catherine's employers, however, were skilled dissemblers, especially the so-called Eight or the war-party (hawks in contemporary parlance), blinded by their passion for political intrigue and persuaded that the unhappy situation had to be settled by arms. Outwardly they were favourable to Catherine's going to Avignon, but in their hearts they were hoping that the Sienese Virgin would whitewash their sins before the Pope and make him understand that failure to obtain peace would be entirely his fault. Catherine, in any case, was more than willing to make an effort for the sake of Christian charity, so she accepted her mission for the good of everyone.

It was perfectly clear to her that one of the real causes of all the political and social discords in Italy, including this Florentine one, was the absence of the Pope from Rome; and, since so many evils would simply disappear and so much happiness follow on his return to Rome, Catherine used the occasion to tell him to his face what she had already written to him more than once. "Keep with true and

72

and holy solicitude (she had written to the Pontiff) your promise to return... Come and console the poor, the servants of God,your children; we await you with loving desire... Come and do not resist the will of God who is calling you. The hungry sheep are waiting for you to take possession once again of the place held by your predecessor and champion, The Apostle Peter, since, as Vicar of Christ, it is also your one and only proper dwelling... God shall be with you".

Catheine did not forget her other great idea, the Crusade, which all generous souls wished to see led by the Pope who had already approved it. But she was absolutely certain that his invitations to all Christian leaders in this enterprise would be much more efficacious if the Pope were to speak from his natural seat in Rome.

She was anxious, therefore, to depart, full of trust in God. She also sent ahead a letter with Blessed Raymond and some ofher other disciples in April 1376; and at the end of May she finally set out with some other Dominican friars and a few sisters of the Mantellate, twenty-three in all.

On June 18 they arrived at Avignon.

AVIGNON

As soon as the Pontiff learned of Catherine's arrival in Avignon, he provided a comfortable house with a chapel for herself and her sisters and decided that two days later she should attend a concistory and perorate on behalf of the Florentines. She spoke, wielding a charming and captivating Tuscan accent and, as she did so, seemed to go into ecstasy. Blessed Raymond stood at her side and translated her words into Latin. Her words wrought such a powerful effect upon the Pope that at the end of her speech he replied:

"Oh Lady, in order to demonstrate to you how sincerely I desire peace, I leave everything in your hands. I am ready to receive as sons the Florentines, and treat them according to your wishes; but always remember to safeguard the honour and welfare of the Holy Church".

Catherine retuned several times to the Papal palace with Blessed Raymond; and she made a special effort to win over to her side those Cardinals and secular rulers who were not interested in concluding a peace. Unfortunately, though, the Florentines were maliciously doing all they could to vitiate Catherine's honest efforts.

The Florentines had promised to send other representives to clarify their intentions to the Pope, but they never arrived and Catherine was so irritated that on June 28 she wrote to the Eight Hawks: You are ruining everything that is being done here. And in fact, if Florence had really desired peace and if the leaders of the many factions had not heeded the voices of their unruly passions and old rivalries, never again, declared Catherine, could such a glorious peace have been reached, considering the generous mood of the Pontiff. But as soon as he became aware of their delaying tactics and dishonest works, Gregory XI rightly exclaimed: "If the Florentines sincerely wanted peace, they would refrain from doing the smallest act against the will of their Holy Father!". And to Catheine he added: "They are trying to make dupes of you and me."

Finally, the other ambassadors arrived from Florence, Pazzino Strozzi, Alessandro dell'Antella and Michele Castellani. Catherine was, at first, overjoyed by their arrival, but soon realized that they were not about to make an open and total act of submission to Gregory: rather, the conditions for peace they were empowered to offer in the name of their Republic were absolutely unacceptable to the Pope. Before setting out Catherine had told their leaders: "If you want me to handle your affairs, give me permission to offer you as perfectly obedient sons to the Holy Father. This, she continued, is the only way; this is the door through which one must enter". The ambassdors, however, behaved rather differently and when speaking with Catherine or with other papal representatives, never once did they betray what was really in their minds; and Catherine did not err when she made a remark about not finding in them "that affectionate love of peace" which she had found in the Pontiff.

But even if the peace talks with the Florentines were deteriorating quickly, the Virgin of Siena was successful in her efforts to obtain her deepest heart's desire: the Pontiff's return to Rome. Before leaving Florence she had sent Blessed Raymond ahead to Avignon with a letter in which she begged Gregory not to delay beyond the end of September and to banish all fears from his mind. And when she arrived at Avignon Catherine used even stronger words in the name of God to convince him to return, even in the presence of the Pope's most powerful opponents who were attempting to undermine his resolve without daring to manifest their opposition in front of Catherine. She was simply marvelous in answering the difficulties raised by the Pope's false advisers and fair-weather friends and exposing their shameful plots; as when somebody openly hinted at the example of Clement IV who, it was said, never made a move without consulting his cardinals. To which Catherine cited the example of Urban V who, when he saw where his duty lay, never wasted time consulting anyone, but followed his own counsel even if nobody agreed with him.

Thus, Gregory did not allow himself to be unduly impressed by a false letter from a certain Fra Peter of Aragon, a holy servant of God and his great friend (though the Pope had never even heard of this Fra Peter) in which he wrote that Gregory should not go to Italy because his dinner-table might be decked with poison. Poison, Catherine declared, could just as easily be found on the dinner-table at Avignon!... She knew all about the attempted poisoning of Urban V in Avignon, when he had decided to retun to Rome! "Go and do not be afraid; God is with you. I have prayed and will continue to pray that the good and sweet Jesus shall banish all base fear from your mind: I order you in the name of Christ to fear not! If you stick to your duty, God will be with you and nobody shall prevale against you... Go at once to your Bride who awaits you and restore some colour to her pale visage...". Gregory XI was a timorous man, but an honest one. He had already vowed in his heart to God to go back to Rome, but he dawdled, while Catherine always made up her mind and acted out her decisions very quickly. She learned of the Pope's vow by means of special illumination from on high and wrote to him urging him to stand firm in his holy resolve and to trust in the Lord, adding: "I hope that you will not despise the prayers that have been offered with such ardent desire and much sweat and tears...".

The Pontiff finally told Catherine openly about his irrevocable will to return to Rome and she replies: "I thank God and Your Holiness that He has strengthened your heart and that he has given you constancy in overcoming all those who wish to block you from returning to your natural home... I pray God that in His infinite goodness He may give me the grace to see you take that first step out the door".

THE CRUSADE

While in Avignon, Catherine's thoughts were not wholly occupied only with the cause of Florence and the return of the Pope to Rome. She took good advantage of her ascendancy over the Pontiff in order to obtain special indulgences and ecclesiastical favours for various Sienese families and her spiritual children, as she revealed in some of her letters to them.

One of the projects closest to her heart was, however, the Crusade against the infedels once the Pope was re-established at Rome. She had already given much time and energy to this project in her letters and particularly, in her talks with the Pisan leader Pietro Gambacorta; and now in Avignon she was able to talk about to Gregory face to face using, as always, Blessed Raymond as her translator.

At one of these audiences, after having listened to Catherine's enthusings, the Pontiff said: "I think it would be better to achieve first peace among Christians and then go on a Crusade". To which, Catherine humbly replied: "Holy Father, you will never find a better way of creating peace among Christians than by means of the Holy Passage. Thus, all these arms that Christians are using against each other shall be used in God's service, to obtain His glory and His forgiveness for our sins. Only the most perverse men will refuse such an opportunity to advance their own salvation. Only in this way can peace be had among Christians who so desire it; and they shall find eternal salvation for their souls".

Charles V was then sitting on the throne of France and Louis, Duke of Anjou, his brother, was more than willing to lead an army in such a Crusade. But the Hundred Years War between France and England was a grave obstacle to such an undertaking. Catherine wrote to the King a letter that combined sweetness and severity, telling him that he must always rule with justice, moderatng it though with charity lest he become like a plant without water. He should not consider his kingdom as if it were his private property but as a gift from God to be used for good ends. And speaking about war and the slaughter of countless innocents she exclaimed: "No more, no more for the love of Christ Crucified!". By engaging in his war against England, he had become, said Catherine, "the enemy of a good cause such as the recovery of the Holy Land for which reason, she added, you should be ashamed of yourself, you and all other Christian rulers!... Make peace, she said, and then go make war upon the heathens. Wake up, because the time is short and you do not know when death will come. She had already won over Charles' brother; and therefore, the Saint told the King: "Your brother, the Duke of Anjou, for the love of Christ is willing to work for this holy enterprise. Your own conscience should goad you to follow his sweet example".

Siena - Basilica of San Domenico - Chapel of the Vaults.
Portrait of St.Catherine (detail)   (A.Vanni 1332-1414)

Siena - **Basilica of San Domenico** - View from the south.

Siena - Basilica of San Domenico
Catherine heals a possesed woman

(A. Vanni, XVI century)

Siena - Basilica of San Domenico
Chapel of St.Catherine - frescoes by Antonio Bazzi called Sodoma (1526) and by Francesco Vanni (1596)

Siena - Basilica of San Domenico
The Relic of St. Catherine's Head
with marble dossal

(G. di Stefano XV century)

Siena - Basilica of San Domenico
Chapel of St.Catherine - **The Saint in Ecstacy** (detail)

(Sodoma - Giov. Antonio Bazzi)

Siena - House of St.Catherine: *Arcades and Basilica of San Domenico in the distance*

Siena - Shrine - House of St.Catherine:
Altar of the Most Holy Crucifix

Siena - Shrine - House of St.Catherine:
Crucifix of the Stigmata (1300)

Siena - Room of St.Catherine's House at the Shrine - House:
The Saint absorbed in prayer, going up the stairs without touching the steps.

(A.Franchi, 1898)

Siena - Room of St.Catherine's Shrine - House at the Shrine - House. *Catherine praying on her knees as a radiant dove descends upon her head.*

(A.Franchi, 1898)

Siena - Room of St.Catherine's House at the Shrine - House.
Catherine cuts off her hair in the presence of Father Tommaso della Fonte.

(A.Franchi, 1898)

Siena - Room of St.Catherine's House at the Shrine - House.
Catherine holding the Infant Jesus in her arms as Our Lady watches.

(A.Franchi, 1898)

Siena - Room of St.Catherine's House at the Shrine - House.
Catherine recognises Jesus in the guise of a beggar to whom she gives some of her fatehr's clothes.

(A.Franchi, 1898)

Siena - Room of St.Catherine's House at the Shrine - House.
The Mystical Marriage of Jesus with Catherine on the Last Day of Carnival, 1367.

(A.Franchi, 1898)

Siena - Room of St.Catherine's House at the Shrine - House.
Jesus offers Catherine two crowns; one of gold and the other of thorns.
The Saint chooses the latter. (A.Franchi, 1898)

On the other hand, Louis was a vain worldly man and Catherine exhorted him to put away all selfish ambitions and control "every disorderly and earthly attachment, for they pass away like the wind and bring death to the soul of he who possesses them", and become a true knight of the Lord. Even though he was younger than Charles, the Sienese Virgin also reminded him of the brevity of life and the unreliability of strong youth. After having heard about a sad incident which had occurred a few days previously during a banquet in the Duke's presence, when one of the walls of the room suddenly collapsed killing some of the participants, Catherine redoubled her warnings to him about not wasting his youth in frivolous vices and urged him even more sternly to dedicate his energies to Christ and to see in the incident a divine judgement.

The young Duke was grateful for the Saint's advice and asked her to inform the Pope of his intentions. She wrote to the Pontiff: "if you are still looking for the right man to lead the Crusade, Holy Father, I have found one for you. The Duke of Anjou for the love of Jesus and out of reverence for the Holy Cross wants to commit himself totally to the arduous and holy enterprise; he is waiting upon your pleasure, most sweet Father... His Lordship wishes to discuss these things with you, so please listen to him, for God's love and grant him his heart's desire".

The young Duke's heart was filled not only with the desire to lead a Crusade, but also to see Catherine and in order to talk to her in a more tranquil atmosphere he invited her to his castle at Villeneuve, near Avignon, where the Duchess his wife was staying. The holy Virgin stayed at his home for three days and she spoke to noble couple about the necessity of renouncing wordly vanities and of the joy that the human soul has in serving God. She invited them to cleanse their consciences of their sins and to work unstintingly for the Crusade.

Catherine prayed intensely and unceasingly for the success of the Crusade. Tommaso Petro, one of the Pope's secretaries, wrote down one of the prayers she pronounced during her ecstasy on the vigil of the Feast of the Assumption. A cetain Fra Tommaso Buonconti of Pisa who also watched her on the occasion tells us that "she was so alienated from her senses and so rigid that it would have been easier to break her body than to bend it..." While speaking to the Lord in prayer she said, among other things: "I have a body which I return and offer up to you; here is my flesh and my blood; rip me apart and destroy me for the sake of those for whom I pray. If it is your will, smash every bone in my body for the sake of your Vicar on earth, the bridegroom of your bride... create a new heart for him, make him grow always in grace, make him strong so that he may hold aloft the banner of the most Holy Cross, so that even the heathens may participate with us in the fruits of the passion and blood of your only- begotten Son, the immaculate Lamb".

THE POPE'S RETURN TO ROME

In that unhappy year of 1376, the obstacles that were blocking the Pontiff's road back to Rome seemed so many and so difficult to overcome, especially the rebellion of Florence and the other Italian Republics against the Papacy.

Many ecclesiastics wanted the Pope to wait for these storms to calm down before going back to Rome, but Catherine, on the contrary, firmly believed and hoped that they would be immediately calmed by means of such a return of the Papacy to its natural residence. With the hindsight of history we may say that the facts were on her side and certainly, divine providence was at the helm guiding a floundering humanity; and Catherine was elected by God as his instrument or as an angel sent by Him to help His vicar on earth to complete the work that had to be done.

Even before leaving for Avignon, the Saint had written to the Pontiff with assurance: "Come; I tell you that those ferocious wolves will lower their heads on your lap like gentle lambs; and they shall ask for your mercy, Holy Father". And she told him the same thing once he finally decided to return to Italy.

Catherine's prayers undoubtedly helped to hasten that happy day. Cheerful and confident as always, she set out with her followers overland towards To- lone. As soon as she arrived there she was surroun- ded by an enthusiastic crowd and even the local bishop paid her a visit. A young mother of great faith who was carrying her sick child in her arms approached Catherine and aroused such pity in her that she instantly healed it. The Saint and her group then continued their long journey by sea in order to avoid similar delays, but a storm forced them to drop anchor at Saint- Tropez. They once again be- gan travelling by land and on Oct. 3rd stopped in Varazze in order to visit the home town of Cathe- rine's famous confrere Blessed Giacomo who had been Archbishop of Genova and author of the ce- lebrated book "Leggenda Aurea"; she found the city, however, devastated by the plague and she advised the citizens to build a chapel in honour of the Holy Trinity, adding a promise that their city would never again be visited by such a loathsome disease. And her promise became reality.

The Pope had begun his journey by sea on the advice of Catherine; he had already constructed a ship on the Rodan without telling anyone why and, suddenly, on September 13th left the Palace. Very few people realized what was happening at first; but all opposition was finally useless, even that of Gregory's aged father who threw himself down on the palace steps in the hope of blocking his son. Catherine's potent words were still sounding in his ears, drowning out those of his own flesh and blood just as Gregory also ignored the pleadings of all the citizens of Avignon among whom the news of this departure had quickly spread like a flash of lightening. The Pope stopped at Marseille where the Cardinals caught up with him, and after a stay of twelve days, a fleet of twenty-two ships with all of them aboard, set sail for Italy on October 2nd. A furious storm which seemed sent by the Devil himself struck them as they approached Monaco, but as God willed, on October 18th the fleet dropped anchor at Genova.

Then some new problems arose. News arrived from Rome about violent riots that were supposed to have taken place thanks to rumors noised abroad by some malcontents in Florence concerning the Pope's intentions. At this point Gregory hesitated, while his cardinals suggested, naturally, that he should go back to Avignon. But on hearing that Catherine was also in Genova he visited her secretly, by night, in order to avoid unecessary observation and comments by the local populace. He had nobody and nowhere else to turn to for help; Catherine was the only person who could advise him on what to do in his unenviable situation. She was, as usual, locked in her room, praying fervently and offering herself as a holocaust for the good of the Church. When Gregory walked in, she threw herself at his feet in total confusion. We cannot even immagine what expressions she used, literally from the bottom of her heart, begging God to give special courage to his Vicar on earth. The Pontiff felt consoled and refreshed after his meeting with Catherine and, without consulting anybody, recommenced his journey on October 29th eventually reaching Leghorn where he was welcomed by the Lord of Pisa, Piero Gambacorta. The Pope remained with his host for eight days and then set sail once again towards Piombino. He disembarked on November 25th and continued his journey by land and by December 5th was at Tarquinia in the Papal States.

Here a letter reached him from Catherine who was still in Genoa exhorting him to persevere against everyone and everything and assuring him of God's constant protection. "I tell you that the sooner you arrive at your destination, the seat of the glorious apostles Peter and Paul, the sooner God will help you to do so. Put your trust in the prayers of the true servants of God who are intereceding so much for you".

While plans were being made at Tarquinia for Gregory XI's solemn entrance into Rome, Catherine decided to stay in Genoa to comfort two of her closest disciples who had fallen gravely ill, Neri di Landoccio and especially Stefano Maconi who had been reduced to an extreme state. He was being literally devoured by an acute fever when Catherine visited him in his room with his confessor and some of her Mantellate. The saint asked him how he was doing and he jokingly replied: "Some people say that I am being sorely tried, but I don't know by what". Catherine touched his forehead and said "Listen to my little son! He has a fever that is consuming him and doesn't even know it! Come, Come, I want you to be healed: get up and begin working again with the others". And Stefano got up and cheerfully resumed his normal life.

When all was ready Catherine left Genoa for Leghorn and, after a brief stop there, went on to Pisa where she disembarked to visit her elderly mother, impatient as ever to see her daughter. She remainded at Pisa for a month and had great pleasure in seeing some old friends once again; the good Fathers of Saint Catherine, the Carthusians at Calci and many other disciples, especially the young widow, Tora Gambacorta, one of her most serious pupils in the ways of Christian perfection. From Pisa she finally arrived in Siena towards the end of December or, perhaps, the beginning of January of the following year.

Meanwhile all the preparations had been completed at Tarquinia and at Rome. Although it had degenerated into desolation and poverty because of the Pontiff's long absence, Rome managed to cloth itself in its former splendour. After leaving Ostia on January 17th 1377, the Pope sailed up the Tiber, lined by cheering crowds and reached the Basilica of Saint Paul's where he disembarked for the last time and processionally made his grand entrance into the heart of the ancient city. The clergy and the whole populace turned out to greet him, many weeping for joy; the streets were strewn with flowers and everyone took up the shout: VIVA GREGORIO! which was nearly drowned out by the ringing of all the bells: at the Porta San Paolo, the Senate reverently offered him the keys to the city.

Thus, after seventy years, the apostolic see was once again established in Rome ending what many writers have called "the Babylonian Captivity".

The pastor had returned to his flock and Catherine, in her bare little room in Siena, gave thanks to the Lord.

NICCOLÒ di TULDO

Ensconced one again in her native city, Catherine would have liked to have passed the rest of he life in silence and retirement; but, once again she was called hither and thither to bring words of peace and to pour into hearts the balm of consolation. Her voice, her affectionate looks, the sighs that issued forth from her breast, and the loving conversations she had with her God and which she shared with her listeners, simply overwhelmed even the most obstinate souls.

The greatest demonstration of her compassion towards sinners, though, was in the episode of Niccol di Tuldo. He was a fiery youth from Perugia, who was accused of having plotted with some friends against the rulers of Siena and was subsequently arrested and condemned to death.

It was in April, 1377, and a certain Father Caffarini went to see the unhappy young man, hoping to hear his confession and, instead, he found Niccol running to and fro in his cell like a madman. His desparate situation made him hurl the most horrendous blasphemies against God and the worst cursings against the priests who tried to induce him to repent of his sins before he died. Finally, Catherine was summoned to come and do what she could and in a letter to Blessed Raymond, she described how the youth met his end: "I went to visit him, of whom you have already heard, and he felt such comfort and consolation that he made his confession and disposed himself very well, making me promise, for the love of God, that at the moment of justice, I should be with him, and so I did. The next morning, before the ringing of the bell, I went to see him and for the first time in many years he received Holy Communion. His will was in total harmony and obedience to God's will, but he was still afraid to face death..." But the unlimited and efficacious goodness of God strengthened him, creating in him such a burning love and desire for God that he could not live without Him saying: "stay with me, don't leave me and I shall be well and die happy and then he laid his head upon my bosom. I also felt happy and even breathed the odour of his blood and of my own which I desire to shed for my sweet spouse Jesus".

I felt this desire growing in my soul and I also sensed his fear, as I said: Don't worry, my sweet brother, because very soon we shall arrive at the nuptials: you shall go bathed in the blood of the sweet Son of God... I shall be waiting for you at the moment of execution.

Just think, Father, how all fear was banished and sadness transformed into joy; he was almost ecstatic, exclaiming: where is all this grace coming from that I should feel such peace of soul, though death be imminent? He was so enlightened that he called the executioner's block holy and said: I shall go to it strong and happy even if the event were a thousand years hence, just knowing that you will wait for me there, and he said other things so sweet to hear about the goodness of God, that would make one weep.

I waited for him, therefore, at the place and seeing me he began to laugh and wanted me to make the sign of the cross over him and when I had done so I said: now to the wedding feast, my dear brother, for very soon you shall reach eternal life. He knelt down with great sweetness and as I fitted his head on the block, I placed my mouth next to his ear and reminded him of the blood of the Lamb. He kept repeating "Jesus" and "Catherine" and as he was speaking, I received his head into my arms, thinking all the while of God's mercy...

Catherine also added that she saw the young man's soul fly heavenward and that she envied his death. Her white habit had been sprinkled by his blood, and she said: "I hated to have had to wash away the stains".

ROCCA D'ORCIA

Catherine was always anxious to seek and delighted to find souls that had seemed lost forever and bring them back to the Lord; and after her brief stay in Siena, she accepted an invitation to visit the awesome castle at Rocca D'Orcia which was situated on an outcropping of the mountain Amiata. The castle was the seat of the great Salimbeni Family, fierce rivals of the equally powerful Tolomei Family.

Two daughters of the Salimbeni faction had recently lost their husbands during a violent skirmish and they were seriously thinking of entering the cloister. Their mother, Monna Bianchina, though deeply sympathetic towards their plight, wanted to keep them at home with herself and begged Catherine to help her accomplish this. As usual, the Saint never ignored an opportunity to exercise her considerable peacemaking prowess.

She left for the "Rocca" in the autumn of 1377 with several disciples including Blessed Raymond, Tommaso della Fonte and Bartolomeo Dominici and as usual, succeeded marvelously in re-establishing peace among the rival families. Hatred disappeared, disagreements were forgotten and promises of moral amendment were really kept. The sight alone of Catherine was enough to soften the hardest of hearts and to reawaken the desire for friendship between former enemies.

One of the worst features of life in the Sienese countryside was the existence of small private armies in the service of great families like the Salimbeni. They were really only bands of outlaws who cared nothing for religion or morality and lived by robbery, a way of life shared even by their women and children.

The coming of Catherine was like the sudden appearance of an angel. Even those people had spiritual souls that had to be saved. A great crowd swarmed around the hillside fortress to hear Catherine speak; most came because of a vague curiosity which soon became a sincere desire to listen. Never before had they heard anybody speak such moving words! Catherine's mere presence, her exhortations, her ardent prayers and humble advice entered those hardened hearts and reawakened their sense of Christian piety. The throng kept growing at an amazing rate and so thick was the press that five priests had to come to help the first three hear all the confessions.

During this period Catherine also revealed a singular talent for dealing with possessed people. The enemy of the human race thought he had found plenty of adherents in that region, but Catherine freed them all with a simple sign of the cross. One poor possessed fellow, who was so absolutely uncontrollable that not even a dozen men could hold him down, was brought up to the "Rocca" with his hands and feet in chains. They led him into the courtyard and sent for Catherine. As soon as she arrived and saw him she asked: "What has this poor man done that he should be so cruelly chained? I beg you, in the name of Jesus Christ, unchain him and do not be afraid". And then, with her eyes lifted heavenward she came beside the man as he lay on the ground like one dead. Catherine said to the onlookers: "Give him some food, don't you see that he is hungry?" The unhappy fellow managed to sit upright and looked around at the bystanders. His eyes met Catherine's eyes and she made the sign of the cross over him. Like a sweet little lamb, he ate something and joyously returned to his family.

The saint prolonged her stay at Rocca d'Orcia for another four months and in Siena the gossips prolonged their uncharitable comments about her. Some even speculated that Catherine was staying there in order to build up her own faction and lead a consipracy of nobles against the Sienese Republic. She immediately wrote a letter to the Magistrates and to some of her disciples, in which she denounced such wicked slanders attributing them to the devil himself who was trying to obtain revenge against Catherine for the loss of so many of his followers; and she added: "I came up here to save souls and I would sacrifice my life a thousand times to do so if it were necessary for their sake. The spirit of God is calling me and I follow His inspiration. And if they continue their calumnies and persecutions I shall continue my tears and prayers...

After leaving Rocca d'Orcia, Catherine went to Sant'Antimo, Montepulciano, Castiglioncello and to the Castle of Belcaro which Nanni di Ser Vanni had given to her so that she could transform it into a monastery for cloistered nuns. And everywhere she went, people came to see her and were moved to compunction for their sins. The priests who accompanied her heard confessions all day and even late into the night, absolving penitents of all their sins. It was tiring work, but they were comforted by the words of Catherine and by the wonders of God's grace.

FLORENCE

There was, however, no rest for Catherine; she
soon had to return to the field of battle for the good
of the Church. Gregory XI had returned to Rome
without difficulty; but the hostile attitude of the Florentine leaders who still refused to bow their heads
and ask for peace, was like a thorn in his heart. For
more than a year now the unhappy city had lain prostrate under the papal interdict: the churches were closed, the faithful could not receive the sacraments and
all religious ceremonies had ceased completely. The
Pope had hoped that such a draconian measure would
help him obtain the city's obedience; Catherine also
shared this hope and had written to the "Eight" announcing the Pontiff's retun to Italy: "The Pope is going
back to Rome, he is coming back tohis Bride, to the
place of Saints Peter and Paul! Run to greet him with
a humble heart!". She understood that peace was absolutely necessary. All the good fruits of the Pope's
return to Rome would be lost unless some sort of
political tranquillity was restored to the Italian city-states, especially Florence. Catherine wrote to Gregory
suggesting that he grant an audience to some of the
Florentine leaders who wanted to talk to him. He was
well aware, though, that most of the other leaders were
intensely ill-disposed towards him and unwilling to
submit to his conditions. The Florentines saw the Pope

as the destroyer of their freedom and in this they were partly right when they witnessed the unheard-of cruelties practiced by the Bretons who had previously been sent by the Pope into Italy. Catherine hoped and worked with all her strength for peace and was deeply displeased to see so much money spent on soldiers rather than on the poor; but the Pope, allowing himself to be swayed by the French Cardinals, insisted on bending the Florentines to his will by the threat of arms. Thus, for a while, both sides waged a war of nerves.

The Florentines, however, made an unbelievable mistake when, at the instigation of their leaders, they publicly violated the papal interdict. When Angelo da Ricasoli, the bishop of Florence, who had left the city upon orders from Gregory XI, was invited to return under pain of amends, he refused, paid the fines and won praise from Catherine for his constancy. The so-called Eight of War had become so powerful that on October 22, 1377 they commanded a solemn Mass to be celebrated in the Piazza Signoria by some reluctant but cowed priests. This flagrant and scandalous violation of ecclesiastical prescriptions certainly merited an exemplary punishment from the Pope; Catherine, however, still pleaded with Gregory to use mercy promising him that Florence would submit to him in the end. She never desisted interceding for the Florentines and begged the Pope to lift entirely the interdict which had been so contemptuously disobeyed.

The Saint realized, on the one hand, that the fault lay with a small group of ill-disposed persons, not with the majority of good people that groaned and suffered in respectful and religious silence under

97

the interdict; on the other hand, she saw how necessary peace was for all Italy and how the lack of it was a great hinderance to the Pope in his efforts to reform the Church and begin a Crusade. Catherine wrote to the Florentines: "Run, run to the arms of your Father. If you do so, you shall have peace, spiritually and socially, you and all Tuscany... I want you to be docile sons, not rebels, obedient subjects for the rest of your lives! My brothers, I tell you with pain and tears from my heart that you are dead! Do not think that God shall overlook the insults offered to his Bride...". She also told Gregory very frankly not to declare war, but to accept peace at any price, even if the Florentine leaders were obstinate in their disobedience.

"You must beat them with the stick of benignity, love and peace rather than with that of war. Do not look at their ignorance, the blindness and the arrogance of your sons. With peace you shall extinguish from all hearts war, rancor and division". She was always thinking of the many souls that could be lost and of the danger of inflamed hatreds, and she put all her trust in the strength of love and forgiveness which conquers all human obstacles and has greater authority than the most sophisticated weapon.

THE COSTA DI S. GIORGIO

Everybody knew that the hostilities of Florence against the Papacy were the creation of a small group of factious men that had seized the reins of power; even Blessed Raymond of Capua was well-aware of what was going on when, in 1377, he paid a visit to the influential Florentine, Niccol Soderini, a sincere admirer of Catherine, who by now placed all his trust in her wisdom and charity, considering the immense prestige she enjoyed with the populace. Catherine tried her best to convert the rebels and had summoned her closest disciple Stefano Maconi, from Siena in order to help her. He was only twenty-seven years old, but he was an accomplished speaker and he knew just what words to use in rebuking the Florentine leaders for having sent Catherine to Avignon as their ambassadress of peace, while secretly plotting against her behind her back. Some of the leaders were willing to listen to reason, but all the others remained hardened in their opposition and, Stefano, had to flee from the city when the rabble was incited by them against him.

Blessed Raymond, meanwhile had been elected prior of the Dominican house, Santa Maria sopra Minerva in Rome and he was thus able to speak face to face with Pope Gregory about these problems. In these audiences he strongly reaffirmed his great trust in Catherine and expressed his conviction that if she were allowed to go to Florence once again the problems would be quickly resolved and he also asked the Pope permission for himself and a few other friars to accompany her. The Pope, however, trusted only Catherine and denied Raymond's request. Catherine offered no resistance to the Pontiff's command; for her, his voice was the voice of God. She left Siena for Florence after having sent a letter announcing her arrival to the Minister of Justice and other officials.

Christmas was at hand, and thinking about how the Florentines, because of the interdict were still being deprived of the sacraments, she tried to arouse their desire for that heavenly food which only the Vicar of Christ could give. "Do not harden your hearts, but humble yourselves now while you still have time; for the soul that humbles itself shall always be exalted. We are not Jews or Saracens, but Christians baptised and ransomed in the blood of Christ. Arise then and run into the arms of the Father. This is the Pasch I desire to share with you". Accompanied by Stefano Maconi, Catherine arrived in Florence on December 13, 1347. She understood at once, though, that hatred had unfortunately hardened those Florentine hearts so much that there was nothing left to hope for. Everyone was too caught up in the labyrinth of political intrigues and the heat of political passions to listen to Catherine, and even the leaders of the Guelf party, who were basically favorable to some kind of reunion with the

Pope, practically ruined such a possibility by maintaining their bitter hostility towards the other parties. Then, on March 27, 1378 news reached Florence of the death of Gregory XI. Peace talks were immediately suspended until the first week in May; and Catherine was overjoyed to see the election of a new Pope, Bartholomew di Prignano, who named himself Urban VI. He was elected on April 8th and solemnly enthroned in Saint Peter's Basilica on the 18th of the same month, which was also Easter Sunday. Catherine had another reason to be happy when Silvestro de Medici, the new Minister of Justice, sent some ambassadors at the beginning of May to resume the peace talks.

In Florence itself, unfortunately, the hatreds grew and the struggles intensified. The whole populace was involved and in the midst of that unhappy confusion the most furious were the members of the Ghibelline party who continually roamed about the streets looking for and threatening to rough up members of the other parties, especially the Guelfs. Among their targets were Niccol Soderini and Ristoro Canigiani who were close and affectionate friends of Catherine; their houses were set on fire and, as if that were not enough, Catherine herself was accused of being the main cause of all the disorders. At that time Catherine was living in a small house, built for her special use by Soderini, near the foot of a slope called San Giorgio beyond the Arno and, one day as she was spending some time indoors with her disciples, a ferocious gang of miscreants broke into the house shouting "Let's grab that wicked woman and burn her intruders alive!" The frightened housekeepers allowed the intuders to enter while Catherine and her little group hid in the garden at the back of the house. The would-be murders, uttering threats of death, ran through all the rooms looking for her, when finally and quite calmly Catherine appeared in front of them, fell down on her knees, raised her head heavenwards and exclaimed "Here I am, take me and kill me. But I beg you, in the name of God, do not touch my little ones". These words, Catherine later told Blessed Raymond, were like a knife that cut right through to the heart of the would-be assassin who lost the courage even to touch her as if his hands had been tied, and he simply replied "Get away from here at once". But Catherine, who desired nothing more than martyrdom said "No, I will stay right here for I have always looked forward to this moment, to give my life for Christ".

The hired killers abruptly left the house without harming anybody, and Catherine sadly reflected "Oh miserable me! I am not worthy to be a martyr! I do not deserve to have my blood poured out for the Mystical Body of the Church!".

THE OLIVE BRANCH TO FLORENCE

As the political fighting continued along its furious way in Florence, Catherine was advised by her disciples to leave the ungrateful city; she listened to them but did not want to abandon her sincere efforts to establish peace. She agreed to spend a few days in a mountain retreat in the Florentine hinterland, near the monastery of Vallombrosa; and writing to her dearest disciple, Alessia Saracini, her sister in the Dominican Third Order, she told her to pray and to have prayers said: "Have prayers said at various monasteries. Tell our Prioress to have our daughters recite special prayers for peace, so that God may show His mercy towards us".

Catherine then wrote to the new Pontiff, whom she had already met in Avignon and, continuing her efforts to obtain peace, said in her letter: "I beg you and command you, for the love of of Christ Crucified, to mercifully welcome back the sheep that have strayed from the flock (because of my own sins); this is the only way to soften their hardness of heart, with a show a gentleness and holiness". And foreseeing the Pope's main difficulty, their incredible stubbornness, added: "If they do not ask for peace, may your Holiness grant it anyway. Doubt not that afterwards they will become your best children".

Urban received this letter while he was at Tivoli with four of his Italian Cardinals. He realized that there was not a moment to lose; in fact, he had had a vague presentment, which rapidly became a terrible certainty, that the French Cardinals were planning to desert him. Of the sixteen Cardinals who had participated in the recent conclave, four were Italian, only one was Spanish and all the others were French. Catherine understood the danger and quickly tried to eliminate it. To Cardinal De Luna, who shortly afterwards betrayed Urban, she wrote a letter informing him that she had advised the Pope not to waste time: "Do not delay in applying a remedy, for the boulder is about to fall on somebody's head".

She had heard about the disagreements that had arisen among the French Cardinals during the summer of that year; "all of which, she said, is an intolerable sorrow for me, because of my fear of heresy (she was really referring to the threatened schism), which undoubtedly will take place thanks to my sins": She also wrote to the pontiff, once again urging him to act quickly to reform the garden of Holy Church, "with good and virtuous plants" and to create "a company of good Cardinals who will work not to increase their personal greatness but as true pastors," who will lead their sheep, who will be "pillars" of strength, who will help the Pope in his "weighty affairs".

The schism, however, was by now inevitable and, if it occurred while Florence and its allies were still in enmity with the papacy, would cause unimaginable harm to all Italy. This was the main reason for which Catherine worked so tirelessly for peace at any price between the Pope and Florence. The supreme interests of the Church and of Italy were at stake and Catherine had the merit of having understood it all. And she also understood the lack of sincerety and false zeal of the French Cardinals who whispered words of revenge in the Pope's ear against Florence and her Tuscan allies under the pretext of defending the honour of the Catholic Church.

Catherine's pleadings finally prevailed upon the Pontiff. On July 18th his messenger entered Florence bearing the traditional olive branch and the entire city rejoiced. Catherine, who was present, thanked the Lord in her heart and wishing the same joy for her fellow citizens of Siena, wrote to Sano di Maco and her other disciples; "The dead sons have been resurrected, the blind see, the dumb speak, crying out in a loud voice: Peace, peace, peace! Now he is called the sweet holy lamb, Christ on earth, who before was called heretic and Patarin... The olive branch arrived Saturday evening ... and I am sending one to you also". Thus she concluded the letter with some actual leaves of olive for the comfort of her followers.

On July 28 the real peace talks began; the Florentines accepted the Pope's conditions and the interdict was lifted. Catherine left for Siena; all the insults, the hardships and treacheries she had had to endure were forgotten; she was simply glad that peace had returned.

THE DIALOGUE

With a heart full of consolation, Catherine returned to her little cell in Siena for a few months of tranquillity, during which her ecstasies became more frequent and more prolonged. She would remain quite insensible during these mystical experiences while her tongue was the only part of the body she could freely move; and it must have been a truly remarkable occasion for any onlookers to see and hear her as she conversed with her Divine spouse, sometimes cheerfully, sometimes weeping.

"O love, o love," she would cry out, "you are the sweetest thing there is, you allow us to have a foretaste of the good and joyous things that we hope to enjoy more fully without ever being satiated in eternal life. O everlasting beauty, hidden so long from the world! O eternal love, grant me the consolation to see all hearts forced open by the strength of your love! I want to enlighten my beloved children: Lord, tear down the wall that divides you from them, so that they may love you totally!".

Catherine's words were addressed now to the Eternal Father, now to the Word Incarnate and she even seemed to change colour: sometimes her face became as white as snow, other times as red as fire; and whoever saw her in these moments felt tears of devotion come to their eyes. Catherine was usually helped by four secretaries: Neri di Landoccio, Barduccio Canigiani, Stefano Maconi and Cristoforo di Gano, all of whom gathered from her own lips such treasures of priceless teachings which, put together, formed an entire book commonly called The Dialogue.

It was completed on October 13, 1378, only three months after it was begun. It is usually thought that Catherine, while in ectasy with her eyes fixed heavenwards, dictated the greater part of it in a small chapel of the hermitage near Siena where she often went. Another famous local worthy and great servant of God, a certain Brother Santi, lived there; and Father Tommaso Caffarini declared solemnly that more than once he saw the holy Sienese virgin utterly absorbed in God while her disciples wrote down her words.

This exquisite book is the ripe fruit of a soul who continually lived in the presence of God and, with good reason, called "The Dialogue", because it is essentially the faithful record of a prolonged conversation in an ecstasy of love between Catherine and God, which explores the depths of Christian spirituality. The work has had, however, various titles such as "Treatise of Divine Providence", "Book of Divine Doctrine", and "Book of Divine Revelation" and it has the following basic structure: a prologue consisting of eight chapters and four longer sections or treatises; on Discretion, on Prayer, on Providence and on Obedience. The longest is the one, on

Prayer, which contains the splendid sub-section "Treatise of Tears".

This book, no less than Catherine's letters is "a monument of wisdom". And it is remarkable how, without any formal schooling, an illiterate young woman, unlike so many grave divines of her time, was able to scale the heights of mysticism and move and breathe in such a rarefied spiritual atmosphere for so many years while immersed at the same time in so many worldly affairs. Pope Pius II was right when he said that Catherine's doctrine was not acquired but infused directly by God, because only He could have given the Sienese virgin such a high and perfect knowledge of His divine perfections, of the sublime excellence of the virtues and of the most efficacious way of arriving at a perfect love of God in this life.

This marvellous book, with her letters, has won for Catherine a secure place among the Doctors of mysticism and among the most eminent Masters of Christian perfection. Her words are not of men, but of God; no other teaching could ever be found in her, save that which springs directly from the fountainhead of divine revelation, for Catherine could neither see nor relate anything which she had not seen with her own limpid gaze in that immense sea of light to which God had raised her.

Thus was she made worthy to become the incomparable guide and outstanding mother of souls with her writings, by means of which she still prolongs the mission that God entrusted to her for the advantage of the whole church.

THE EUCHARIST

All the spiritual vigour that characterized St. Cat
herine came to her from that perennial centre of
light and life, the most holy Eucharist. This heavenly bread was, literally, her life, for all her early
biographers fully agree that it sustained her spiritually and materially; and it must be truly said that her
entire earthly life was one great eucharistic miracle.
"By the power of the Holy Eucharist, wrote Cornelius a Lapide, she became an angelical virgin in such
wise as to be called the wonder of the ages". For
many years, from the first day of Lent to the feast
of the Ascension, the Divine Sacrament was her only
food: it was quite sufficient to satisfy her, and when
because of illness or other serious reasons she could
not receive it, she felt such an intense hunger for
it, that she begged her confessor with tears in her
eyes: "Father, I am hungry; for the love of God
give food to my soul".

In order to satisfy the desire she had to receive
the celestial bread every day, Pope Gregory XI granted her the priviledge of using a small portable altar
which is still preserved today among her other relics
in the Church of San Dominico in Siena. The priests
who accompanied Catherine on her journeys celebrated Mass early in the morning wherever she hap-

pened to be lodging and, after havng received Holy Communion, she would remain immobile for many hours and her heart would beat so strongly that everyone heard it.

Wondrous things occurred during these Holy Communions. While it was still in the hands of the priest, the Sacred Host would move by itself and, sometimes, abruptly fly from them and place itself on Catherine's tongue. She often saw, as she solemnly declared, Jesus himself in the form of a small boy in the Host; the altar appeared to her gaze as though it were surrounded by angels and at times it seemed to be enveloped by flames as the burning bush did to Moses. At these moments the visage of the Senese virgin was transfigured: whoever saw her thought she was a seraphim. Indeed angels themselves sometimes brought Catherine Holy Communion even when no priest was present, bearing the sacred species on a white cloth; and she used to reveal to others that sometimes, for several days, the taste of blood stayed in her mouth.

An interesting episode took place in Lucca in 1375. A certan priest who didn't believe all the extraordinary things that people told him about Catherine decided to put her to the test by means of a gross imposture. She was in bed, unwell; and the said priest came to visit and asked if she wished to receive Holy Communion. Catherine accepted the offer most willingly; so the priest returned to his Church, took a small pyx, placed an unconsecrated host in it, and then with a great show of candles, songs and a procession of people carried it back to the house where Catherine was staying. As he entered the room, he noticed that while everyone else fell to their knees, she did not make any outward sign of reverence, but seemed rather disturbed and even angry.

The priest was on the point of scolding her as a woman of little faith; but she, inflamed with holy zeal, rebuked him for having tried to sacrilegiously trick her with common bread. The unworthy priest left, humiliated and derided by all; and Catherine was consoled by a vision of angels who miraculously gave her a real Holy Communion.

In the dialogue and the letters, the holy virgin says many beautiful things about the Most Holy Sacrament; in fact one could put together an entire treatise on the Eucharist from the various passages in which she speaks about it. St. Paul and St. Thomas Aquinas are her obvious masters in these matters and she even conversed with these two saints about it in her visions.

The devotion to Jesus in The Blessed Sacrament was one that transported Catherine to Jesus Crucified of whom she was a living image. That which she said about another person in particular was indeed applicable to her: that is, she had chosen as her dwelling place the wounded side of Jesus Christ, finding there in His pierced Heart the source of her love for God and other people.

The Sienese virgin was one of the first saints to whom it pleased Jesus to reveal the secrets of His divine Heart. The feet of Christ, nailed to the cross, were for Catherine the first rung of the ladder that led to His side where He manifested the secrets of His Heart. In a letter to her disciples she exhorts them thus: "With feet of love we must climb up to the love of Jesus Crucified. In His side inflamed with love He shows us the secrets of His Heart ... Truly, He is the fountain of living water and with great sweetness of love invites us...".

There are several splendid pages in her writings about the necessary dispositions for receiving the benefits of the heavenly food and, in particular, on the necessary purity of the ministers of God for celebrating the holy sacrifice. "The very angels, she says, should purify themselves for such a mystery, if it were possible that their nature could be so purified". For this reason Catherine wanted deep reverence to be shown to the ministers of God, even if they were unworthy of it, and rebuked everyone who did not give all due respect to their priestly dignity. To the rulers of Florence, who had rebelled against the common Father of all the faithful she tries to explain how hurtful it was for them "to deprive themselves of that dilection for which the Divine Son gives himself as food and calls us to a covenant of peace. Whoever does not obey Christ in this world cannot participate in the benefits of the blood of the Son of God, for He holds the key to that blood, and God has decided to grant us this blood only through His hands". We owe, therefore, immense respect to Pastors and Priests "because even if they were to act like devils incarnate, we owe it not simply for what they in fact are, but

112

out of obedience to Christ whose blood they administer".

Daily communion in those days was very unusual; and some people dared to reprove Catherine because she received the Holy Eucharist every day, quoting St. Augustine who neither praised nor criticized such a practice. To which she replied, "if St. Augustine does not disapprove of it, why sir, do you? While you ally yourselves to him, he opposes you".

She ceaselessly counseled everybody to keep their hearts pure in order to receive more abundantly the grace of the Blessed Sacrament; but the simple excuse of being unworthy in a very general sense was not, according to her way of thinking a good enough reason for abstaining from the Eucharist. To the famous painter Andrea Vanni who was also her disciple, she once wrote that Holy Communion must never be neglected neither by the devout nor by sinners under the pretext of unworthiness. "If a sinner is not well-disposed, he must become so; if one is a pious Christian, he must not abstain out of humility saying: "I am not worthy of such a great gift: only when I am ready shall I receive it. One must never act thus, one must never think that one can become really worthy; and if one were to become worthy, he would still remain unworthy, cloaking pride with humility"". Speaking again on the same subject, Catherine once cried out: "Oh foolish humility! And does He not see that you are unworthy? Do not delay, for you shall be no worthier of it at the end than at the beginning;

notwithstanding all our efforts, we shall never be worthy of it".

So Catherine, who nourished herself totally on this celestial food, who sought to attract her spiritual children towards it, who was the pioneer of all the future eucharistic awakenings, showed herself to be a true daughter of St. Dominic, who was himself one of the greatest lovers of the Holy Eucharist and who always celebrated Mass with tears streaming down his face; and a true sister of St. Thomas Aquinas, who was the great theologian and poet of the Divine Sacrament and merited the title of "The Eucharistic Doctor".

THE DISCIPLES

Many people were attracted to a life of more intimate union with God thanks to Catherine; not only the other tertiaries and pious women generally, but also men of various ages and conditions, were influenced by her words, examples and writings. Most of them were children of the times; some came from illustrious families, passionate lovers of the things of this world who were saved by Catherine just at the edge of abyss in which they were about to fall. With her help their hearts became gradually inflamed with love for spiritual things and, under her patient and loving tutelage, they progressed greatly in the ways of virtue and, quite a few, entered the religious life. They repaid her efforts with deep affection and close tenderness, sanctified and elevated by grace even though, in many cases, such attachments began as merely a vague liking for Catherine due to her moral superiority.

In this way she was able to wield a very special maternity with all the instincts and tenderness of a real mother. All these generous children which she called dearest ones in Christ accompanied Catherine on all her journeys and shared all her hardships; and they loved being with her. She encouraged them to travel along the ardous ways of sacrifice and exercised such a sweet dominion over them as very few saints have done with their followers in the history of the Church.

They could not help loving Christ Crucified in Catherine for she was a living image of Him. For the whole of her brief life, while she was literally tormented and consumed by the love of God, she also felt deeply for them according to the words of St. Paul: "Every day I labour to give birth in the presence of God": She wanted all her sons and daughters to be intimately united to God with words of love; and like a mother-eagle that almost forces her young to learn how to fly, Catherine incited them to renounce the things of this world and dedicate themselves to God. In fact, her efforts were so successful, that the love of God triumphed over all else in their hearts and they realized that they had been born anew. Society mocked them and nicknamed them "Catherinites"; but they could not have cared less.

These bright young people soon became ready to act as Catherine's closest collaborators in the new task for which God had destined her and His earthly vicar. Some of them, particularly Stefano Maconi, had already rendered important services to her, and she had always found in them an incomparable docility; but now their assistance was going to be required as never before and their childlike devotion to her, whom they called "mama", was going to be tested in the crucible.

Little more than a year of life remained to Catherine and it was a year of intense hard work for the good of a troubled, uncertain Church and an

Italy threatened by new unsuspected dangers; it was also, for Catherine, a year of indescribable sorrows. It must have been a profoundly moving and remarkable sight: Catherine at work, surrounded by a brave band of gallant youths who, under her generalship, with true religious spirit, were dedicating themselves like armoured knights, for the triumph of the cause that lay closest to her heart, the welfare of the Church and the defense of the Vicar of Christ.

The young people of our own day who declare themselves able and willing to do the same work for the Church and the Supreme Pontiff, even if it costs blood, sweat and tears, will never find a better and more inspiring "General".

ROME

The Pope who succeeded Gregory XI, Urban VI, ex-Archbishop of Bari, was a man of austere virtue, animated by a lively desire to reform the decadent moral life of the clergy. Catherine was not unknown to him and he was fully aware of how unstintingly she had helped his predecessor in his difficult moments, almost injecting her own energy into his own veins.

He was so desirious of having her near him that he sent Blessed Raymond to persuade her to come to Rome. Catherine replied that she was willing to come, but wanted Raymond to bring a written request to that effect from the Pope in order to avoid the usual "gossip"; meanwhile she prepared for departure.

Catherine saw quite clearly that, once again, she had been chosen to enter the field and participate in a fierce struggle; and writing to Urban in humbly accepting accepting his invitation, she told him: "I wish that I was already in the midst of battle, suffering and fighting for you even unto death". In another letter, written to her dear spiritual daughter, Sister Danielle who had received the Dominican habit at Orvieto, she said: "The time for weeping is at hand. Cease not to pray for the Vicar of Christ, that he may be granted light and strength to resist the blows of the incarnate demons, lovers only of themselves, who want to contaminate our Faith".

Catherine was right in shedding tears for the new calamity that had struck the Church. Those same Cardinals who had elected the Pontiff and had rendered him the usual official homage and had asked him special favours, were now rebelling against him when they saw that he was in deadly earnest about uprooting vices and weeding out abuses in the Church. "As soon as he bagan to irk them, wrote the Saint, they immediately lifted up their heads". They met together at Tondi on September 18th, 1378 and, with the full support of the local nobleman Count Gaetani, elected as anti-Pope Cardinal Robert of Genevra, who took the name Clement VII. He was the same man who as commander of the Bretons sent into Italy a few years back against Catherine's advice, had devastated the region of Romagna and allowed his soldiers to commit horrific massacres, especially during the siege of Cesena.

There was never any doubt about the legitimacy of Urban's election. On Easter Sunday, which fell on April 18th that year, of the twenty-three Cardinals who made up the Sacred College, sixteen had performed the formal act of obedience in St. Peter's in Rome; the other six who had remained in Avignon shortly afterwards did likewise and even raised the papal banner high above the walls of the castle. So the election of the anti-Pope was open rebellion, totally unjustified.

119

Catherine, once again, had her work cut out for her; and trusting fully in God, left her beloved Siena towards the middle of November, intuiting perhaps that she would never return, and arrived in Rome on the twenty-eighth of the same month. Various other Mantellate went with her, Alessia Saracini, Francesca Gori, Lisa Colombini and Giovanna di Capo; some priests, the Dominican Bartolomeo Dominici, the hermit Fra Santi, the Augustinian Giovanni Tantucci; and three young men who acted as her secretaries, Barduccio Canigiani, Neri di Landoccio and Gabriel Piccolomini. After having stayed in a few different places here and there in the city, they finally took a house in Via del Papa, known today as Via Santa Chiara, that belonged to a certain Paola del Ferro. This house was used quite often as a sort of hotel by Sienese pilgrims.

Catherine did not waste a minute in presenting herself to the Pope, who received her with great joy and deep respect in the company of several Cardinals and, after having heard her speak, exclaimed: "It is not this woman who speaks, but the Holy Spirit who speaks through her". And while they were all thinking of their own fates because of the worsening of the schism, they exclaimed: "This little lady confounds us! We are afraid and she is fearless".

In fact, the rebels had seized the Castle of Saint Angelo and the Pope was considering abandoning the Vatican and withdrawing to Santa Maria in Trastevere. The political intrigues, the misunderstanding and, above all, the wicked operations of Urban's enemies, had gained for the anti-pope the explicit support of almost the whole of France, the Savoy and some of the Piemonte and Naples, which was split into two factions, one in favour of and the other against the legitimate Pope, including the Queen, Giovanna who bitterly opposed Urban.

Thus, Catherine was perfectly right when she previously insisted on peace at any price between the Papacy and Florence back in the days of Gregory XI. The powerful position that Florence had obtained, the alliance she had with Milan, the wide influence she wielded over all Italy, expecially in Tuscany, all contributed to the fact that if, at the beginning of the schism, Florence were to actively assist the anti-pope, the whole of Italy would be plunged into a deplorable betrayal.

Catherine, therfore, was the intrument chosen by God to keep her country from religious and political ruin.

THE PRAYER CRUSADE

The Great Schism caused Catherine such piercing sorrow that the mere thought of it was enough to break her heart. She had always feared such an event and had written: "Any other evil, compared to this one, is like straw or a shadow: just thinking about it makes one tremble!". This is why, in accepting the Pope's call to come to Rome, she threw herself heart and soul into the struggle showing a contagious energy that touched Urban himself. "Come now, be fearless, she told him, participate in this battle!".

Certainly, the greatest weapon she possessed was her humble and fervent prayer, to which she added mortifications and vigils, reducing herself in the process to extreme bodily weakness. But if the flesh was weak, the spirit was ready and vigorous. Catherine was in constant agony. "Sometimes, the pain is simply too much for me to bear... Normal sweat is not enough to satisfy the holy and ardent desire I feel ...I want to sweat blood!".

The letters and prayers that poured forth from Catherine's lips during this last period of her life are full of such ideas. She dictated them standing upright, with a loud voice and often in ecstasy, especially after Holy Communion. She would burst forth in acts of thanksgiving and love, expressing her desire that all hearts might be filled with the fire of love. The Sienese virgin prayed for the Church, asking God to free Her from the hands of the devil, and to grant Her strength and victory against all enemies; and she prayed for the Supreme Pontiff asking God to give him a manly heart. "I will never cease, she told her God, knocking at the door of your mercy my beloved, until you exalt him, until you make him burn with bold desire, so that with benignity, charity, purity and wisdom he may proceed in all his acts, and drag the whole world to himself". She prayed for the Cardinals, that instead of becoming superfluous and sterile branches in the Church, they might produce fruit with the examples of their own virtuous lives; and even for her adversaries, she prayed that their hardness of heart might be softened and she offered herself as a victim-soul saying: "Punish their sins in me. Behold my body, let it become the anvil for them, so that their sins may be expiated". And with singular affection, Catherine addressed the Blessed Virgin Mary, "temple of the Trinity, bearer of fire and of mercy, producer of fruit, giver of peace, fructiferous soil from which we receive the fragrant flower of the only-begotton Word of God, chariot of fire that brought to us the fire which was hidden under the ashes of His humanity". To Our Lady, she entrusted the sweet bride of her most sweet Son, and His Vicar on earth and His entire people. Catherine also prayed, especially, for her own spiritual children, that they might become "inflamed coals, burning with love for God and neighbour".

This was the crusade proclaimed by Catherine for the benefit of the Church at that terrible moment. During Lent of that 1379, she practised the Way of the Stations. According to an ancient custom, beginning on Ash Wednesday, the pious faithful in Rome would every day visit various fixed churches that were famous for their relics of martyrs in order to obtain the Holy Indugences. In that year Catherine tried to gather all her followers and bring them with her on these visits for the edification of everybody, thus invigourating more and more the powers of her soul with the remembrance of those champions of the faith. Tired and pained as she was, Catherine never complained while she made her daily rounds, leaning for support, more often than not, on the arm of her dear Barduccio and raising her eyes to heaven. She even visited the Vatican Basilica everyday; and, near the Confession of St. Peter she would remain for hours, often in ecstasy. "When it is the third hour (mid-morning, we should say) she wrote to Blessed Raymond, and I get up from the table, you will see a corpse walking towards St. Peter's, and there I shall stay until the hour of vespers". She prayed to the great Apostle asking him to defend his successor against the powers of hell.

Catherine requested prayers from those who were far away: she remembered, above all, her dear Company of the Virgin, located in Siena, which was a centre of religious fevour. Many of her disciples who had remained behind gathered together there and, in her absence, called themselves "the lost sheep". This pious society supported the real Pope, and the zeal with which they did so rapidly extended to the entire city. When the anti- pope's ambassador, Alderigo Albertinelli, announced his arrival, the whole populace responded that it was ready to stone him to death in the streets if he dared enter the city; so he decided not to make his visit. Catherine herself seemed to be working in those fervent disciples, encouraging and stimulating them to remain solid in their obedience to the Vicar of Christ.

To everyone she addressed her message of prayer, to those near, to those distant, to religious and to laypeople. "Cease not to pray for Holy Church", she urged her sons and daughters in Siena, "and for our Lord Pope Urban VI, for it is most necessary to do so... By means of the prayers and the loving anxious desires of his servants, God will grant mercy to the world. Sons and daughters, tell everybody that now is the time to weep to pray and to sigh for the sweet bride of Christ and for the entire Christian people so heavily afflicted by its own sins".

It is simply astonishing to see how many hardships Catherine took upon herself, adding them to all her prayers and pains of expiation. In these last months of her life, she rose above all her contemporaries and, rather than acting in a mild-mannered way, dominated them. She thought out a defense plan that consisted in two great actions: to sustain with all her strength the legitimate election of Urban VI, and maintain in total union with him all the dispersed members of the Church, including Italy. History attests that this humble woman made the most valid contribution to the worthy cause at that moment.

What we must really admire in her is not the daughter of the dyer of Fontebranda, but a miracle of God. The Pope was not deceiving himself when he said that in Catherine he had found "a divine help".

FOR THE UNITY OF THE CHURCH

The powerful love that Catherine had for the Church of Jesus Christ made her consider any attack against its unity as a great crime and a true work of diabolical perfidiousness. Whoever separated himself from this unity was for Catherine a putrid member, excluded from participating in the Blood, deprived of the divine lymph that flows in every part of the mystical body of Christ. Thus she approved of any means available in order to spare the Church from such a disaster, even if it meant giving her own life. This was a holy and noble desire on Catherine's part against all those degenerate sons of the Church, who with their petty ambitions and cowardly fears were trying to break the bonds that bound them to the Common Father.

Together with her prayers and penances, Catherine made immense efforts to win over many secular rulers to the cause of Urban VI. She turned to the King of Hungary and Poland, Louis the Great, telling him to make peace with Venice, and to obey Pope Urban who had also asked him for assistance, "because those who should have been the pillars and defenders of the holy faith have abandoned it and become blind and leaders of the blind". The King, who knew their lies, ought to always protect the

Holy Church against heretics and false Christians. "And will you sit back and allow the anti-Christ, a follower of the devil, and a certain female (the Queen of Naples n.d.t.) to touch our faith in order only to ruin it and throw it into darkness and confusion? Have pity on our Father, Pope Urban VI. Truly, he should seek comfort in God alone and place all faith and hope in Him. But he also hopes that God will persuade you to share this burden for His honour and the good of the Holy Church".

To Charles of Durazzo, called Charles of the Peace, Catherine sent a letter by means of Martin of Taranto, one of the Pope's chamberlains, asking him for help against the rebels, who "having renounced their sonship, had become slaves of the devil, of the world and of the flesh. Be a valiant knight: after having won the interior battle in your soul, take part in the external battle and, as a pillar of the Church, come to her assistance. How shameful and unpleasant in the sight of God to see so much coldness in the hearts of the lords of this world who have only words to offer to this most sweet Bride".

Catherine probably wrote a letter to Richard II, King of England, which unfortunately has been lost. In order to keep the English under obedience to Urban and convince them to use their influence on the other nations of Europe, she sought the services of William Flete, the celebrated English hermit who did continue to work for the noble cause even after the death of Catherine.

To the King of France, Charles V of Anjou, who had allowed himself to be dragged to the side of the anti-pope, she wrote: "I am rather surprised that a Catholic man who wants to be brave and God-fearing should permit himself to be led astray like a small boy and not notice the ruin he is causing for himself and others". And if he still had any doubts, he ought to consult the doctors at the Sorbonne. "You have the fountain of all knowledge there", she told him; and, in fact, the famous University had declared itself in favour of Urban, but then changed its opinion because of political intrigues.

In order to keep Italy in Urban's camp, Catherine spoke to all those who had some authority in the major Italian cities, admonishing them to provide for the defence of the Church and the good of the nation. Florence, which had resumed friendly relations with the Pope, now energetically sustained him. And Catherine, who had suffered and worked so much to obtain that peace, wrote to the Gonfalniere of Justice and the Priors of the Arts telling them to quickly eliminate the seeds of discord from their city because, "nothing weakens states so much as internal divisions. Urban VI, true High Pontiff and Vicar of Christ on earth, has forgiven you with great charity, treating you as though you had never even offended him. Be grateful and respectful! because gratitude is that virtue which nurtures piety and it invites God Himself to increase and multiply His graces".

She repeated the same message to the Rectors of Perugia. "If we do not help our father, we shall be in great danger, because we shall place ourselves outside the fortress and become weak. The arm of the Holy Church has not been broken: and from its momentary atrophy it will be strengthened as well as all those who trust in it. God will be wrathful and will punish us if we do not assist our Pope Urban VI and our faith... Forgive me, but the necessities of the Holy Church and your own salvation force me to speak thus".

And she thought particularly of her own Siena. To it she sent the very learned Augustinian Cardinal, Bonaventure Baduario of Padua, who preached in the Cathedral on Pope Urban's legitimacy; and, later on, she even urged her fellow- Sienese to send not only money but arms to help the Pontiff. If anyone refused to lend a hand because of the personal failings of Urban, she said: "He is really a good, virtuous, God-fearing man who acts with right and holy intentions as nobody else has done for a long time in the Church of God; and anyway, whether or not he is a good or a bad man, reverence is owed to him not only for what he is in himself but for the blood of Christ and for the dignity and authority of God who has given him to us. This authority and dignity is not diminished for any defect he may have, nor does his ministry lose any of its power; our reverence and obedience towards him must never diminish".

Venice remained in union with the Pontiff thanks to Catherine, who, writing to the Bishop, Angelo Corario, later Pope Gregory XII, wanted him to openly declare for Pope Urban VI, and wanted the city of lagoons to resist the pressures of the anti-pope and his representatives: "Be the master of this city and bravely proclaim the truth about Pope Urban VI the true High Pontiff; and do your best to keep all the citizens in the faith, reverence and obedience they owe to the Holy Church and to His Holiness".

Catherine also looked for help among professional soldiers such as Count Alberigo of Belbiano, head of the famous Company of St. George, consisting of four-thousand infantry and four-thousand cavalry. She exhorted him to fight for Urban's cause while regreting the sad fact that she could do nothing but pray. "We shall do what Moses did; when the people fought Moses prayed, and while he was praying, the people won". The great Captain, in fact, came to Rome, defeated the forces of the anti-pope and, on April 29, captured the Castle of Sant'Angelo which they had been holding; the rulers of Rome offered Alberigo the keys to the Castle and, thanks to his victory, the Pope was able to leave Santa Maria in Trastevere and return safely to St. Peter's. The Pope never thought to make such a triumphant re-entry; he went barefoot, as in a penitential procession and was praised by Catherine who, writing to the seven Councillors of Rome and urging them to be grateful to God, said: "The example has been given by our Father, Pope Urban VI with which he thanks God for His graces, humbling himself and performing what has not been done for a very long time, going on procession barefoot. As sons and daughters, let us follow the tracks of our Father and thank God for His graces".

Catherine wanted them to also thank the military Company which had done so much to help them; and with a mother's heart, she thought of the "poor wounded" left over after the battle and sought help for them in all their needs. She also wanted the Romans to be grateful to the Keeper of the Castle, John Cenci, who with care and loyalty, a pure heart and great prudence assisted them in liberating the imposing fortress.

Writing about it all to Urban himself, she expressed her joy thus: "I am happy, holy Father, and my heart is uplifted, for my eyes have seen the will of God accomplished in you.., namely in that humble action, not performed in ages, of the holy procession. Oh, how pleasing it must have been to God". Catherine thanked the Virgin Mary and the glorious Apostle Peter, to whom she was deeply devoted. "I rejoice in this sweetest Mother, Mary and in Peter, prince of the Apostles, who have restored you to your place...".

And even if the hateful schism did not end immediately because of the obstinacy of the anti-papal party, the efforts of this humble woman to save the church from total destruction will always arouse admiration. She was also the perfect instrument of God to keep her own nation, Italy, faithful to the true succesor of Peter at the moment in which its defection from the Church seemed inevitable.

AGAINST THE ARMIES OF THE EVIL ONE

It is difficult to summarize, even briefly, the many phases of the struggle carried on by Catherine in Rome in 1379 and during the first months of 1380, by the side of the Pontiff against those who, denying the legitimacy of his election and trying to drag along to their party all of Christendom, appeared to her eyes as "the armies of the evil one against Christ on earth". If history had not left us a most faithful record of it all and if the most reliable witnesses had not testified to the absolute truth of the facts, it would be unbelievable that such a humble woman should had dared and obtained so much. It must have been amazing to see her, exhausted and consumed by tears and by the sorrow she carried in her heart. Her life seemed to hang on the thinnest of threads, but under that tenuous thread lay hidden the soul of a giantess, who fought with indomitable courage as long as God sustained her, refused to listen to voice of human prudence, did not surrender in front of difficulties, and did not mitigate the vigour of her zeal; a true victim of love who defended at all costs the violated honour of her Groom, whose real living image she saw in the Roman Pontiff. The letters through which up to that moment she had carried on her singular apostolate and in which she tried to inflame other hearts with the fire of divine love, by destroying the roots of hate and discord, became more than ever before mighty weapons, fiery arrows against all kinds of enemies to awaken their conscience and induce them to change their ways. Francesco Malavolti, one of her secretaries in Rome, has described Catherine's method of dictating. Very often she would have three secretaries simultaneously at her disposal and she would begin speaking without interruption on various topics, addressing her words now to one, now to another, smoothly directing the verbal flow and flawlessly picking up an argument exactly where she had previously left off. She would fix her gaze heavenwards, fold her arms, hide her face in her hands and her speech was sometimes punctured by groans and weeping.

The well-known and ferocious letter that Catherine wrote to the three Italian Cardinals, Pietro Corsini of Florence, Giacomo Orsini of Rome and Simon Borzan of Milan who, after having elected and supported Urban vilely abandoned him, belongs to the first months of 1379. "You wish to persuade us that you elected Urban out of fear! Whoever says this lies in his throat! I am not obliged to speak to you with respect, because you do not deserve any respect!" She calls them "blind and stupid" and tries to make them reflect on the dastardliness into which they had fallen by separating themselves from the head of the body. They are no longer flowers that emanate pleasant odours, lights shining brightly from on high, angels who fight for us against the hellish enemy, but exactly the opposite. They have become cruel children towards the mother who has nourished them at her breast and have deserved a thousand deaths.

She regrets the fact that they are not there in front of her, because if they were, whe would "sting them with her living voice". And, in Catherine's opinion, being Italians, their fault was even more serious. "Humanly speaking, Christ on earth is an Italian, and you are Italians and yet you have no love for your country like the ultramontanes". If she could not thus rebuke foreigners, she could assurredly rebuke those three for being traitors to their own country. She ends the letter with a hope for their conversion and expresses the desire to see them "bathed in the blood of the lamb shed for us with fiery love and restored to the bosom of the Father".

No less severe were the reprimands which Catherine launched against Count Onorato Gaetani of Fondi who, having previously been loyal to the Church, was now playing the host to those rebellious cardinals who had elected the anti-pope in his city.

She begins by calling him "most dear Father", but then attacks him at once for having consigned himself over to the "tyrannical whim of self-love", thus changing the garden of his soul into a dark forest. "In your heart of hearts, she says, you believe that Urban VI is the one, true Pontiff. I know that God has given you enough light to see the truth: but now your own egoism has made you deny it.

For the love of God do not continue in this way! It is human to err; but it is diabolical to persist in error. Return to yourselves, for sin will not go unpunished, particularly when it is committed against the Holy Church. Leave your errors before it's too late; death comes soon and we don't even think about it and we shall find ourselves in the hands of the High Judge".

Catherine also crossed swords with one of the most corrupt women of her age: Joan, Queen of Naples. She was the daughter of the Count of Anjou, called Lackland by the Italians, nephew to Philip the Fair. Catherine had once already written to and exhorted Joan, because of her title as Queen of Jerusalem, to be a faithful servant of the Holy Church; but when the rebellion broke out against the legitimte Pope, Joan passed over to the French party and, it was said, lent a helping hand in the election of the anti-pope.

"From what they say, wrote Catherine, he was elected with the help of your arm". And she begged her "to turn back. For if you do not, you will be seen for what you really are, an unstable woman. Eliminate the poison from your soul and then my soul shall rejoice to see the fruit of your obedience, for I care deeply about your salvation. I only wish I could do more than just write words against those who plant heresy in the mystical body of the Holy Church".

Catherine would have liked to go to Naples herself and talk to the mis-informed queen, but the

Pope would not hear of it. She satisfied her desire by sending her dear disciple Neri di Landoccio to accompany the Abbot Lisolo Brancacci, chosen by the Pope, with some letters for several influential people. She even wrote another letter to the same queen, always hoping for a change of mind on her part. "I have noticed a great change in your person for which I can no longer call you mother, because you have become the slave of the devil who is the father of all lies... You are already dead spiritually and you shall be so even bodily if you do not desist".

Catherine also had a few more things to say about the anti- pope whom Joan defended, revealing the cunning and double-dealing of his electors: "Where is this right man they have elected as anti-pope? What kind of man have they really chosen? A holy man? By no means, but a wicked man, a demon, for he acts like one. The real demon tries to hide from the truth and this fellow does the same. And why did they not choose the right man? Because they knew perfectly well that the "right" man would have preferred death rather than accept their election!".

She stoutly denied the charge that her own mind was unclear and turned it against the Queen whose own passions had obscured the light of truth. And she closes, admonishing Joan once again to convert "in order to void the rod, to remember death, to give no thought to riches, status, dignity, nobility or people, for nothing and nobody will be able to save her from the Tribunal of Christ the Judge!... With heartfelt sorrow, I tell you this, for I tenderly love your salvation".

Unfortunately, the ambitious queen did not desist from her unhappy rebellion, though the Neopolitans themselves and their Archbishop kept the faith by supporting Urban VI. Joan even reached the point of trying to capture and imprison the Pontiff and slay his closest adherents, sending a certain Rinaldo of the Orsini to accomplish it all, and she invited the anti-pope to Naples offering him one of her castles. That beautiful city thus became the rock of the anti-Christ against the Roman See.

THE FAREWELL TO THE FATHER

Catherine was so occupied in protecting the interests of the Church, that she had hardly any time to think about herself; she lived only for its cause, struggling with God by means of prayers, tears, groans and with men by uprooting from their hearts pride and cupidity, the real causes of all those terrible discords.

The best proof that she did not think of herself was her willingness to be deprived of her only earthly comfort. Blessed Raymond of Capua had been her spiritual director and she was keenly aware of her need for his wise and loving support. And yet Catherine herself more than once advised him to leave her in order to better serve the interests of the Church wherever necessary. For example, in that year 1379, Raymond went to Naples to speak to Queen Joan. As we know, Catherine would have liked to have gone there, but since at that very moment St. Catherine of Sweden, daughter of St. Brigette, who was aquainted with the Queen of Naples, was in Rome, the Pontiff desired both Catherines to go together. The Swedish princess, however, had valid reason for excusing herself from such a mission and Raymond dissuaded the Pope from sending two virtuous young women to that corrupt court. When the Sienese Catherine got wind of it, she let Raymond have a piece of her mind: "If Catherine (of Alexandria n.d.t.), Margaret, Agnes and the other holy virgins had been held back by such cowardliness, they would never have won the crown of martyrdom! Do not all good virgins have a Spouse who can defend them from wicked men?" Raymond felt chagrined and, at the same time, full of admiration for the unshakable faith of this remarkable woman.

Raymond's prudent fears were, however, not totally unfounded; but Catherine's virtues were so superior to his estimates of them, that what he called prudence, she called cowardice. His caution in not wanting to see her involved with people who were accustomed to perform the most nefarious deeds and did not shrink from staining their hands with innocent blood must have seemed a bit strange to her heroic fearlessness and unquenchable thirst for martyrdom.

Since things were getting worse in Italy, thanks to the machinations of the followers of the antipope, a Crusade was necessary for the defence of the successor of Peter, especially in southern Italy, where Joan stubbornly continued to protect Clement. Catherine's rebuke was still ringing in Raymond's ears when Urban VI summoned him and told him that, as by birth he was a subject of the Queen, he should begin it by going to Naples and trying to reason with Joan. Unfortunately he was unable to bend the Queen, who tried, at first, to bend him with her charms and a large sum of money, which

Raymond indignately refused, and then, with threats upon his life. Catherine was always praying for him and he was saved.

The Pontiff, meanwhile, seeing how ardently Raymond preached the new Crusade, hoped for good results by sending him to Charles, King of France in order to convince that sovereign to stop supporting the schism. Urban officially nominated him as his legate and entrusted him with several letters for the King and other influential people. As Raymond prepared for his departure, Catherine added her own instructions, "I want you to openly preach and defend the truth against the libelous schismatics". She realized, however, the nature of the sacrifice that God was asking of him and she was certain that, having only a few more months of life on earth, the loss of such a good spiritual father, would be a very hard blow for her to accept. Raymond himself was most unhappy about being separated from her whom he called both daughter and mother at the same time: but both were used to such heroic renunciation for the good of the chruch. On December 19, 1379, Raymond sailed down the Tiber to Ostia with Catherine at his side. The pontifical galley was waiting for him there, and the sweet virgin gave her last farewell to the father of her soul who had gladly let himself be called by her "son": "my son, everything has been accomplished. You will not see me again in this life. Go and do not be afraid. The sign of the cross will protect you, but you shall not see your mother ever again in this life!". The ship was already moving as

Raymond boarded and from the stem he waved farewell for the last time to his sweet mother who was kneeling on the shore. She watched the ship until it disappeared from the horizon with her father and guide. Raymond, though, was exposing himself to terrible risks. Queen Joan's ships roved up and down the Tyrrhenian sea ruling the waves and rigidly controlling entrance to all ports, so that only by a hairsbreadth, thanks to the craftiness of the sailors, was his ship able to safely reach Genova. At this point, Raymond thought it best to prosecute his journey on land and headed for Ventimiglia; but even the overland roads were patrolled by the officers and spies of Queen Joan who set traps for the unwary and once captured one of Raymond's travelling companions. They were in some danger of death and on the advice of another of his confreres, Raymond decided to turn back. The legation to France thus came to an unexpected halt and Raymond tried to continue in Genoa his mission of defending the Church with even more zeal after having been elected shortly afterwards Provincial of the Dominicians in Lombardy and, then, Master General of the whole Order. But Catherine, with her uncontrollable enthusiasm saw only weakness in Raymond's decision to turn back even if he had run the risk of being murdered and she sent him a bittersweet reproof. "You were not fit to enter the fray! And like a little boy you have been tossed out of it. My naughty little father, how beautiful our souls might have become, if with your blood you had cemented a rock in the edifice of the Holy

Church for the love of Jesus! Let us leave behind such childish fears, and like a grown man, let us run back to the battle field ... drown yourself in the blood of Christ crucified, and bathe yourself in that blood, console yourself in it, exult in it, grow and fortify yourself in it and fly as a brave knight to seek the honour of God and the good of the Holy Church". In another letter she tells him that before his return, she will receive a wonderful grace, for she will leave this world. He instead shall remain. And she says with all honesty that he is not yet ready to give his life for Christ. Therefore, he must continue working without fear or weakness. "If you are a man in your promises, do not be womanish when the nail is hammered into you, for I would have you remember Christ crucified and Mary. Be a man, always!". Raymond never saw Catherine again, but her words and examples were, for the rest of his life, the greatest stimulus he could have wished for in his work for the good of the Church and, particularly, in his call to the whole Dominican Family, which he governed for twenty years, to return to its primitive fervour.

THE APPEAL TO THE DISCIPLES

In the struggles that Catherine gallantly undertook to keep as many people as possible faithful and obedient to the true Pope and to expose the wily schemes of the schimatics, she sought help from all her children. Like a captain who gathers his best men around him in the hour of greatest danger, so she wanted to have her disciples around her in Rome, especially her fellow Siennese who had assisted her so loyally in various other tasks. She attracted them with the love of a sister and mother; and though they were far away from her, they were always with her in their hearts and thoughts, hoping that she would not collapse under the strain of work. Catherine's three faithful secretaries were already with her in Rome along with some of her other daughters, Lisa, Alessia, Cecca and Giovanna di Capo. Stefano Maconi had to remain in Siena because of some family problems; perhaps his mother, Monna Giovanna, knowing and worrying about how impulsive and independent he was, wanted to keep him at home under her watchful eye. Among the Dominican religious, Fra Bartolomew Dominici, who had accompanied Catherine to Rome, was now back in Siena as Prior of San Domenico, and Blessed Raymond, as we have seen, had already left her forever. The invitation she sent to these dearest friends to come to Rome and fight and suffer with her are deeply moving. To Stefano especially, Catherine sent many affectionate letters; and Barduccio, who usually wrote most of these for her, privately added some of his own sentiments in them. To Stefano and to all the members of the Company of the Virgin Mary, she said with firm hope: "if you become what you must become, you will set all Italy on fire!". And even while, with jocular intimacy, she calls Stefano an "unworthly and ungrateful little son" she says to him "I want you to act like a man. The blood of many glorious martyrs buried here in Rome, who with so much fire of love gave their blood and lives for love of Life is boiling and inviting you and the others to come and fight for the glory and praise of God's name and of the Holy Church": Stefano had previously asked Catherine to obtain certain indulgences, as usual, from the Holy Father personally, for himself and some others; but for once, in order to arouse him to come, she thus replied: "About those indulgences you asked me to procure for you, let me tell you not to expect them or anything else from me, if you don't come here yourself to get them ..." She repeated the same invitation to others, including a certain Peter di Giovanni Ventura: "let me see if you really want to leave home and come here. If you do, hurry up and finish whatever you still have to do ..." Many religious belonging to various Orders, holy men all of them, had become disciples of the Saint; and, during those last months of her life, she asked them to help her with their talents. To Don Giovanni delle

Celle, a monk at Vallombrosa, she wrote: "Necessity calls us, duty impels us. Do you not see today, as never before, in the Holy Church, how necessary it is for all her children, nourished at her breast, to rise up and help her and the Father?". And she wants him "to enter the battle with a manly heart" and if need be, to give his life. "Now is the hour for all the servants of God to come forth and work". For all those who might complain about so many religious going to Rome, she has a ready answer: "you are not coming here in order to obtain prelacies, but to work; the dignity that you seek consists in sweat, tears, vigils and continual prayers!" Catherine turned to even the more strictly enclosed monks, such as the Carthusians, manifesting the Pope's desire "to have the servants of God at his side". To Don Bartholomew Serafini, prior of Gorgona, she made a special plea and sent him a list of the monks that he should send: "Do this as quickly as you can and do not waste time for the Church of God has no need of slackers. Put aside all other projects even if they are important, and order the ones whose names are on the list to come here at once. Do not hesitate, please, for the love of God; come and work in this garden!". So the good Father Serafini did as Catherine wished bringing other confreres with him. Other people summoned by Catherine were the Dominican fra Leonardo of Monteplciano and the three hermits of Monte Luca near Spoleto, fra Andrea of Lucca, Fra Naldo and Fra Lando. Here is how the Saint invited these three to leave their hemitage: "Stick your heads

146

out and come and fight for the truth. You must not retire for any reason, neither for the hardships you might have to face nor for hunger, thirst, death or the desire to live quietly". Using the example of a dog that barks to wake up its master, she added: "For the infinite goodness and mercy of God has provided for the needs of the Holy Church by giving her a good and upright pastor, who wants to have around himself these dogs that bark for the love of God continuously, that are wide-awake and watchful, so that they may wake others ... I beg you and order you to come here immediately and accomplish the will of God and of the Vicar of Christ, who gently calls you and the others". Even Andrea of Lucca, old and feeble as he was, exposed himself to the hazards of the journey and went to Rome. Catherine also sent urgent appeals to the Augustinian hermits of Lecceto. In that holy monastery, about three miles from Siena, there was among the other monks under the direction of the Master Giovanni Fantucci, an Englishman named William Flete, nicknamed the Bachelor, to whom the Saint wrote many letters. Flete lived in a cave deep in the nearby woods during the daylight hours and returned to the monastery in the evenings. Catherine had sometimes gone to visit him there and now she would have liked him to come to Rome; but Flete absolutely refused to leave his tranquil oasis. She judged him rather severely for this inopportune desire of peace and quiet, which was only a thinly disguised egoism on his part; and, writing to one of Flete's brother monks, Fra Antonio, Catherine cited the example of the great patron of all monks and hermits, St. Anthony of Tebaide, who though preferring to live in fervent solitude away from cities, had no difficulty in travelling to Alexandria in order to defend persecuted Christians. This, she said, has always been the custom of the true servants of God, to come foreward in times of necessity and adversity "Leaving the solitary life for a short period does not damage the spirit The spirit is weak in the worst way, if it loses itself simply because of a change of place. As if God were an acceptor of places and could he found only forests! Do not worry about leaving the woods: even here you will still be surrounded by them; come, do not hesitate, do not sleep now dearest sons: it is time to wake up". The needs of the Church occupied the first place in her thoughts and the unity of the Church was her main interest. The Master, Giovanni Fantucci and Fra Antonio obeyed her summons and went to Rome; William Flete obstinately remained in his woods. We must remark, however, that from his lonely hermitage he worked for the good of the Church, writing letters to his friends in England and thus, keeping that nation firm in its obedience to the true Pope. For all this, Catherine was the living personification of the Church in danger, waiting to be helped by the love and sacrifices of her children. She used to compare the Church to a ship and say that she was carrying it on her shoulders, feeling all its weight. And around her, fatigued and literally consumed by slow martyrdom, were gathered, thanks to God, her most loving sons and daughters.

THE DEATH OF CATHERINE

During these last few months of her life, news had been reaching Siena of Catherine's deteriorating state of health. She even had to stop her daily visits to St. Peter's Basilica where she used to go using a cane and leaning on the arm of her beloved Barduccio, remaining there until evening in prayer. As soon as she heard about Catherine's condition, her elderly mother, Lapa went down to Rome. We can well imagine her reaction when she saw her daughter lying on a miserable cot, totally exhausted, a shadow of what she once had been.

Barduccio who assisted Catherine continuously, spoke incessantly of the pains and hardships that afflicted her during the last months of 1380. "Notwithstanding that infermity, she always applied herself to prayer, which to us seemed a miracle for the frequent humble sighs and bitter weeping that gushed forth from her heart". Everyday she received Holy Communion and, though weakened by atrocious pains, managed to raise her eyes to heaven with joy and say, "I thank you, eternal Spouse, that everyday you give me, your miserable servant, so many and such marvellous graces!". Thus, she literally dragged herself along right up to the Sunday preceeding the Feast of the Ascension which turned out to be the last day of her life. In the meantime, another of her dearest and most beloved disciples arrived in Rome, Stefano Maconi. Catherine had written to him, "When you hear a voice calling, answer it". And behold, one night, he heard a loud clear voice crying: "Go, run to Rome, for your mother is about to depart". He obeyed immediately. Catherine welcomed him with indescribable affection saying: "Finally you have come! Now go to confession, then come back to me and I shall let you know the divine will." Stefano obeyed, and when he returned to the bedside of his holy mother, who by now was unable to speak above a whisper, together with Baruccio Francesco Malavolti and other disciples, he heard from her lips her last testament of love: "My children, love each other always. So shall you be my joy and my crown". Then, calling them individually, Catherine advised one to retire to a hermitage, another to do works of charity in the world, another to become a priest; and when it was Stefano's turn, reaching out to touch him with her feeble hand, she said: "Stefano, I command you, in the name of God and in holy obedience, to enter the Carthusian Order. To this God is calling you". Up to that moment such a thought had never entered Stefano's head. But the will of his holy mother was to him the voice of God and he did as he was told; and the facts of history attest that he became an honour to the Carthusian Order by leading a most holy life. The venerable Abbot of St. Antimo was also present and, seeing that death was nigh, gave Catherine absolution and the last anointing. Af-

150

ter this, everybody noticed that she began acting rather oddly, as though the Evil One was, for the last time, trying to tempt and disturb her. And she began to say: "I have sinned, Lord, have mercy on me", which she repeated sixty times, simultaneously raising her right arm each time and letting it fall upon the bed. Then, another sixty times, but without moving her arms or any other part of her body, she exclaimed: "Oh Holy God, have mercy on me". Catherine then began to say many other things: and with her head resting on the bosom of Alessia, who was sitting on the bed, almost breathless with groaning and weeping, she confessed the sins that she remembered having committed during life; when, suddenly, she appeared to be greatly distressed by something. She remained silent for a few minutes and, with as much force as she could muster in her voice, exclaimed: "Vainglory? No, never, but true glory in Christ Crucified". Catherine was undergoing the last assault of the devil who, knowing how many good works she had accomplished in her life, was trying to suggest that she had done everything for her own selfish glory when, in truth, she had alaways given all the credit and honour to God. It was extremely touching to see poor, desolated Lapa standing next to the bed, asking her daughter's blessing, while she asked her mother for her blessing. Calling for the last time all her beloved sons and daughters around her, she said in a sure voice: "know all of you that Urban VI is the true Pontiff and may none of you hesitate to die for him". She immediately lost consciousness. Shortly afterwards

Catherine awoke and said "You are calling me, o Lord; I am coming to you, not thanks to my own merits, but only because of your mercy!". After another brief silence, she shouted: "Blood, blood, blood!". Lastly with hardly a thread of voice, she whispered: "Father, into your hands I entrust my soul and my spirit" Catheine looked up to heaven for a moment, then lowered her head and died. She was thirty-three years and thirty-five days of age. It was the twenty-ninth of April and the Church was celebrating the feast day of the Dominican, St Peter Martyr.

THE SORROW OF THE CHILDREN

For the entire afternoon and evening of that day, Catherine's devoted family, now cruelly orphaned, sighed and wept. They decided not to reveal her death to anyone outside, thinking that the news of it might arouse a tumult among the locals. The door to the house remained jealously closed, so that nobody could enter. Far into the night, in agreement with the Prior of the Dominicans at the Minerva, Catherine's corpse was transported secretly to their Church by Stefano himself, wrapped in a simple sheet. The following morning, the Saint's virginal body was placed behind the gate of St. Dominic's Chapel where it was visited by people from all over Rome; it remained there for seven days during which many extraordinary healings and graces were obtained by invocations to her.

Meanwhile Lapa with Alessia and all the other dear disciples, holed up in their little house in Via del papa, were completely disconsolate, bearing a great emptiness in their hearts. They did not weep for Catherine, though; they were all certain that she had already joined the blessed in heaven and was praying for them; but they were sad at feeling themselves orphans in the world, unsure about the future, deprived so soon of she who had been in every occasion their guide, not only in spiritual matters, but in all the circumstances of life, especially in the work they had begun for the love and defence of the Church to which Catherine had always urged them. Pope Urban VI expressed his deep sorrow for the death of Catherine who had been his finest supporter in his darkest hours; and he ordered a solemn funeral to be celebrated at the Minerva, at his own expense on May 2nd with the entire clergy of the city present, while a second funeral celebration was held a few days later by order of Giovanni Cenci, Senator of Rome, as an act of homage by the whole populace. Another high-placed prelate who sincerely mourned Catherine's death was Tommaso Petra, Apostolic Pronotary and personal Secretary of the Pontiff; ever since the day he had met Catherine in Avignon he had felt a high esteem and profound veneration for her. Their friendship blossomed quickly and he assisted her in her last hours. And, naturally, we cannot fail to be moved by the poignant sorrow of the Saint's disciples, who, during those difficult first days, in their efforts to bravely bear up under the impact of her death, wrote consoling letters one to another. To the dear Barduccio, who must have keenly felt the pain of his loss, Giovanni delle Celle wrote: "How shall we live now that our mother, our joy, has left us? There is nothing we can do but weep hot tears over our misfortune. I know, the angels in heaven are celebrating a great feast in her honour, but I weep, for it is the sweetest thing for me to do". Neri di Landoccio was in Naples at the time and knew nothing as yet about Catherine's passing until Neri di Duccio wrote to him: "Know that our dearest and treasured mother has gone to heaven. I feel like an orphan, for all my comfort was in her and now I can't stop crying... I do not cry for her, but for myself, because I have lost the most precious thing on earth. We are all now like sheep without a shepherd". The most devastated of all was, undoubtedly, Stefano Maconi. After having done all he could for the dead Catherine, after having poured out torrents of tears and kisses on her closed coffin, he returned to Siena with a broken heart and in a state of uncontrollable mental anguish, for now he had nobody to guide him and he was uncertain of his future. He felt the need of disattaching himself totally from the world, as his holy mother had commanded him to do in her last moments; but for a while, he did not know where to go or how to do so and for days on end he just wandered aimlessly around the countryside near Siena. Some thought he had gone mad. Catherine's invisible hand was helping him, though. Hardly a year had passed when he received the religious habit in the Carthusan Monastery in Pontignano. The sufferings of Catherine's sons and daughters after her death was not sterile. They all rememebered her in their hearts, her life and her dynamic love; and following her teachings and examples became in different ways, according to their individual preferences and conditions, humble instruments for the salvation of souls and the good of the church.

CANONIZED

The extraordinary graces granted through the intercession of Catherine, especially to those who with faith visited her sacred remains in the Church of Santa Maria Minerva, or touched one of her relics, or simply invoked her name, were indeed innumerable and confirmed the title of Blessed and Saint which the whole Roman populace had already attributed to her. Catherine's fame spread rapidly, everyone wanted an image or some kind of remembrance of her, the letters and other writings were conserved like priceless treasures, the great biography composed by Blessed Raymond of Capua was eargely awaited and read by all; and a substantial body of literature began to grow up around her, of whom other saints, Popes and illustrious personages sang praises. Catherine's remains soon received the honours usually reserved only to the Servants of God and, after three years of repose in a cypress coffin in the little cemetary attached to the Dominican Priory of the Minerva, was transported on October 3rd, 1383 into the Church and enclosed in a marble tomb by blessed Raymond, who was now Master General of the Dominican Order; and on that same occasion, in order to please her fellow citizens of Siena, he separated the head from the body and sent Fra Ambrose Sansedoni and Fra Tommaso della Fonte with it to them while one of Catherine's fingers was given to Stefano Maconi. On May 5, 1384, with a pomp never seen before in Siena, the sacred head was brought into the Church of San Domenico which became the most famous santuary of the Saint. The entire city participated in the magnificent spectacle; four hundred small girls dressed in white sang hymns and strew flowers while four Dominican religious carried the precious relic enclosed in a bust of gilded copper under a rich canopy. It must have been a most touching thing to see Lapa, Catheine's eighty year old mother walking in the procession, propped up by the good Alessia Saracini and to hear all the people call her blessed, while their holy strains wafted towards heaven. All the Saint's children showed up for the ceremony. The most conspicuous among them were Neri dei Pagliaresi, Neri di Landoccio, Barduccio Canigiani, Christopher di Gano, Francesco Malavolti, Gabriel Piccolomini and many others. And, at the head of them all stood Stefano Maconi who had rushed down to Siena from Pontignano in order to help the city Fathers and the Bishop organize the memorable event. The Sacred Head was greeted by an impressive host of Dominicans from all over Tuscny who gratefully guarded it in the Church of San Domenico. To another Domenican saint, Antonio Pierozzi, prior of the Minerva in Rome and later, Archbishop of Florence, fell the happy task of erecting a most worthy resting place for his illustrious sister in St. Domenico. He commissioned the sculptor Isaiah of Pisa to build the actual urn with a little statue of the Saint next to it; the urn was then placed in the Chapel of the Rosary surrounded by angels holding various written praises in their hands. The official process of canonization, began in 1411 was, unhappily, suspended because of the Great Western Schism which continued to afflict the Church until the Council of Constance, during which the Pope Martin V was elected finally putting an end to it all. The overwhelming joy of elevating Catherine to the honours of the altar fell to a Sienese Pope, Pius II, formely known as Enea Silvio Piccolomini; and the solemn canonization took place on June 29, 1461, the feast day of the Holy Apostles Peter and Paul, in the Vatican Basilica. Some years later, the Pontiffs, Urban VIII and then, Benedict XII officially asserted the authenticity of the stigmate that Catherine had received during her life and a special feast was granted to celebrate that event, particularly in the Dominican Order and the whole of Tuscany. Throughout the ensuing centuries many other honours have been bestowed upon St. Catherine; for example, several churches and altars erected in her name and in 1637 the transfer of the walls of the room in which she died to a tiny room behind the sacristy of the Minerva; and special mention must be made of the solemn homage paid in 1855, upon the completion of repairs done to that Church, by the whole of Rome, when the body of St. Catherine was carried in stately magnificence through the streets of the city, and then placed once again in its urn under the main altar of the Minerva which had been consecrated by Pope Pius IX, who with a decree of April 13, 1866 declared St. Catherine Co-Patroness of Rome. Pope Pius XII, with his decree of June 18, 1939, proclaimed St. Catherine, patroness of Italy, along with St. Francis of Assisi as Patron of the same. And, on October 4,1970, Pope Paul VI officially declared St. Catherine of Siena, Doctor of the Church.

THE HOMAGE OF ART

The fine arts which flowered in their greatest splendour especially in Tuscany in the XIV century, did not neglect to pay their respects to St. Catherine. A most lifelike portrait was done just ten years after her death by one of her fervent disciples Andrea Vanni; originally part of a larger frescoe, it was disattached in 1667 and placed in the well-known Chapel of the Vaults in the Church of San Domenico where it may still be seen today above a small altar. After Catherine's death many artists diligently conserved her effigy and reproduced her in paintings and frescoes, now by herself, now next to the Virgin Mary and other Saints, or in some episode of her life, particularly the mystical marriage with Jesus, or when she was imprinted with the sacred stigmata. Unfortunately, several other portraits have been lost during the centuries even though Blessed Raymond ordered then to be painted in so many churches belonging to the Order. The custom of portraying Catherine with St. Dominic began quite early; later on other saints were sometimes added, especially our Lady in the act of giving both the holy rosary. Many of these works were true masterpieces, one of the most celebrated being that of Sassoferrata which is now in the Church of Santa Sabina in Rome. But more than enough works have survived to demonstrate the enthusiasm above all of the Sienese, in glorifying with gentle and attractive colours their great Saint, even before Pius II canonized her. They painted Catherine not only in the churches and smaller oratories, but also in the hospitals, their homes and in their very own town Hall; and they particularly loved to represent Catherine on the lids of coffins in order to place their dear deceased under her protection, always showing her in a most virginal pose with a lily in one hand and a book in the other. They often painted her in the company of the great Saint Bernardino canonized in 1450. The most famous portraitists of Catherine have belonged to the Sienese school: Giovanni di Paolo, Sano di Pietro, Lorenzo the Vecchietta, Francesco di Giorgio, Neroccio di Lando, Girolamo of Pecchia, Balducci, and towering above then all, Antonio de Bazzi, nicknamed Sodoma who was so struck by the spirirtual beauty of the great woman, that he portrayed her in three sublime frescoes which are considered to be the best works produced by his brush. These three still admirably adorn the chapel where, just above the marble altar exquisitely sculptured by Giovanni di Stefano, is kept the treasure of the Sacred Head of Catherine. The three frescoes represent the stigmatization of the Saint, one of her esctasies in which an angel offers her the Host and the tragic beheading of the callow youth from Perugia, Nicola di Tuldo, whose soul was seen by Catherine as it flew to heaven. Francesco Vanni covered the other wall of the Chapel with the frescoe of the liberation of a possessed woman and, under the archways he painted the two first biographers of Catherine, Raymond of Capua and Tommaso Caffarini. The house where the angelic little girl was born and raised, her father's shop and the small orchard were all transformed by the art of the cinquecento, and became one of the most holy shrines in Siena, full of rich artistic memorials, affectionately guarded and constantly refurbished. Only one hundred years ago Alessandro Franchi painted with much finesse and rare piety the tiny austere bedroom which had been the scene of so many prodigies performed by God in the Sienese virgin. The same homage was repeated in various places: for example the Priory of Fiesole, built by another great disciple of Catherine, Blessed Giovanni Dominici, as part of an august altarpiece, now conserved in London, and the Dominican artist, Beato Angelico painted his sister with her head surrounded by supernatual rays. In Rome itself and in many other italian cities and around the whole world, the cult of St. Catherine was eventually established, thanks to efforts of the artists who brought honour also upon themselves by offering their fairest flowers of homage. Upon the tomb of the great Pontiff Pius IX who ardently exalted her, there is a mosaic portrait of St. Catherine according to the design of 'Lodovico Seit,' as the protectress of the Papacy, in the act of holding up high the tiara and bringing it back to Rome. Thus all the plastic arts have offered their gracious homage to the great Saint whom Cornelius a Lapide called "the wonder of the world" almost as a humble token of love and gratitude for the incredible burst of enthusiasm with which she wholeheartedly embraced the church and all humanity in one great act of faith and love.

F I N E

PUBBLICAZIONI CATERINIANE
DELLE EDIZIONI CANTAGALLI

Nelle librerie cattoliche o richieste direttamente a
EDIZIONI CANTAGALLI - Via Massetana Romana, 12
Casella Postale 155 - 53100 Siena - Tel. 0577 42102 Fax 0577 45363
e-mail: cantagalli@edizionicantagalli.com
www.edizionicantagalli.com

Stampato da Edizioni Cantagalli
Siena - Via Massetana Romana, 12 - Tel. 0577/42102 Fax 45363
nel Giugno 2002